T0323397

Fiscal Capacity and the Colonial State in Asia and Africa, c. 1850–1960

This book examines the evolution of fiscal capacity in the context of colonial state formation and the changing world order between 1850 and 1960. Until the early nineteenth century, European colonial control over Asia and Africa was largely confined to coastal and island settlements, which functioned as little more than trading posts. The officials running these settlements had neither the resources nor the need to develop new fiscal instruments. With the expansion of imperialism, the costs of maintaining colonies rose. Home governments, reluctant to place the financial burden of imperial expansion on metropolitan taxpayers, pressed colonial governments to become fiscally self-supporting. A team of leading historians provides a comparative overview of how colonial states set up their administrative systems and how these regimes involved local people and elites. They shed new light on the political economy of colonial state formation and the institutional legacies they left behind at independence.

Ewout Frankema is Professor and Chair of Rural and Environmental History at Wageningen University. He is editor-in-chief of the *Journal of Global History* and research fellow of the UK Centre for Economic Policy Research (CEPR).

Anne Booth is Professor Emerita at SOAS, University of London. She has researched on the economies of Southeast Asia in both the colonial and post-colonial eras, and has written and edited a number of books on the region as well as articles in journals.

Cambridge Studies in Economic History

Cambridge Studies in Economic History comprises stimulating and accessible economic history which actively builds bridges to other disciplines. Books in the series will illuminate why the issues they address are important and interesting, place their findings in a comparative context, and relate their research to wider debates and controversies. The series will combine innovative and exciting new research by younger researchers with new approaches to major issues by senior scholars. It will publish distinguished work regardless of chronological period or geographical location.

A complete list of titles in the series can be found at:
www.cambridge.org/economichistory

Fiscal Capacity and the Colonial State in Asia and Africa, c. 1850–1960

Edited by

Ewout Frankema
Wageningen Universiteit, The Netherlands

Anne Booth
School of Oriental and African Studies, University of London

CAMBRIDGE
UNIVERSITY PRESS

CAMBRIDGE
UNIVERSITY PRESS

University Printing House, Cambridge CB2 8BS, United Kingdom

One Liberty Plaza, 20th Floor, New York, NY 10006, USA

477 Williamstown Road, Port Melbourne, VIC 3207, Australia

314–321, 3rd Floor, Plot 3, Splendor Forum, Jasola District Centre,
New Delhi – 110025, India

79 Anson Road, #06–04/06, Singapore 079906

Cambridge University Press is part of the University of Cambridge.

It furthers the University's mission by disseminating knowledge in the pursuit of
education, learning, and research at the highest international levels of excellence.

www.cambridge.org
Information on this title: www.cambridge.org/9781108494267
DOI: 10.1017/9781108665001

First published 2020

Printed in the United Kingdom by TJ International Ltd. Padstow Cornwall

A catalogue record for this publication is available from the British Library.

Library of Congress Cataloging-in-Publication Data
Names: Frankema, Ewout, editor. | Booth, Anne, 1946– editor.
Title: Fiscal capacity and the colonial state in Asia and Africa, c. 1850–1960 /
edited by Ewout Frankema, Wageningen Universiteit, The Netherlands, Anne
Booth, School of Oriental and African Studies, University of London.
Description: New York : Cambridge University Press, 2021. | Series: Cambridge
studies in economic history – second series | Includes bibliographical references
and index.
Identifiers: LCCN 2019037674 (print) | LCCN 2019037675 (ebook) | ISBN
9781108494267 (hardback) | ISBN 9781108665001 (epub)
Subjects: LCSH: Fiscal policy – Africa – History. | Fiscal policy – Asia – History.
| Europe – Colonies – Administration – History.
Classification: LCC HJ1441 .F54 2021 (print) | LCC HJ1441 (ebook) | DDC
339.5/209509041–dc23
LC record available at https://lccn.loc.gov/2019037674
LC ebook record available at https://lccn.loc.gov/2019037675

ISBN 978-1-108-49426-7 Hardback

Contents

Figures and Maps

Figures

Maps

Tables

Contributors

KLEONIKI ALEXOPOULOU, Eberhard Karls University of Tübingen

ANNE BOOTH, SOAS, University of London

KENT DENG, London School of Economics

EWOUT FRANKEMA, Wageningen University

LEIGH GARDNER, London School of Economics and Stellenbosch University

ABEL GWAINDEPI, Stellenbosch University

MONTSERRAT LÓPEZ JEREZ, Lund University

TIRTHANKAR ROY, London School of Economics

KRIGE SIEBRITS, Stellenbosch University

MARLOUS VAN WAIJENBURG, University of Michigan

Acknowledgements

The historiography of colonial fiscal development has received increasing scholarly attention in the past decade. There is a growing conviction that the intricate processes of colonial state formation, which have left such a deep imprint on large parts of Asia, Africa and the Americas, can only be understood when the development of fiscal systems are placed at the core of historical analysis. Tax and non-tax revenues formed the financial backbone of the colonial state and strengthening fiscal capacity was viewed as a crucial part of colonial state building. The idea of bringing experts on colonial fiscal history together in an attempt to discuss and synthesize their work on Africa and Asia began in 2012, at the World Economic History Conference in Stellenbosch, South Africa. In 2015, during the World Economic History Conference in Kyoto, the idea was picked up again and funding was sought to organize two workshops on the theme, one in June 2016 and another in February 2017, both held at the SOAS, University of London.

This book project has been made possible by the financial support of the European Research Council under the European Community's Seventh Framework Programme (ERC Grant Agreement no. 313114) as part of the project 'Is Poverty Destiny? A New Empirical Foundation for Long-Term African Welfare Analysis' and the Netherlands Organisation for Scientific Research for the project 'Is Poverty Destiny? Exploring Long Term Changes in African Living Standards in Global Perspective' (NWO VIDI Grant no. 016.124.307). We are grateful for invaluable comments and advice from William Gervase Clarence-Smith, Tony Hopkins, Debin Ma, Patrick O'Brien, Alice Sindzingre and from two anonymous reviewers. For their comments on various drafts of the book's introduction we thank Leigh Gardner, Marlous van Waijenburg and Elise van Nederveen Meerkerk. Special thanks are also due to Michael Watson and Lisa Carter of Cambridge University Press, who have assisted us in many ways during the preparation of the manuscript. Finally, we are greatly indebted to the exceptional commitment and effort put in by all the chapter contributors. They have responded without protest to our many requests for the changes necessary to turn a collection of conference papers into a coherent volume of synthesis. We hope readers will appreciate both the detail of the case studies and the deeper patterns that emerge when the different colonial experiences are placed in a comparative framework.

1   Fiscal Capacity and the Colonial State: Lessons from a Comparative Perspective

Ewout Frankema and Anne Booth

Introduction

This book examines the comparative development of fiscal capacity in a number of Asian and African colonial states.[1] We situate this study in the context of the changing world order in the long century between 1850 and 1960. The end date signals the termination of colonial rule in most of sub-Saharan Africa, with the exceptions of Portuguese Africa (1975) and the semi-autonomous status granted to the Union of South Africa (1910).[2] The starting date of 1850 is more arbitrary, as colonial control began earlier in some parts of both Asia and Africa. But, broadly speaking, it was only after 1850 – and indeed in many of the colonies which are examined in this book, several decades later – that the colonial powers began to develop the fiscal systems of the territories which came under their control.

We define 'fiscal capacity' as the ability of the state, or its representative agents, to collect revenues in order to provide public goods and services. In this definition, fiscal capacity refers not just to the power of the state to assess and collect taxes, but also to its ability to extract non-tax revenues from state monopolies, from enterprises such as railways or from foreign aid. Moreover, fiscal capacity also refers to the ability of the state to raise loans to supplement both tax and non-tax revenues, especially for capital works. All the chapters in this book examine the long-term development of colonial fiscal policies, using this definition of fiscal capacity. They also

[1] Ewout Frankema gratefully acknowledges financial support from the European Research Council under the European Community's Seventh Framework Programme (ERC Grant Agreement no. 313114) as part of the project 'Is Poverty Destiny? A New Empirical Foundation for Long-Term African Welfare Analysis' and the Netherlands Organisation for Scientific Research for the project 'Is Poverty Destiny? Exploring Long Term Changes in African Living Standards in Global Perspective' (NWO VIDI Grant no. 016.124.307).
[2] Most Asian colonies obtained independence, or a large measure of self-government, in the years between 1946 and 1957.

1

explore how different colonial administrations tackled the problem of revenue centralization, and what factors influenced both the revenue mix and changing expenditure policies. The chapters also address wider questions on the use of forced labour, debt creation, the impact of increasing global and local trade, and the development of financial systems.

We will argue in more detail that existing concepts and theories of fiscal development have had little to say about the nature and determinants of fiscal development in a colonial setting. Until now, the historical literature has paid much more attention to the rise of the fiscal state in Europe and its offshoots in the Americas, than to the development of fiscal systems in the former colonies and protectorates in Africa and Asia. Fiscal histories that employ a global comparative outlook have either concentrated on the comparative features of fiscal state formation in Eurasia (Yun-Casalilla & O'Brien 2012, He 2013), or have focused on the North-South divergence in the Americas (Engerman & Sokoloff 1997, North, Summerhill & Weingast 2000, Sokoloff & Zolt 2006, Grafe & Irigoin 2012). While there has been a recent upsurge of studies in the fiscal history of African and Asian colonies (Booth 2007a, Frankema 2011, Gardner 2012, Wahid 2013, Frankema & van Waijenburg 2014, Huillery 2014, Alexopoulou & Juif 2017), the findings of these studies have yet to be synthesized. This volume brings the experiences of colonies in Asia and Africa into a global comparative framework in order to clear the ground for new theories on the relationship between colonial state-building and the development of fiscal capacity.

The Colonial State in a Changing World Order, 1850–1960

The fiscal systems analysed in this book all developed during the wave of global imperialism that emerged between the independence wars in the Americas (c. 1776–1830) and the end of colonial rule in Africa. The spread of the Industrial Revolution from Britain to the wider Northern Atlantic basin opened up new possibilities to bring overseas areas under direct control. The heightened pace of technological change, and accumulation and application of scientific knowledge brought solutions to a range of problems, including the treatment and prevention of tropical disease (e.g. quinine to treat malaria, smallpox vaccination), communication over large distances (e.g. telegraph) and the preservation of perishable commodities (e.g. refrigerators). Moreover, the major revolutions in transportation, railways and steam ships, in particular, greatly enhanced global trade and opportunities of colonization (Kuznets 1974, 168,

O'Rourke & Williamson 1999, Williamson 2011, Frankema, Williamson & Woltjer 2018). The colonial states, no matter how weak and understaffed many of them were, occupied a critical place in this compulsory process of globalization (Hopkins 2002, 6–7; see also Burbank & Cooper 2010, chapter 10). Colonial states were responsible for maintaining law and order, and for creating a political space for infrastructure development, trade and capital investment, in order to create profitable export sectors. All these aims required money. The fiscal system, it can be argued, formed the backbone of the colonial state.

The expansion of formal and informal empire was led by a handful of Western European powers, but was not an exclusively European undertaking. The United States annexed the Philippines, and replaced its Spanish government in 1900. Threatened by Western incursions in the mid-nineteenth century, Japan decided that an empire was necessary if it was to be taken seriously by the other global powers. In the late nineteenth century, Meiji Japan became an imperial power by adapting foreign production technologies and by engaging in rapid military capacity building.

Although the physical distance from metropolitan centres provided the colonial state with some degree of policy autonomy, improved transportation and communication technologies also meant that metropolitan supervision was more effective than it had been in the early modern era. Both internal and external factors caused changes in colonial policy, including fiscal reforms. In Indonesia, pressures from within the colony and in the Netherlands brought an end to the cultivation system and a transition to the so-called liberal era in the 1860s and 1870s (Fasseur 1991). In India, the rebellion against British East India Company rule in 1857–8 induced a reorganization of the colonial army as well as the government administration and the financial administration (Prakash 2004). The Meiji reforms in Japan involved a reorganization of the fiscal apparatus, which in turn influenced later Japanese imperialism. The discovery of diamonds in 1867 had an enormous impact on subsequent economic and political development of South Africa, including revenue and expenditure policies (Feinstein 2005, 108–9, Gwaindepi & Siebrits, Chapter 9, this volume).[3]

While major investments in fiscal development in sub-Saharan Africa were made only after the scramble of the 1880s and 1890s, many African societies experienced major changes in the relations with their trading partners, both African and European, during the middle decades of the

---

[3] When they are not supposed to cause much confusion, we will use anachronistic geographic denotations throughout this volume.

nineteenth century. Even though the shift from slave exports to commodity exports occurred at different points in time, this 'commercial transition' coincided with improving terms of trade for African commodity exports and rapidly expanding export volumes. The expansion of 'legitimate commerce' across the nineteenth century, in turn, created new opportunities for financing the colonial state (Law 1995, Frankema & van Waijenburg 2014, Frankema et al. 2018).

By the end of the nineteenth century, when the scramble for Africa had largely been completed, European empires reached the territorial size that they would retain until the 1940s. In this period, the growth of colonial populations, output and trade accelerated, despite the problems caused by the First World War and the Great Depression. While the transport and communication revolution transformed the logistics of empire-building, innovations in military technologies, including improved naval vessels and machine guns, enhanced the superiority of the metropolitan 'cores' over the colonial 'peripheries'. Investments in railways, roads and harbours opened up the more promising hinterlands to increasing numbers of European merchants, engineers and occasional settlers. Their activities concentrated mainly on export production, but food production for domestic consumption also became a policy concern as populations expanded (especially in parts of Asia) or to supply major mining areas (especially in parts of Central and Southern Africa). The gradual and radical shifts in the global division of labour associated with 'modern imperialism' also provoked new flows of migrants, capital and commodities within and across both continents. It is in this context of a changing world order, characterized by sharply increasing flows of cross-continental trade and investment capital, that colonial administrations attempted to strengthen and consolidate the fiscal capacity of the colonial state.

Fiscal Capacity Building in a Colonial Context

In most of the colonies of Africa and Asia there was little scope for an 'organic' evolution of government structures and fiscal systems, as had occurred in the metropolitan countries over a span of centuries. Until the early decades of the nineteenth century, European colonial control over Asia and Africa had been largely confined to coastal and island settlements, which often functioned as little more than trading posts. Officials charged with running these settlements had neither the resources nor the need to develop new fiscal instruments.

With the expansion of imperialism in the course of the nineteenth century, the costs of maintaining colonies rose. The reluctance of home governments to place much of the financial burden of imperial expansion on the backs of metropolitan taxpayers pressed colonial governments to expand their revenue base as quickly as possible and become fiscally self-supporting. In fact, in several cases they were asked to make contributions to the metropolitan economy, and to this end new fiscal duties were often imposed upon the local population. Colonial administrators could rely to varying extents on revenue institutions that were already in place, but these were often imperfectly understood, and local elites had good reasons for hiding the extent to which they were taxing their people. Therefore, it was not unusual for local people to be confronted with additional revenue demands from colonial officials while at the same time continuing to pay pre-colonial imposts to local rulers. This was especially the case when colonial governments adopted 'indirect rule' and left local power structures largely in place.

In the European context, scholars have analysed the rise of the 'fiscal-military' state, where the ability of countries to wage war was predicated on growing flows of both tax and non-tax revenues. These imposts were often accepted by the population as temporary demands to meet legitimate defence needs, although in many cases the new taxes became permanent (Tilly 1990, Bonney 1999, Hoffman 2015). In most Asian and African colonies, external threats were largely eliminated by the late nineteenth century, and the revenues raised by the colonial state were not primarily intended to fight off external powers. The First World War (1914–18) had some fiscal impact on many colonies, especially through the contraction in world trade which affected revenues. Those colonies which provided significant numbers of troops to the metropolitan country, such as India, shouldered most of the costs of their upkeep (Roy, Chapter 3, this volume). Yet, on the whole, colonial revenues were first and foremost needed to secure *internal* order. Colonial control often required considerable investments in local armies and police forces, as well as roads, railways and ports. Moreover, revenues were needed to pay the salaries of government officials who administered the government departments. Without the trust and commitment involved in the defence of a 'nation', raising revenues on behalf of a foreign government, which often had little legitimacy in the eyes of local people, required a more intensive combination of coercion and co-option. In many colonies across Asia and Africa, officials found this combination difficult, if not impossible, to implement.

One of the ideas advanced by the *bellicist* theory of fiscal development in Europe, is that constant interstate warfare resulted in an imagined 'social contract' between citizens and the state. Gradually, this would become an increasingly important marker of 'national' identity, solidarity and unity in the face of the violence perpetrated by outsiders. Indeed, nationalism was one of the major social-political forces in Europe both before and during the period of our study (c. 1850–1960). But on whose behalf did colonial governments collect revenue and provide public services? Many subject populations were ethnically heterogeneous, if not fragmented, and did not share a common identity. Moreover, co-optation of specific ethnic groups, social classes or elite factions hampered the idea of a state working in the public interest. The legitimacy problem of the colonial state was aggravated by the importation of labour from India and China into parts of East Africa and Southeast Asia, as well as from Korea into the Japanese colony of Manchuria. This gave rise to economies where small- and medium-scale businesses were owned by people who were neither locals nor from the metropolitan country. To the extent that national identities were sharpened during colonial occupation, it was generally in response to perceived oppression from the colonial power, and to the migrant workers from other parts of the world, who were either regarded as tools of colonial exploitation (e.g. coolies) or as colonial middlemen (e.g. tax farmers, entrepreneurs). Rather than underpinning colonial state formation and fiscal capacity expansion, nationalist ideologies promoted by independence movements thus became a major destabilizing factor of existing political-fiscal arrangements.

Fiscal Extraction and the Costs and Benefits of Empire

The national historiographies which have developed on the colonial experience of particular metropoles, not just in European countries but also in the United States and Japan, reveal great variation in their assessment of the costs and benefits of empire. In Dutch, Belgian and Portuguese historiography the consensus view is that the possessions in Asia and Africa were, on the whole, beneficial to the development of the metropolitan economy.[4] Assessing the contribution of empire to Portuguese economic growth in the early-modern era, Costa, Palma and Reis (2015, 1) concluded that "eliminating the economic links to empire would have reduced Portugal's per capita income by at least a fifth". For the modern era, Lains (1998) has argued that the net benefits of Portuguese Africa to the Portuguese economy between 1885 and 1975 were also substantial.

---

[4] It has also been widely acknowledged that silver receipts from Spanish America kept the Spanish-Habsburg war machinery in Europe going for centuries and also supported the survival of the Spanish American empire in the face of British and French encroachment (Marichal 2007).

The net contribution of the Netherlands Indies to the Dutch treasury was also considerable. At the peak of the *cultuurstelsel* (cultivation system) in the mid-nineteenth century, it has been estimated at 52 per cent of the total metropolitan budget (Fasseur 1991, van Zanden & van Riel 2000, 223). The Dutch experiment (c. 1830–60) inspired the Belgian king Leopold II to set up a similar system in the Congo Free State (Frankema & Buelens 2013). Although the rates of extraction were less clear after 1870 (van der Eng 1998, Gordon 2010), private sector remittances remained substantial, especially from the plantation and mining sectors in both Indonesia and the Congo (Booth 1998, 210–14; Buelens & Frankema 2016). Scholars have pointed to the exceptional profitability of Belgian investments in Congolese mining and plantation sectors during the 1920s to 1950s (Buelens & Marysse 2009, Vanthemsche 2010).

The debates in Britain and France have been less conclusive and often more politicized (e.g. Gann & Duignan 1967, Ferguson 2002, Lefeuvre 2006). Davis and Huttenback (1988) argued that empire-building not only brought about a redistribution of resources between the United Kingdom and its colonial dependencies, but also transferred resources within British society from the general British taxpayer to a select class of merchants, entrepreneurs and investors who greatly benefitted from the 'free' naval and military protection of their overseas activities (O'Brien & Prados de la Escosura 1998, Offer 1993, Edelstein 1994, 213–14). More recently, scholars have explored the extent to which British colonies benefitted from access to metropolitan capital markets and favourable conditions for government loans (Ferguson & Schularick 2006, Gardner 2017).

Marseille (1984) and Lefeuvre (2006) have argued that French colonies received substantial net inflows of funds to the detriment of French taxpayers, especially in the decades after 1930. Marseille (1984) has also pointed out that in the interwar years in particular, uncompetitive traditional industries were sustained by captive colonial markets after the loss of European markets, with adverse effects on the competitiveness of French industries. Following earlier incomplete attempts by Bobrie (1976), Coquery-Vidrovitch (1982) and Marseille (1984) to calculate the net transfers between France and its colonies, Huillery (2014, 1) estimated that the net payments to French West Africa (the AOF) were negligible, on average 0.29 per cent of total metropolitan public expenses, while the burden on African subjects was high. This view finds support in the work by van Waijenburg (2018), who has shown that the implicit tax burden of forced labour in French West Africa was extremely severe, particularly up to the 1920s.[5]

---

[5] Although the literature on the costs and benefits of empire to the metropole is dominated by European scholars, Asian and African scholars have taken up the issue as well. As Roy

The Japanese case is also important, not least because many students of comparative colonialism, following the influential work of Myers and Peattie (1984), have tended to accept that Japanese policies in Taiwan, Korea and Manchuria were more 'developmental' compared with the extractive or exploitative policies pursued by the European powers. In fact the evidence is mixed. In Taiwan, the Japanese government transferred funds to the colonial budget in the early years of colonial occupation, but, after 1909, surpluses from the colony were used to fund transfers on both government and private account to metropolitan Japan (Booth & Deng 2017, 94). But both Korea and Manchuria maintained large balance of payments deficits, funded by inflows from Japan. An American study of the Japanese economy came to the conclusion that, at the end of the 1920s, from a fiscal point of view the colonies were a liability rather than an asset (Moulton 1931, 180). Large capital inflows to both Manchuria and Korea persisted until the 1940s.

Fiscal Development and Economic Growth

The debates on the costs and benefits of empire for European metropoles are closely connected to the debates on the (long-term) consequences of colonial extraction for colonial societies. An influential strand of literature stresses the intimate link between colonial repression, fiscal extraction and institutions designed to exploit colonial populations (Jamal 1978, Young 1994, Acemoglu, Johnson & Robinson 2001). Other studies, especially on sub-Saharan Africa, have argued that colonial state budgets were small and, if anything, led to understaffed bureaucracies and underinvestment in public services rather than high tax burdens (Kirk-Greene 1980, Frankema 2011, Gardner 2012). In the context of Asian colonies, the impact of the cultivation system on living standards in Java and the role of the colonial state in the Indian famines of the late nineteenth century have been extensively debated (see for Java: Elson 1984, chapter 11; see for India: Roy 2012).

The scanty evidence we have suggests that colonial economies did grow over extended periods of time, mostly in the order of an annual 0.5 to 1.0 per cent per capita (see for Africa 1870–1950: Prados de la Escosura 2012; see for Asia 1870–1950: Maddison 2010). This growth was largely driven by the expansion of export sectors and related infrastructural investment. Rapid growth was realized in times of mineral or cash-crop

(Chapter 3) points out in this volume, there exists an influential strand of Indian scholarship investigating the drain theory, and especially the impact of the so-called home-charges that were transferred from the Indian budget to the British state coffers.

export booms, but these usually tapered off after one or two decades at best. Structural change and economic diversification, and in particular the development of competitive manufacturing industries, remained weak. The biggest exception among the cases studied in this book is South Africa, where greater political autonomy after 1910 facilitated the adoption of import substitution policies in the industrial sector from 1924. Along with systematic labour repression, these policies resulted in a manufacturing share of 20 per cent in GDP by 1960, in addition to 13 per cent for mining (Feinstein 2005, 144, Austin, Frankema & Jerven 2017, 356). Yet, pervasive racial discrimination meant that little of the growth translated into improvements in living standards for the indigenous African majority (Feinstein 2005, 67–71).

To what extent has fiscal development stimulated or limited colonial economic growth? In the absence of a historical counterfactual it is hard to formulate even a tentative answer to this question. The few countries that, at least in name, remained independent (e.g. Liberia, Ethiopia, Thailand) did not fare any better than their colonial neighbours, but it remains questionable to what extent this tells us anything about the relationship between fiscal development and economic growth. Some have argued that the access of colonial states to metropolitan capital markets has enhanced their possibilities to borrow and invest cheaply, in contrast to poor countries that remained independent (Ferguson & Schularick 2006; see for a critique: Accominotti et al. 2010). However, colonial powers in general tended to be rather conservative in the supply of colonial loans and could have done much more if they had wanted to. Only after 1945, were substantial grants-in-aid provided for investment in colonial development programmes. Moreover, in many African colonies, marketing boards were syphoning off export sector surpluses that remained unutilized for capital investments or expansion of local banking.

Investments in health and education received low priority, although there was considerable variation across colonies and metropolitan powers. For instance, the United States channelled much more resources into the education system of the Philippines than the Dutch did in Indonesia under the so-called 'ethical policy' (Frankema 2013). Whereas school enrolment rates in British Africa rose faster than in French Africa before 1940, the British relied much more on private funds supplied by missionary organizations to finance mass education, while the French emphasized the role of public educational investment by the colonial government (Frankema 2012, Cogneau & Moradi 2014).

Any evaluation of the relationship between fiscal development and colonial economic growth will have to consider the transition that colonial states made from a 'night-watchman state' with minimal resources towards a more 'developmental state' (Booth 2007b, 67–8), with small but growing investments in health, education and infrastructure. This transition was supported by increasing opportunities for borrowing in metropolitan capital markets, increasing grants in aid, and some degree of tax diversification towards 'modern' personal and corporate income taxes and general sales taxes. All these developments reflected the ambition to 'modernize' the colonial state, but the effect of these reforms has remained limited in the majority of cases.

This brings us to one of the key insights of this book: colonial economies and societies were difficult to engineer and the solution to the revenue problem thus varied enormously both *across* and *within* empires. Since local economic, political and social conditions were crucial in shaping the opportunities and constraints to fiscal capacity building, the economic legacy of the colonial 'fiscal state' may be best considered as unique to each colony and often even each region. Specific blends of political, legal and commercial institutions evolved which, in most cases, required significant modification to support a process of 'modern' economic growth.

Fiscal Capacity and the Colonial State: a Theoretical Vacuum

We now return to the issue of fiscal capacity, and its relation to state capacity. The existing literature accepts that state capacity includes fiscal capacity, but they are not synonymous concepts. State capacity also involves the ability to protect subjects of the state against the threat of internal or external violence, expropriation and other offences; to effectively implement government policies; and to run a state bureaucracy. State capacity also includes the concept of 'legal capacity', which Besley and Persson (2009) define as the capacity of the state to support markets with appropriate institutions. In this book, we use the term 'colonial state' to refer to a governance system imposed on indigenous people in a distinct territory by a foreign power for a prolonged period of time, whereby the central government ultimately relies on the military, administrative and technological backup of the metropole to secure internal order.

The colonial state thus defined made use of foreign agents to run key positions in the administration, the army and, in most cases, the major export sectors of the local economy. Almost all colonial states analysed in this book were states where local or *indigenous* inhabitants comprised a large majority of the population; the main exception was British Malaya, where large-scale in-migration from China and India had resulted into a minority position for the indigenous population by the 1930s. Native populations were at least partially integrated into the colonial fiscal system in all colonies. This distinguished them from the much smaller number of settler colonies where indigenous populations remained largely outside the fiscal system, or were even pushed entirely beyond the settler's land frontier.

It was argued earlier that economic and political theories aiming to explain the dynamic relations between fiscal capacity and state capacity have been mainly inspired by the European experience (Tilly, 1990, Besley & Persson 2009, 2010) and, to a lesser extent, by the cases of China and Japan (He 2013). This leaves an important gap in the literature. The theoretical models of Besley and Persson emphasize the complementary nature of fiscal capacity and legal capacity. Their models reveal, in line with Tilly's argument, that the positive feedback loops between fiscal capacity and state support for markets are enhanced by war threats, and constrained by the presence of natural resources, which erode incentives to invest in fiscal capacity and market development.

The concept of 'fiscal modernization' offers another framework with which to evaluate specific stages in colonial fiscal development. In his comparative study of Britain, Japan and China, He (2013, 3–13) defined 'fiscal modernity' in terms of several criteria. The first relates to the capacity of the state to collect revenues at a local level and to transfer these into a central consolidated fund. According to He, revenue centralization requires a threshold level of commercialization and monetization to levy sufficient indirect taxes on both foreign trade (import and export taxes) and domestic transactions (excises), which can be remitted to the centre using bills of exchange or other methods. The second condition is that the central state uses its revenue generating capacity to establish a long-term floating debt position. In the military-fiscal states of early-modern Europe, governments could borrow to finance exceptional expenses such as warfare. However, after military campaigns had ended, states often redeemed their debts in order to start the next war with a blank sheet. The transition towards structural floating debt is thus a key feature of fiscal modernity (Dincecco 2009, 2011).

A third condition relates to the expenditure side of the budget. In order to justify taxes and other imposts, states had to be seen to be delivering goods and services which protected, and indeed enhanced, the welfare of taxpayers. The idea that the state, instead of churches or other charitable institutions, had a responsibility to look after the welfare of the general populace gained ground in parts of Europe and North America during the nineteenth century. This idea was tightly connected with a fourth condition, fiscal modernity, or the transition towards responsible and representative government. Improved accountability and extension of the franchise in Europe and the western offshoots had considerable implications for fiscal policy, as negotiations over the distribution of the tax burden and the provision of public goods became more open. These negotiations were conducted by representatives of most social groups, and went hand in hand with the rise of political parties representing class interests. The push for responsible state government in the British North American colonies developed, in part at least, as a result of the resentment against British refusal to delegate taxation powers to the local population, and was expressed in the famous slogan "no taxation without representation".

These theoretical and conceptual approaches have clear limitations for understanding the varying patterns of fiscal capacity building under colonial rule. One key reason was that the feedback loops between fiscal capacity and legal capacity, as well as the balance between tax legitimacy and tax enforcement were fundamentally different in a colonial setting. In fact, most colonial fiscal systems found it difficult to progress beyond the first criterion of fiscal modernity as defined by He (2013). The borrowing capacity of the colonial state, for instance, did not depend primarily on the risk assessment of private investors, but rather on the political decisions taken by metropolitan officials who would weigh the value of colonial development projects – mainly infrastructure – against the risk of default (Sunderland 2007).

Although by the early twentieth century, the European imperial powers were justifying their control over much of Asia and Africa in terms of a 'civilizing' mission, they did not define this in terms of establishing 'responsible government', let alone a welfare state. The lack of tax legitimacy was usually compensated by higher degrees of coercion, often exercised through intervention in land and labour markets. Even though commercialization was a priority for all colonial governments, a positive feedback loop between fiscal capacity and legal capacity was not self-evident. Factor markets had to be controlled in order to push the price for labour, capital and land below what a free market would have established. In addition, export sectors had to be taxed in order to syphon off part of the income from international trade, including mineral exploitation. The presence of natural resources did not always crowd out other taxes either, because direct taxes or coercion were often needed to make labour available for the exploitation of mines or plantations. Public expenditures were often not intended to strengthen domestic economic linkages, but rather to open up specific production and consumption opportunities to metropolitan investors, producers and consumers. Fiscal capacity was thus stimulated by, and in turn used to strengthen, monopolies and monopsonies.

A complicating factor was that the great majority of colonial populations were poor, and could not reasonably be expected to pay more than a small fraction of their meagre incomes to the government. Even before the problems brought about by the world depression in the 1930s, colonial governments faced the threat of tax revolts if governments made excessive demands. Colonial governments without effective institutions of representative government could limit the risk of revolt by pursuing various strategies, including outright violence to enforce tax compliance. But this required a credible commitment on the part of the state to use force, and in the longer run could make the problem of legitimacy worse. In most cases, the compromise reached was to limit the range of taxes imposed, and their amount. This minimalist strategy involved the avoidance of direct taxes, if possible, and a strong emphasis on less visible indirect taxes.[6]

Colonial states also critically depended on indigenous rulers to enforce taxes in the expectation, not always realized, that these rulers had greater legitimacy in the eyes of local people. This meant that part of the revenues had to be shared with indigenous intermediaries such as sultans, chiefs, local warlords, or village heads, many of whom had good reason to frustrate attempts at centralizing revenues. But in many indirectly ruled territories, colonial revenue officials had no alternative. Since taxation with representation was by definition impossible, the legitimacy deficit could only be overcome by force, by reliance on indigenous elites acting as intermediaries in the process of revenue centralization or by keeping taxes low.

The growing difference between metropolitan and colonial approaches to revenue mobilization had important implications for the composition of revenues. In particular, the colonial state permitted the use of policies to extract resources that might have been used in the metropolitan country in earlier times, but had fallen into disuse, or had even been declared illegal under the modern fiscal state. For example, colonial governments in parts of Asia continued to rely on revenues from the sale of opium, long after the sale and use of the opium derivatives had been either banned or strictly controlled in the metropolitan countries. This 'narco-colonialism', to use

---

[6] It is unlikely that many colonial officials were familiar with the Italian school of public finance, which only became known in the English-speaking world after 1960. Writers such as Puviani developed the concept of fiscal illusion, which challenged the assumption of rationality on the part of taxpayers. Puviani claimed that the form through which revenues were extracted could influence taxpayer perceptions of how much they pay; often taxpayers were less aware of indirect taxes, such as import duties and excises, than direct income taxes (Wagner 2003). It is likely that colonial officials felt that indirect taxes were easier to levy in a colonial setting, although they may have exaggerated the extent of fiscal illusion.

the phrase of Bayly and Harper (2004, 33), sustained the growth not just of British colonialism, but also French and Dutch activities in Asia.

An even more striking example was the large-scale use of forced labour. Although colonial occupation in many parts of Africa was justified by the suppression of the slave trade and slavery, the use of forced labour was often defended, not just in Africa but in Asia as well, as part of the overarching civilizing mission. Forced labour, it was argued, would improve labour discipline among 'lazy natives'. In fact, it was often considered the only policy tool available to stimulate commercialization and economic development among indigenous populations who were reluctant to abandon their traditional, subsistence-oriented way of life for the uncertainties and indignities of wage labour (e.g. see for French West Africa: van Waijenburg 2018; see for the Netherlands Indies: Bosma 2013). Another example is large-scale alienation of land, which was then leased or sold to foreign investors, made available for railway and road construction or just appropriated in order to push more indigenous people into the wage labour market.

This is not to say that constraints to fiscal expansion paralysed colonial governments. The emancipatory forces that were unleashed by the deployment of African and Asian soldiers in the First and Second World Wars forced many colonial states to revise their expenditure priorities. Even though colonial soldiers were selectively recruited, with a focus on ethnic groups that were both trusted and supposed to have martial qualities, such as the Sikhs or the *tirailleurs Sénégalais*, colonial administrators felt the need to strengthen the legitimacy of the colonial state. As this need was translated into more explicit development agendas, some restrictions on the use of forced labour were introduced.

These restrictions were supported by the new international organizations that emerged in the early twentieth century, especially the International Labour Organisation, which was founded in 1919. All European colonial powers became members, although some, such as France and Portugal, were more reluctant to abolish forced labour than others, such as Britain (van Waijenburg 2018). Increasingly, British colonies in both Africa and Southeast Asia dealt with the problem of labour shortages by encouraging in-migration from the Indian sub-continent and China. The Dutch were reluctant to allow in-migration but encouraged the Javanese to move to the less densely settled islands outside Java.[7] But they continued to impose labour

---

[7] This involved the movement of people to the areas in northern Sumatra, where there was a rapid growth in labour demand on large agricultural estates. In addition, the colonial state funded land settlement projects in both Sumatra and other islands outside Java, although the numbers which had moved up to 1941 were quite small. For a discussion of

obligations (*heerendiensten*) on indigenous populations outside Java until 1942.

The greater emphasis on development expenditures, to the extent that they occurred, eventually also placed a time bomb under the colonial state-building project. Educated indigenous elites, some of whom had studied at universities in the metropole, started to play an important role in the rise of various independence movements in Asia and Africa. There was no way that the call for emancipation and representation could be accommodated by administrations whose survival was predicated on restricting access to political as well as economic markets in order to safeguard the interests of European, American and Japanese settlers, planters, merchants and enterprises.

Lessons from a Comparative Approach

Globalization and Colonial Fiscal Development

What then, are the lessons that can be learned from the comparative approach taken in this book? First of all, the comparative evidence indicates that the opportunities to engage in international or imperial trade were *the single most important determinant* of the cross-colony variation in budget size. Figure 1.1 shows the correlation between per capita export revenues (y-axis) and per capita government revenues (x-axis) in 1911 (a census year in the British empire) on a logarithmic scale. This relationship remained strong throughout the colonial era. In most colonies, a large part of the revenues from international trade came from custom duties, and especially import duties. But there were also a range of other taxes that co-evolved with international trade. These included state revenues from shares in export companies (e.g. mining firms), corporate and individual income taxes, harbour duties, excises and export taxes. Government monopolies on items such as salt, alcohol and opium were also important in some colonies, as these were often viewed as a way of taxing Asian migrant workers, including Indians and Chinese, who were otherwise considered hard to reach. In Africa, the revenues from state marketing boards also became significant, especially from the 1930s onwards.

Figure 1.1 also shows that there was no sharp distinction between the per capita export revenues generated in African and Asian colonies. In both regions, the development of exports showed considerable variation.

---

transmigration policies in both the colonial and post-colonial eras, up to the early years of the Suharto era, see Hardjono (1977).

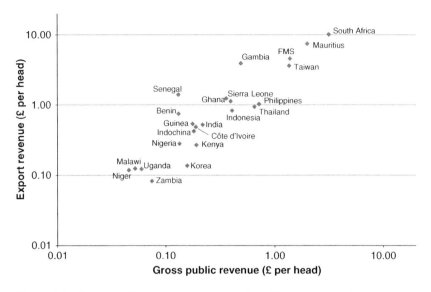

Figure 1.1 Gross public revenue per capita (x-axis) versus export revenue per capita (y-axis), c. 1911 (current £)
Source: Gross public revenue from the various contributions to this volume, export revenues from Mitchell (2007, table E1); Asian population from Maddison (2010); and African population from Frankema and Jerven (2014).

Booth (Chapter 2, this volume) argues that colonial governments in the Philippines, Indonesia and British Malaya boosted tropical export crops such as sugar, coffee, tea, fruits, rubber, palm oil and tobacco. They did this through facilitating the establishment of large estates, usually owned by interests in the metropolitan country, although in the Philippines local investors were also involved. In addition, smallholder cultivators of export crops were important in Indonesia, Thailand, Burma and South Vietnam,

Roy (Chapter 3, this volume) argues that the problem of fiscal inertia in British India (i.e. a persistently small tax base in per capita terms) was partly due to a reluctance to squeeze the agricultural sector too hard, and partly due to a lack of alternatives, including limited per capita involvement in international trade. Most colonies in sub-Saharan Africa and Southeast Asia experienced an impressive terms of trade boom during the nineteenth century (Williamson 2011, Frankema et al. 2018), but British India did not experience a similar windfall. On the other hand, the early abolition of taxes and other restrictions on domestic trade led to the establishment of a vast customs union across the Indian sub-continent, in which the main urban economic zones were connected by railroads. In other words, even with a small central budget and a limited basis for indirect taxation, domestic markets became significantly better integrated under colonial rule (Studer 2008, Bogart & Chaudary 2013).

Frankema and van Waijenburg (Chapter 6, this volume) argue that the coastal colonies in West Africa enjoyed a notable advantage over inland colonies, and that this locational advantage led to different fiscal policies in British and French colonies. The federal structure adopted in French West Africa functioned as a vehicle to integrate areas that were by themselves fiscally unsustainable. Per capita exports in French West Africa remained low from 1913 to 1938 in comparison with Ghana, and most parts of colonial Asia, including the Federated Malay States, which were part of the larger federation of British Malaya (Booth 2008, table 3). The French also created a fiscal federation in Indochina, as López Jerez (Chapter 4, this volume) explains, although here too, export revenues per capita were low in comparison with other Asian colonies.

Gardner (Chapter 7, this volume) also indicates that in the settler colonies of East Africa, lower volumes of trade in the early colonial era put a limit to fiscal expansion and supported the introduction of direct taxes, which were both more costly to levy and more directly felt by local tax-payers. Differences in export development also played a role in Portuguese Africa. Alexopoulou (Chapter 8, this volume) shows that Mozambique had to rely more on direct taxes, while the Angolan government relied more on trade taxes, including those derived from lucrative diamond exports. Gwaindepi and Siebrits (Chapter 9, this volume) show how the mineral discoveries in South Africa created ample opportunities for fiscal expansion, which they see reflected in high railway investments and which also encouraged heavy state intervention in the labour market.

The disadvantage of dependence on trade taxes was the vulnerability of colonial budgets to world market volatility. The great depression of the 1930s hit the budgets of the main commodity exporters particularly hard and resulted in austerity measures in colonies as diverse as Ghana, Indonesia, British Malaya and Angola. The terms of trade of most tropical commodities underwent a prolonged decline during the first four decades of the twentieth century. Falling relative prices were compensated by expanding production volumes or by the introduction of new commodities, such as the rubber and palm oil in British Malaya and Indonesia (Booth 2007a, 56–60, Buelens & Frankema 2016). But even in these colonies, the depression years certainly imposed hardship on many people who lost access to wage employment, and had to accept lower prices for most export commodities.

Local Conditions versus Metropolitan Visions

This volume also offers support for the view that *local* economic, social and political conditions were more important in the design of colonial fiscal systems than metropolitan blueprints for fiscal governance (Frankema & van Waijenburg 2014). Apart from the different opportunities for the creation or expansion of export markets, some of which developed spontaneously, while others were enforced, the nature of precolonial tax systems also mattered a lot. In some places, such as Equatorial Africa, there was no system available that could be adopted by the colonial government. Squeezing revenue out of the local population through forced labour seemed to be the only option.

In British India, on the contrary, the Raj was very reluctant to introduce new taxes and modified the existing system of land taxes as a financial basis for the colonial state (Roy, Chapter 3, this volume). This system proved inelastic. In French Indochina, the French decision to impose indirect rule in most regions meant that existing power structures remained in place right down to the village level. Local elites had little incentive to alter existing revenue systems and the French lacked the capacity to force them to change. New revenues imposed by the French thus added to existing tax obligations for most rural people (López Jerez, Chapter 4, this volume).

That metropolitan visions of fiscal organization, whatever they might have been, were of limited influence, is obvious when we look at revenue outcomes across colonies in Asia and Africa in the early twentieth century (Figure 1.1). Revenue systems adopted within particular empires varied considerably. Alexopoulou (Chapter 8, this volume) shows that even within Mozambique there were three distinct revenue systems geared towards local economic and political structures, with limited opportunity to impose a uniform system. If we examine the much larger French and British empires, the variation is even more striking. Revenues range from land and opium taxes in India and parts of Southeast Asia to 'plural wives' taxes in Tanzania, from cattle taxes in French West Africa to rice export taxes in Indochina. Local economies and polities thus shaped both the opportunities and the constraints to fiscal capacity building.

This does not mean, however, that metropolitan identity did not matter at all. The different preferences of the metropolitan powers for direct or indirect rule, for the use of forced labour and the availability of investment capital from the metropolitan economy or elsewhere all had a bearing on different practices of revenue generation. In addition, the fiscal systems of the home governments undoubtedly had some impact on colonial practice. As López Jerez (Chapter 4, this volume) points out, the French only began to implement an income tax in France in the late 1930s; before that they depended very largely on indirect taxes and non-tax revenues. In Indonesia, income taxes assessed on both individual and corporate incomes grew in importance in the last decades of colonial rule, as they did in British India (Kumar 1983, table 12.7). To a considerable extent, this reflects British and Dutch practice at home, although it should be noted that in British Malaya, income taxes were not imposed until after 1945.

Metropolitan visions of colonial development were expressed more clearly in the expenditure side of the budget. For instance, the contrast in education spending between the Philippines and Indonesia reveals a very different view of the long-term aims of colonial rule (Booth, Chapter 2, this volume). For the Americans, education was the principle means of preparing the indigenous population for self-government, and eventual independence. For the Dutch, who considered their colonial role in the Indies as a permanent condition, the drive to increase access to education was much more limited.

As independence movements developed in India, Indonesia and Vietnam in the early twentieth century, British, French and Dutch colonial governments feared that too much access to education in the language of the colonial power would create unrealistic expectations about employment, which would in turn lead to more demands for self-government if not complete independence. Differences in metropolitan visions were also clear in the attitudes towards Christian missionaries and their role in the provision of 'public' services such as health and education (Cogneau & Moradi 2014, Frankema 2012).

As Booth and Deng (Chapter 5, this volume) demonstrate, Japanese policies in Korea and Taiwan were predicated on the idea of forcible assimilation, and their spending patterns prioritized this goal. This was reflected especially in programmes of railway construction, and in the large-scale private investments in both colonies, as well as in Manchuria in the 1930s. Access to primary education was also expanded, although there were few opportunities for young people in the colonies to get access to post-primary education. The figures on numbers enrolled in education as a percentage of the total population varied considerably across colonial Asia in the late 1930s. The highest figure was in the Philippines, followed by Taiwan and Thailand where many young people were enrolled in monastic schools. This was also true for Burma, where the figure was about the same as for Korea; Indonesia and Indochina were lower, although still higher than in Ghana or Nigeria (Booth 2008, table 12).

Of course, all expenditure decisions were taken within the context of tight budgets, but the relative shares of the budget that went into the security forces, both soldiers and police, varied enormously. Roy (Chapter 3, this volume) shows how the Indian army ate away a big chunk from already limited budgets, not only to maintain order in India, but also to secure it in other parts of the empire. Alexopoulou (Chapter 8, this volume) also indicates that the size of the Portuguese African army was comparatively large, and that security expenses remained very high up to the 1930s. Other colonies could rely much more on external assistance in case of need, from, for example, the British Navy, or imperial recruits, thus supressing the costs of a large permanent local army.

Alexopoulou and Frankema (2018) have argued elsewhere that such resource pooling mechanisms were easier to organize in the British Empire than in the empires of the weaker metropolitan states, such as Portugal or the Netherlands. Indonesia, along with Manchuria and independent Thailand allocated over 30 per cent of budgetary outlays to law and order and defence in the 1930s, compared with only 8 per cent in the Philippines and 7 per cent in Taiwan (Booth and Deng, Table 5.8, this volume). Defence expenditures in both the Federated Malay States and Ghana were even lower, at less than 3 per cent (Booth 2008, table 6). In the Philippines, there was a small military presence which was paid for from the American budget, while 36 per cent of Philippine budgetary outlays went to health and education compared with 12 per cent in Indonesia and only 4 per cent in French Indochina.[8] In Portuguese Africa, where the government spent much larger amounts on the security forces compared with the more advanced parts of British Africa, the budget available for welfare spending remained very small (Alexopoulou & Frankema 2018; Gardner, Table 7.3, this volume).

Africa versus Asia: Distinct Patterns?

Were there distinctive 'Asian' and 'African' patterns of colonial fiscal development? It appears from Figure 1.2 that the average Asian colony had a somewhat larger budget in 1911, but the variation in budgets and in population size was too large to make strong inferences on the basis of these estimates. In terms of spending capacity, the variation within both

---

[8] By the late 1930s, Ghana was spending a higher proportion of its budgetary outlays on health, education, public works and agriculture than most Southeast Asian colonies, although in per capita terms, expenditure was lower than in most colonies except the Philippines and French Indochina (Booth 2008, table 6).

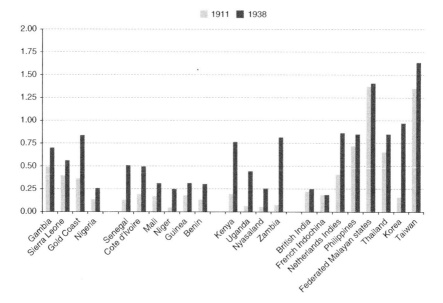

Figure 1.2 Gross public revenue per capita in 1911 and 1938 (in current £)
Sources: Revenue data supplied by contributors to this volume, occasionally complemented by data from Mitchell (2007, Table G6). Population data for African colonies from Frankema and Jerven (2014), for Asian colonies from Maddison (2010).

regions appears at least as large as the cross-continental differences. It seems that individual colonies followed distinct patterns of fiscal development, some of it based on mining (Zambia, South Africa), others on tropical export crops (Uganda, Ghana, Nigeria, French Indochina) or a combination of both (Indonesia, Malaysia, Belgian Congo, Angola). There was a group of landlocked African colonies where revenues remained small because of limited opportunities (e.g. Niger, Chad, Mali) and two large Asian colonies (British India, French Indochina), where central governments found it difficult to centralize fiscal revenues that were well established at local levels.

Three generalizations may be made, notwithstanding the exceptions that are present in all cases. First, colonial states in Asia tended to have had a longer experience of colonial governance, at least in their core areas. With the exceptions of French Indochina, the Japanese colonies and the Cape Colony (South Africa), Asian colonial governments had more time to integrate, impose, expand or consolidate fiscal policies than colonial governments in sub-Saharan Africa. Second, tax systems in Asia were, on the whole, more deeply rooted in local agricultural systems, and were underpinned by more fine-grained systems of tax assessment (income, wealth, especially land and consumption). Put differently, by the early twentieth century, Asian colonial states had a better capacity to collect information-intensive taxes. A third generalization relates to the greater emphasis colonial governments in Asia placed on agricultural development, and on developing infrastructure, especially irrigation systems, to boost agricultural output.

The development of land taxes illustrates the second of these points. By the early twentieth century, land taxes were important in several parts of colonial Asia, but remained virtually absent in colonial Africa. Historical differences in the spread of sedentary agriculture probably played an important role in explaining this difference. Nomadic pastoralism was more deeply rooted in various tribal societies living in Africa's extensive savannah belts, large parts of which were too dry for crop cultivation. Farmers were probably more mobile in forested parts of sub-Saharan Africa than in the rice producing regions in Asia, where farmers had adapted to (or were earlier coerced into) more sedentary lifestyles. Taxing shifting cultivators at the central level was very difficult as Frankema and van Waijenburg (Chapter 6, this volume) argue. The absence of land taxes in most parts of Africa and their importance across many parts of colonial Asia, also implied differences in pre-colonial administrative structures.

In African states, the role of slavery in fiscal systems was larger, while feudal relations were more developed in parts of Asia. But even within Asia, there were considerable differences in the extent to which governments assessed land taxes, and their importance in local and central revenue systems. Some colonial authorities viewed accurate land cadastres as essential not just for assessing taxes but also for establishing property rights, and estimating output of key staples such as rice.

Given these benefits, some governments were prepared to invest considerable sums in drawing up and maintaining accurate land records, but in other regions, land cadastres either did not exist, or were considered very inaccurate. Even within one colonial jurisdiction, there were often wide variations. The Dutch had very accurate records for Java and Bali, but in most other islands, little attempt was made to develop accurate land records. Within British India, land taxes formed a much higher proportion of agricultural output in Burma than elsewhere in India, or indeed in most other Asian colonies (Booth 2014, table 2).

Taxes on domestic consumption at the retail level were another indicator of a more fine-grained system of tax assessment. Even though a general sales tax, let alone a value-added tax, was not implemented anywhere in colonial Asia or Africa, there were a variety of excises and consumption taxes in Asia, and their contribution to the budget was, in many cases, substantial. These consumption taxes were often first introduced as revenue farms, auctioned by the central government, but later integrated into central collection systems (Wahid 2013). Consumption taxes also existed in African colonies, but not on a similar scale. In African colonies a combination of custom duties, poll, head or hut taxes and railway revenues tended to dominate the revenue mix.

A longer legacy of revenue centralization also had implications for state investments in administration, infrastructure and other public services. Again, one has to be careful not to overstate the Asia–Africa differences. The wealthiest colonies in Africa did perform better than the poorest colonies in Asia. But if we look at the four indicators listed in Table 1.1, it is difficult to escape the conclusion that the Asian colonies included in this book did have higher railway densities, higher per capita output of electricity (except for the major mining areas in Africa), more currency in circulation per head of the population, a significant lead in educational attainment and higher literacy rates. At the same time, Table 1.1 illustrates the variation within both regions, and especially the impressively rapid development of infrastructure in the Japanese colonies of Korea and Taiwan (Booth & Deng, Chapter 5, this volume) and the distinct development path of South Africa (Gwaindepi & Siebrits, Chapter 9, this volume).

The third generalization relates to investment in agricultural development. The evidence, although not conclusive, does suggest that government expenditure on agricultural development in Asia was not just higher, but also more focused on food crop cultivation, especially in those areas that were densely settled and where colonial officials were worried about food security. The Dutch had invested heavily in developing irrigation systems and transport networks in Java from the late nineteenth century to 1930, and were turning their attention to other islands when the global depression forced them to curtail expenditures. The French invested heavily in irrigation and drainage projects in both the Red River and the Mekong deltas (López Jerez, Chapter 4, this volume). Although there were some attempts to develop irrigation systems in West Africa, they appear to have been poorly planned, and were not successful in raising food output. In view of the very different paths of rural transformation in Asia and Sub-Saharan Africa after 1950, deeper comparisons of the role of the colonial state in agricultural development seem to be warranted.

Fiscal 'Modernization' under Colonial Rule: a Contradiction in Terms?

In what sense can we talk about fiscal modernization under colonial rule? All the chapters in this volume indicate that colonial governments managed, sooner or later, to increasingly centralize revenues. In large parts of Africa, where pre-colonial states were either weakly developed or entirely absent, resources were mainly pooled at communal or tribal levels. In some regions, the colonial state had to build fiscal systems from scratch. State-controlled slave production systems were difficult to incorporate into colonial revenue policies, as were farmers practising shifting cultivation, nomadic pastoralists and other households that remained largely outside the monetary economy. In addition, colonial officials often had to tolerate taxes in labour and kind, because they lacked the ability to stop them, or because they did not want to alienate indigenous leaders.

Centralization of revenues did not necessarily imply diversification. High revenues per capita could be extracted by the state with a limited number of tax and non-tax instruments. The case of British Malaya illustrates this point; in both the Straits Settlements and the Federated Malay States, revenues per capita were high by Asian standards, but mainly derived from excises on opium, tobacco, alcohol and petroleum products, together with non-tax sources (Booth, Chapter 2, this volume). Elsewhere colonial officials had to make a greater effort to diversify revenue sources. In Africa, the need for diversification was especially great in colonies that lacked an economically significant foreign trade sector. In Ghana and Nigeria, where exports per capita had increased quite rapidly between 1900 and 1940, direct taxes and customs duties accounted for a higher proportion of total revenues than in any Asian colony by the late 1930s (Booth 2008, table 8). But in other parts of West and East Africa, there was a heavy reliance on forced labour to put the wheels of commerce in motion (van Waijenburg 2018, Frankema & van Waijenburg, Chapter 6, this volume).

Forced or corvée labour declined in importance in most Asian colonies, and in Thailand after 1900, but it persisted in some parts of Indonesia (Booth, Chapter 2, this volume). The fiscal systems of the major mining economies were relatively straightforward, but also proved vulnerable to world market shocks. The treasuries of British Northern Rhodesia and the Belgian Congo, for instance, became increasingly dependent on copper receipts after 1950, but this led to a dramatic collapse in the 1970s when world copper prices plummeted and both countries fell back to the very bottom of the African national income rankings (Abbeloos 2013).

We should be careful not to push too far the argument that indirect trade taxes crowded out more information-intensive direct taxes. After all, the revenues from trade taxes stimulated investments in bureaucratic capacity, which were in turn a necessary condition for the development of a more sophisticated tax administration. The poorest African colonies may have relied to a larger extent on direct taxes, but the hut, poll or head taxes collected by local chiefs did not reflect greater 'administrative capacity'. They did not entail a detailed assessment of the incomes accruing from indigenous farms, households or enterprises, let alone their total wealth. Nor did colonial governments necessarily have firm control over the chiefs or village heads who collected direct taxes. Many had good reasons for under-reporting the amounts they were collecting. More in general, tax avoidance remained a structural phenomenon.

He (2013) has emphasized the importance of commercialization in facilitating the rise of the fiscal state in both Britain and Japan, and it is probable that in many colonial territories the development of a modern financial system was hampered by the fact that most of the population participated in the cash economy only to a limited extent. Outside the main cities, few people had access to banks, and savings were often held in gold, cattle or land. By the early twentieth century, governments were borrowing to fund infrastructure projects but the borrowing was almost always conducted in metropolitan financial markets. Even so, the domestic money supply did grow relative to GDP in some colonies, although greater monetization was restricted to urban dwellers, and those rural producers who marketed all or part of their output (see, for example, on India and Japan: Goldsmith 1983; see on Indonesia: Van Laanen 1990).

When we examine the evidence on government borrowing, we again see striking differences between colonies. The Portuguese regime under Salazar after 1933 was extremely reluctant to expand colonial debt (Alexopoulou, Chapter 8, this volume). But this reluctance was not widely shared. British India, Nigeria and South Africa adopted different policies. In India, a large unified currency zone emerged with a greater reliance on internal debt financing, and a rising share of local investors in government bonds (Roy, Chapter 3, this volume). In South Africa, the mineral discoveries set the stage for large investments in railway infrastructure and created ample leverage for debt financing by the colonial government. Moreover, as Gwaindepi and Siebrits demonstrate, the autonomy of South Africa granted in 1910 also freed the way for the creation of a modern fiscal system that was more advanced than in any of the other African or Asian colonies discussed in this volume (Chapter 9, this volume). Indeed, the size of national income, whether driven by large population numbers or abundant mineral resources, expanded the possibilities of colonial debt creation.

In many parts of Asia and Africa by the early twentieth century, we observe major cross-colony differences in expenditures on health and education, but nowhere did they come close to the amounts that were being spent in the metropoles. The Americans did channel a substantial share of the annual budget in the Philippines into education, but elsewhere allocations to health and education were much lower (Booth & Deng 2017, table 4). In the Southeast Asian case, we have the counterfactual of independent Thailand, but while the Thai government did not lag far behind most Asian colonies in terms of development, neither did it forge ahead (Table 1.1). On numerous occasions between 1850 and 1950, the Thai government prioritized defence expenditures over development expenditures on, for example, irrigation or education. The main non-colonized counterfactual in Africa was Ethiopia, which also ran a central budget that was large enough to field a substantial army in its attempt to avoid Italian invasion. At most, we can argue that colonial states in Africa initiated revenue centralization in those regions which did not have a central polity, and that they accelerated welfare spending compared with what might have happened in the absence of colonial control. But this is speculative, as indeed it is in most parts of colonial Asia.

The final criterion of fiscal modernization, the development of accountable government, was by definition impossible under colonial rule. Even though independence movements managed to obtain some political concessions and exercise greater influence in some colonies, fiscal sovereignty was only achieved after decolonization. But nowhere did this transition result in the kinds of constraints on executive power that operated in metropolitan countries such as Britain, France, the United States or the Netherlands. Institutions such as effective audit boards were often slow to develop after independence, and in many former colonies they are still weak, or non-existent. Fiscal sovereignty became more difficult to achieve in the 1980s, as structural adjustment programmes made independent governments subject to conditions imposed by foreign donors and international organizations such as the IMF. In the early twenty-first century, the majority of African states still cope with external financial dependence, while the majority of Asian states enjoy greater sovereignty in fiscal and monetary affairs.[9]

---

[9] For the twenty-seven low-income African countries, the share of Official Development Assistance (ODA) of GDP averaged c. 13 per cent in 2000–5 and c. 9 per cent in 2013–14 (OECD, African Economic Outlook 2014, p. 49).

Table 1.1 *Comparative indicators of economic development in Africa and Asia, c. 1950*

	Railway density 1950	Electricity output 1950	Currency in circulation 1938	Years of school attainment 1950
	Km/1000 Km²	*kwh per capita*	*£ per capita*	*population 15+*
British West Africa	3.6	7.8	0.44	0.6*
French West Africa	2.1	2.0	0.27	0.6
British East & Central Africa	1.9	7.6	–	1.1
Portuguese Africa	2.5	6.0	0.25	0.5**
South Africa	17	876	1.61	4.2
India	17	14	0.39	1.0
Indochina	1.9	6.2	–	2.0
Indonesia	11	8.4	0.26***	1.1
Philippines	3.8	25	0.98	2.8
Federated Malayan states	25	93	1.32	2.1
Thailand	6.1	3.4	0.71	3.4
South Korea	28	20	0.90	4.5
Taiwan	26	172	1.09	4.3

Sources: Railway length, electricity output and currency from Mitchell (2007; tables F1, D24, G1). Attainment estimates from Barro and Lee (2013). Population data for African colonies from Frankema and Jerven (2014), for Asian colonies from Maddison (2010). * Population weighted average of Gambia, Sierra Leone and the Gold Coast, excluding Nigeria. ** Mozambique only, no data for Angola. *** The Indonesian estimate probably excludes paper currency and is therefore too low.

Future Agenda

Now that the first steps towards a comparative understanding of fiscal developments in colonial Asia and Africa have been made, it is worth asking which lines of research are worth pursuing in future work. We see three interrelated priorities.

First, and most important, we need to connect the largely separate literatures on colonial and post-colonial fiscal development. Are there any common patterns in fiscal development after independence, which can be traced back to a shared colonial heritage, or should we rather focus on understanding cross-country variations? One of the reasons we grapple with the question of 'colonial legacies' is that we lack a sound analytical framework to distinguish the structural conditions of fiscal capacity building which emerged under colonial rule, from the changes brought about by the many political revolutions in Africa and Asia since independence. In addition, civil or interstate wars, exogenous economic shocks caused by volatile world markets and the unpredictable dynamics of global political relations have all affected fiscal policies. The structural conditions inherited from the colonial era are important for understanding path dependence in both fiscal resources and the institutions underpinning country-specific systems of public finance. The more contingent events are important in analysing deviations from the historical path. Such an analytical framework is crucial in explaining not just the persistence of specific taxes in the post-colonial era, but also changes in the composition of revenue and the allocation of government expenditure. More broadly, we need a framework to understand the political economy of fiscal reforms in the post-colonial era.

Second, and directly connected with the above, there is a need for a deeper analysis of the development of public debt spanning the colonial and post-colonial eras. One of the most influential and widely shared episodes of post-colonial public finance was the debt crisis of the 1980s. To what extent did colonial legacies play a role in this crisis, and to what extent did the responses to this crisis erase these legacies? On the eve of independence, all countries were indebted to varying degrees, but nowhere did government borrowing reach proportions that could overturn the entire fiscal system. This changed in the third quarter of the twentieth century, but the mechanisms driving this change remain poorly understood, at least from a historical perspective. The evolution of government borrowing in the global South is an extremely important aspect of both political and financial globalization, linking fiscal policy-making at the country level to global financial relations, but there is a need for more comparative research on this topic.

Third, in spite of improved quantitative data that can be used to estimate and interpret fiscal developments across countries, there are more subtle changes in the conduct of fiscal policy which are harder to monitor. Changes in information technology have enabled some states to organize the assessment and collection of taxes, as well as the implementation of government expenditures in a much more efficient and transparent way. These changes in turn facilitate more complex methods of socio-economic governance and targeted expenditures than was feasible fifty years ago. In this respect, the changes in countries such as South Korea, Taiwan and South Africa have been nothing short of revolutionary. At the same time, there are many countries, especially in Africa, where the development of reliable flows of information needed for the functioning of the fiscal state has remained disappointing. To date, we understand only imperfectly to what extent varying colonial legacies can explain the development of state capacity in the post-colonial era, although it is clear that the education and training of government officials, both before and after independence, must have played an important role.

In other words, more comparative research is needed to obtain a deeper understanding of the complexities of fiscal state formation. We hope this volume will serve as a valuable contribution to this broader agenda.

Bibliography

Abbeloos, J-F. (2013). Mobutu, Suharto, and the Challenges of Nation-Building and Economic Development, 1965–97. In E. Frankema & F. Buelens (Eds.), *Colonial Exploitation and Economic Development: The Belgian Congo and the Netherlands Indies Compared*. London: Routledge, 251–73.

Accominotti, O., Flandreau, M., Rezzik R., & Zumer F. (2010). Black Man's Burden, White Man's Welfare: Control, Devolution and Development in the British Empire, 1880–1914. *European Review of Economic History*, 14(1), 47–70.

Acemoglu, D., Johnson, S., & Robinson, J. A. (2001). The Colonial Origins of Comparative Development: An Empirical Investigation. *American Economic Review*, 91(5), 1369–401.

Alexopoulou, K., & Frankema E. (2018). Imperialism of Jackals and Lions: The Militarization of Portuguese Africa in the British African Mirror, c. 1850–1940, Paper presented at the XVIII World Economic History Congress 2018, Boston.

Alexopoulou, K., & Juif, D. (2017). Colonial State Formation without Integration: Tax Capacity and Labour Regimes in Portuguese Mozambique (1890s–1970s). *International Review of Social History*, 62 (2), 215–52.

Austin, G., Frankema, E., & Jerven, M. (2017). Patterns of Manufacturing Growth in Sub-Saharan Africa: From Colonization to the Present. In K. H. O'Rourke & J. G. Williamson (Eds.), *The Spread of Modern Industry to the Periphery since 1871*, Oxford: Oxford University Press, 345–73.

Barro, R. J., & Lee, J-W. (2013). *A New Data Set of Educational Attainment in the World, 1950–2010*. NBER Working Paper No. 15902.

Bayly, C., & Harper, T. (2004). *Forgotten Armies: Britain's Asian Empire and the War with Japan*. London: Allen Lane.

Besley, T., & Persson, T. (2009). The Origins of State Capacity: Property Rights, Taxation, and Politics. *American Economic Review*, 99(4), 1218–44.

Besley, T., & Persson T. (2010). State Capacity, Conflict, and Development. *Econometrica*, 78(1), 1–34.

Bobrie, F. (1976). Finances publiques et conquête coloniale: le coût budgétaire de l'expansion française entre 1850 et 1913. *Annales*, 31 (6), 1225–44.

Bogart, D., & Chaudhary, L. (2013). Engines of Growth: The Productivity Advance of Indian Railways, 1874–1912. *The Journal of Economic History*, 73(2), 339–370.

Bonney, R. (Ed.). (1999). *The Rise of the Fiscal State in Europe, 1200–1815*. Oxford: Oxford University Press.

Booth, A. (1998). *Indonesian Economic Development in the Nineteenth and Twentieth Centuries: A History of Missed Opportunities*. London: Macmillan.

Booth, A. (2007a). *Colonial Legacies: Economic and Social Development in East and Southeast Asia*. Honolulu: University of Hawai'i Press.

Booth, A. (2007b). Night Watchmen, Extractive, or Developmental States? Some Evidence from Late Colonial South-East Asia. *Economic History Review*, 60(2), 241–66.

Booth, A. (2008). West Africa in the Southeast Asian Mirror: The Historical Origins of the Post-1960 Divergence. *Itinerario (European Journal of Overseas History)*, XXXII (3), 61–90.

Booth, A. (2014). Land taxation in Asia: An Overview of the 19th and 20th Centuries. *Oxford Development Studies*, 42(1), 1–18.

Booth, A., & Deng, K. (2017). Japanese Colonialism in Comparative Perspective. *Journal of World History*, 28(1), 61–98.

Bosma, U. (2013). Dutch Imperial Anxieties about Free Labour, Penal Sanctions and the Right to Strike. In A. Stanziani (Ed.), *Labour, Coercion, and Economic Growth in Eurasia, 17th-20th Centuries*. Leiden: Brill, 63–86.

Buelens, F., & Frankema, E. (2016). Colonial Adventures in Tropical Agriculture: New Estimates of Returns to Investment in the Netherlands Indies, 1919–1938. *Cliometrica*, 10(2), 197–224.

Buelens, F., & Marysse, S. (2009). Returns on Investments during the Colonial Era: the Case of the Belgian Congo. *Economic History Review*, 62(S1), 135–66.

Burbank, J., & Cooper, F. (2010). *Empires in World History: Power and the Politics of Difference*. Princeton: Princeton University Press.

Coquery-Vidrovitch, C. (1982). Le financement de la 'mise en valeur' coloniale, Méthode et premiers résultats. In *Etudes africaines offertes à Henri Brunschwig*, Paris: EHESS, 237–52.

Cogneau, D., & Moradi, A. (2014). Borders That Divide: Education and Religion in Ghana and Togo since Colonial Times. *The Journal of Economic History*, 74(3), 694–729.

Costa, L. F., Palma, N., & Reis, J. (2015). The Great Escape? The Contribution of the Empire to Portugal's Economic Growth, 1500–1800. *European Review of Economic History*, 19(1), 1–22.

Davis, L. E., & Huttenback, R. A. (1988). *Mammon and the Pursuit of Empire: the Economics of British Imperialism* (Abridged edition). Cambridge, MA: Cambridge University Press.

Dincecco, M. (2009). Political Regimes and Sovereign Credit Risk in Europe, 1750–1913. *European Review of Economic History*, 13(1), 31–63.

Dincecco, M. (2011). *Political Transformations and Public Finances: Europe, 1650–1913*. Cambridge; New York: Cambridge University Press.

Edelstein, M. (1994). Imperialism: Cost and Benefit. In R. Floud & D. McCloskey (Eds.), *The Economic History of Britain since 1700, vol. 2: 1860–1939*. Cambridge: Cambridge University Press, 197–216.

Elson, R. E. (1984). *Village Java under the Cultivation System*. Sydney: Allen and Unwin for the Asian Studies Association of Australia.

Engerman, S. L., & Sokoloff, K. L. (1997). Factor Endowments, Institutions, and Differential Paths of Growth among New World Economies: A View from Economic Historians of the United States. In S. Haber (Ed.), *How Latin America Fell Behind: Essays on the Economic Histories of Brazil and Mexico, 1800–1914*. Stanford, CA: Stanford University Press, 260–304.

Fasseur, C. (1991). Purse or Principle: Dutch Colonial Policy in the 1860s and the Decline of the Cultivation System. *Modern Asian Studies*, 25(1), 33–52.

Feinstein, C. H. (2005). *An Economic History of South Africa: Conquest, Discrimination and Development*. Cambridge, UK: Cambridge University Press.

Ferguson, N. (2002). *Empire: the Rise and Demise of the British World Order and the Lessons for Global Power*. New York: Basic Books.

Ferguson, N., & M. Schularick. (2006). The Empire Effect: the Determinants of Country Risk in the First Age of Globalization, 1880–1913. *The Journal of Economic History*, 66(2), 283–312.

Frankema, E. (2011). Colonial Taxation and Government Spending in British Africa, 1880–1940: Maximizing Revenue or Minimizing Effort? *Explorations in Economic History*, 48(1), 136–49.

Frankema, E. (2012). The Origins of Formal Education in Sub-Saharan Africa: Was British Rule More Benign? *European Review of Economic History*, 16(4), 335–55.

Frankema, E., & Buelens, F. (2013). Introduction. In E. Frankema & F. Buelens (Eds.), *Colonial Exploitation and Economic Development: the Belgian Congo and the Netherlands Indies Compared*. London: Routledge, 1–17.

Frankema, E., & Jerven, M. (2014). Writing History Backwards or Sideways: Towards a Consensus on African Population, 1850–2010. *The Economic History Review*, 67(4), 907–31.

Frankema, E., & van Waijenburg, M. (2014). Metropolitan Blueprints of Colonial Taxation: Lessons from Fiscal Capacity Building in British and French Africa, c. 1880–1940. *Journal of African History*, 55(3), 371–400.

Frankema, E., Williamson, J. G., & Woltjer P. J. (2018). An Economic Rationale for the West African Scramble: the Commercial Transition and the Commodity Price Boom of 1835–1885. *The Journal of Economic History*, 18(1), 231–67.

Gann, L. H., & Duignan, P. (1967). *Burden of Empire: An Appraisal of Western Colonialism in Africa South of the Sahara*. Stanford University, Stanford, CA: Hoover Institution Press.

Gardner, L. A. (2012). *Taxing Colonial Africa: the Political Economy of British Imperialism*. Oxford: Oxford University Press.

Gardner, L. A. (2017). Colonialism or Supersanctions: Sovereignty and Debt in West Africa, 1871–1914, *European Review in Economic History*, 21(2), 236–57.

Goldsmith, R. W. (1983). *The Financial Development of India, Japan and the United States: a Trilateral Institutional, Statistical, and Analytic Comparison*. New Haven: Yale University Press.

Gordon, A. (2010). Netherlands East Indies: the Large Colonial Surplus of Indonesia 1878–1939. *Journal of Contemporary Asia*, 40 (3), 425–43.

Grafe, R., & Irigoin, M. A. (2012). A Stakeholder Empire: the Political Economy of Spanish Imperial Rule in America. *Economic History Review*, 65(2), 609–51.

Hardjono, J. M. (1977). *Transmigration in Indonesia*. Kuala Lumpur: Oxford University Press.

He, W. K. (2013). *Paths towards the Modern Fiscal State: England, Japan and China*. Cambridge: Harvard University Press.

Hoffman, P. T. (2015). What Do States Do? Politics and Economic History. *The Journal of Economic History*, 75(2), 303–32.

Hopkins, A. G. (2002). *Globalization in World History*. New York: Norton.

Huillery, E. (2014). The Black Man's Burden: the Cost of Colonization of French West Africa. *The Journal of Economic History*, 74(1), 1–38.

Jamal, V. (1978). Taxation and Inequality in Uganda, 1900–1964. *The Journal of Economic History*, 38(2), 418–38.

Kirk-Greene, A. H. M. (1980). The Thin White Line: the Size of the British Colonial Service in Africa. *African Affairs*, 79(314), 25–44.

Kumar, D. (1983). The Fiscal System. In D. Kumar & M. Desai (Eds.), *The Cambridge Economic History of India, vol. 2: c.1757-c,1970*. Cambridge: Cambridge University Press, 905–44.

Kuznets, S. (1974). Modern Economic Growth: Findings and Reflections. In S. Kuznets (Eds.), *Population, Capital and Growth: Selected Essays*. London: Heinemann Educational Books, 165–84.

Lains, P. (1998). An Account of the Portuguese African Empire, 1885–1975. *Revista de Historia Económica*, 16(1), 235–63.

Law, R. (Ed.). (1995). *From Slave Trade to Legitimate Commerce: the Commercial Transition in Nineteenth-Century West Africa*. Cambridge: Cambridge University Press.

Lefeuvre, D. (2006). *Pour en finir avec la repentance coloniale*. Paris: Flammarion.

Ma, D. (2013). State Capacity and Great Divergence: the Case of Qing China. *Eurasian Geography and Economics*, 54(5–6), 484–99.

Maddison, A. (2010). *Historical Statistics on World Population, GDP and Per Capita GDP, 1–2008 AD*. www.ggdc.net/maddison/.

Marichal, C. (2007). *Bankruptcy of Empire: Mexican Silver and the Wars between Spain, Britain and France, 1760–1810*. Cambridge, MA: Cambridge University Press.

Marseille, J. (1984). *Empire colonial et capitalisme français. Histoire d'un divorce*. Paris: Albin Michel.

Mitchell, B. R. (2007). *International Historical Statistics: Africa, Asia & Oceania, 1750–2005*. 5th ed. Basingstoke: Palgrave Macmillan.

Moulton, H. G. (1931). *Japan: An Economic and Financial Appraisal*. Washington, DC: Brookings Institution.

Myers, R. H., & Peattie, M. R. (1984). *The Japanese colonial empire, 1895–1945*. Princeton, NJ: Princeton University Press.

North, D. C., Summerhill, W., & Weingast, B. R. (2000). Order, Disorder and Economic Change. In B. Bueno de Mesquita & H. L. Root (Eds.), *Governing for Prosperity*. New Haven: Yale University Press, 17–58.

O'Brien, P. K. (1988). The Costs and Benefits of British Imperialism, 1846–1914. *Past and Present*, 120(1), 163–200.

O'Brien, P. K., & Prados de la Escosura, L. (1998). The Costs and Benefits for Europeans from Their Empires Overseas. *Revista de Historia Económica*, 16(1), 29–89.

OECD. (2014). *African Economic Outlook 2014: Global Value Chains and Africa's Industrialisation*. African Development Bank, Organisation for Economic Co-operation and Development, United Nations Development Programme.

Offer, A. (1993). The British Empire, 1870–1914: a Waste of Money? *Economic History Review*, 46(2), 215–38.

O'Rourke, K., & Williamson, J. G. (1999). *Globalization and History: The Evolution of a Nineteenth-Century Atlantic Economy*. Cambridge, MA: The MIT Press.

Prados de la Escosura, L. (2012). Output per Head in pre-Independence Africa: Quantitative Conjectures. *Economic History of Developing Regions* 27(2), 1–36.

Prakash, O. (2004). *Mutiny and Its Aftermath*. New Delhi: Anmol Publications.

Roy, T. (2012). *Natural Disasters and Indian History*. New Delhi: Oxford University Press.

Sokoloff, K. L., & Zolt, E. M. (2006). Inequality and Taxation: Evidence from the Americas on How Inequality May Influence Tax Institutions. *Tax Law Review*, 59 (2), 201–76.

Sunderland, D. (2007). *Managing British Colonial and Post-Colonial Development*. Woodbridge: Boydell & Brewer.

Tilly, C. (1990). *Coercion, Capital, and European States, A.D. 990–1992*. Cambridge, MA: Blackwell.

Van der Eng, P. (1998). Exploring Exploitation: The Netherlands and Colonial Indonesia 1870–1940. *Revista de Historia Económica*, 16(1), 291–321.

Van Laanen, J. T. M. (1990). Between the Java Bank and the Chinese Moneylender: Banking and Credit in Colonial Indonesia. In A. Booth, W. J. O'Malley & A. Weidemann (Eds.), *Indonesian Economic History in the Dutch Colonial Era*, Monograph Series 35. New Haven: Yale University Southeast Asia Studies, 244–66.

Van Waijenburg, M. (2018). Financing the African Colonial State: the Revenue Imperative and Forced Labour. *The Journal of Economic History*, 18(1), 40–80.

Van Zanden, J. L., & van Riel, A. (2000). *Nederland, 1780–1914: Staat, Instituties en Economische Ontwikkeling*. Amsterdam: Balans.

Vanthemsche, G. (2010). *La Belgique et le Congo l'impact de la colonie sur la métropole*. Bruxelles: Le Cri Ed.

Wagner, R. E. (2003). Public Choice and the Diffusion of Classic Italian Public Finance. In D. Fausto & V. de Bonis, (Eds.), *The Theory of Public Finance in Italy from the Origins to the 1940s, Il Pensiero Economico Italiano, anno XI(1)*, 271–82.

Wahid, A. (2013). *From Revenue Farming to State Monopoly: the Political Economy of Taxation in Colonial Indonesia, Java c. 1816–1942*. PhD Thesis, Utrecht University, Utrecht.

Williamson, J. G. (2011). *Trade and Poverty when the Third World Fell Behind*. Cambridge, MA: MIT Press.

Young, C. (1994). *The African Colonial State in Comparative Perspective*. New Haven: Yale University Press.

Yun-Casalilla, B., & O'Brien P. K. (2012). *The Rise of Fiscal States: A Global History 1500–1914*. Cambridge: Cambridge University Press.

2 Towards a Modern Fiscal State in Southeast Asia, c. 1900–60

Anne Booth

Introduction

This chapter examines the changing role of the state in Southeast Asia in the decades from 1900 through to 1960, a period which covers the last phase of colonialism in the region, and the transition to independence.[1] Southeast Asia is a particularly interesting part of the world in which to study comparative colonial policies as by the end of the nineteenth century the three main European colonial powers, Britain, France and the Netherlands, all controlled substantial territories in the region. The Spanish, who had occupied the Philippine islands since the seventeenth century, ceded control to the Americans after their defeat in the Spanish-American War at the end of the nineteenth century. Thus, by the early twentieth century, four colonial powers were active in the region, while Siam, which became Thailand at the end of the 1930s, had managed to remain independent, although at the cost of losing territory to both the British and the French. The Thai government accepted British financial advisers, and although their influence varied considerably, their advice was often important on monetary, trade, exchange rate and fiscal policies.

Each of the colonial powers controlling both island and mainland Southeast Asia endeavoured in the latter part of the nineteenth century to establish effective administrative structures which prioritized the centralization and reform of fiscal systems (Elson 1992, 149–54). Thailand also carried out major reforms of government fiscal policy (Ingram 1971, chapters 8 and 9). On the revenue side, the metropolitan powers wanted tax systems under the direct control of the colonial administrations which were sufficiently buoyant to provide enough revenues to fund current expenditures while at the same time providing a surplus for investment in infrastructure. Old practices of revenue farming, and the widespread use

---

[1] This chapter draws on previous work, including Booth (2007a), (2007b) and (2013).

of corvée labour, were largely, if not entirely, eliminated over the last decades of the nineteenth and the early twentieth century in favour of more 'modern' revenue systems relying on trade taxes, on domestic excises and sales taxes and in some cases on corporate and individual income taxes. As Butcher (1993, 42) argued, by the early twentieth century, the state in Southeast Asia was a very different institution from what it had been a century earlier when corvée demands were the only way that governments could obtain scarce labour for government projects, and revenue farms enabled the often rather weak indigenous governments to secure more money income, usually by appointing the commercially powerful Chinese as tax farmers. By the early 1900s, a very different view of the fiscal functions of the state was taking hold, a view based on the idea of a strong central state taking responsibility for both revenue raising and expenditures. At least some of the expenditures would be devoted to the provision of infrastructure which was increasingly demanded by private investors.

Given the emphasis that all the colonial powers were placing on the reform of revenue policies after 1900, and their increasingly ambitious plans for government expenditure, it might have been expected that there would have been some convergence of both revenues and expenditures on a per capita basis by the latter part of the 1930s across Southeast Asia. But this was far from being the case. By 1938, when most economies in the region were recovering from the ravages of the depression of the early 1930s, per capita government revenues and expenditures showed considerable variation. In that year, per capita revenues varied from US$30 in the Straits Settlements to only US$2 in Vietnam (Table 2.1). There was also considerable variation in the structure of tax and non-tax revenues, and in the composition of expenditures. Tax revenues varied as a proportion of total revenues from 80 per cent in Burma to only 34 per cent in the Straits Settlements (Table 2.2). After 1945, there was even greater variation in the composition of revenues and expenditures, both in those British territories which remained under colonial control, and in the newly independent states. This chapter explores the reasons for these variations, and also discusses the extent to which a modern fiscal state can be said to have emerged in Southeast Asia in the decades from 1900 through to 1960.

The Evolution of Tax and Revenue Policies before 1942 in Southeast Asia

Two factors stand out in the economic development of Southeast Asia in the nineteenth and early twentieth centuries. First, population growth

Table 2.1 *Revenues per capita (US$), 1929, 1938 and 1952*

Colony	1929	1938	1952
British:			
Burma	6	4	9
Straits Settlements/Singapore[a]	29	30 (16)[b]	63
Federated Malay States	28	17	42
Unfederated Malay States	11	10	[a]
Brunei	n.a.	20	465
North Borneo (Sabah)	n.a.	6	25
Sarawak	n.a.	5	29
Other:			
Taiwan	16	12	27
Philippines	6[b]	5[c]	12
Indonesia	5	4	9
Thailand	4	3	8
Vietnam	3	2	3 (1950)
US GDP Deflator	115	100	199

Sources: 1929 and 1938: Taiwan: Mizoguchi and Umemura (1988, 288); Vietnam: Bassino (2000, 286–88); Netherlands Indies: Creutzberg (1976), population data from van der Eng (2002); Philippines: Commonwealth of the Philippines (1941, table 100) and Birnberg and Resnick (1975); Thailand: Ingram (1971, 329–37); Burma: Andrus (1948, table 37); Federated Malay States, Straits Settlements: Department of Statistics (1939), with additional data from Fraser (1939), appendix A and Colonial Office (1955, 33–56). Brunei, Sarawak and Sabah: Colonial Office (1955, 107, 125, 146); 1952: International Monetary Fund (1952–60), *International Financial Statistics*, various issues between 1952 and 1958, with additional data for Federation of Malaya, Singapore, Brunei, Sabah and Sarawak from Colonial Office (1955, 33, 56, 107, 125, 146) and for Philippines and Indonesia from Central Bank of the Philippines (1956); Bank Indonesia (1956). Exchange rate for Taiwan in 1952 from Sato et al. (2008, 369). Other exchange rates from van Laanen (1980, table 8) and Bidwell (1970).
Notes: a. After 1945, the Federated and Unfederated states were amalgamated into the Federation of Malaya. Singapore became a separate crown colony, and the other parts of the Straits Settlements (Malaka and Penang) became part of the Federation of Malaya; b. Figure in brackets excludes the payment from the Currency Guarantee Fund; c. Figures include local government revenues.

accelerated to over 1 per cent per annum, a much faster rate than in China or the Indian sub-continent, and almost certainly faster than in most parts of sub-Saharan Africa. In 1800, the population of the region was probably

Table 2.2 *Percentage breakdown of government revenues in Southeast Asia, 1938*[a]

Country	All taxes	Land taxes	Income taxes	Excises	Trade taxes
Burma	81.4	33	11.6	14	22.2
North Borneo	72.5	16.7	0	[b]	54.6
Philippines	64	n.a.	28.3 (19.3)	17.1	15.9
Indonesia	62.8	6.7	22	13.8	16.1
Thailand	61.5	6.3	8.6 (6.5)	15.0 (8.7)	30.8
Sarawak	58.8	0	0	[b]	43
Vietnam	58.7	n.a.	10	17	31.7
FMS	49.3	0	0	11.1 (8.3)	38.2
Brunei	36.8	0	0	[b]	25.2
Straits Settlements	34.4	0	0	27.1 (9.2)	0

Sources: Vietnam: 1938: Bassino (2000, 286–88); Indonesia: Creutzberg (1976, 67); Central Bureau of Statistics (1947, 133); Philippines: Commonwealth of the Philippines (1941, table 102); Thailand: Central Service of Statistics (1940, 274–9); Burma: Andrus (1948, table 37); Federated Malay States and Straits Settlements: Department of Statistics (1939, 238–41); Brunei, North Borneo and Sarawak: Colonial Office (1955, 107, 125, 147).

Notes: a. Figures in brackets for the Philippines refer to the license and business tax; for Thailand the capitation tax, and the opium *regie*; for the SS (Straits Settlements) and FMS (Federated Malay States), opium revenues. For Burma, the FMS and the SS, stamp duties and other license fees are included in tax revenues; b. Total tax revenues include other duties including some excises and licenses.

no more than 35 million people, and many parts of the region were very lightly populated. By 1931, when census data were available for most parts of Southeast Asia, the total population was slightly above 130 million. Part of this growth was the result of in-migration from other parts of Asia but most was the result of higher fertility and lower mortality, compared with both China and the Indian subcontinent, and with much of Africa. Population growth continued to be rapid over the latter part of the twentieth century, and by 2018 was estimated to be 650 million (Population Reference Bureau 2018). In 1800, it is probable that the population of Southeast Asia was only about 10 per cent of China; by 2018 it was 46 per cent. Recent projections suggest that by 2050, the percentage will increase to around 58 per cent.[2]

The second factor which had an important influence on the region's development was the growing involvement of the region in international

---

[2] The estimate for 1800 is given by Boomgaard (2014, 133). More recent data and projections are from Population Reference Bureau (2018).

trade. In the 1830s, exports from Southeast Asia comprised less than 10 per cent of total exports from Asia; by 1937 this had risen to 37 per cent (Booth 2004, table 2). In 1937, the region accounted for about one third of all exports from the tropical world, as estimated by Lewis (1969, table 9). The growth of population facilitated export growth, by providing more labour, and export growth in turn facilitated the growth and diversification of government revenues. Not surprisingly, there was a significant relationship between export growth and revenue growth in all colonial territories. Long-run elasticities of both government revenues and expenditures with respect to exports were close to unity in most parts of the region, which indicates that they increased in the same proportion as export revenues (Booth 2007a, table 6). But the channels through which export growth affected revenue growth varied across the region. Taxation of exports accounted for only a small proportion of total revenues in most colonies; the main exception was the Federated Malay States, where it accounted for around 15 per cent of total revenues. The corporate income tax, which fell on companies producing exports, was quite an important revenue source in the Netherlands Indies, but not elsewhere. In most colonies, and in independent Thailand, non-tax revenues accounted for a substantial part of total revenues; in the Straits Settlements they accounted for over 60 per cent of all revenues.[3] These non-tax revenues varied across time and space; they included profits from government enterprises, and also revenues from forests and civil administration. More controversially, they included revenues from government monopolies, including those on the production and sale of opium. I turn now to a more detailed discussion of both tax and other revenue policies in different parts of Southeast Asia.

Taxing Agriculture

Given that agricultural output accounted for a significant part of total output in most parts of Southeast Asia until well into the twentieth century, it might have been expected that agricultural taxation would have been given high priority by colonial authorities. One way of taxing agriculture was to levy a tax on agricultural land. In Taiwan, the Japanese administration, aware of the role land taxes had played in Meiji Japan, devoted considerable resources to drawing up land cadastres so that land taxes could be levied (Ho 1984, 355), although actual revenues remained

---

[3] The 1938 figures were exceptional, in that there were large revenues from "other sources", which included a large payment from the Currency Guarantee Fund, but in previous years, even without this additional source of revenue, less than half of all revenues were derived from taxes.

quite low until the 1930s. Detailed cadastral surveys were also carried out in Burma and Java, and in some of the more settled regions outside Java, on the basis of which land taxes were levied as a fraction of the income which cultivators were assumed to be deriving from the land. Furnivall, who had extensive knowledge of the Burmese system and studied the Dutch colonial land tax in Java in the 1930s, argued that the tax in Java was simpler, and that the pressure of the tax on cultivators was lighter than in Burma (Furnivall 1934, 21).[4] Van der Eng (2006, table 4) has estimated that the land tax was a smaller percentage of gross value added in agriculture in Java than in Japan until 1920, although between 1920 and 1940 the percentage was higher in Java.[5] Less progress was made in assessing land taxes outside Java and Bali, or in French Indochina where cadastral surveys were far less accurate and the assessment of land taxes a hit-or-miss affair, and often very inequitable (Thompson 1937, 193–4; 232–3; see also López Jerez, Chapter 4, this volume).

In spite of the efforts made by the Dutch colonial authorities, land taxes never accounted for a large share of government revenues in Indonesia after 1915, and by 1937 were under 7 cent of total revenues.[6] Only in Burma did land taxation account for a significant share of total revenues (Table 2.2). In Thailand, land taxes grew quite rapidly in nominal terms until the latter part of the 1920s, but fell thereafter, and by 1938 were around 6 per cent of total revenues. They were light in comparison with colonial Asia in both per hectare and per worker terms (Booth 2014, table 3). In Thailand as elsewhere, farmers were given remissions as agricultural prices fell through the early parts of the 1930s. Ingram (1971, 243) argued that in the 1930s, the agricultural sector was lightly taxed, although as Thompson (1967, 550–1) pointed out, in those regions where the marketed surplus of rice was small, the capitation tax and the modest land tax together comprised heavy imposts for many households. In other parts of the region, land taxation was also not an important

---

[4] Furnivall's argument that the land tax was a heavier burden on cultivators in Burma than in Java is borne out by the ratio of land revenues as a proportion of net domestic product from agriculture as estimated by Aye Hlaing (1965, 288). In 1938/39 the ratio was 11.4 per cent, which was more than twice the ratio estimated by van der Eng for Java over the 1930s. Land tax per agricultural worker was also higher in Burma than in other parts of Asia over the 1930s (Booth 2014, tables 2 and 3).

[5] A survey of economic conditions of the indigenous population of Java and Madura, carried out by W. Huender in 1921, argued that 'it is impossible to maintain that the indigenous population is not taxed heavily enough'. Fear of rural unrest on the part of Dutch officialdom was probably the main reason why both land taxes and other imposts, including head taxes, were not increased after 1920, at least in Java. For a translation of part of the Huender report, see Penders (1977, 91–6).

[6] Land taxes included the tax on agricultural land, the house and property tax and the ground tax.

source of revenue. In the Philippines, agricultural land was under-taxed in the Spanish era, and this continued under the American administration (Luton 1971, 143). To the extent that land was taxed at all, it was the responsibility of local governments, often under the control of large land-owners, who were hardly in favour of land taxes, or indeed other taxes whose incidence fell on agricultural producers. Only in the larger cities did taxes on land contribute significant amounts to local budgets (Corpuz 1997, 235).

The other tax which fell on agricultural producers was the export tax, although in fact export taxes were not widely used on agricultural commodities before 1940.[7] In the FMS, most of the revenues from export taxes were from tin exports, with rubber accounting for only a small share. In Thailand, export taxes accounted for less than 5 per cent of government revenues in 1938, although they became more important after 1950. In the Netherlands Indies, a special export cess on native rubber was levied in the mid-1930s as a means of reducing smallholder production. In 1936, the tax amounted to almost 19 per cent of total tax revenues of the central government (Central Bureau of Statistics 1947, 133). But it caused considerable hardship for native producers. O'Malley (1979, 241) argued that even after world rubber prices started to rise again in the mid-1930s as a result of the international restriction scheme, many farmers found their incomes reduced. Outbreaks of violence occurred in some parts of Sumatra, and the Dutch authorities removed the special cess in 1937.

Taxing International Trade

Even if export taxes were low in most parts of Southeast Asia before 1940, import taxes were often an important source of revenues. By the latter part of the 1930s, export and import taxes together accounted for almost 55 per cent of all government revenues in North Borneo, 43 per cent in Sarawak, and 38 in the Federated Malay States. In the non-British colonies the proportion was lower, but still over 30 per cent of the general budget revenues for Vietnam, and for Thailand (Table 2.2). In the Philippines and Indonesia, where tax systems were more diversified, trade taxes were a lower percentage of total government revenues, but still quite significant. Singapore was a free port and there were no taxes on

---

[7] The extent to which the incidence of an export taxes falls on domestic producers rather than foreign buyers depends on the elasticities of domestic supply and foreign demand. It has been argued in the context of most Southeast Asian agricultural exports in the 1960s and 1970s that the incidence of export taxes fell largely on domestic producers (Booth 1980).

imports or exports, although excises were levied on a range of imported products, including alcoholic drinks, tobacco and gasoline, and accounted for most of the revenues from taxation.

Taxing Incomes

By the latter part of the 1930s, there were striking differences across Southeast Asia in the role of income taxation. In both the Straits Settlements and the Federated Malay States, there were attempts to tax incomes during the First World War, but the revenues raised were small and met with fierce resistance from both the European and the Chinese business communities (Thompson 1943, 166). Arguments for and against income taxation continued, but the business communities across British Malaya managed to prevent the imposition of either corporate or personal income taxes until the Japanese arrived in 1942. The situation across the straits in Indonesia was very different. By the late 1930s, taxes were levied on both corporate and personal incomes and wages. They amounted to over one fifth of all government revenues in 1938 (Table 2.2). Estate companies operating in both colonies complained to the Dutch colonial authorities about what was seen as an 'unfair' tax, but the Dutch authorities were unmoved.

In the Philippines, the *cedula* and the *industria* had evolved by the late nineteenth century into roughly graduated taxes on personal and business incomes, but the American administration was determined to modernize the revenue system and introduce more equitable taxes on income and profits. They immediately ran up against powerful interests in both the business and the agricultural sectors. The proposed tax on corporations was dropped from the 1904 Revenue Law, as was the tax on legacies and inheritance (Luton 1971, 137). A low tax on corporate incomes was imposed in 1913, but the license and business tax was the main burden on the business sector and was often arbitrary in its incidence. It still accounted for around 20 per cent of total revenues in the late 1930s, compared with under 10 per cent for income taxes (Table 2.2).

In French Indochina, the Doumer reforms of the late nineteenth century were intended to centralize and modernize the revenue system, and to lay the groundwork for economic diversification into industry, mining and plantations (Brocheux & Hemery 2009, 117; see also López Jerez, Chapter 4, this volume). Following French post-revolutionary practice, indirect taxes were favoured over direct taxes. This was not popular with the indigenous populations; according to Thompson (1937, 184) they preferred the older direct taxes. It seems probable that the net effect of the Doumer reforms was to add to the tax burden of many Vietnamese.

Income taxes were imposed in the early twentieth century but only accounted for around 10 per cent of total government revenues by 1938, which was a slightly lower proportion than in Burma (Table 2.2). In independent Thailand, an income tax and a tax on business and the professions were imposed in the 1930s, and although revenues grew rapidly, they only accounted for 2 per cent of total government revenues in 1938. The older head tax accounted for a further 6.5 per cent of revenues. A reform of the revenue system was enacted into law in 1938 which was intended to shift the burden of taxation from the rural farmer to business and high income groups in urban areas. But as Ingram (1971, 184) pointed out, there was little change in the structure of taxation and non-tax revenues before the Pacific war; after 1942 accelerating inflation posed new problems for government revenue collection.

The Role of Opium

One of the more controversial issues in fiscal policy in most parts of Southeast Asia was the reliance on revenues from opium sales. The British, French and Dutch regimes were all, by the early twentieth century, justifying their colonialism in terms of a "civilizing mission", bringing enlightened standards of government to the benighted populations of Asia. How could they justify deriving often substantial revenues from a narcotic whose sale and consumption was increasingly controlled, if not completely banned, by governments in the metropolitan countries? In the Philippines, where the American administration was committed to replacing the "repressive" Spanish revenue system with one which would enhance economic and social uplift, the opium levy was seen as especially reprehensible, although it had only accounted for about 3.3 per cent of total government revenues in the fiscal year 1896/87 (Corpuz 1997, 193–4). The Americans were the first colonial power to cease deriving government revenues from the sale of opium. They also fought hard for the prohibition of opium trading, except for medical purposes, throughout Asia in the early part of the twentieth century, although other colonial powers, including the British, were reluctant to support more than its 'gradual' withdrawal (Foster 2003, 112).

The British had good reason for their reluctance, as the opium levy was an important source of revenue in all three parts of British Malaya. Indeed Bayley and Harper (2004, 33) argued that British rule in both Burma and Malaya was "supported by narco-colonialism on a colossal scale". This is an exaggeration, although there can be no doubt that, as late as 1919, opium was a very important revenue source in British Malaya. In the Unfederated States, especially Johore and Kedah, revenues from opium sales comprised over 40 per cent of total revenues in 1919 (Lim 1967, 351). The reliance on opium fell after 1920, as revenues from other sources, including customs duties, increased. In Kedah, the opium monopoly only accounted for around 12 per cent of revenues in the late 1930s. A similar decline took place in the Federated Malay States, where opium revenues accounted for around 20 per cent of total revenues in 1920, but had fallen to under 10 per cent by the late 1930s. The Straits Settlements were more reliant on opium revenues, mainly because of the absence of customs revenues, or revenues from income taxation. In the latter part of the 1930s, they still accounted for more than 20 per cent of total budget revenues (Department of Statistics 1939, 238).[8]

The other colony where opium revenue was an important, if controversial, source of government revenue was French Indochina. In the first decade of the twentieth century, gross receipts from the opium *regie* were around 25 per cent of total revenues accruing to the general budget, although the net revenues were considerably lower (Descours-Gatin 1992, 223–5). The *regie* was in effect a government monopoly which meant that the government had to bear the cost of buying and processing the opium; one estimate was that these costs amounted to around 30 per cent of the gross revenues (Guermeur 1909, 178). Both gross and net receipts declined as a proportion of total revenues after 1910, and after 1913 revenues from all monopolies (salt and alcohol as well as opium) declined as a proportion of total revenues accruing to the central budget. Bassino (2000, 286) estimated that in Vietnam, revenues from the monopolies fell from around half all revenues in 1913 to around 19 per cent in 1940. As in British Malaya, the reason for the decline was not an absolute fall in receipts from monopolies, but a rapid growth in other revenues, especially those from customs duties and indirect taxes.

In Indonesia, revenue farms were an important source of income for the colonial government until the end of the nineteenth century, and the opium farm was the most important (Diehl 1993, 199: Chandra 2010). Reforms after 1900 led to the conversion of opium farms into a government monopoly, which yielded a diminishing proportion of total government revenues, especially after 1914. Chandra (2010) estimated that the gross revenues from the opium *regie* fell from 13.5 per cent of total revenues in 1914 to 1.7 per cent by 1939.[9] Once again the main reason for the decline was the increase in revenues from income and

---

[8] In 1937, the opium levy accounted for almost 24 per cent of all revenues in the Straits Settlements; the fall in 1938 was due to the jump in miscellaneous receipts, mainly from the Currency Guarantee Fund.
[9] Chandra (2010) showed that the net profits from the *regie* fluctuated between around 70 to 80 per cent of total revenues, which was roughly the same as in French Indochina.

excise taxation and trade taxes, at least until 1930, although over the
1930s government revenues fell in absolute terms. Much the same trends
occurred in independent Thailand where revenues from sale of opium
were around 20 per cent of total revenues in 1905, and rose to almost
26 per cent by 1919. But they fell to less than 10 per cent in the late 1930s,
while revenues from other tax and non-tax revenues grew rapidly.

One reason why taxes on opium – and indeed other 'sin taxes' including
excises on alcohol and tobacco – however obnoxious to public opinion,
were favoured by colonial governments, and by the Thais, was that they
were seen as a way of taxing the Chinese, who were considered more
affluent than the indigenous populations, and were usually very reluctant
to pay income tax, even in those colonies where it was levied. But in fact
the evidence indicates that many among the indigenous populations in
Southeast Asia consumed opium, alcohol and tobacco. In Indochina,
Descours-Gatin (1992, 214) estimated that the Chinese were only
22 per cent of all opium smokers in Cochinchina and a much smaller
percentage in other parts of Vietnam, although they were around
60 per cent of all smokers in Cambodia. In Indonesia, data for the
1930s showed that indigenous Indonesians accounted for most of the
licensed opium smokers, although Chinese dominated among unlicensed
users (Central Bureau of Statistics 1947, 143). The assumption among
colonial officials appeared to be that users were relatively affluent,
although that might not always have been the case, and dependency on
opium could well have reduced many users, whether Chinese or indigenous, to penury.

Taxes in Labour

Colonial governments in many parts of Southeast Asia viewed labour
shortages as the main constraint on the rapid development of both
export-oriented agriculture and industries based on the extraction and
processing of minerals. In most parts of the region, pre-colonial governments imposed labour demands on the populations under their
control, and slavery and debt bondage were not uncommon.[10]
Colonial governments tackled the problem of labour shortages in
different ways. In British Malaya the government decided that indigenous Malays were usually unwilling to work for wages at all, and
certainly reluctant to take on arduous regular employment on estates
and in mines. They were encouraged to stay in their reservations and

---

[10] Lasker (1950) gives a comprehensive historical overview of serfdom, debt bondage and
   compulsory public services in Southeast Asia from pre-colonial times to the 1940s.

pursue traditional occupations as farmers and fishermen. Labour was procured cheaply from China and India, and came in large numbers. The 1931 census showed that 1.71 million Chinese lived in the Straits Settlements and the Malay states, and 624,000 Indians. Together these two groups comprised over half the total population of 4.4 million. In Burma, the number of migrants from India also grew rapidly, taking up many of the unskilled jobs in urban areas. In 1931, there were 1.02 million Indians living in Burma, out of a total population of 14.65 million. In both colonies, those migrants who had some knowledge of English and some entrepreneurial skills moved into non-agricultural jobs as clerks, shopkeepers and traders. A small number moved into the professions. But most were trapped in unskilled jobs, and were prepared to work long hours, which removed any necessity on the part of the British to force indigenous workers into unpaid labour in public works or as plantation workers.

Other colonies faced different problems. In Indonesia, the 1930 Census found that there were 1.23 million Chinese, around 2 per cent of the total population. Some were recent migrants, but many came from families which had already been in the country for several generations. Only a small number of recent migrants took up employment as estate labourers or unskilled workers on public works projects. The Dutch authorities encouraged young men from Java to move to the plantation sector in North Sumatra, usually as indentured labourers with penal clauses in their contracts. The harsh treatment of these workers led to campaigns in both Indonesia and the Netherlands to improve their conditions, and a labour inspectorate was established in the early years of the twentieth century.[11] But given the long history of labour coercion through the nineteenth century, both in Java and elsewhere, the Dutch were slow to abolish the various forms of forced labour which had been used by both the colonial government and indigenous rulers. The formal abolition of the cultivation system in the 1870s, and the introduction of more liberal policies which relied on free markets had some impact, and obligations under the *pantjendiensten, desadiensten* and *heerendiensten* were reduced or eliminated in Java, with the exception of the native states, by the early twentieth century (Kloosterboer 1960, 42, Lasker 1950, 176–9, Furnivall 1944, 181–7). But as will be seen, outside Java, *heerendiensten* demands for public works continued

---

[11] Controversies over the impact of the labour inspectorate, and other efforts to improve the conditions of estate labourers in Sumatra continue; see Breman (2002) for one side of the debate.

until the late 1930s, and imposed a considerable burden on the indigenous populations.

In Thailand, where a large part of the population had traditionally been obliged to work for nothing for the aristocracy and local patrons, the whole system of corvée labour underwent considerable change over the nineteenth century. There were several reasons for these changes. Migrants from China grew in numbers, and many were willing to work for wages on projects such as canal building. As the rural economy became more monetized, many Thai men began to pay a money tax in lieu of their corvée obligations; these payments were then used to hire Chinese workers, or those Thais who were willing to work for wages (Ingram 1971, 58–9, Baker & Phongpaichit 1995, 24–5). By the early twentieth century, most forms of forced labour had been eliminated in central Thailand although it persisted in parts of the north and the south of the country, where laws and regulations passed in Bangkok were implemented more slowly.[12] As late as the 1930s, Andrews (1935, 160) argued that many Thais were still reluctant to work for wages, and a high proportion of non-agricultural wage labour was carried out by Chinese migrants.

In Vietnam, the French authorities introduced regulations which abolished forced labour in Cochinchina in 1898, and in other parts of French Indochina soon after, but implementing these regulations proved difficult (Lasker 1950, 194–5). More regulatory controls on the use of forced labour were issued and, in December 1936, a law was passed which banned forced labour in Laos and Cambodia, as well as in Vietnam. Thompson (1947, 186) reported that by the late 1930s "forced labor still existed but only as a vestige" and in the more remote parts of Indochina. The exceptions were obligations to provide labour for public works, although the 1936 law stated that these could be commuted for cash payment in all parts of Vietnam. The length of annual service was reduced to between sixteen and twenty days. There were also more controls over the labour contracts used to attract workers from the north into wage employment in the south (Thompson 1947, 204–7). Wages in Saigon were almost twice those in the north in 1931, which should have been a strong incentive for workers to move, and the French government was keen to develop a more unified labour market in Indochina. But employers in Tonkin were worried that large-scale migrations from north to south might deplete their own supplies of cheap

---

[12] Terwiel (2011, 216–17) discusses the reforms in system of corvée in the late nineteenth and early twentieth centuries. He stresses that there was considerable variation in the nature of corvée obligations, and the extent to which individuals could pay a ransom instead of contributing labour.

labour, and there appears to have been little change in differentials over the 1930s.

Most studies of forced labour in colonial Asia and Africa agree that it should be viewed as a form of taxation, although placing a value on the labour supplied under coercion is not straightforward, given that labour markets in many parts of Asia were undeveloped until well into the twentieth century, and segmented by region and ethnicity. But where the practice of making money payments to escape corvée duties was widespread, it is possible to value the labour supplied by those who chose to work out their corvée obligations, using the amounts of "ransom" paid by those who decided to make a cash payment. Estimates for the outer islands of Indonesia (both the native states and the directly governed territories) in selected years from 1925 to 1937 are given in Table 2.3. In 1930, usually considered the last year before the full impact of the global depression hit the regional economies outside Java, numbers paying the ransom were higher than those contributing labour in the directly governed territories, and the value of labour was thus estimated to be lower than the ransom. But by 1934, when the full impact of the global slump was being felt in Indonesia, numbers choosing to pay the ransom fell sharply, while the amount of the ransom increased in the directly governed territories, although it fell in the native states. There was some increase between 1934 and 1937 in the amount of ransom paid, although the total amount of both ransom and work contributed was still less in 1937 than in 1930.

The Dutch authorities claimed that the continued use of corvée labour on public works (*heerendiensten*) outside Java was justified as most regions outside Java were not assessed for the land tax. But in 1930, the total amount of the corvée (ransom plus actual labour) was greater in per capita terms than the land tax in those regions where it was assessed. This confirms the argument that the burden of taxation on the regions outside Java in the 1930s was higher than on Java, although it is worth noting that in the native states of Java, and in directly governed Bali and Lombok, cultivators were assessed for the land tax as well as being liable for *heerendiensten* obligations.[13] While the land tax revenues fell sharply over the 1930s, numbers liable for *heerendiensten* fell only slightly in the directly governed territories and actually grew in the

---

[13] Numbers obliged to contribute *heerendiensten* labour in the native states of Java in 1933 amounted to around 362,000 people, or 8.7 per cent of the total population. Most of these (around 275,000 people) were in Surakarta.

Table 2.3 *Numbers liable to* heerendiensten, *ransoms per worker, total ransoms and value of labour, 1925, 1930, 1934 and 1937*[a]

Sector	Numbers liable ('000)	Ransom per worker (guilders)[b]	Total ransom (Million guilders)	Value of labour (Million guilders)	Total (Million guilders)
1925					
DGOJ	1,366	6.51 (41)	3.7	5.2	8.9
NSOJ	1,142	5.87 (24)	1.6	5.1	6.7
1930					
DGOJ	1,469	7.67 (58)	6.5	4.1	10.6
NSOJ	1,306	6.65 (30)	2.6	5.4	8
1934					
DGOJ	1,432	5.39 (16)	1.2	5.7	6.9
NSOJ	1,295	4.17 (12)	0.6	4.3	4.9
1937					
DGOJ	1,421	5.47 (23)	1.8	5.1	6.9
NSOJ	1,367	4.10 (22)	1.2	4.1	5.3

Source: Indisch Verslag 1938: Part II, Statistical Abstract for the Year 1937, tables 405, 427.
Notes: a. DGOJ refers to directly governed territories outside Java; NSOJ refers to the native states outside Java; b. Figures in brackets show the percentage of all those liable who paid the ransom.

native states outside Java, although the value of the ransom per worker paying it did fall after 1930 (Table 2.3).

The continued use of corvée in colonial Indonesia attracted adverse comments internationally, given that other colonial territories in Asia had largely abolished it by the interwar years, and a convention of the International Labour Office banning forced labour was ratified in 1930, and became operative in 1932. The Netherlands was a member of the ILO and its conventions applied, at least in principle, to colonies as well as to the metropolitan state. In fact the value of the *heerendiensten* by 1930 as estimated in Table 2.3, was less than 3 per cent of total government revenues. Why was it not abolished, and replaced by paid labour? The most probable answer is that the colonial government was determined to improve infrastructure outside Java, but doubted that sufficient labour would be available at wages which the Dutch authorities deemed reasonable. The only alternative was to maintain the old practices of forced labour, albeit with some restrictions.

Revenue Performance: A Summing Up

The differences in revenue performance between countries in Southeast Asia can be explained partly by differences in taxable capacity, as prox-ied by per capita GDP. British Malaya, including Singapore, had the highest per capita GDP in the region after 1913, and also the highest per capita revenues, although the composition of revenues was less diversi-fied than in other colonies, especially Indonesia. In many colonial terri-tories, officials were reluctant to increase taxes on the indigenous populations for fear of provoking unrest. But in spite of this reluctance, a frequent criticism of colonial revenue systems in Asia was that they were regressive. Critics pointed to the high reliance on land taxes, excises and export duties whose incidence fell mainly on the indigenous populations living in rural areas. Income taxes on both corporations and individuals were either not assessed at all, as in British Malaya, or assessed at low rates with many exemptions. The main exceptions were Indonesia and the Philippines, although in the Philippines, the business taxes were often not progressive in their incidence. Excises on petroleum products, tobacco and alcohol, and revenues derived from the sale of opium were thought to fall more heavily on the Chinese who were on average richer than indigenous populations. But, by the 1930s, there were worries about their incidence, especially as many poorer labourers, whether Chinese, Indian or indigenous, spent a significant part of their incomes on these products. All colonial governments, as well as the administration in Thailand, had to strike a balance between raising more revenues which could lead to popular unrest, and curbing expenditures.

Changing Expenditure Patterns

On the expenditure side, the early years of the twentieth century saw a marked change in the role of governments in many parts of the region. The colonial governments across Southeast Asia began to assume respon-sibility for a much broader range of activities than simply the maintenance of law and order and the collection of revenues. In Indonesia, the ethical policy, introduced in 1901, emphasized policies which were intended to enhance the productivity of indigenous workers in agriculture and also equip at least some workers with the skills which would allow them to take on employment outside the rural sector. Increasingly, it was recognized that ambitious programmes of infrastructural development were neces-sary for the economic development of both indigenous and foreign enter-prises, and that these programmes would have to be funded, or at least subsidized, by government rather than the private sector, with government funds derived in part at least from loan finance.

Government expenditures had grown in real terms continuously after 1870, and by 1920 public works (including railways) accounted for almost 40 per cent of total government expenditure (Booth 1990, table 10.5). Government spending on irrigation, railways and tramways had already grown rapidly in real terms after 1870; after 1900 expenditures on roads and harbour works also increased (de Jong & Ravesteijn 2008, 66). Although government spending on infrastructure was drastically cut back after 1930, by the late 1930s Java had the highest ratio of roads per square kilometre of area of any colony in Southeast Asia, and higher than in Taiwan or Korea. Length of railways per square kilometre of area was also higher than in any other colony except Taiwan (Booth 2007b, table 4.7). But outside Java, both road and rail development was very limited, and transport of goods was often done on the backs of people or animals, along rough jungle tracks or by river.

In Burma, civil public works accounted for almost 24 per cent of government expenditures by 1901–4, although the percentage fell somewhat thereafter (Aye Hlaing 1965, table 22). In Indochina, especially the three parts comprising what is now Vietnam, public works already accounted for 20 per cent of total government expenditures in 1901; by 1909 the share had risen to over 40 per cent. The concept of "*mise en valeur*", stressed by successive French administrators after 1900, meant in effect increased expenditures on public works, in order to facilitate the exploitation of the colony's natural resources (Simoni 1929). Road building was also given high priority in both the Philippines and British Malaya, although railway development lagged behind both Java and the Japanese colonies of Taiwan and Korea. In all the Southeast Asian colonies, with the exception of British Malaya, electricity generation was also well behind both Taiwan and Korea (Booth 2007b, table 4.7). Paradoxically, it was independent Thailand which was slow to develop a national road system. Writing in the late 1930s, Thompson (1967, 506) called Thailand "virtually a roadless land" where outside Bangkok and a few other towns, much of the transport of both people and goods took place by river and canal, or by carts along old caravan routes. Railways were built up to the Mekong region in the north and down to the border with British Malaya in the south. Although the motive for building railways in Thailand was mainly for defence, they played an important role in transporting both goods and people.

In spite of the increased emphasis on infrastructure, there were marked differences in spending priorities across colonial Southeast Asia. The comparative study carried out by Schwulst (1932) showed that the

Table 2.4 *Percentage breakdown of government expenditures by sector, 1931*[a]

Sector	Philippines	Siam	Indonesia	FMS	French Indochina
Education	28	6	9	5	3
Health	8	2	3	15	1
Public works	8	12	6	20	30
Agriculture	10	3	1	8	6
Administration	31(8)	45(9)	38(6)	34(6)	35(1)
Military	0	22	26	2	13
Public debt	12	9	13	9	4
Other	3	1	4	7	8
Total	100	100	100	100	100

Source: Schwulst (1932, 57).
Notes: a. Percentages in brackets refer to expenditures on law and order. Figures for the Philippines and French Indochina refer to central government expenditures only. All figures are for ordinary budgets only and may understate some capital expenditures.

percentage of ordinary budgetary expenditures on the armed forces varied from over 20 per cent in the Netherlands Indies and Siam to virtually nothing in the Philippines, where the cost of the small military presence was charged to the American budget until the latter part of the 1930s (Table 2.4). The percentage of ordinary expenditures devoted to public works and agriculture also varied considerably from 30 per cent in French Indochina, to only 6 per cent in Indonesia. The percentage on health and education was under 15 per cent in most colonies; the exceptions were the Philippines and the Federated Malay States. Particularly striking is the Philippines, where the government was spending over a third of the budget on health and education, compared with only 4 per cent in French Indochina.

The percentages shown in Table 2.4 are for one year, 1931, which was already affected by budgetary cutbacks in several colonies as the impact of the global depression began to be felt. In the case of Indonesia, the cutbacks affected expenditures on public works, which would have accounted for a much higher proportion of total expenditures a decade earlier. They also excluded expenditures by sub-national levels of government which might account for the low percentages spent on health and education in French Indochina, which was divided into five components, all of which had their own budgets.[14] But the evidence which we have on

[14] Slocomb (2010, 49–50) argues that in Cambodia, there was a considerable improvement in roads and telephone communications after 1910, especially within and between the

educational enrolments in the late 1930s does suggest that enrolments as a percentage of total population were much lower in French Indochina than in other colonies (Furnivall 1943, 111). In the Philippines, Furnivall found that enrolments as a percentage of the population were higher than in any other colony, or in Thailand. The 1939 population census in the Philippines found that 48 per cent of the population over fifteen was literate, a very high proportion by Asian standards. Although the percentage was higher for men than women, 41 per cent of women over fifteen were literate in 1939, again a very high figure in comparison with other parts of Asia, and with most states in Central and South America (UNESCO 1957).

The relatively high expenditures on the army and navy in Thailand reflected the very high priority which the government placed on maintaining its independence by posing a credible threat to those foreign powers, mainly the British and the French, which might have wished to take more territory. In fact, the figure of 22 per cent for 1931 was lower than in the early years of the twentieth century when expenditures on the army and navy reached 28 per cent of total expenditures in all government departments. To foreign observers, and indeed to some Thais, these expenditures seemed extravagant and unnecessary. Edward Cook, the influential British financial adviser from 1925 to 1930, was very critical of the rapid rise in government spending, especially on defence and on the royal household (Batson 1984, 17). In the latter part of the 1930s, another British financial adviser, W. Doll, warned that continuing heavy spending on defence was causing budgetary problems (Thompson 1967, 560). Although ordinary expenditures were usually lower than ordinary revenues in the years from 1926 to 1939, the resulting surpluses were often not enough to cover capital expenditures, which necessitated borrowing. As will be discussed, the Thai government was reluctant to increase borrowing, and over the 1930s placed more emphasis on debt redemption. In several other colonies, including Indonesia, government spending on defence increased over the 1930s, as the Dutch became more worried about the threat from Japan.

One important consequence of the expansion in government expenditures in Southeast Asia was the growth in public sector employment, much of which was taken up by indigenous employees. Censuses carried out in the 1930s showed that indigenous workers comprised between 87

---

main towns. But progress in spreading modern healthcare and formal education was slow. There were plans for schools in every village teaching an eight- to ten-year cycle. But this never happened; by 1940 around 72,000 children were enrolled in primary schools and fewer than 1,000 in secondary and technical schools. Altogether, school enrolments accounted for around 2 per cent of the total population in 1940.

and 97 per cent of total employment in government and the professions (Booth 2007b, table 6.4). It was perhaps not surprising that the percentage was high in independent Thailand where very few foreigners were employed in government service, or the Philippines which had been granted self-government in 1935, and where very few Americans remained in government by the time of the census in 1939. In both Thailand and the Philippines, the Chinese were either discriminated against in public sector employment, or preferred to work in the private sector. This was also the case in Indonesia, where the employment of indigenous Indonesians increased quite rapidly in the 1920s, although they seldom managed to move into the highest ranks of the public service, or the judiciary. The main exception to these trends was British Malaya. In the Straits Settlements, only 20 per cent of workers in government and the professions were indigenous; in the Federated Malay States the proportion was around one third. This resulted from the failure of most Malays to gain access to English-language education. Those who did manage to get government employment usually worked in unskilled jobs.

The Growth of Government Borrowing and Monetary Development

In most parts of Southeast Asia over the first four decades of the twentieth century, increased government revenues led to increased government expenditures. But expenditures did not always move in step with revenues, and in Vietnam, the Philippines and Indonesia the elasticity of expenditures with respect to exports was slightly higher than revenues (Booth 2007a, table 6). This partly reflected the tendency to run deficits in years when revenues fell sharply, as they did in the early part of the 1930s, when GDP contracted in most parts of Southeast Asia. It also reflected the fact that in boom periods when exports and total output were growing rapidly, it was easier for governments to access loan finance to fund increases in expenditures.

According to the budgetary principles followed, at least in principle, by the European powers, loans could be contracted to fund at least part of the investment in public works which would then yield returns over a long period. But this rule was not always applied in all colonies. It was estimated that over the period 1900–25, loans covered about 21 per cent of the cost of all public works carried out by the central and local governments in French Indochina (Simoni 1929, 141). In Indonesia, the ethical policy led to a rapid increase in budgetary expenditures on both current expenditures and capital works, and this in turn caused a widening deficit by the end of the second decade of the twentieth century. In 1923, the

Table 2.5 *Public debt per capita (US$)*

Country	1935	1955[a]
British Malaya	18	27
Indonesia	16	17
India	12	18
Philippines	5	28
Thailand	5	11

Sources: 1935: British Malaya: Department of
Statistics (1936) and Federation of Malaya (1956:
90); Indonesia: Creutzberg (1976, table 7) and
Bank Indonesia (1956, 75); Thailand: 1935:
Central Service of Statistics (1940, 416); 1955
(Ingram 1971, 301). Philippines and India:
United Nations (1948); Philippines: Central Bank
of the Philippines (1956, 111); India: 1955 from
International Monetary Fund (1952–60),
International Financial Statistics 1958; Exchange
rates for 1935: as for Table 2.1; 1955 from
International Monetary Fund *International
Financial Statistics*, various issues between 1957
and 1960.
Note: a. For 1955, official exchange rates are used
to convert to US dollars in all cases.

public debt amounted to 21 per cent of GDP and debt service charges
were around 6 per cent of exports. These figures would not be considered unduly high today, but they alarmed the Dutch government,
or at least those people in the Netherlands who opposed the ethical
policy on other grounds. Through the 1920s, the government implemented a more austere spending policy, but by the early 1930s, the
debt to GDP ratio had increased, not just because of heavier borrowing but also because of a contraction in nominal GDP (Booth 1998,
146). By 1935, public debt per capita was around sixteen dollars,
which was high by Asian standards, although British Malaya was
higher (Table 2.5).

Even in fiscally conservative Thailand, government debt and debt
service charges grew in the early part of the twentieth century, and by
1935 the debt servicing/export ratio was over 6 per cent (Sompop
1989, 176). The influential British financial adviser, Edward Cook,
argued in the latter part of the 1920s that Siam should build up
a reserve to avoid recourse to further loans, and that a debt

redemption reserve should be established (Thompson 1967, 560, Batson 1984, 18). Schwulst found in his interviews with Thai officials in early 1931 that they were determined to liquidate the outstanding government debt. Since 1927, following Cook's advice, substantial sums were taken from current revenues to set up a fund for the purpose of retiring outstanding debt (Schwulst 1932, 46). The policy of reducing the debt, both in absolute terms and relative to total budgetary revenues continued through the 1930s.[15] The total government capital liability at the end of the fiscal year 1938/9 was 5.7 million pounds, which was about half what it had been a decade earlier. Debt charges fell from a peak of 12.3 per cent of total budgetary revenues in 1931/32 to 5.8 per cent in 1938/9.[16] By 1935, total public debt per capita was lower than in the Philippines and much lower than in the Netherlands Indies, British Malaya and India. British Malaya had the highest debt per capita in the mid-1930s among the Asian colonies (Table 2.5). This reflected not just borrowing to fund public works, but also the tendency for the government to resort to borrowing to maintain current expenditures as revenues fell in the early 1930s.

To what extent did the tendency to resort to borrowing lead to the development of local capital markets in Southeast Asia? He (2013, 128–30) argues that the severe deflationary policies implemented in the early 1880s in Japan, while having a very serious impact on rural welfare, reduced investment expenditures and made it easier for the government to sell bonds to the public as well as to the corporate sector. Most of the colonial governments in Southeast Asia made only limited attempts to develop a modern financial system. Capital markets were undeveloped and most banks were branches of those based in the metropolitan country. In Indonesia, which by the 1920s had the largest economy in absolute terms, "there was no well-organised framework . . . within which credit transactions could be arranged between borrowers and creditors, either through the intermediary of the banks . . . or the Stock Exchange" (van Laanen 1980, 31). Van Laanen (1990, 250) argued that most foreign enterprises chose to keep their surpluses in foreign financial centres. This was especially true of some of the most profitable companies, such as the Batavian Petroleum Company, which kept its profits in the Netherlands, and only remitted back funds which were needed for investment in further expansion. Government bond issues were conducted in the Netherlands, London and New York.

---

[15] Because of falling export values in the early 1930s, the debt service to export ratios increased to around 6 per cent in 1935. It fell after that (Sompop 1989, 176).

[16] These figures are taken from Central Service of Statistics (1940).

While the Dutch did develop a credit system designed to encourage savings and provide loans to indigenous Indonesians, especially in Java, the system was not linked in to the western banking system, or indeed to that of the Chinese.[17]

Van Laanen's conclusion that there was little scope for an independent monetary policy in Indonesia until 1942 also holds for the other colonies in Southeast Asia. In the Philippines, a stock market was established in Manila in 1927, and local banks were established, usually with government deposit guarantees. But the fixed exchange rate against the dollar together with few controls on inward and outward flows of capital gave little scope for independent monetary policies. In Singapore, which had emerged as the leading port and financial centre in the region by the 1920s, a monetary board was established early in the twentieth century to cover the Straits Settlements. By 1938, the board was extended to cover all the Malay states. As Drake (2004, 123–4) pointed out, the advantages of the monetary board were that it was simple to operate, relieved officials of the need to conduct monetary policy and prevented any over-issue of local currency which strengthened confidence in the stability of the currency, thus allowing a fixed rate of exchange with sterling.

The main disadvantage of the monetary board was that the authorities had to hold sterling reserves equal to 100 per cent of the local money stock. These reserves yielded low returns, and the funds could probably have been used more profitably to finance investments within the colony. In his survey of monetary arrangements in the British Empire in the early 1950s, Hazelwood (1954, 311–12) wrote that "the fundamental disadvantage of the present colonial monetary arrangements is, in most territories, the investment of funds in sterling securities which is enforced by the currency regulations". In many territories, officials who were beginning to draw up development plans were frustrated by the fact that they could not invest more of their reserves in domestic projects. Another disadvantage was that in times of instability in foreign earnings, "the monetary needs of the domestic economy are made subsidiary to external balance" (Drake 2004, 124). Huff (1994, 88–9) estimated that there was a very sharp reduction in base money in British Malaya from 1926 until 1933, and only a slow recovery thereafter. The monetary contraction had a serious impact on the real economy; real GDP, as estimated by

---

[17] A discussion of the colonial initiatives in credit provision in Java, and how they influenced post-colonial policies is given in Booth (1998, chapter 4). The successful rural credit programmes of the 1990s were lending less, in real per capita terms, than the colonial programmes of the 1930s.

Sugimoto (2011, 185) contracted by 40 per cent between 1929 and 1932. British banks faced with liquidity problems could access loans from their London headquarters, but in the absence of a central bank in Singapore, local Chinese banks experienced difficulties. So did firms and individuals using the informal financial sector. The segmented nature of the capital market was to persist into the post-1945 period.

Only Thailand, as an independent kingdom, could have pursued an independent monetary policy along Japanese lines. But Ingram (1971, 170–4) pointed out that in fact the government pursued very conservative policies, designed to stabilize the baht against sterling, and keep the currency fully convertible. The interests of foreign banks and foreign bondholders were always placed above national interests including the rapid development of the country's resources. Government borrowing, even for capital projects which would have yielded good returns, was always cautious, and from the late 1920s onwards the aim was to pay down foreign debt, and build up more reserves in foreign currencies and gold. Although there had been some discussion about establishing a central bank at the turn of the twentieth century, the idea was shelved, and the Bank of Thailand was founded only in 1942 (Vichitvong 1978, 421). Several writers have argued that the main reason for the conservative attitude to the development of the financial sector, and to economic development more broadly defined, was the fear of further foreign intervention if the Thai government were to acquire a reputation for irresponsible financial and economic policies. According to Brown (1988, 175) economic policy was determined "by the overriding need to defend the political sovereignty" of the country. But the cost of this conservatism was very slow economic growth compared with other parts of colonial Asia. The estimates of Sompop (1989, 251) showed that there was only a very slight increase in per capita GDP between 1870 and 1913, and a slight decline between 1913 and 1938. By 1938, per capita GDP in Thailand was estimated to be below that of British Malaya, the Philippines and Indonesia (Table 2.6).

The Transition to Independence: Philippines, Burma and Indonesia Compared

In the aftermath of the Japanese defeat in August 1945, nationalist movements in several parts of Southeast Asia expected that they would rapidly be given self-government or complete independence. Several independence leaders had cooperated with the Japanese, and were influenced by their nationalism and patriotism, even if they resented their occupation. The Americans, who had granted self-government to the Philippines in

Table 2.6 *Per capita GDP in 1913, 1939, 1952 and 1960 (1990 international dollars)*

Country	1913	1939	1952	1960
Southeast Asia				
Singapore	1,367	2,379	2,280	2,310
Malaysia	900	1,609	1,471	1,530
Philippines (1939)	988	1,508	1,186	1,476
Indonesia	869	1,046	901	1,015
Thailand	841	826[a]	869	1,078
Vietnam	727	n.a.	694	799
Laos	n.a.	n.a.	628	679
Cambodia	n.a.	n.a.	504	671
Burma	685	740[a]	449	564
Other Asia:				
Japan	1,387	2,816	2,336	3,986
Taiwan	807	1,380	1,028	1,353
Korea (South)	485	804	835	1,226
India (1943)	673	674	629	753

Source: www.ggdc.net/maddison/maddison-project/home.htm, 2013 version.
Note: a. data for 1938.

1935, honoured their previous pledge regarding independence, which was duly granted on 4 July 1946. Parts of the Philippines had been devastated in the fighting between the Americans and the Japanese in 1945, including the capital, Manila. Per capita GDP in 1952 was still well below the 1938 figure (Table 2.6). The Americans offered considerable financial aid to the new republic, and promised continued access to the American market for sugar and other exports.[18] The American action in conceding independence rapidly on favourable terms, followed by the British decision to leave India, led the independence leaders in both Burma and Indonesia to expect the speedy end of colonial occupation in both countries. But in both countries the transition was far from smooth.

In Burma, the economy had been devastated by the war. The retreating British had destroyed infrastructure in 1941/2 in the face of the Japanese

---

[18] But the Americans were either unable or unwilling to alter the exchange rate of the peso, which Hooley (1996, 296) argued was overvalued from 1904 right through to the devaluation of 1962. This almost certainly adversely affected growth of exports and overall economic growth, in both the colonial era and afterwards.

advance, and the fighting between the advancing British and Japanese forces in 1944/5 had also been violent and prolonged. It was officially estimated that GDP in 1947/8 was only 72 per cent of the figure in 1938/9; it only returned to the pre-war level in 1958/9, by which time population had increased substantially (Ministry of National Planning 1960, 16). The Maddison Project estimates show that per capita GDP in 1960 was still well below the 1938 level (Table 2.6). While most of the population wanted independence, a range of political parties had emerged which were divided by ideology, ethnicity, religion and personal animosities. An already chaotic situation was made much worse by the assassination of Aung San and five other leaders in July 1947. The British granted independence in January 1948 to a government headed by U Nu, but immediately after independence the country showed every sign of becoming a failed state (Bayly & Harper 2007, 322). Plagued by ethnic and regional rebellions, Burma never managed to achieve the political stability of India or the relative prosperity of British Malaya, although as will be seen, there was some progress in restoring the public finances after 1950.

In Indonesia, the Dutch in 1945 were determined to re-occupy their huge Asian colony. Their main motive was economic: the Dutch economy had been badly damaged by the German occupation and leading economists, together with the great majority of the Dutch population, feared that the loss of the Indies, and its remittances, would have serious implications for economic recovery in the Netherlands. Many Dutch administrators were convinced that Sukarno and Hatta were tools of the Japanese and had little following among the Indonesian masses who wanted nothing more than to return to the peace and stability of the Dutch *raj*. Four years of bitter fighting followed; only after the failed Communist uprising in Madiun did the Americans realize that the Indonesian revolution was nationalist rather than communist and deserved their support. After protracted and often difficult negotiations, the Dutch finally agreed to a transfer of power in late 1949, under conditions which were far from favourable to the infant republic (Lindblad 2008, Booth 2016, 36–9).

In all three countries, the advent of political independence led to rising expectations among the local populations, which the governments found difficult to meet. National income had fallen in per capita terms in all three countries, which reduced the tax base. In addition, there was considerable resentment that colonial-era taxes, which many people felt were inequitable, continued to be assessed, albeit with difficulty. In Indonesia, many nationalists had exaggerated ideas of the revenues from exploitation of natural resources, especially petroleum and other minerals, which they assumed could accrue to the government once remittances abroad were

Table 2.7 *Revenues per capita and inflation
in 1954 (1938 = 100)*

Country	Revenues per capita	Prices
Indonesia	1,449	2,340
Thailand	2,422	1,330
Burma	513	380
Philippines	311	329

Sources: International Monetary Fund (1952–60),
International Financial Statistics, various issues,
with additional data for Burma from Ministry of
National Planning (1960); Central Bank of the
Philippines (1956); Bank Indonesia (1956);
Ingram (1971, 329–30). Price indices for
Indonesia from Central Bureau of Statistics (1961,
229–30); for Burma from Ministry of National
Planning (1960); for Thailand from Ingram (1971,
164, 222).
Note: Price indexes for Burma: GDP deflator; for
Indonesia: Average retail prices in Jakarta of 30
home-produced and imported products; for
Thailand: Cost of Living index in Bangkok and
after 1951 GDP deflator; for the Philippines:
Cost of Living of lower income groups in
Manila.

halted. A further problem was that inflation had been high throughout the
1940s, and by the time power was handed over to the governments in the
Philippines, Indonesia and Burma, as well as in independent Thailand,
the salaries of civil servants had been considerably reduced in real terms.
This affected morale, and made the collection of taxes more difficult, as
officials were more tempted to take bribes in order to reduce tax assessments. In addition, many took second jobs to increase their incomes,
which reduced the time and commitment they gave to their tasks as tax
officials.

In both the Philippines and Indonesia, inflation in the years from 1938
through to 1954 was higher than the increase in per capita government
revenues; in other words, their value was lower in real terms than in 1938
(Table 2.7). In spite of the recourse to deficit spending, especially in
Indonesia, real per capita expenditures were lower in Indonesia in 1958
than in 1938, while in the Philippines there was little change (Table 2.8).
In both Indonesia and the Philippines, government investment

Table 2.8 *Index of real per capita government expenditures in local currencies (1953 = 100)*

Country	1938	1953	1956	1958
Indonesia	130	100	66	117
Philippines	129	100	170	130
Burma	58	100	94	104
Thailand	52	100	91	89

Sources: Indonesia: Creutzberg (1976, table 4); Central Bureau of Statistics (1971, 317); population date from van der Eng (2002). Burma: Ministry of Planning (1960) Philippines: Commonwealth of the Philippines (1941, 164) and Central Bank of the Philippines (1956, 1960) Thailand: Ingram (1971, 329–30) Deflators: Indonesia: Papanek and Dowsett (1975, 184); from 1953 onwards ECAFE (1964, 240), Burma: Ministry of Planning (1960), Philippines and Thailand, as for Table 2.7.

comprised only about 2.6 per cent of GDP in 1957, which was a lower ratio than that in Japan, Taiwan and South Korea (Booth 1998, 167). In Indonesia, the demise of parliamentary democracy and the return to the 1945 constitution at the end of the 1950s was accompanied by much talk of "Indonesian socialism", but in fact government control over the economy in the early 1960s weakened. An over-valued exchange rate led to massive smuggling of export commodities to Malaysia and Singapore, which in turn further reduced tax collections. By the early 1960s, the government was caught in a vicious downward spiral of inflation and smuggling leading to poor revenue performance, leading to budget deficits which fuelled further inflation, and eventually hyper-inflation. The economy was only stabilized after the change of regime in 1966.

In spite of its difficult transition to independence, and the chaotic situation which prevailed in the immediate aftermath of the transfer of power, Burma did manage to increase government revenues in real terms and as a proportion of GDP in the 1950s. As a proportion of GDP, government receipts, excluding loans and revenues from government boards and corporations, increased from almost 12 per cent in 1938/9 to 23 per cent in 1954/5, but had fallen back to less than 17 per cent by 1958/8 (Table 2.9). Government revenues from all sources comprised 49 per cent of GDP in 1952/3, and grew relative to GDP over the decade. Budgetary expenditures also increased after 1950, although a direct comparison with 1938 is difficult because over the 1950s expenditures of

Table 2.9 *Burma: government revenues and expenditures as a percentage of GDP*

	1938/9	1952/3	1954/5	1958/9
Receipts	11.8	17.4	23	16.7
Total revenues	n.a	48.6	49.1	51.2
Total expenditures	8.2	46.6	59.1	54.1
Of which: capital	0.3	7.1	11.2	7.8

Sources: Total revenues from 1952/53 onwards refer to revenue and loan receipts plus revenues from boards and corporations. Total expenditures from 1952/53 onwards refer to consolidated expenditures of the government sector, including current and capital expenditures of ministries, departments, boards and corporations. Revenues and expenditures as reported in Central Statistical and Economics Department (1963: 281). GDP data from Ministry of National Planning (1960, table 1A) and Central Statistical and Economics Department (1963, 273).
Note: Government receipts refer to central and net state and local revenues excluding loans and revenues from government boards and corporations as given in Ministry of National Planning (1960, table III).

government boards and corporations increased rapidly, and accounted for a substantial part of the total growth in consolidated budgetary expenditures (Central Statistical and Economics Department 1963, 281). By 1954/5, budgetary expenditures accounted for 59 per cent of GDP, and capital expenditures about 11 per cent, although there was some reduction in these percentages by the end of the decade.

The growth in the role of government in the economy of Burma after independence was the result of a conscious decision on the part of the government to adopt a socialist economy, at least in the non-agricultural sector. This meant building new state enterprises in industry, transport and utilities and adopting marketing boards for key export crops, especially rice. Farmers had to sell rice to the marketing board at a price which, at least in the early 1950s, was well below the world price. These policies met with considerable criticism, especially from the American advisers which the government had contracted to provide them with economic advice (Brown 2013, 120–4). Both the foreign advisers and some Burmese economists threw doubt on the extent to which the increased budgetary expenditures were being used to enhance the productive capacity of the economy, especially given that the agricultural sector was still largely in private hands, and was increasingly penalized through low procurement prices and starved of investment in irrigation and other infrastructure.[19] Although total GDP had regained 1938/9 levels in 1958/9, real value added in agriculture was still lower. In December 1958, the caretaker government led by Ne Win terminated the contract of the foreign advisers, but there was little change in policy.

The Transition to Independence in Malaya, Singapore, Brunei, North Borneo and Sarawak

Apart from Burma, the various parts of the British Empire in Southeast Asia were slower to achieve independence, at least partly because of fears that communist-backed insurgents might take over large parts of the Malayan peninsula. What became known as the Malayan Emergency lasted until the late 1950s. The Federation of Malaya was formed from the three components of British Malaya after 1945, excluding Singapore which was administered separately. The Federation and Singapore were finally granted self-government in 1957 and 1959 respectively, and, in 1963, both joined the new federal state of Malaysia. This federation also included the British-controlled territories of Sabah (North Borneo) and Sarawak on the island of Borneo. Strains emerged almost immediately between Singapore, with its Chinese majority, and the Malay-dominated government in Kuala Lumpur, and Singapore left the federation to become an independent republic in 1965. But the rest of the federation has survived until the present day.

In the 1930s, the revenue base in the three parts of British Malaya depended heavily on excises and trade taxes (with the exception of Singapore which was a free port), and a range of non-tax revenues. In per capita terms these revenues were high compared with most other parts of colonial Asia (Table 2.1). Colonial officials were under pressure not to increase taxes further, especially on incomes. In North Borneo and Sarawak, per capita revenues were much lower, and little different from the Philippines. The comparative data assembled by Schwulst showed that the Federated Malay States were spending about 20 per cent of the budget on public works and a further 20 per cent on health and education. These were high percentages compared with most other regions (Table 2.4). Conversely, defence expenditures were very low, and remained low over the 1930s. In the Straits Settlements, a higher proportion of the budget was allocated to the military.

---

[19] Brown (2013, 162–3) discusses the growth of the marketing board for rice after 1948, and the adverse impact it had on producer incentives.

After 1948, the various parts of Southeast Asia still controlled by the British underwent considerable changes in both revenue and expenditure policy. The most important reform was the introduction of an income tax in both the Federation of Malaya (FOM) and Singapore; by 1953 this accounted for 43 per cent of total revenues in Singapore and 27 per cent in the FOM. The FOM also received some assistance from the UK Colonial Development and Welfare Fund. The absolute amounts were lower than those granted to Ghana or Nigeria, and until 1957 they amounted to less than 10 per cent of total budgetary revenues (Markandan 1960, 50). In terms of pounds per capita, the reforms led to a substantial increase in revenues in both Singapore and the FOM compared with 1938 (Table 2.10).[20] The increases in Brunei, Sabah and Sarawak were much higher. In Brunei the increase from just four pounds per capita in 1938 to almost 200 pounds in 1953 was mainly the result of the exploitation of the sultanate's oil resources, which began after 1945, although not all the increased revenues were spent in Brunei. In Sabah, revenues from the Colonial Development and Welfare Grants accounted for almost 14 per cent of total revenues in 1953; in addition, over 60 per cent accrued from customs duties and revenues from forests, license fees and income taxes (Colonial Office 1955, 125). In Sarawak, revenues from trade taxes, and license fees, income taxes and other revenues accounted for almost all revenues.

The increased revenues per capita in Singapore, FOM, Sabah and Sarawak led to increases in expenditures after 1950. But what were the increased revenues spent on? In the FOM, the battle against the communist insurgency led to a sharp increase in spending on police and defence. By 1953, this amounted to over one quarter of the budget, which was considerably more than the proportion spent on health, education and welfare, or on public works (Table 2.11). In Singapore by contrast, expenditures on health, education and welfare comprised almost 26 per cent of expenditures, and public works a further 20 per cent. Singapore experienced rapid population growth after 1947, mainly because of rapid natural increase but also because of continued in-migration (Huff 1994, 292). This put considerable strains on the housing stock; by the early 1950s many people were living in crowded apartments in the city or in shanties around the periphery. It is probable that the extreme overcrowding and lack of sanitation was one reason for the higher infant mortality in Singapore than in the Malay states, both in the 1930s and the 1940s (Smith 1952, 54). Only after Singapore

---

[20] Estimates of the purchasing power of the pound indicate that 10 pounds in 1938 could buy the same amount of goods and services as 22 pounds and 16 shillings in 1953.

Table 2.10 *Revenues and expenditures per capita (£), 1938, 1953 and 1957*

Colony	1938	1953	1957
Revenues:			
Straits Settlements/Singapore[a]	3	25	19
Federation of Malaya[a]	3	13	15
Brunei	4	200	215
Sabah	1	10	16
Sarawak	1	8	9
Expenditures:			
Straits Settlements/Singapore	4	18	19
Federation of Malaya	4	16	15
Brunei	5	45	65
Sabah	1	11	15
Sarawak	1	6	9

Sources: Revenue data: Colonial Office (1955) with additional data for 1957 for the Federation of Malaya from Markandan (1960, 60) and Lim (1967, 352). 1957 figures for Sabah, Sarawak, Singapore and Brunei from Annual Reports of North Borneo, Sarawak, Brunei and Singapore. Population data from Jones (1966, table 19). Expenditure data; Federation of Malaya: Colonial Office (1955). Additional data from Markandan (1960, 60), State of Brunei Annual Report 1958, 20–1; Colony of North Borneo Annual Report 1959, 33–6; Sarawak Annual Report 1958, 18–19.

Notes: a. 1938 figure refers to the Straits Settlements, not just Singapore, and to the sum of the figures for the Federated and Unfederated Malay States. Revenues in Singapore in 1938 exclude the transfer from the Currency Guarantee Fund; for the Federation of Malaya they include railway revenues.

became an independent republic in 1965 was there a concerted attempt by the government to build more housing, and initiate a family planning programme.[21]

---

[21] The report on the Social Survey of Singapore, carried out in 1953/4, found that 20 per cent of households were living in acutely overcrowded conditions compared with 21 per cent in 1947. Acutely overcrowded was defined as two adults and four children, at least one over ten years, living in one room (Goh 1956, 73). A further 28 per cent lived under conditions of overcrowding, and only 15 per cent were deemed to be living in spacious conditions. The main author of the report, Dr Goh Keng Swee became deputy prime minister after Singapore became independent in 1965, and was instrumental in initiating ambitious programmes in public housing and birth control.

Table 2.11 *Percentage breakdown of government expenditures, 1953*

Colony	Police & Defence	Health & Education	Public Works	Other
FOM	26.8	4	14.1	55.1
Singapore	18	25.7[a]	20.5	35.8
Sabah	6.6	8.3	12.4	72.7
Sarawak	10.5	10.7	11.4	67.4
Brunei[b]	2.4	7.5	13.5	76.6

Source: Colonial Office (1955, 34,57,108, 126, 147).
Notes: a. Includes spending funded through the colonial development and welfare schemes;
b. 1952.

In Sabah, Brunei and Sarawak, the proportion of government spending on health and education was lower than in Singapore. All these territories faced considerable challenges in raising literacy from the very low levels prevailing in the 1940s, but given limited government funding, progress was slow. A UNESCO report published in 1957 included North Borneo, Sarawak and Brunei among the areas of the world characterized by high illiteracy. In North Borneo, the 1951 Census found that 83 per cent of the population was illiterate, with not much difference across age groups, indicating that there had been little improvement in schooling in the preceding two decades. Illiteracy was also high in Sarawak and Brunei according to the 1947 Census, although especially in Brunei there was some improvement in the younger age groups. Inadequate data make any estimation of mortality rates in Borneo before 1950 very difficult, although Jones (1966, 48) found that there was some tendency for infant mortality in Brunei to fall over the 1930s. But it remained higher than in peninsular Malaysia. After 1945, population growth accelerated in Sabah, Sarawak and North Borneo, which Jones (1966, 111) attributed to both increased fertility and falling mortality, in turn the result of better social services and better communications.

By the late 1950s, when the former British territories in Malaya, Singapore and Borneo had achieved or were about to achieve independence, a more activist fiscal state had emerged. Government revenues per capita had increased, and the revenue systems had become more diversified. Government expenditures were also increasing in per capita terms, and the state was assuming responsibility for a broader range of functions, including health and education as well as continuing to spend on public works and civil administration. There was also some progress towards a more diversified banking system, especially in Singapore where the three main Chinese banks made an increasing contribution to financing local industry and commerce. In addition, the European banks were more willing to lend to local business than before 1942 (Huff 1994, 287–8). The Currency Board remained in place after 1945, and expanded its geographic coverage after 1950 to the British Borneo territories (Drake 2004, 115). Only in 1959 was a central bank established (Bank Negara Tanah Melayu), with jurisdiction over the Federation of Malaya, excluding Singapore.[22] As Drake (2004, 137) pointed out, the new bank inherited a monetary system in which domestic liquidity was largely a function of swings in the balance of payments, and the scope for domestic monetary policy was very limited.

Conclusions

This chapter has discussed the differences in revenue and expenditure policies across Southeast Asia in the last decades of colonial rule, and the impact of the transition to independence. The first conclusion is that there were marked variations in revenues and expenditures per capita across colonies and in Thailand. There were also striking differences in the allocation of expenditures across different sectors. These variations reflected the different goals of the colonial powers. The Americans, aware of the domestic unpopularity of their occupation of the Philippines, promised self-government and thus promoted the rapid development of an English-speaking upper class, which was to dominate politics after 1946. One-third of the budget went on health and education, a much higher proportion than elsewhere. At the other extreme, French Indochina spent very little of the federal budget on health and education, but much more on public works, administration and the army. This was also true in Indonesia.

But in spite of these differences, there were also some features of fiscal policy common to all countries, and to independent Thailand. By the early twentieth century, all parts of the region were becoming more involved with the global economy. In many parts of the region, large corporations in the agricultural and mining sectors were producing a range of commodities for export and employed thousands of workers. In addition, millions of smallholder producers were involved in producing for export. When a severe depression hit the global economy in the early 1930s, this affected government revenues in all colonies. Some governments resorted to borrowing, but the conservative attitude of home

---

[22] Schenk (1993) examines the background to the establishment of this bank, which became the Bank Negara Malaysia.

governments limited the extent to which they could borrow. When they did, they borrowed in the metropolitan countries, or in the London market. This in turn hampered the development of money markets within the colonies.

The Philippines was granted independence in 1946, and Indonesia in 1949, after a protracted struggle with the Dutch. Both countries struggled to increase government revenues in step with population growth, and by the mid-1950s, revenues in real terms were below the pre-1940 levels. Especially in Indonesia, real government expenditures also fell in per capita terms. In Burma, by contrast, real revenues grew in per capita terms, and both revenues and expenditures increased relative to GDP. But this expansion of the public sector had its critics; by the late 1950s, some thought that the government sector, together with state enterprises, was too big and the private sector, especially agriculture, was being squeezed to fund the expansion of unprofitable state enterprises. Singapore, the Federation of Malaya and the British Borneo territories remained under British control until the early 1960s. They all experienced considerable growth in both government revenues and expenditures. But the currency board system remained in place, giving little scope for the development of an independent monetary policy.

There remains the puzzle of Thailand, which, as an independent country, had an opportunity for conducting more developmental, or growth-promoting, monetary and fiscal policies. But in fact the Thai state failed to promote growth even compared with neighbouring colonies, and between 1900 and 1952, per capita GDP changed little. Larsson (2012, 33) has argued that the Thai state from the late nineteenth century onwards became "actively non-developmental in order to protect its sovereignty in the context of geopolitical vulnerability". The result, as Schwulst observed, was not a small government by the standards of the time, but one which placed most emphasis on building up a national system of administration and a defence force, rather than on economic development. Several studies of Thai policy in the years from 1900 to 1940 have stressed the influence of the British advisers in urging caution regarding the implementation of costly public works projects which would have necessitated foreign loans. While this was probably true, the evidence suggests that it was senior Thai officials who made the final decisions. Even after 1950, when control by Britain or France was no longer a credible threat, the Thai government continued to pursue a cautious approach to fiscal and monetary policies, and left economic growth mainly to the private sector.

Bibliography

Andrews, J. M. (1935). *Siam: Second Rural Survey 1934–1935*. Bangkok: Bangkok Times Press.

Andrus, J. R. (1948). *Burmese Economic Life*. Stanford: Stanford University Press.

Aye. H. (1965). *An Economic and Statistical Analysis of Economic Development of Burma under British Rule*. PhD thesis, University of London.

Baker, C., & Phongpaichit, P. (1995). *Thailand: Economy and Politics*. Kuala Lumpur: Oxford University Press.

Bank Indonesia. (1956). *Annual Report 1956*. Jakarta: Bank Indonesia.

Bassino, J.-P. (2000). Public Finance in Vietnam under French Rule 1895–1954. In J.-P. Bassino, J.-D. Giacometti & K. Odaka (Eds.), *Quantitative Economic History of Vietnam 1900–1990*. Tokyo: Hitotsubashi University, Institute of Economic Research, 269–92.

Batson, B. A. (1984). *The End of the Absolute Monarchy in Siam*. Singapore: Oxford University Press.

Bayly, C., & Harper, T. (2004). *Forgotten Armies: Britain's Asian Empire and the War with Japan*. London: Penguin Books.

Bayly, C., & Harper, T. (2007). *Forgotten Wars: the End of Britain's Asian Empire*. London: Penguin Books.

Bidwell, R. L. (1970). *Currency Conversion Tables: a Hundred Years of Change*. London: Rex Collings.

Birnberg, T. B., & Resnick, S. A. (1975). *Colonial Development: an Econometric Study*. New Haven: Yale University Press.

Boomgaard, P. (2014). Population Growth and Environmental Change: a Two-Track Model. In N. G. Owen (Ed.), *Routledge Handbook of Southeast Asian History*, Abingdon: Routledge, 133–43.

Booth, A. (1980). The Economic Impact of Export Taxes in ASEAN. *Malayan Economic Review*, 26(1), 36–61.

Booth, A. (1990). The Evolution of Fiscal Policy and the Role of Government in the Colonial Economy. In A. Booth, W. J. O'Malley & A. Weidemann (Eds.), *Indonesian Economic History in the Dutch Colonial Era, Monograph Series 35*, New Haven: Yale University Southeast Asia Studies, 210–43.

Booth, A. (1998). *The Indonesian Economy in the Nineteenth and Twentieth Centuries*. Basingstoke: Macmillan Press.

Booth, A. (2004). Linking, De-linking and Re-linking: South East Asia in the Global Economy in the Twentieth Century. *Australian Economic History Review*, 44(1), 35–51.

Booth, A (2007a). Night Watchman, Extractive, or Developmental States? Some Evidence from Late Colonial South-east Asia. *Economic History Review*, 60(2), 241–66.

Booth, A. (2007b). *Colonial Legacies: Economic and Social Development in East and South East Asia*. Honolulu: University of Hawaii Press.

Booth, A. (2013). Colonial Revenue Policies and The Impact of the Transition to Independence in Southeast Asia. *Bijdragen tot de taalland- en Volkenkunde*, 169, 1–31.

Booth, A. (2014). Land Taxation in Asia: an Overview of the 19th and 20th Centuries. *Oxford Development Studies*, 42(1), 1–18.

Booth, A. (2016). *Economic Change in Modern Indonesia: Colonial and Post-colonial Comparisons*. Cambridge: Cambridge University Press.

Breman, J. (2002). New Thoughts on Colonial Labour in Indonesia. *Journal of Southeast Asian Studies*, 33(2), 333–9.

Brocheux, P.,& Hemery, D. (2009). *Indochina: an Ambiguous Colonization 1858–1954*. Berkeley and Los Angeles: University of California Press.

Brown, I. (1988). *The Elite and the Economy in Siam c.1890–1920*. Singapore: Oxford University Press.

Brown, I. (2013). *Burma's Economy in the Twentieth Century*. Cambridge: Cambridge University Press.

Butcher, J. (1993). Revenue Farming and the Changing State in Southeast Asia. In J. Butcher & H. Dick (Eds.), *The Rise and Fall of Revenue Farming*, Basingstoke: Macmillan Press, 19–44.

Central Bank of the Philippines. (1956). *Seventh Annual Report 1955*. Manila: Central Bank of the Philippines.

Central Bank of the Philippines. (1960). *Annual Report 1960*. Manila: Central Bank of the Philippines.

Central Bureau of Statistics. (1947). *Statistical Pocketbook of Indonesia 1941*. Batavia: G. Kolff.

Central Bureau of Statistics. (1961). *Statistical Pocketbook of Indonesia, 1961*. Jakarta: Biro Pusat Statistik.

Central Bureau of Statistics. (1971). *Statistical Pocketbook of Indonesia, 1968 and 1969*. Jakarta: Biro Pusat Statistik.

Central Service of Statistics. (1940). *Statistical Yearbook of Thailand, No 20*. Bangkok: Central Service of Statistics.

Central Statistical and Economics Department. (1963). *Statistical Year Book 1961*. Rangoon: The Revolutionary Government of the Union of Burma.

Chandra, S. (2010). Economic Histories of the Opium Trade. In R. Whaples (Ed.), *EHNetEncyclopedia*, accessed 2010/02/05. http://eh.net/encyclopedia/article/chandra.opium.

Colonial Office. (1955). *An Economic Survey of the Colonial Territories, Volume V: The Far Eastern Territories*. London: Her Majesty's Stationery Office.

Commonwealth of the Philippines. (1941). *Yearbook of Philippine Statistics 1940*. Manila: Bureau of Census and Statistics.

Corpuz, O. D. (1997). *An Economic History of the Philippines*. Quezon City: University of the Philippines Press.

Creutzberg, P. (1976). *Changing Economy in Indonesia, Volume 2: Public Finance 1816–1939*. The Hague: Martinus Nijhoff.

Department of Statistics. (1936). *Malayan Year Book 1936*. Singapore: Government Printing Office.

Department of Statistics. (1939). *Malayan Year Book 1939*. Singapore: Government Printing Office.

Descours-Gatin, C. (1992). *Quand l'Opium Financait la Colonisation en Indochine*. Paris: L'Harmattan.

Diehl, F. W. (1993). Revenue Farming and Colonial Finances in the Netherlands East Indies 1816–1925. In J. Butcher & H. Dick (Eds.), *The Rise and Fall of Revenue Farming*. Basingstoke: Macmillan, 196–232.

Drake, P. J. (2004). *Currency, Credit and Commerce: Early Growth in Southeast Asia*, Aldershot: Ashgate.

Elson, R. (1992). International Commerce, the State and Society: Economic and Social Change. In N. Tarling (Ed.), *The Cambridge History of South East Asia, Volume 2, Part 1*. Cambridge: Cambridge University Press, 127–91.

ECAFE. (1964). *Review of Long-term Economic Projections for Selected Countries in the ECAFE Region*. Bangkok: United Nations Economic Commission for Asia and the Far East.

Federation of Malaya. (1956). *Federation of Malaya Yearbook 1956*. Kuala Lumpur: Malay Mail Press.

Foster, A. L. (2003). Models for Governing: Opium and Colonial Policies in South East Asia, 1898–1910. In J. Go & A. L. Foster (Eds.), *The American Colonial State in the Philippines: Global Perspectives*. Durham: Duke University Press, 92–117.

Fraser, H. (1939). *Annual Report on the Social and Economic Progress of the People of the Federated Malay States for 1938*. Kuala Lumpur: FMS Government Press.

Furnivall, J. S. (1934). *Studies in the Social and Economic Development of the Netherlands East Indies; 3d, the Land Revenue System*. Rangoon: Burma Book Club Ltd.

Furnivall, J. S. (1943). *Educational Progress in Southeast Asia*: New York: Institute of Pacific Relations.

Furnivall. J. S. (1944). *Netherlands India: a study of plural economy*, Cambridge: Cambridge University Press.

Goh, K-S. (1956). *Urban Incomes and Housing: a Report on the Social Survey of Singapore, 1953–54*. Singapore: Government Printing Office.

Guermeur, H. (1909). *Le Regime Fiscal de l'Indochine*. Paris: L'Harmattan.

Hazelwood, A. (1954). The Economics of Colonial Monetary Arrangements. *Social and Economic Studies*, 3, 291–315.

He, W. (2013). *Paths towards the Modern Fiscal State: England, Japan and China*, Cambridge: Harvard University Press.

Ho, S. P-S. (1984). Colonialism and Development: Korea, Taiwan and Kwantung. In R. Myers & M. Peattie (Eds.), *The Japanese Colonial Empire, 1895–1945*. Princeton: Princeton University Press, 347–98.

Hooley, R. (1996). A Century of Philippine Foreign Trade: a Quantitative Analysis. In E. DeDios & R. Fabella (Eds.), *Choice, Growth and Development: Essays in Honor of Jose Encarnacion*. Manila: University of the Philippines Press.

Huff, W. G. (1994). *The Economic Growth of Singapore: Trade and Development in the Twentieth Century*. Cambridge: Cambridge University Press.

Indisch Verslag. (1938). *Indische Verlag II, Statistisch Jaaroverzicht van Nederlandsch-Indie over het Jaar 1937*. Batavia: Landsdrukkerij.

Ingram, J. C. (1971). *Economic Change in Thailand, 1850–1970*. Kuala Lumpur: Oxford University Press.

International Monetary Fund (1957–60). *International Financial Statistics*. Washington DC: International Monetary Fund (monthly publication).

Jones, L. W. (1966). *The Population of Borneo: a Study of the Peoples of Sarawak, Sabah and Brunei*. London: Athlone Press.

Jong, F. de & Ravesteijn, W. (2008). The Rise and Development of Public Works in the East Indies. In W. Ravesteijn & J. Kop (Eds.), *For Profit and Prosperity: the Contribution made by Dutch Engineers to Public Works in Indonesia*. Leiden: KITLV Press, 244–66.

Kloosterboer, J. (1960). *Involuntary Labour since the Abolition of Slavery: a Survey of Complusory Labour throughout the World*. Leiden: E.J. Brill.

Laanen, J. T. M. van (1980). *Money and Banking 1816–1940, Volume 6: Changing Economy of Indonesia*. The Hague: Martinus Nijhoff.

Laanen, J. T. M. van (1990). Between the Java Bank and the Chinese Moneylender: Banking and Credit in Colonial Indonesia. In A. Booth, W. J. O'Malley & A. Weidemann (Eds.), *Indonesian Economic History in the Dutch Colonial Era* Monograph Series 35. New Haven: Yale University Southeast Asia Studies, 244–66.

Larsson, T. (2012). *Land and Loyalty: Security and the Development of Property Rights in Thailand*. Ithaca: Cornell University Press.

Lasker, B. (1950). *Human Bondage in Southeast Asia*. Chapel Hill: University of North Carolina Press.

Lewis, W. A. (1969). *Aspects of Tropical Trade 1883–1965*. Stockholm: Almqvist and Wiksell.

Lim, C-Y. (1967). *Economic Development of Modern Malaysia*. Kuala Lumpur: Oxford University Press.

Lindblad, J. Th. (2008). *Bridges to New Business: the Economic Decolonization of Indonesia*. Leiden: KITLV Press.

Luton, H. (1971). American Internal Revenue Policy in the Philippines to 1916. In N. G. Owen (Ed.), *Compadre Colonialism: Studies on the Philippines under American Rule, Michigan Papers on South and Southeast Asia, Number 3*. Ann Arbor: University of Michigan, 129–55.

Markandan, P. (Ed.). (1960). *Report on Finance, Commerce and Industry Federation of Malaya 1960*. Singapore: Far Eastern Features Service.

Ministry of National Planning. (1960). *The National Income of Burma*. Rangoon: Ministry of National Planning, Central Statistical and Economics Department.

Mizoguchi, T., & Umemura, M. (Eds.). (1988). *Basic Economic Statistics of Former Japanese Colonies, 1895–1938: Estimates and Findings*. Tokyo: Toyo Keizai Shinposha.

O'Malley, W. J. (1979). The Bengkalis Hunger Riots of 1935. In F. van Anrooij-Dirk, H. A. Kolff, J. T. M. van Laanen & G. J. Telkamp (Eds.), *Between People and Statistics: Essays in Modern Indonesian History*. The Hague: Martinus Nijhoff, 235–49.

Papanek, G. F., & Dowsett D. (1975). The Cost of Living 1938–1973. *Ekonomi dan Keuangan Indonesia*, XXIII, 181–206.

Penders, Chr. L. M. (Ed.). (1977) *Indonesia: Selected Documents on Colonialism and Nationalism 1830–1942*. St Lucia: University of Queensland Press.

Population Reference Bureau. (2018). *2018 World Population Data Sheet*, Washington: Population Reference Bureau.

Sato, M. et al. (2008) *Asian Historical Statistics: Taiwan*, Tokyo: Toyo Kezai Inc for the Institute of Economic Research, Hitotsubashi University.

Schenk, C. R. (1993). The Origins of a Central Bank in Malaya and the Transition to Independence, 1954–9. *Journal of Imperial and Commonwealth History*, 21(2), 409–31.

Schwulst, E. B. (1932). Report on the Budget and Financial Policies of French Indochina, Siam, Federated Malay States and the Netherlands

Indies. In *Report of the Governor General of the Philippines Islands 1931*. Washington: United States Government Printing Office, 42–59.

Simoni, H. (1929). *Le Role du Capital dans la Mise en Valeur de l'Histoire de L'indochine*. Paris: Helms.

Slocomb, M. (2010). *An Economic History of Cambodia in the Twentieth Century*. Singapore: NUS Press.

Smith, T. E. (1952). *Population Growth in Malaya*, London: Royal Institute of International Affairs.

Sompop M. (1989). *Economic Development of Thailand, 1850–1950*. PhD-thesis, University of Groningen, The Netherlands.

Sugimoto, I. (2011). *Economic Growth of Singapore in the Twentieth Century: Historical GDP Estimates and Empirical Investigations*. Singapore: World Scientific Publishing Co.

Terwiel, B. J. (2011). *Thailand's Political History: from the 13th Century to Recent Times* (Revised edition). Bangkok: River Books.

Thompson, V. (1937). *French Indo-China*. London: George Allen and Unwin.

Thompson, V. (1943). *Postmortem on Malaya*. New York: The Macmillan Company.

Thompson, V. (1947). *Labor Problems in Southeast Asia* New Haven: Yale University Press.

Thompson, V. (1967). *Thailand: The New Siam* (2nd ed.), as reprinted by Paragon Book Reprint Corporation, New York.

UNESCO. (1957). *World Illiteracy at Mid-Century: A Statistical Study*, Paris: UNESCO.

United Nations. (1948). *Public Debt 1914–46*. Lake Success: Department of Economic Affairs.

van der Eng, P. (2002). Indonesia's Growth Performance in the Twentieth Century. In A. Maddison, D. S. Prasada Rao & W. Shepherd (Eds.), *The Asian Economies in the Twentieth Century*. Cheltenham: Edward Elgar, 143–79.

van der Eng, P. (2006). Surplus mobilization in farm agriculture: a comparison of Java and Japan, 1870–1940. *Bulletin of Indonesian Economic Studies*, 42, 35–58.

Vichitvong na Pombhejara. (1978). Thailand's Monetary Development in the 1930s. In Vichitvong na Pombhejara (Ed.), *Readings in Thailand's Political Economy*. Bangkok: Bangkok Printing Enterprise Co. Ltd, 414–23.

3   Why Was British India a Limited State?

Tirthankar Roy

Introduction

Discussions on the state in early-modern Europe employ the concept of the 'fiscal state' to suggest a process of interdependent growth in coercive and financial capacity, and the creation of institutions, like securitization of public debt, to sustain the process. This scholarship also suggests that "the motor" of fiscal change in these senses "was expenditure on war" (Bonney 2000, 161; see also Frankema & Booth, Chapter 1, this volume), and that the emergence of fiscal states contributed to the beginning of modern economic growth in Western Europe.

The colonization of India by the British East India Company began in the late-eighteenth century. This chapter focuses on the fiscal development of British India during the period of Crown rule between 1858 and 1947. With the British legacy of a fiscal state behind it, did the Company's attempts to construct a state in India use some of these lessons? Was British India a distinct form of state from the indigenous ones? Did the distinctness rest in institutional innovation? Was warfare the spur of these innovations? Did state formation aid or obstruct economic growth in colonial India? We know the answers to some of these questions already. Significant institutional interventions and reforms (like securitization of debt) did underpin the origin of the British Indian fiscal system. On coercive capacity, administrative reach, securitization and centralization of the revenue system, the state enjoyed greater success than the Mughals and their successors did. Some of the institutional reforms were undertaken during a time when the Company was trying to raise more money to fight wars. British India, in other words, was in some sense a legacy of the fiscal state in Britain.

The outcome of the process, however, presents us with two puzzles. The first puzzle is that the institutional reforms still delivered a small state. And the second puzzle is that, to the extent that the pattern of economic change can be attributed to the state, the effect was inequality rather than growth. During the colonial era, private enterprise in trade, transport, finance and industry experienced robust growth, whereas peasant agriculture remained trapped in low yields, and low and mostly stagnant real wages. The small capacity of the state did not hurt capitalistic businesses, but represented a failure to bridge the growing inequality between the modernizing port cities and the countryside. The present chapter asks two questions about the relationship between fiscal modernization and economic change in British India. Why did the state remain small? And, how might state capacity contribute to inequality?

The key stylized fact for this chapter is that the government of British India was a small government. It was small not only in comparison with Britain, the metropolitan power, but also with other emerging economies of the time such as Imperial Russia and Meiji Japan, the two countries that were the 'natural paradigms for India' (Charlesworth 1985, 545). Government revenue in India amounted to 6.7 per cent of GDP in 1910. The proportion was 11 per cent in Japan and 9 in the UK. These proportions convert into a revenue per head in India that was one third that in Japan and one seventeenth of Britain. Even in comparison with the British, Dutch and French colonies in Asia, British India was a poor government. Between 1920 and 1930, the government of the Federated Malay States spent on average more than ten times the money spent in British India per head. That of Ceylon spent more than three times, those of the Philippines and Indonesia more than double, and those of Thailand and French Indochina 40–50 per cent more (Roy 1996).

Not only was the government of India small, it shrank in relation to the size of the British government during the period of Crown rule in India. Between 1870 and 1940, Indian revenue per head as a proportion of British revenue per head fell steadily, from 10 per cent to less than 2 per cent. Whereas in the interwar years, the revenue/GDP ratio rose more than three times in Britain (from 7 to 25 per cent), it did not move in India from the already low level of about 6 per cent (Figures 3.1 and 3.2). An inertia took hold of public finance.

Explaining this inertia remains a challenging task. The suggestion that a "British tradition of conservative finance" was behind the Indian record (Thomas 1939, 430) is not persuasive because Britain did not apply the same rule to itself. There was something distinctly 'colonial' about Indian finances. But what was colonial about the fiscal system that imposed limits on its capacity to achieve sustained growth? A similar question has been asked in a growing literature on colonial public finances worldwide, to which this chapter relates closely. The literature suggests that the state formation project usually followed a distinct pathway in the colonial

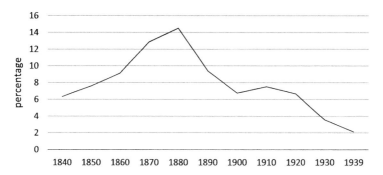

Figure 3.1 British Indian revenue per head as a percentage of British revenue per head, 1840–1939
Source: For Figures 3.1 and 3.2, India, *Statistical Abstracts of British India*, Calcutta, various years; and The Bank of England's Three Centuries Macroeconomic Dataset, Version 2.3 – 30 June 2016, www .bankofengland.co.uk/research/Pages/onebank/threecenturies.aspx (accessed 1 February 2017).

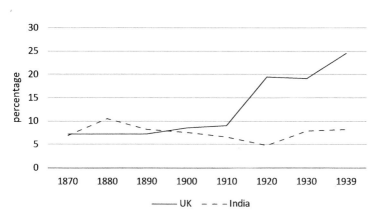

Figure 3.2 Government revenue as % of GDP, 1870–1939
Source: See Figure 3.1.

territories. Practices like indirect rule, negotiations with indigenous elite, settler power and information scarcity imposed limits on the taxable capacity of the colonial governments, despite institutional changes that enabled certain flexibilities (Frankema 2010, Gardner 2012, Frankema & van Waijenburg 2014, Frankema & Booth, Chapter 1, this volume). This chapter confirms the general hypothesis that the emergence of a modern kind of state, even a fiscal state, in India did occur, but in a constrained manner.

The constraint arose, the chapter suggests, not from elite power, indirect rule or information asymmetry, but from a different source. The relevant colonial element in the public finances could be found in the division of duties between India and London. India looked after the fiscal system and London the monetary system and public debt raised in London. Any push to grow would have required the two heads to coordinate as well as agree on a common developmental goal. When ideologically such agreement became more likely, late in the interwar period, strains in the British economy, the collapse of the debt market, the nationalist movement and world politics, reduced room to manoeuvre.

The rest of the chapter is divided into four sections: historiography of public finance, revenue, expenditure and developmental implications of a limited state.

Historiography of Public Finance

There are two strands in the interpretive scholarship on colonial public finance. One of these focuses on expenditure, and the other on revenues. The main problem for the former set of writings is to explain Indian poverty with reference to the actions of the state. The main question the latter explores is why it was difficult for the government to grow, with reference to particular heads of revenue.

The former literature, which originated in the writings of Indian nationalists and was endorsed and developed by Marxist writings on colonialism, explains Indian poverty as an outcome of the nineteenth-century globalization maintained by free markets for commodities and factor movements that the British Empire insisted on and imposed on the territories under its control until the interwar period. For India, openness meant, on one side, a persistent trade surplus, and on the other, a persistent deficit in factor payments (remittance, interests and repatriated profits). Trade funded the services. Therefore, any criticism of the service side of the account implied a criticism of free trade. The nationalists criticized the deficit calling it a "drain" or a waste of savings available for domestic investment, and held drain to be responsible for economic stagnation. Historians of a later generation saw it as one instrument among many of surplus appropriation on a world scale. "[A] large part of India's social surplus", write the authors of a popular textbook, " ... was appropriated by the colonial state and misspent" (Chandra et al. 1999, 13; see also Chandra 1991).

The argument that this item in the balance of payments caused Indian poverty and stagnation rested on the assumption that some of this money, for which the government was responsible (salaries and pensions paid to expatriate officers out of the budget, and interest on public debt), contained an element of unnecessary and excessive payment. The Indian army, for example, was employed for imperial wars in various places. The salaries were excessive. And debt service accounted for "the biggest part of the drain" (Chandra 1960, 678).

Although some of these criticisms have substance, the 'drain theory' of Indian poverty cannot be tested with evidence, for several reasons. First, it rests on the counterfactual that any money saved on account of factor payments abroad would translate into domestic investment, which can never be proved. Second, it rests on "the primitive notion that all payments to foreigners are 'drain'", that is, on the assumption that these payments did not contribute to domestic national income to the equivalent extent (Kumar 1985, 384; see also Chaudhuri 1968). Again, this point cannot be tested. Third, as a large literature on the colonial borrowing activity has underscored, raising debt in London carried an implicit subsidy for the colonies because it entailed lower transaction costs relative to similarly placed independent countries (Accominotti et al. 2011, Ferguson 2012, Gardner 2017). Within the empire, Indian debt was especially well placed. Fourth, while British officers serving India did receive salaries that were many times that of the average income in India, a paper using cross-country data shows that colonies with better-paid officers were governed better (Jones 2013). For all of these reasons, most commentators today would consider the debate over the drain as an explanation for Indian poverty impossible to resolve (Balachandran 2015). That is not saying that there was no element of waste in public expenditure. There was, but we can neither measure it nor weigh its significance for long-term development.

Whatever its defects, the drain theory did draw attention to public investment. One of the first systematic research projects on national accounts in post-independence India focused on the historical saving-investment data. In the 1960s, Bina Roy and M. J. K. Thavaraj wrote several research papers reconstructing national investment, or capital formation, and, in the context of that research, estimated public investment (Thavaraj 1960, 1972, Roy 1967).

More recent scholarship again draws attention to public expenditure. Economists interested in patterns of regional inequality in India show an indirect interest in the colonial fiscal system, by asking how the supply of public goods varied geographically (Chaudhary 2010, Banerjee et al. 2011). Contributors to this debate identify some institutional features, such as tax settlements between the state and the landowners, which made for differential fiscal ability between the provinces. While important in its own way, this scholarship does not comprise a systematic analysis of public finance.

Quite different from the expenditure-oriented projects linking development and public finance, are a set of works that analyse public finance as such. A serious interest in the subject developed in the 1930s in the wake of the establishment of provincial legislatures (1919–37), and encouraged several books and articles. The most detailed work by far was P. J. Thomas' magisterial *Growth of Public Finance in India*, first published in 1939. These works problematized the small size of the state, but offered only tentative explanations for it. A modern interpretive history in the same tradition, which explores the politics behind finance is Sabyasachi Bhattacharya's elegantly written *Financial Foundations of the British Raj*, first published in 1971 and recently republished (Bhattacharya 1971). The book exposes the conflicts and negotiations that lay behind what appeared to many administrators as an unsustainable fiscal system.

Both the descriptive history and *Financial Foundations* reveal several influences, including conflicts between the centre and the provinces or between London and Calcutta, over tax policy. These influences suggest a reason for the structural inertia that beset revenue efforts in British India. Lord Canning, Governor General and later the first Viceroy of India in 1858, said that, "danger for danger", the prospect of living with a small state was better than risking unpopular taxation (quoted in Thomas 1939, 81). This was by no means the generally accepted view of taxation policy, as fierce debates between the centre and the provinces over an income tax showed. But the sentiment behind it was common enough. With specific reference to the suggested income tax, J. B. Maltby, a Madras civilian, said that "since a foreign rule must always in itself be distasteful to a people, . . . [it] requires to be attended with strong palliative advantages" (Thomas 1939, 80). Other officers and publicists saw the benevolent rule of the late-sixteenth-century Mughal emperor Akbar as the ideal for the British in India, implicitly rejecting the rule of the late-Mughal king Aurangzeb who raised taxes to fund warfare. "Would Akbar have done this?" – words like these appeared in official exchanges for some time after the Indian Mutiny (Bartle Frere, cited in Thomas 1939, 79–80).

If this sentiment explains inertia immediately after the Mutiny, it does not explain the subsequent ninety years of the Raj when only limited efforts could be made to raise revenues. Research published in the 1970s and the 1980s re-established the link between development and public finance, now with reference to the inertia, but did not offer a new paradigm on the inertia itself. Raymond Goldsmith's overview of financial development, and Dharma Kumar's survey of the fiscal system only illustrated the problem. Neil Charlesworth, though confined to the interwar period, took that discussion into the realm of comparative history (Goldsmith 1983, Kumar 1983, Charlesworth 1985). These studies elaborate the fact that something like a revenue trap was present, and that it was due to over-reliance on land taxes. They highlight the inflexibility or inelasticity of the revenues of British India. The colonial state inherited a fiscal system from the British East India Company that taxed agricultural land and the consumption of articles like opium and salt, taxed trade to a limited extent and did not tax income and wealth. Charlesworth showed that this inheritance became increasingly dysfunctional in the twentieth century. Whereas income, wealth and customs did rise after World War I, the rise was just enough to compensate for the losses in taxes on land, opium and salt. I have added to this discussion an emphasis on the geographical context. Low and, in some regions, falling land yields made the government's reliance on the land tax particularly damaging, and limited scope for raising money through consumption taxes (Roy 2016a).

But why was there an overreliance on land tax in the first place? That the government was afraid of taxing the rich would be too simplistic an explanation. Many wealthy and undertaxed Indians like landlords and business houses supported the empire, but the empire did not regard that support to be as valuable as it did the support of the peasants. The crucial missing link in the interpretive scholarship is public debt. This could be the escape route from the land productivity constraint, and a key – perhaps the only one available but a major one – to fiscal modernization.

Quite clearly, the borrowing option was underutilized by British India. British India was a government with three heads. One of its heads was in the India Office in London, which managed currency and security market operations. The second head was the Viceroy's office and council of advisors in India, which managed the fiscal system. The third head, and the lowest in the hierarchy, was in the provinces, which oversaw spending on such essential public goods as healthcare and education. The India Office was the dominant partner for most of these years, because of its role as unofficial broker in the London securities market from which the British Indian government borrowed until World War I (Sunderland 2013). The burden of debt was kept relatively low (less than a quarter of GDP until the end of World War I). The reason it was low was that a larger debt service put pressure on the currency, which would be unpalatable to the administration, and a larger debt service was also unpalatable to the Indian critics of policy, who believed that "the biggest part of the drain arose on account of interest in borrowed capital" (Chandra 1960, 678).

Had the government borrowed more in India, it would have reduced the currency and political risks and grown more freely without fear of affecting trade. Why did it not take that road? Again, geography or structural conditions provides an answer. The obvious answer is that the Indian money market was extremely expensive, and borrowing in India would have put pressure on the budget. It was expensive because the main economic activity, agriculture, was a highly seasonal activity owing to the tropical monsoon climate. Money rates rose to astronomical levels during the busy season (November–March, usually), and since money was hoarded during the slack season, little was available for long-term non-agricultural uses (Roy 2016b).

This fundamental structural weakness of the Indian money market, which made it a particularly expensive market to operate at any time of year, reinforced the position of the India Office as money manager, increased reliance of the British Indian government on the London money market, added currency risk to any innovation in the budget, and thus weighed against innovations in the budget. In the long run, the more British India relied on the London money market, the more cautious it needed to be about public debt, and the more the size of the Indian government shrank in comparison with the British government.

Government Income

The Company Era

For about forty years (1840–80), decades which span the rule of the Company (ending in 1858) and the Crown, British India experienced rising fiscal and state capacity (Figure 3.1). This was a 'modernization', but one meaningful only in the context of the eighteenth century political economy, which the Company state reformed.

Land tax was the mainstay of the precolonial regimes, and collected through semi-independent agents who enjoyed some sovereign powers including tax-collection rights. In north India they were called *zamindars*. The Company wanted to de-arm and yet remain friendly with these magnates. That military-political imperative and a physiocratic faith in private property in land induced Company officers to take over tax collection powers, introduce ownership rights in land in 1793, and give them away to the zamindars. In Bengal, the new understanding led to the

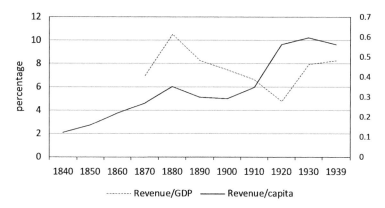

Figure 3.3 Revenue/GDP (%, left-hand axis) and revenue/capita (£, right-hand axis), 1840–1939
Source: See Appendix: Data Set Used.

Permanent Settlement, where the zamindars received proprietary right over the villages they once collected taxes from, but ceased to enjoy sovereign and military power over these villages. The new proprietors often proved incompetent as entrepreneurs, and divided, sold off and mortgaged estates, ending up poorer than before. But the state succeeded in the twofold aim: to reduce the threat of rebellion and raise more money. A similar reform in spirit was introduced in western and southern India in the 1820s, only here the ownership right was delivered to actual cultivators. The removal of a military-political intermediary class between the state and the peasantry enabled the state to collect more revenue from land. The burden was borne in some regions by the former magnates and in others by the peasants.

The rising phase of the line in Figure 3.1 reflects the impact of the reforms. But the effect was wearing off after the Indian Mutiny (1857–8), and especially the Deccan Riots (1875). Thereafter, raising tax burden on the peasantry became, politically, out of bounds. A new modernization paradigm was needed, one that would focus on trade and income taxes rather than land taxes, and here the state clearly failed to rise up to the challenge.

India fell behind Britain in the pace of government growth after 1880. In money terms, it was a growing state throughout and was growing somewhat faster than British fiscal capacity between 1840 and 1880 (Figure 3.3 shows per capita revenue in current prices). Although revenue per head did increase in the long run, deflated by agricultural prices, the increase would look quite modest, if still positive (Figures 3.3 and 3.6).

Land Tax

The dependence of the budget upon the land tax remained significant until the 1930s (Figures 3.4 and 3.5). This was a tax on an asset, and was not sensitive to the changing productive value of that asset over time. The exceedingly low yield of land, and consequently the low value of land and the relatively high administration cost (collection charges were 15–20 per cent of total expenditure in the 1860s) limited the amount collected. The struggle to grow revenues, therefore, depended on the ability to collect taxes from other heads. Between 1840 and 1880, the rise in revenue (Figure 3.4) was derived from agricultural area expansion, thanks in part to railway and canal projects, and to the lucrative opium trade with China. Between 1880 and 1900, land tax collection fell due to repeated famines, and the opium trade was in decline. Customs duties, excises and taxes on assessed income and wealth, so far negligible, began to grow in importance in the early twentieth century.

Because of the sustained effort to reduce dependence on land revenues, and the controversial and unwanted dependence on taxing the peasant, the importance of land tax in revenue fell steadily in the long run. So did land tax collected per head, measured in constant prices (Figures 3.5 and 3.6). The peasants did get a reward for their loyalty, and those in the more commercialized zones like the Punjab, who captured the gains of the worldwide rise in the agricultural terms of trade, were rewarded even more. Some nationalist publicists, like Romesh Dutt, complained about taxation of land (Chandra 1991). He probably had the beleaguered landlords of Bengal, the zamindars, in mind. They earned a rent from peasants. As nominal rents were legally

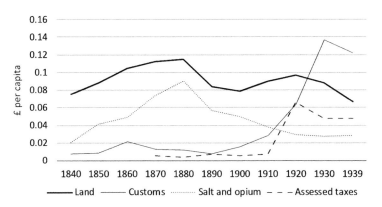

Figure 3.4 Main heads of revenue (£/capita), 1840–1939
Source: See Appendix: Data Set Used.

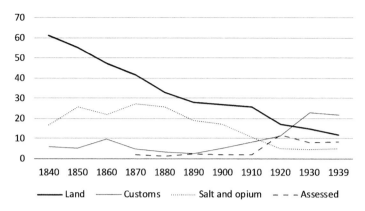

Figure 3.5 Main heads of revenue (% of total revenue), 1840–1939
Source: See Appendix: Data Set Used.

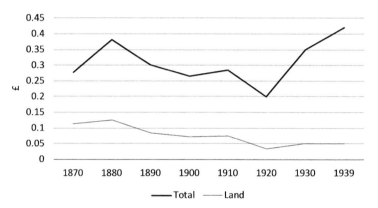

Figure 3.6 Revenue per capita (£) at 1873 prices
Source: See Appendix: Data Set Used.

controlled through the Tenancy Acts passed in 1859 and 1885, the land-lords' real income would have fallen at the same time as the government's own real income from land also fell. This was a redistribution between rural classes, from the rich to the less rich, rather than a redistribution from earners to the state.

Opium and Salt

Two taxes of a special nature contributed greatly to government finance in the third quarter of the nineteenth century. These were special

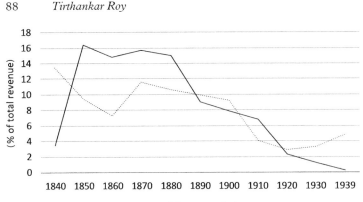

Figure 3.7 Salt and opium revenue (% of Total revenue)
Source: See Appendix: Data Set Used.

because they were taxes on consumption and taxes that entailed a fiscal monopoly. One of these was levied on the export of opium, and the other on the sale of salt. They were relics from an earlier era, salt being 'a tax handed down from time immemorial' (Thomas 1939, 41). Together, the taxes on these two items accounted for about a quarter of government revenue in the 1860s, the highest point of their contribution. Opium was a special commodity also because the moral justification for the trade was in question in the late nineteenth century. Salt was controversial because a tax on salt fell in equal extent on the rich and poor alike, for both consumed the same quantity. This fact, together with the low levels of taxes assessed on income and wealth made the tax system regressive. Politically, therefore, salt and opium taxes were not sustainable. Facing near bankruptcy in the 1930s, the government tried to revive the salt tax (Figure 3.7), with disastrous political effects.

Trade Taxes

A breakthrough of some kind was achieved with customs duties in the interwar period. The Company had inherited a loose system of trade and transit duties from the indigenous rulers, especially in the former Mughal provinces. These duties had proliferated and were used in an extortionate manner by local landlords in the late eighteenth century. Reforms in 1845 brought the local and provincial tariffs and transit duties into some uniformity. The main duty from then onward was customs rather than inland transit duties.

Figure 3.8 Industrialization and customs collection, 1871–1939
Source: See Appendix: Data Set Used.

Customs duties thereafter made a modest but positive contribution to the public finances until 1920, when the extent of collection turned sharply upward (Figure 3.8). In the nineteenth century, Manchester textile producers lobbied against protective duties on cloth, and Bombay's millowners lobbied for a protective duty. The government settled the matter with a small revenue tariff and a countervailing excise on domestic production. Chaudhuri (1983, 868), describing this struggle, suggests that a depreciation of the currency towards the end of the nineteenth century, may have afforded Indian industry a measure of protection. In view of the poverty of the government, there was little choice but to move in the direction of raising the duty. The outbreak of World War I made that move politically acceptable. The first three years of war were traumatic for Indian industry, but thereafter, Indian industry recovered and made a significant contribution to the war effort. This was rewarded with protection, which was a rule-based system and not indiscriminate. This left room for dissatisfaction. But the tariff instrument was also used quite flexibly in the case of Tata Steel to nurse the firm through a post-war recession (Roy 2017). While protection did achieve revenue gains, whether it accelerated industrialization or not remains debatable. Indian industrialization began without protection. Industrial growth accelerated after protection, and yet, that acceleration led to inefficiency. An example was the growing obsolescence of a section of Bombay's mills that, with protection, had a chance to survive.

Income and Wealth Taxes

The need to collect more of the so-called assessed taxes was raised from time to time after 1858. The earliest occasion was a famous dispute between the central and the Madras governments over a proposed Income Tax Bill. Although it was shot down on the grounds of political advantage, it is not entirely clear how far politics explains the limited use of this instrument for the next seventy years. Charles Trevelyan, a protagonist in the 1858 debate, argued against the tax by saying that it would be administratively impossible to create a fair system because it would rely too much on information which could be manipulated by local officers to extract bribes (cited in Thomas 1939, 76). It is indeed the case that the fiscal system had a bias against taxes that were information-intensive and demanded considerable administrative resources. In this way, the small size and limited capacity of government reinforced a bias towards staying small.

Public Debt

The crisis in the 1930s did not owe as much to a fall in revenues raised in India as to the government's reduced ability to raise credit in London. The general depression in prices in the mid-1930s in fact increased the level of collection of revenues in India in constant prices. Credit was another matter. To understand the roots of the crisis, we should first see what role public debt played in the budget until the 1930s.

Public debt was a legacy of the Anglo-French wars at the turn of the nineteenth century. Before that, the Company borrowed little, and when it did, it relied on Indian bankers for temporary loans. The practice continued for some time. Debt volume, however, began to rise from around 1800. The government sold securities, which expatriate Europeans and wealthy Indians bought. During the Mutiny, 90 per cent of the debt stock was held within India. However, after the Mutiny, as British capital started flowing into the railways, the government found it easier to raise capital in London. Thereafter, London's share rose rapidly. Throughout, Indian stocks carried a lower interest rate in London than in India, which justified the shift. The relative position of London changed only when the Reserve Bank of India was established in 1935. Thereafter, the volume of securities traded in India rose again.

For most of these years, the British Indian government managed to keep debt within stable limits. The debt/GDP ratio was modest, and below the average for pre-war Britain. In keeping with the rise in prices, and nominal expenditures, debt per person registered an increase in the long run (Figure 3.9). This was almost purely a price adjustment, for in constant

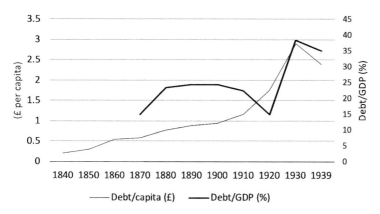

Figure 3.9 Public debt stock as debt/GDP (%, right-hand axis, thick line) and debt/capita (m £, left-hand axis, thin line), 1840–1939
Source: See Appendix: Data Set Used.

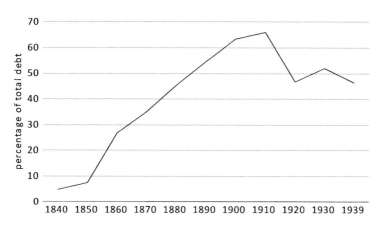

Figure 3.10 Public debt raised in the UK (% of total), 1840–1939
Source: See Appendix: Data Set Used.

prices, there was little change in debt stock per head between 1870 and 1920. Until then, government debt, which was mainly contracted in Britain (Figure 3.10), was not a crucial instrument either to meet a current deficit or to finance capital expenditure. The government in most years earned a revenue surplus.

A crisis began in the 1920s and the 1930s because the revenue surplus disappeared, and the government found it increasingly difficult to meet its obligations to Britain from its budget. Net increases in liability to meet public investment rose from an average of 10 per cent of investment in the pre-war period to 35 per cent in the interwar period. Following the Great Depression there occurred a controversial episode of monetary management, as the India Office refused a currency depreciation fearing the government would fail to meet the home charges (as we shall discuss) if it did so. The resultant fall in trade and prices made the government face the deficit in its domestic obligations. As British India stared at bankruptcy, its stocks were less attractive in London, and indeed failed on some occasions (Figure 3.10).

Expenditures

Army

British India was a small state, but it was not a weak one. It spent a large proportion of the government budget on maintaining an army (Figure 3.11). The standing army originated in the troops raised and maintained in Bengal, Bombay and Madras. They were known as the Presidency Armies. From the mid-eighteenth century, British regiments were sent to fight in India. Until 1784, the expense of British regiments in India was paid from the British budget; thereafter, the Board of Control (the body appointed by the Parliament to manage the governance of India) could hire British regiments and pay the cost with Indian revenue. Limits were set on the numbers to be hired from Britain. From the early nineteenth century, the cost of the army was paid mainly from the Indian revenues (Heathcote 1995). When the

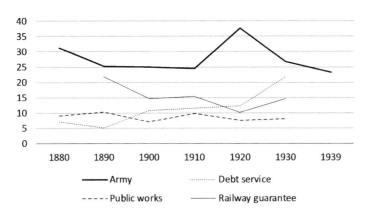

Figure 3.11 Four main heads of expenditure (% of total expenditure), 1880–1930
Source: See Appendix: Data Set Used.

Mutiny began, about 350,000 military personnel received pay from the Company. They consisted of British and European infantry, cavalry and artillery, and 'native infantry' regiments and battalions numbering over 200,000. The Mutiny broke out among the native infantry. Almost all of the cost was paid out of Indian revenues.

Why was the army so large? The answer depends partly on the legacy left behind by the East India Company. The Company's largely successful effort to raise revenue enabled it to form a standing army, whereas the armies of its rivals were formed of smaller standing armies and much larger numbers of irregulars, mercenaries and soldiers contributed by feudal chieftains and warlords. In 1765, the Company's military expenditure was £1.5 million; in 1793, £3 million; in 1834, £7 million; and in 1846, £12 million. It is hard to be exact on the other heads of expenditure, but it is likely that the share of the army in expenditure was as high as three-fourths in 1765, and fell to around one-third in 1856. Well before this date, the main rivals of the Company had shrunk in power. While centralization of the fiscal system enabled the Company to raise taxes and spend them on the army, among the rivals, such as the Maratha rulers, warfare empowered the regional and local warlords and reduced the power of the state (Roy 2013).

The Company's legacy was left intact. Running a state with a handful of foreign officers was always a survival issue, as the Mutiny showed. The army also ensured political and economic integration on a scale that the region had never known before. There is a sense in which the map of South Asia as we know it today was a product of the military capability of the British Indian state. Until World War I, British military power depended vitally on the Indian army. It was funded out of the Indian revenues. Whether it could be used for British campaigns in other parts of the world was not negotiable between Britain and India until 1923, when Britain agreed to pay a fee for the services of the Indian army.

Military expenditure overwhelmed every other item. Among these other items, railway guarantees and direct expenditure on state railways dominated in the nineteenth century, and debt service in the twentieth century. Other infrastructural investment or 'public works', consisting mainly of canals and roads, formed a low if steady share.

Expenditure in England

The government's payments abroad were embedded in these heads of expense. By far the most controversial item in public expenditure was the expenditure of the government of India in England, popularly (but not in official statistics) known as the home charges (Figure 3.12). About half of the home charges in the pre-war years consisted of interest payment on loans

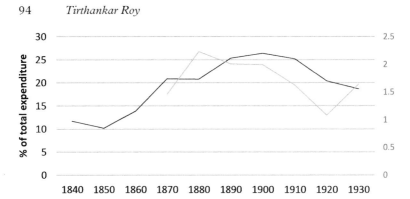

Figure 3.12 Gross expenditure of India in England, 1840–1930
Source: See Appendix: Data Set Used.

raised to finance construction of railways and irrigation works. The item next in importance was payment for the maintenance of the army and marines. A third component was pension payments for officials who had served in India and retired to Britain. India Office expenses and stores purchased, formed the other items of expenditure. The volume of these charges in relation to total expenditure or GDP rose in the nineteenth century, and then started to fall. At its peak, these formed a quarter of the expenditure and 2.2 per cent of GDP.

Directly or indirectly, most of the discussion on the controversial 'drain' and the value of government payments abroad came to rest on military expenditure. Army and civil administration officers numbered 6,400 in 1872, and European soldiers 64,000. The numbers are not large in an adult male workforce of 6.2 million (1872). But these people received extraordinarily high salaries. The salary of the highest-ranking civil or military officer was 200 times the per capita income, and about ten times the average salary of administrative office workers in 1872. Foreign soldiers were paid three times the salary of Indian soldiers on average. The combined salary of the Europeans in public administration and the military formed 1.3 per cent of the income of all adult male workers in 1872, and 1.5 per cent in 1895. The proportions were not small, and the salary (rank) differentiation was outrageous (some of the figures come from Atkinson 1902).

Still, whether or not they support the theory that this was a pure drain or tribute extracted by Britain is speculative. Salary difference as such does not indicate *overpayment* or drain or a waste of resources. The opportunity cost of European personnel was set by salaries in Britain or in European firms in India. Overpayment depends on whether Indians were available to perform the same task for less. In 1872, the answer to the question might be, perhaps not many. But by 1900, the answer would surely be many more than before. Hiring and salary practices almost certainly did not adapt to Indian capability fast enough: racialist ranking systems, petrified into conventions, caused a great deal of anger among the upwardly mobile Indian middle classes, and fuelled the nationalist movement. But no matter how we measure it, the remittance part of the overpaid foreign salaries was too small to sustain a thesis, which the drain theory was, that the home charges caused serious economic distress, and even caused underdevelopment.

The government was not the only agency making net factor payments abroad. On a significant but somewhat uncertain scale, private actors like factories, trading firms, banks and insurance companies also remitted money as salaries, repatriated profits or business expenses (Banerji 1982). In the case of both the government and the private sector, the purchase of services abroad reflected openness rather than colonial politics. By comparison with the present time, anywhere in the world, the transaction cost of hiring someone from abroad was practically zero in British India. The government, of course, hired military officers and top bureaucrats abroad not only because it was easy to do, but also for political reasons. There was an ill-concealed racial bias in granting promotions, though people affected by it formed a small number and accounted for a fraction of the home charges. If there were items in the home charges that represented political fears and racial prejudices, and surely there were, these items were overwhelmed by debt service.

Administration and Investment

The administrative departments that managed the entire operation of the state in India generated a small (usually less than 5 per cent) proportion of national income. But the proportion rose in the interwar period, as the real scale of the operation expanded. The provincial autonomy played a large role in forcing public administration to enlarge (Figure 3.13). Ordinarily, about a quarter of total expenditure consisted of investment, which went to the construction and repair of national assets (Table 3.1). If we consider only net investment – that is, creation of new assets – the percentage was smaller. Depreciation accounted for about one-third of gross investment in the pre-war period, and over half of gross investment in the middle of the 1930s.

Given the commitment to debt service and the army, the government had limited capacity to make investments in infrastructure. The crisis of the 1930s caused by the rise in debt burden eroded even that capacity.

Table 3.1 *Gross public investment as a proportion of public expenditure, 1898–1938 (%)*

	Investment/expenditure ratio
1898–9 to 1913–14	23.5
1919–20 to 1929–30	23.4
1930–1 to 1937–8	15.7

Source: Thavaraj (1960, 219).

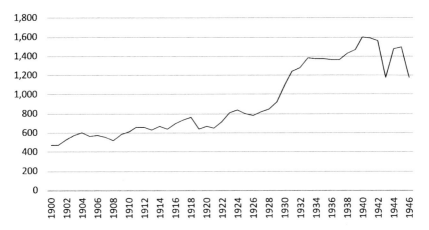

Figure 3.13 National income in public administration, 1900–1946 (Rs m 1938–9 prices)
Source: See Appendix: Data Set Used.

The percentage of investment in expenditure fell quickly towards the end of the interwar period, as debt service and administrative commitments took priority over investment. The major heads of capital expenditure were irrigation, roads, railways (after full nationalization in 1925) and posts and telegraphs (Table 3.2). Increasingly from the interwar period, investments under these heads went into depreciation rather than new assets.

The regional distribution of government expenditure in major infra-structure projects reflects shifting priorities. The first large-scale nine-teenth-century canal projects occurred in two deltas in the Madras Presidency, and the later projects mainly in the Punjab. The Madras

Table 3.2 *Regional distribution of public investment in irrigation, roads and power, 1860–1946 (% of total)*

	Madras	Bombay-Sind	Punjab	UP	Burma	Bengal	Others
1860–1 to 1918–9	16.6	15.5	8.8	8.8	24.0	6.9	19.2
1919–20 to 1946–7	16.2	21.7	11.9	1.8	21.9	5.8	20.7

Source: Thavaraj (1972, 5, 8, 10, 12).

share was high throughout, and that of Punjab rose. The government spent more money on roads in the less accessible Deccan Plateau (both the Madras and Bombay-Sind shares show this) and in Burma. The Deccan expenditure was largely motivated by the famines that took place in this region in the late nineteenth century. On the other hand, in the heart of the Indo-Gangetic Basin, Bengal and the United Provinces (UP), the density of the railways was much higher, but the government spent relatively little on the other heads of expenditure. These were the more populated regions, and, in per capita terms, expenditure was biased towards arid geographies. This was so because in those regions where the state collected taxes from landlords, known as zamindari, there was an expectation that the landlords would invest in public goods; whereas in regions where the state collected taxes from the peasants, known as ryotwari, the state was by default responsible for such investment. Ryotwari regions tended to be concentrated in the drier tracts. Besides this factor, in the dry lands of Punjab, canal projects also had a political angle. Punjab was a border zone, and had stood broadly loyal to British India during the Great Indian Mutiny (1857–8).

Provinces

Public finance operated within a federal structure. During the early years of Company rule, there were three provincial governments. These became nine in 1919. These were Madras, Bombay, Bengal, United Provinces, Punjab, Burma, Bihar and Orissa (all administered by Governors or Lieutenant Governors), Central Provinces and Assam (under Chief Commissioners). Several other territorial units (British Baluchistan, North-West Frontier Province, Ajmer-Merwara and Coorg) were governed by Chief Commissioners.

During the Company's rule, the finances of the three major 'presidencies' of Bombay, Bengal and Madras were effectively autonomous. But after 1870, there was a tendency to centralize control over finances (Kumar 1983, 907). Around 1882, the structure of fiscal federalism was well established. The central government was responsible for raising certain heads of revenue (mainly customs, salt tax, opium tax and railway income) and for making certain types of expenditure (mainly army, debt service and railways). The provinces received a share of land revenue and excise, and the receipts of provincial administrative departments such as law and justice or education. The shares varied between provinces and were set by precedent. The provinces were responsible for spending on local administration, education and health. Only the centre could borrow.

The system was fraught with tensions. The provinces believed that they were given inflexible sources of revenue such as the land tax, the other heads being quite small, and were made responsible for expenditures that would necessarily grow with population. To the extent their income from local sources depended on regional standards of living, per capita tax burden and per capita expenditure varied between provinces. The centre's own investment priorities, as we have seen, followed a geographic logic, and less naturally endowed regions tended to get more money per head for economic or strategic reasons. Provinces under Permanent Settlement raised less revenue on average and spent less. Provinces such as Bombay or Madras raised more on average and spent more.

During World War I, the government made an implicit promise of self-government to the Indian public, in return for their contribution to the war, which included more than a million Indian soldiers. The promise was kept insofar as provincial legislatures were created in 1919. The Government of India Acts of 1919 and 1935, and the legislative assemblies that were created after the 1919 Act, restructured federal finance and exposed it to organized pressures from elected representatives. The divided heads of revenue were abolished. Land revenue was given over to the provinces. The centre took the income tax. The central budget now had to be balanced by contributions made to the provinces, which added another bone of contention. These changes did little to meet the grievances of the provinces. The 1935 Act went a little further in giving a larger share to the provinces (Table 3.3). The idea of a five-yearly Finance Commission to review the structure of federal finance, an institution that continues today, was a result of this Act.

The provinces oversaw health and education, as well as local roads. During much of the nineteenth century, demand for public education or

Table 3.3 *Shares of the centre and the provinces in gross public investment,*
1920–37 (%)

	Centre	Provinces	Total (incl. municipalities and local governments)
1920–1 to 1929–30	56	35	100
1930–1 to 1937–8	46	39	100

Source: Thavaraj (1960, 223).

public health remained subdued. Perhaps the expectation was that private investment would supplement the limited effort the state made in these areas. In the twentieth century, the demand for these expenditures gained strength. Although the limited legislative reforms did not satisfy the nationalists, provincial budgets became responsible for education and health after the reforms. High levels of illiteracy and mortality showed that being a colony of Britain for over half a century had done little to enable India to approach British standards of social development. A slight rise in the proportion of public spending on education and health in the interwar period reflects an attempt to redress this neglect. The attempt, however, was a limited one, given the government's poverty and other expenditure commitments.

World War II and the End of Colonial Finance

Just as Indian finances were recovering from the Depression, the World War II re-imposed a deficit. The government had to spend much larger sums and proportions of the budget on defence not only on its own behalf, but also on behalf of Britain's war efforts on promise of repayment from Britain later. While taxes and borrowings increased, these were insufficient to cover the deficit. However, a central bank had been established in 1935, which now printed money, and started buying government securities on an unprecedented scale. Between 1939 and 1941, the nominal value of new issues of government securities increased from Rs 0.3 to 1.5 billion, reaching Rs 3.8 billion in 1947. As the demand for goods expanded, the supply of essential goods, including food-grains, was diverted to the war effort. The net effects were a massive inflation, erosion of real incomes and a fall in the burden of private debt. Inflation and diversion of food caused a famine in Bengal in 1943, where some half a million people died of starvation and disease.

The last days of the war saw government control over supplies of essential commodities consolidate. The food ration system was the precursor of a public distribution system with which independent India has been familiar. The end of the war also saw a steady liquidation of India's accumulated foreign debt. This was a result of Britain's obligations to India because of the war. India thus entered independence with 'substantial reserves of foreign exchange' (Vaidyanathan 1983, 948).

Public Finance and Colonial Development

The small size of the government did not cause economic stagnation in colonial India, but gave economic change an extremely unbalanced character. We would miss this fundamental characteristic of economic change in colonial India if we stay too focused on per capita income. To see this, consider Figure 3.14, which reports growth in real national income by dividing the economy of late-colonial India into three parts – peasant cultivation, government and a mixed basket of capitalistic enterprise dominated by trade, transportation, banking and manufacturing industry. The figure reveals a divergence within India between peasant agriculture on the one hand, where growth was small overall, and near zero when adjusted for population growth, and capitalistic businesses on the other hand, where growth was significant, and, when adjusted for working population, showed evidence of productivity gains. If we are to explain the divergence between colonial India and contemporary Europe or North America on average income, we must show how conditions of peasant farming were dissimilar between these world regions. In respect

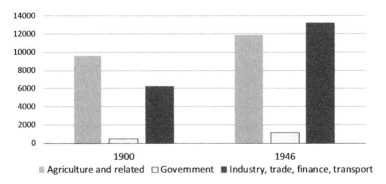

Figure 3.14 GDP by major activities in British India, 1900 and 1946 (in m Rs 1938–9 prices)
Source: See Appendix: Data Set Used.

of capitalistic enterprise like trade and industry, there was *convergence*, and we need to show why capitalistic enterprise faced substantially similar conditions, if India is compared with Europe. Neither of these two tasks has been taken up in a serious manner in the study of Indian economic history.

How is public finance relevant to the discussion? Smallness of the state hurt agriculture badly, but it did not affect business as badly. British Indian administration prided itself on looking after the interests of the peasants. National income statistics reveal that the belief that the government was performing this role successfully was no more than a reassuring myth. The government knew what was needed for 'improvement': investment in irrigation. But it could perform the task only to a limited extent. And this is revealed by the tiny share of government in investment. On the other side, the government was not necessary as an agent to promote trade or industrialization. Private investment by merchants and bankers took care of that need well enough. Many of these people gained from the open economy, insofar as they benefited from trade or were able to access capital and labour from abroad. The government facilitated that process by maintaining open borders to both trade and factor market transactions, by enabling railway construction and by creating a giant customs union within the empire. Aided by this open environment, business growth sustained itself (Figure 3.15). Between 1870 and 1940, cities including Bombay, Ahmedabad, Madras, Calcutta, Kanpur and Karachi had been linked to the agricultural interior by railways and telegraph. They shipped abroad huge quantities of cotton, grain, seeds, indigo and opium, and imported British textiles, machinery and metals, and chemicals from Germany and Belgium. The cities hired many foreigners to work in the firms and the factories. Merchant firms engaged in these businesses consisted of Indian, European and Indo-European firms, and they usually had branches in several cities within India, and sometimes in Southeast and East Asia, and even Europe.

Profits from trade were invested in large-scale mechanized factories, especially cotton and jute textiles, plantations, mining and banking. Between 1860 and 1940, employment in factories increased from near zero to two million. The growth was comparable with that in two other emerging economies of the time, Japan and Russia, but without parallel in the tropical world. India led the contemporary developing world in two leading industries of the industrial revolution, cotton textiles and iron and steel. In 1910, 55 per cent of the cotton spindles installed outside Europe, North America and Japan were in India. In 1935, 50 per cent of the steel produced outside Europe, North America and Japan was produced in India. At the time of independence in 1947, the port cities were home to

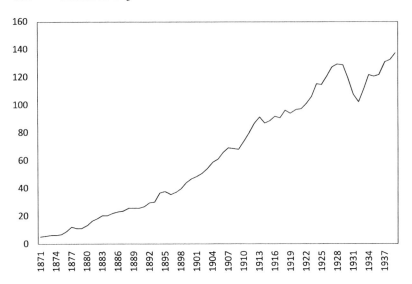

Figure 3.15 Volume of goods carried via rail and sea: 1871–1937 (m tons)
Source: See Appendix: Data Set Used.

some of the best schools, colleges, hospitals, universities, banks, insurance companies and learned societies available outside the western world. A big part of that infrastructure had been created by the Indian industrialists themselves. After the Great Depression, this industrial elite turned their back on openness, demanded protection and funded nationalist politics.

What, then, was the main failing of the fiscal system from a developmental point of view? Public finance could potentially bridge the gap between the cities and the agricultural interior, by investing in schools, roads, hospitals and agricultural technology across the country. That the minimalist state did not do this, and did not distribute opportunities more widely, was its decisive failure. Persistent inequality between the business cities and the countryside was the price Indians paid for small government.

The failure was compounded by the appalling record of colonial India in universal healthcare and education. In 1933, the UK government spent on average £2.4 per person on defence, and £4.5 per person on social welfare, including education. The Indian government spent £0.13 on defence and £0.05 on social welfare. Literacy rate on average was 5 per cent in the Indian subcontinent in 1900, and rose to 19 per cent in 1951 in the Indian Union. UNESCO (1957) data show that around

1950, India's illiteracy rate (80.9 per cent) was one of the highest in the world. Only a few regions, such as Haiti, Sarawak, North Borneo and Portuguese Guinea, exceeded this rate. Parts of North Africa came close to it. The record in East and Southeast Asia excluding the regions mentioned was considerably better than India's. Infant mortality rate (IMR) was 200 in 1900, so India belonged in a set of countries with exceptionally high child mortality (Chandrasekhar 1959). IMR was sensitive to famines and epidemic outbreak of malaria, plague, cholera and influenza. Only after 1921, with control of epidemic diseases and the scarcity of famines, did IMR fall, reaching 146 in 1947. This was still high in comparison with other Asian colonies such as the Philippines.

Literacy rates varied enormously between communities. The overall female literacy was near zero in 1901, but was over one-third among the Parsi community in Bombay. Similar cultural variations can be found in IMR too. Generally, IMR was higher in North and Central India relative to Eastern and Southern India. And the female IMR was higher than the male one in the former regions. These facts suggest that more public investment would not have been a sufficient condition for improvement in education and health outcomes, as cultural factors were important. That it was a necessary condition cannot be disputed.

Conclusion

Post-colonial India did reshape its public finances in some respects, although in other ways it inherited and preserved the colonial legacy. The areas of change were public debt which was raised mainly at home, and that subsidies and transfers were used more liberally. The legacies that persisted were the large army, and the limited success with direct taxes.

There was one dramatic change. Nationalists had long criticized the minimalism of British India. That certainly changed after 1947. The government size grew, from 5 per cent of GDP in 1920 to reach 20 per cent in 1980. However, when we investigate the means that were used to achieve this growth, and the obstacles that these means tried to overcome, similarities in structural features are revealed. For example, the effort to raise direct taxes was only partly successful; it was somewhat more successful with corporate tax than personal income tax. The expenditure on defence remained large, and social services continued to be underfunded. And reliance on commodity and trade taxes continued.

How then was the enlargement of the government achieved? The answer, if we exclude foreign aid which was important in the 1950s and the 1960s, is public debt. Borrowing was one of the instruments that the government of the Indian Union used to side-step limited ability to raise direct taxes after 1947. It borrowed more from the public, nationalized banks and diverted credit to itself. After independence, the government progressively regulated interest rates and agricultural credit to reduce its own borrowing costs. This comprehensive 'financial repression' was necessary for the state to grow, but the social costs of the strategy remain under-researched.

The consequences of growth in size were enormous. Public investment sustained industrialization for about twenty years; and budgetary investment and transfers sustained the Green Revolution. The rise in agricultural productivity and rural wages bridged the inequality between the countryside and the cities to some extent, although the 1990s liberalization has widened it again.

Bibliography

Accominotti, O., Flandreau M., & Rezzik, R. (2011). The Spread of Empire: Clio and the Measurement of Colonial Borrowing Costs. *Economic History Review*, 64(2), 385–407.

Atkinson, F.J. (1902). A Statistical Review of Income and Wealth in British India. *Journal of the Royal Statistical Society*, 65, 209–283.

Balachandran, G. (2015). Colonial India and the World Economy c. 1850–1940. In L. Chaudhary, B. Gupta, T. Roy & A. Swamy (Eds.), *A New Economic History of Colonial India*. London: Routledge, 84–99.

Banerjee, A., Iyer, L., & Somanathan, R. (2011). History, Social Divisions and Public Goods in Rural India. *Journal of the European Economic Association*, 3(1), 39–47.

Banerji, A. (1982). *Aspects of Indo-British Economic Relations, 1858–1898*. New Delhi: Oxford University Press.

Bhattacharya, S. (1971). *The Financial Foundations of the British Raj. Ideas and Interests in the Reconstruction of Indian Public Finance 1858–1872*. Simla: Indian Institute of Advanced Study.

Bonney, R. (Ed.). (2000). *The Rise of the Fiscal State in Europe c. 1200–1815*. New York: Oxford University Press.

Chandra, B. (1960). *The Rise and Growth of Economic Nationalism in India*, Delhi: People's Publishing House.

Chandra, B. (1991). Colonial India: British versus Indian Views of Development. *Review*, 14(1), 81–167.

Chandra, B., Mukherjee A., & Mukherjee, M. (1999). *India since Independence*. Delhi: Penguin.

Chandrasekhar, S. (1959). *Infant Mortality in India 1901–55*. London: George Allen and Unwin.

Charlesworth, N. (1985). The Problem of Government Finance in British India: Taxation, Borrowing, and the Allocation of Resources in the Inter-War Period. *Modern Asian Studies*, 19(3), 521–48.

Chaudhary, L. (2010). Land Revenues, Schools and Literacy: A Historical Examination of Public and Private Funding of Education. *Indian Economic and Social History Review*, 47(2), 179–204.

Chaudhuri, K.N. (1968). India's International Economy in the Nineteenth Century: An Historical Survey. *Modern Asian Studies*, 2(1), 31–50.

Chaudhuri, K.N. (1983). Foreign Trade and Balance of Payments (1757–1947). In D. Kumar (Ed.), *The Cambridge Economic History of India, vol. 2: 1757–1970*. Cambridge: Cambridge University Press, 804–77.

Ferguson, N. (2012). *The Ascent of Money: A Financial History of the World*. Harmondsworth: Penguin Books.

Frankema, E. (2010). Raising Revenue in the British Empire, 1870–1940: How 'Extractive' Were Colonial Taxes? *Journal of Global History*, 5(3), 447–77.

Frankema, E., & van Waijenburg, M. (2014). Metropolitan Blueprints of Colonial Taxation? Lessons from Fiscal Capacity Building in British and French Africa, c. 1880–1940. *Journal of African History*, 55(3), 371–400.

Gardner, L. (2017). Colonialism or Supersanctions: Sovereignty and Debt in West Africa, 1871–1914. *European Review of Economic History*, 21(2), 236–57.

Gardner, L. A. (2012). *Taxing Colonial Africa: The Political Economy of British Imperialism*. Oxford: Oxford University Press.

Goldsmith, R. (1983). *The Financial Development of India 1860–1977*. New Haven: Yale University Press.

Heathcote, T.A. (1995). *The Military in British India: The Development of British Land Forces in South Asia, 1600–1947*. Manchester: Manchester University Press.

Jones, P. (2013). History Matters: New Evidence on the Long Run Impact of Colonial Rule on Institutions. *Journal of Comparative Economics*, 41(2), 181–200.

Kumar, D. (1983). Fiscal System. In D. Kumar (Ed.), *The Cambridge Economic History of India, vol. 2: 1757–1970*. Cambridge: Cambridge University Press, 905–44.

Kumar, D. (1985). The Dangers of Manicheism. *Modern Asian Studies*, 19(3), 383–6.

Roy, B. (1967). Capital Formation in India: 1901–51. *Economic and Political Weekly*, 2(17), 807–11.

Roy, T. (1996). The Role of the State in Initiating Development: A Study of Interwar South and Southeast Asia. *Indian Economic and Social History Review*, 33(4), 373–401.

Roy, T. (2013). *An Economic History of Early Modern India*. London: Routledge.

Roy, T. (2016a). The British Empire and the Economic Development of India 1858–1947. *Revista de Historia Economica – Journal of Iberian and Latin American Economic History*, 34(2), 209–36.

Roy, T. (2016b). Monsoon and the Market for Money in Late Colonial India. *Enterprise and Society*, 17(2), 324–357.

Roy, T. (2017). The Origins of Import Substitution in India. *Economic History of Developing Regions*, 32(1), 71–95.

Sunderland, D. (2013). *Financing the Raj: The City of London and Colonial India, 1858–1940*. Woodbridge: Boydell and Brewer.

Thavaraj, M. J. K. (1960). Capital Formation in the Public Sector in India: A Historical study, 1898–1938. In V. K. R. V. Rao et al. (Eds.), *Papers on National Income and Allied Topics*. Bombay: Asia Publishers, 215–230.

Thavaraj, M. J. K. (1972). Regional Imbalances and Public Investment in India (1860–1947). *Social Scientist*, 1(4), 3–24.

Thomas, P.J. (1939). *The Growth of Federal Finance in India*, London: Humphrey Milford.

UNESCO. (1957). *World Illiteracy at Mid-Century*. Paris: United Nations Educational, Scientific and Cultural Organization.

Vaidyanathan, A. (1983). The Indian Economy since Independence. In D. Kumar (Ed.), *The Cambridge Economic History of India, vol. 2: 1757–1970*. Cambridge: Cambridge University Press, 947–94.

Appendix: Data Set Used

Table A.1 *Finance, national income, population, exchange rate*

Unit	Revenue	Expenditure	National Income	Population of British India excl. Burma	Exchange rate
	Million £	Million £	Million £	Million	(Rupee/£)
1840	20.1	22.2		164	13.3
1850	27.5	27.0		172	13.3
1860	39.7	51.9		180	13.3
1870	50.9	50.8	728	188	13.3
1880	68.5	69.7	650	195	13.3
1890	64.3	61.5	777	214	13.3
1900	64.7	65.1	862	222	14.9
1910	80.7	77.7	1,208	232	14.9
1920	132.0	147	2,775	234	
1930	153.8	170.7	1,943	257	13.3
1939	166.8	161.8	2,017	296	

Sources: Revenue and expenditure: India, *Statistical Abstracts of* British India, various years, Calcutta. The exact title varies.

National Income: S. Sivasubramonian, National Income of India in the Twentieth Century, New Delhi: Oxford University Press, 2000 for 1900–39; and Alan Heston, 'National Income,' in Dharma Kumar, ed., *The Cambridge Economic History of India, vol. 2: 1757–1970*, Cambridge: Cambridge University Press, 1983, for 1870–90. National Income (or Net National Product) are reported in constant prices (1946–7 prices in Heston and 1938–9 prices in Sivasubramonian). These are converted into current prices using the price index (1873=100) in Michelle McAlpin, 'Prices and Economic Fluctuations', in Kumar, ed., *Cambridge Economic History*. National Income figures refer to the Indian Subcontinent, and may underestimate any ratio in which income appears as a denominator. Having said that, in the figures for national income, the figures for the Indian territories outside British India were usually approximate, and likely underestimates.

Population: India, *Statistical Abstracts*, for 1880–1939. For 1840–80, I have applied the growth rates of population of the Indian subcontinent used in medium-range estimates of J. D. Durand on British Indian population in 1880. Durand's estimates are reported in Pravin and Leela Visaria, 'Population,' in Kumar, ed., *Cambridge Economic History*, for 1870–90. Also used for reference, M.D. Morris, 'The Population of All India 1800–1951', *Indian Economic and Social History Review*, 1974, 309–13.

Table A.2 *Main heads of revenue and expenditure (m £)*

	Income					
	Land	Excise & forest	Assessed Tax	Customs	Salt	Opium
1840	12.3	0.8		1.2	2.7	0.7
1850	15.2	1.1		1.4	2.6	4.5
1860	18.8	1.7		3.9	2.9	5.9
1870	21.1	2.7	1.1	2.4	5.9	8.0
1880	22.5	3.5	0.8	2.3	7.3	10.3
1890	18.0	5.1	1.6	1.7	6.4	5.9
1900	17.5	5.2	1.3	3.4	6.0	5.1
1910	20.9	8.8	1.6	6.6	3.3	5.5
1920	22.6	16.3	15.5	15.0	3.8	3.0
1930	22.7	16.1	12.2	35.1	5.1	1.9
1939	19.7	9.4	14.2	36.2	8.1	0.4

	Expenditure			
	Army	Debt service	Public works	Railway
1840				
1850				
1860				
1870				
1880	21.7	4.9	6.4	
1890	15.5	3.1	6.3	13.4
1900	16.3	7.1	4.6	9.5
1910	19.1	9.0	7.6	11.9
1920	55.3	18.0	11.3	15.1
1930	45.7	37.0	14.0	25.1
1939	37.7			

Notes: Budget reporting changed in 1939 in a manner that makes the data not perfectly comparable with the earlier heads.

Table A.3 *Public debt stock (m £)*

1840	34.5
1850	53.0
1860	98.1
1870	108.2
1880	151.7
1890	189.5
1900	210.0
1910	270.0
1920	412.0
1930	746.4
1939	708.2

4   Colonial and Indigenous Institutions in the Fiscal Development of French Indochina

Montserrat López Jerez

> The idea of this experiment (Indochina) as a unity of diverse ethnically, historically and geographically countries is either an absurdity or the essence of federalism
>
> Touzet (1935, 100)

Introduction

French Indochina was a paradoxical state for several reasons. First, it was a federal state, in contrast to the metropolitan government itself.[1] Second, within the federal arrangement, Cochinchina was the only colony. The other four regions that constituted Indochina became protectorates, with different levels of intervention, although French rule was mostly indirect. An important implication of these political arrangements was that the different parts of French Indochina fell under different ministries in Paris (the Ministry of Colonies and the Ministry of Foreign Affairs). This added political and institutional complexity to the administration of the federation, which was often plagued by conflicting military, political and economic interests. Third, French Indochina has often been characterized as one of the most extractive cases of colonial taxation (Acemoglu, Johnson & Robinson 2002, 1266). Scholars such as Popkin (1979, 142–3) argued that French tax demands were a crushing burden on many indigenous people. But this contrasts with the evidence that official revenue collections in Vietnam were in fact low compared with most other colonies in East and Southeast Asia (Booth, Chapter 2, this volume, Table 2.1). For instance, in 1929, revenues per capita in Burma and the Philippines were twice as much as in Vietnam and even five times as much in Taiwan. The only way to reconcile these different views is to examine the pre-colonial fiscal

[1] I thank the editors and the participants of the two project workshops for comments and inspiring discussions. I am especially grateful to Debin Ma, Christer Gunnarsson and Sara Torregrosa Hetland for feedback on earlier versions of the chapter. I gratefully acknowledge partial funding by the Swedish Research Council (VR 2011–2137).

institutions which survived under French colonial rule, but have not been adequately recorded in the official figures.

This chapter argues that there were two fiscal states co-existing from the turn of the nineteenth century to the Japanese invasion in 1940, and this meant that the real tax burden per capita was higher than the aggregated French data show. This dualism created forces which both favoured and prevented institutional change. The colonial 'fiscal state' was dependent on the growth of the monetized economy, both from the expanding export economy and from the internal consumption of products such as opium, salt and alcohol, on which excises were levied. By contrast, the indigenous economy remained a domain system where taxation was a village responsibility and closely tied to land levies and corvée (Khoi 1981: 353). Their interaction is fundamental to an understanding of the major economic changes of this period, relating to ownership of land, the main economic asset, and to the capacity of the economy to generate fiscal surpluses.

Consequently, it is argued that the remarkable institutional and economic differences among the different parts of French Indochina conditioned the choices made by the colonial administrators in designing fiscal policies, and the impact of these policies.[2] The federal arrangements, in some respects, concealed these differences, while not fundamentally altering them. Some differences were obvious. Cochinchina was a frontier region that had been recently settled by the Kinh people. The kingdoms of Kampuchea (Cambodia) and those that became Laos had low population densities, and were relatively poor. Parts of Annam and Tonkin had very high populations relative to the arable land and suffered from repeated subsistence crises.

It is a truism that colonialism had an impact on institutional developments in all these regions, since the imposition of colonial rule in itself represented a major institutional change. French colonialism left important legacies for what, towards the end of the twentieth century, became the three countries of Vietnam, Cambodia and Laos. But, in order to evaluate the long-term consequences for fiscal policy, as for other aspects of policy, we must understand the mechanisms at work. These were, in turn, intrinsically associated with the formation and evolution of the colonial state. This chapter tries to clarify the conditions which shaped French choices in developing revenue sources and in implementing expenditure programmes. The case of Indochina can be initially seen as an example of fiscal modernization, in that tax revenues were centralized,

---

[2] This institutional and economic heterogeneity bears some clear resemblance to the situation in Portuguese Mozambique; see Alexopolou, Chapter 8, this volume.

and the tax base changed along with the economic transformation of the colony (as defined by He 2013). A range of infrastructural projects in transport, water control and irrigation were implemented. At the end of the colonial period, Vietnam and the rest of Indochina remained predominantly agrarian, but there were important differences in the level of commercialization. By the 1930s, Cochinchina was the richest part of the federation, but also well known for its economic inequalities, especially in land tenure and payment of rents. However, even in this region the process of fiscal modernization was at best partial.

In sum, this chapter contends that the role of local conditions and pre-colonial fiscal institutions must be brought to light in order to develop a deeper analytical understanding of the transformations that were to take place after French government was established. These institutions set both incentives and constraints for the local populations in their interactions with the colonial state. The chapter examines village administrative institutions and stresses the remarkable geographical differences. But first, we need to define what it is meant by French Indochina.

French Indochina: a Constructed Federal State

While contact with various Europeans can be traced back to the seventeenth century, the colonization of Indochina started with the conquest of the three eastern provinces of Cochinchina in 1862. Nine consecutive admirals ruled Cochinchina until 1879, when a civilian government controlled by the Colonial Council (consisting of colonists, merchants and officials) was formed. At this point, the six provinces of Cochinchina were all under French influence, if not direct French control. In 1887, the three parts of what is now Vietnam (renamed by the French as Tonkin, Annam and Cochinchina) and Cambodia were incorporated into the Indochinese Union. Laos, understood as the Kingdom of Luang Prabang and the southern territories, was added in 1893 after the Franco-Siamese war (Stuart-Fox 1997, 24–9). The territory of Guangzhouwan was incorporated in January 1900 (see Map 4.1). It is widely accepted that there were significant geopolitical reasons for this territorial expansion; the French government wanted to stake clear claims to territory to prevent rival claims from Great Britain to the west and the south and China in the north (Ennis 1936, Dommen 2001).

The General Government of French Indochina was established in 1898. The centralization of the budgets of the Indochinese Union was a result of Paul Doumer's federalization efforts, from 1897 to 1902. One of the principal objectives of these reforms was to assimilate the colonial 'local' budgets into a centralized budget and reduce the fiscal autonomy

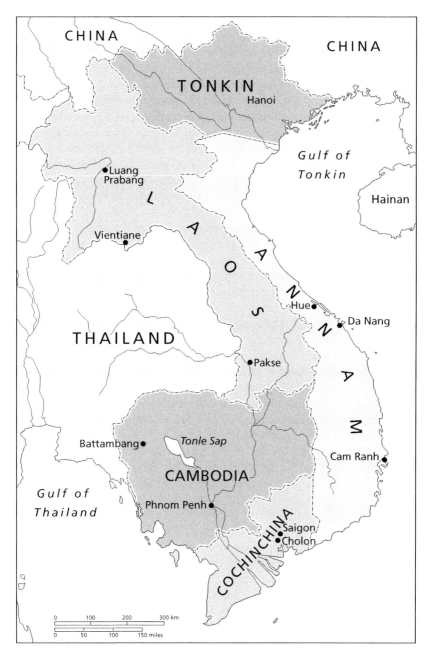

Map 4.1 Territories of French Indochina, 1887–1940

of each region (in 1889, the protectorate of Annam-Tonkin was divided into two). The outcome was the formation of six different budgets differentiated by the nature of revenues and expenditures; the local budgets were in charge of local expenditures and financed by direct taxes, while indirect forms of taxation comprised the central, general, budget (Doumer 1902, 12). We argue that this transformation might be also understood as an effort to centralize tax revenues and compensate for the differences in fiscal capacities between the parts of the federation, as was also evident in the case of French West Africa (Frankema & van Waijenburg, Chapter 6, this volume). For instance, in 1899, the total amount of the largest local budget, Cochinchina's, was less than half of the revenue obtained from indirect taxes, which was then part of the central budget (Guermeur 1909/1999, 55–8).

The concern for the financial precarity of Annam and Tonkin was central in the reporting by Doumer (1902, 5–15). The pacification of Tonkin and Annam (1874–95) cost almost four times as much as the conquest of Cochinchina from 1859 to 1895, and all the budgets were, by the end of the nineteenth century, running a deficit. But the option of taking over the Vietnamese empire's entire fiscal system was not feasible at the time. Éliacin Luro, the inspector of indigenous affairs in Cochinchina, bluntly stated that it was impossible to know the precise amount of revenue collected by the Empire (Luro 1897, 171). Paul Bert, resident general in Annam and Tonkin, attempted to tap into the indigenous tax revenues to finance the conquest of that region, but it proved impossible. These constraints, together with the growing difficulty in obtaining financial support from Paris, led to substantial contributions from Cochinchina's budget to the military expenses of conquering the two northern regions (Isoart 1961, 161). This was facilitated by the budgetary surplus in Cochinchina derived from increasing rice exports and the sale of land concessions (Brocheux & Hémery 2009, 78–9).

These difficulties should not be interpreted as an inability on the part of the French to modify the indigenous fiscal regime. The French paper trail of reforms is extensive, and created a body of knowledge centred on the intentions and implications of frequent policy changes. In fact, one of the main characteristics of French rule was a lack of consistency as governors changed frequently (Ennis 1936, 59; Thompson 1968, 425). This caused problems in the implementation of new policy initiatives, since the institutional apparatus for execution was often not in place, and the governors might be recalled before the policies could be implemented. Attempts at direct rule, even in Cochinchina, were abandoned as a result of either local resistance or a lack of administrative resources (Guermeur 1909/1999, 35–6, Popkin 1979,

171, Brocheux & Hémery 2009, 74–5). Stuart-Fox (1997, 29–33) examined the problems facing the French in Laos, and Owen et al. (2005, 362) and Slocomb (2010, chapter 1) have looked at Cambodia. Most scholars have concluded that the French learnt early on that 'you do not rule against the elites', and policy reforms had to be kept to a minimum (Brocheux & Hémery 2009, 90). But even so, popular protests against increased tax demands were not unusual. For instance, 8,000 farmers of Di Loc, Quang-Nam province (Annam), demonstrated against the French authorities and provincial mandarins and notables in 1908 as a result of an increase of labour corvée from six to nine days, which meant, in effect, an 18 per cent rise in personal tax levels (Brocheux & Hémery 2009, 298). The protests spread to other provinces. During the 1930s, protests and riots became more commonplace and political resistance more organized. An example was the march of 5,000 Vietnamese in western Cochinchina against tax levies; these protestors also demanded a more equal distribution of land (Ennis 1936, 188).

The capital of the Union was moved from Saigon to Hanoi in 1902, and remained there until the Japanese occupation in 1940. This move did not imply a shift in the economic centre: the frontier economies of Cochinchina, and also at least partly Cambodia, remained the main contributors of revenues during the colonial occupation. But the French, by moving the capital to Hanoi, gained proximity to other sources of revenue, especially the coalfields in Tonkin (run by the *Société Française des Charbonnages du Tonkin*). The political organization of the colony may have acted as a catalyst for the polarization between Saigon and Hanoi, and the progressive displacement of Hue (Annam) as the political capital (see Map 4.1). But, during the colonial period, Hue remained the imperial capital and residence of the Nguyen dynasty and experienced some fiscal autonomy (Anh 1985, 150).

French Indochina was thus a colonial construct, comprising different kingdoms and peoples, with their own pre-existing economic centres, over which the colonial powers ruled indirectly. With the exception of the surplus derived from taxing opium and other consumables, which was an important revenue generator for most of the colonial period, the French economic endeavour was based on land and the exportable surplus derived from it. On the export side, rice was undoubtedly the most important commodity, although its relative importance declined over the period. Other primary products such as maize and rubber gained in importance, especially in the 1920s and 1930s, while the shares remain stable for dried fish, skins, copra, pepper and cinnamon. Mining and manufacturing products, coal and cement, contributed around 4 per cent and 1 per cent of the total value of Vietnamese exports from 1913 to 1946 (Bassino & Huong 2000, 306).

The industrialization of Indochina had a limited impact on both employment, and the tax base, although there were some developments in the interwar years (Nørlund 1991). In 1914, private investment in industries and mines accounted for almost half of the total; by 1940, these sectors accounted for 60 per cent of the total (Brocheux & Hémery 2009, 163). Private investments were mainly located in Saigon and Hanoi, and linked to the mining of coal and cement, rubber plantations, a small textile industry and distilleries. Yet, the official statistics showed only French private investments (Robequain 1944, 158). Chinese investments in the cement industry and in most of the rice milling companies in Cholon (Cochinchina), as well as investments in local handicrafts and textile production, were not reported (Nørlund 1986, 43). Chinese and Indian capital played a crucial role in the trading of rice, maize, silk and tropical products (Robequain 1944, 159).

Throughout the colonial period, companies tended to complain about the scarcity of labour, especially during the harvest season. This was most acute in Tonkin where, despite its large population, the urbanization rate was low (about 4 per cent) and the majority of the population remained linked to the rice economy, which was one of the most labour-intensive wet rice systems in Southeast Asia (Lopez Jerez 2014, 79–104). In the rubber plantations, some labour was imported from Java, at least until the Great Depression of the early 1930s (Goudal 1938, 250). Migrants from Tonkin remained in the south for three years and then returned back, so their net numbers were small (Robequain 1944, 56). There were few possibilities through labour migration to transform the main sources of income for most of the population, and hence to expand the tax base. Land remained the key factor of production during the colonial period, and this perpetuated the domain fiscal state that had ruled the village economies prior to colonial times. Given the fact that the French administration lacked modern land cadastres and an effective rural civil service, land and personal taxes were levied by the indigenous village administration, even in Cochinchina.

French colonial supervision of the village administrations was also very weak in the case of Cambodia and Laos, where the French presence was confined to the capitals. The link between French administrative decrees and their effective implementation also remained weak. In Vietnam, the French administrative control was only slightly better (Popkin 1979, 143). In Tonkin, the supervision of the native budgets was confined to villages with more than 2,000 inhabitants (500 registered males), which meant that 85 per cent of the village budgets in the region were either not supervised, or only superficially. None were supervised in Annam (Rouilly, cited by Popkin 1979, 150). This had major implications for the fiscal performance of the local administrations, and it also weakened the potential impact of colonial policies on the majority of the population.

At the same time, because of the centralization of the public finances, the surplus generated in the southern regions contributed to the budgets of the other protectorates, which were running deficits (Bassino 2000a, 272). Cochinchina became the third largest exporter of rice in the world and an important player in the regional rubber market in the 1920s. This is not unique to Indochina; the French resorted to a similar fiscal strategy in West Africa (Frankema & van Waijenburg, 2014). But, as a consequence, any understanding of economic change in French Indochina as a whole must be linked to the economic transformation of Cochinchina and the changes in its fiscal capacity. Why then was the colonial state's fiscal capacity so limited compared to other colonies Southeast Asia?

A Dual Fiscal State: Taxing Commerce versus Taxing Land

From 1900, Indochina's public finances were made independent from the French government in Paris (Bassino 2000a, 270). An Act of 13 April 1900 established the principle of Indochina's financial autonomy from the metropolis and cut the ties between the French treasury and the local and central colonial budgets (Robequain 1944, 150). However, the contributions to the metropolitan economy remained important; Indochina was the only colony to contribute a significant share to France's military budget from 1899 to 1913. It also contributed to the additional pay of French troops serving in the colony and to military pensions, as well as other French activities in Asia. This accords with the argument that the financial burden of colonization rested mainly upon the local populations, and not the French (Huillery 2014, van Waijenburg 2018). By 1938, Indochina was second in importance after Algeria in terms of total budget size (Brocheux & Hémery 2009, 97).

The French fiscal system in Indochina was divided into three levels: central, local and provincial (mainly in Cochinchina) as illustrated in Figure 4.1. The central account derived its revenues in large part from indirect taxes, including foreign trade taxes and taxes on consumer goods. The production and sale of opium, salt and alcohol were run as state monopolies. Expenditures were supposed to benefit the Union as a whole and included the payments related to public debt, and the colony's share of defence expenditures (the annual quota paid to the French budget for defence services rendered by France). Also included were the costs of the central administration (administrative and judiciary services). The local governments were responsible for the collection of direct taxes. On the

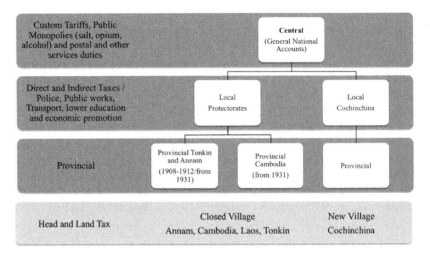

Figure 4.1 Levels of colonial government in French Indochina up to the village
Source: Author's own estimates.

expenditure side, they paid for the police, some public works (with the exception of the railways, which had a special account), transport subsidies to companies, lower education and other targets of socio-economic development. The word 'local' in this context is, however, misleading since the French administration allowed the village authorities, and even provincial and township governments, to keep their own administrations, which functioned as autonomous entities.

The main sources of revenue were customs tariffs and public monopolies (salt, opium, alcohol). Other direct and indirect taxes were less important. This led to a significant asymmetry in the budgets of the different levels of government. The fiscal system was very similar in all the protectorates, both in revenues and in expenditures, although the tax rates were normally higher in Vietnam than in Laos and Cambodia until the 1920s, which benefited from larger exemptions (Bassino 2000a, 271). This was an outcome of the greater French administrative presence in Hanoi and Saigon, and of the asymmetric economic development of the regions.

The General Budget was an intrinsic component of the federal state and grew partly as a result of the transfer of responsibilities over taxing export and import trade. Cochinchina's government fiercely resisted this process of centralization but had to agree to a reduction of its budget by more than two-thirds in 1899, the year the central budgets were approved. This, however, did not alter its political strength. Saigon was the only city in Indochina to have a municipal council elected by universal suffrage. The Colonial Council of Cochinchina remained in charge of the land concessions of less than five hundred hectares (Brocheux & Hémery 2009, 82). As most land concessions were granted in Cochinchina, this was a major source of revenue and of autonomy (White 1981, 34–5).

As land transactions and the export economy became the dominant sources of revenue, public investment in land development and cultivation, and the transport of export commodities, were government priorities. Public works comprised around 18 to 20 per cent of the entire budget from 1900 to 1939 (Brocheux & Hémery 2009, 157). The composition of these investments varied over time; from 1899 to 1923, railways, roads and ports accounted for 68.1 per cent of all infrastructure investments while 20.5 per cent was spent on agricultural hydraulics, dredging and inland navigation. The remainder of the infrastructure budget went to personnel and miscellaneous expenses (Brocheux & Hémery 2009, 157). Cochinchina was the recipient of the initial investments made to improve the navigability of the Mekong River. From 1890 to 1930, new transport and irrigation canals were dredged, exceeding 165 million cubic metres in volume. This was a remarkable engineering achievement, comparable in scope to the 210 million cubic metres dredged to construct the Panama Canal or the 260 million cubic metres for the Suez Canal. The outcome was that almost 1.5 million hectares of land were cleared and put under cultivation from 1886 to 1930, at a cost of 52 million piastres (Brocheux 1995, 21). The local budget and three large loans from France financed these activities (Nørlund 1991).

Another major area of investment was in railways in Tonkin, including the Haiphong port, and the line joining Hanoi and Saigon, which was completed in 1936. The lines connected most of the mining centres, facilitating the transport of both produce and people. The objectives of moving what the government considered the excess population of the north to the south, and of moving rice from the surplus areas in the south to the deficit districts in the north, remained an important policy priority during the colonial period. After the 1926 floods in Tonkin, when the water level in the rivers around Hanoi went from two to almost twelve metres, the French became more systematic and methodical in the construction of different hydraulics projects (Gourou 1945, 267). There were more dam reinforcement projects between 1926 and 1931, which, in turn, led to increases in land under cultivation. The overall efforts, which amounted to excavations of 40 million cubic metres from 1915 to 1930, cost 12 million piastres up to the end of 1930 (Goudal 1938, 201). This was equivalent to 10 per cent of the value of exports for the whole of

Indochina in 1931 (Bassino 2000b, 337). Yet, the per capita level of these investments was limited as population pressure increased during the 1930s, partly as a result of the return migration derived from the Great Depression. In Cambodia, the local government invested in the electrification of provincial towns, extensive road construction and the railway between Phnom Penh and the Siam boarder, but made limited direct investments in cultivation (Owen et al. 2005, 363–4).

In spite of these achievements, most expenditures of the central budget were not on public works, which fell under the responsibility of the local colonial budgets, but on administration and the payment of debt, transfers to the local budgets and transfers to France. During the 1920s, an average of 75 per cent of the total was spent on administrative costs, transfers and subsidies and debt service (Indochine Francaise 1930a). This situation did not change much during the 1930s, although the share of debt service declined relative to subsidies and public works (Robequain 1944, 152). The question arises as to why, under indirect rule, did the majority of the expenditures go into administrative and military costs? In order to answer this, we need to understand the asymmetries of budgetary organization under French rule.

The Central and the Local Budgets: an Asymmetric and Complex Relationship

Even if we set aside the criticism that the French tended to present statistics in order to disguise information about the realities of colonial development (Ennis 1936, 70), the available data indicate that French rule had two major characteristics: a large bureaucracy, located disproportionally in the major cities, and a large central budget relative to those of lower levels of government.

According to Brocheux and Hémery (2009, 81), the French Indochinese Civil Service, formed in 1898, was modelled on that of the British Indian Civil Service. The high salaries were an incentive for recruiting high-quality personnel. These efforts led to a large civil service relative to the population. Cochinchina, by 1900, had 290 European civil servants and more than 1,000 other French officials. That was one for every 7,900 inhabitants compared to one for every 76,000 inhabitants in Java (Brocheux & Hémery 2009, 82). Prior to the conquest, Cochinchina was run by fifty mandarins and a small staff. But because the budget of Cochinchina was larger than in other regions, the personnel expenditures were smaller as a proportion of the total. Brocheux and Hémery (2009, 83) reported that administrative expenditures in Cochinchina declined from almost 36 per cent of the local budget in 1913 to 24.5 per cent in 1938. In Annam, Tonkin and Cambodia the percentage of administrative expenditures in the local budgets during

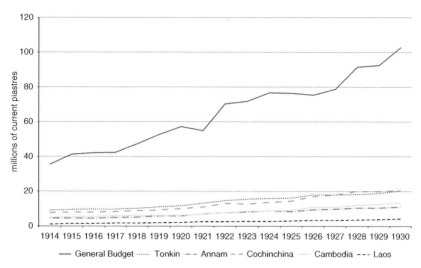

Figure 4.2 Budgets of the general and local governments in Indochina (millions of current piastres)
Source: Indochine Francaise (1930a, 49).

this period was around or above 40 per cent; in Annam, it reached 57 per cent in 1938. In Cambodia, Adolphe Messimy (cited in Brocheux & Hémery 2009, 82) stated that fourteen French civil servants were employed in 1910–11, and, according to his assessment, they were not very busy. Given that nine out of ten Cambodians lived in the countryside, these servants had little contact with the great majority of the population and had an ill-informed understanding of local conditions, such as land distribution or tenure arrangements. Indeed, they did not even know the total population with any accuracy (Owen et al. 2005, 362).

Despite the larger numbers of civil servants employed, there were only 2,860 Europeans in French Indochina in 1897, and several thousand Vietnamese for a population of over 10 million people. By 1911, there were 5,683 Europeans, and 12,200 indigenous civil servants (Brocheux & Hémery 2009, 82). Yet, since public servants and administrators were mainly located in Hanoi and Saigon, the distance to the majority of the Vietnamese population remained large. Relative to the population, the European staff was small in Annam and Tonkin.

Given that the majority of the colonial revenues collected were indirect, and they accrued to the federal budget, the local budgets remained underfunded. Figure 4.2 depicts these asymmetries. The situation did improve as a result of Governor Serraut's decentralization efforts during his mandate (1911–14 and 1917–19). Of the local budgets, Tonkin had

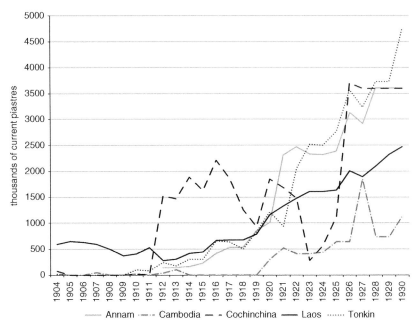

Figure 4.3 Transfers from general budget to local, 1904 to 1930 (thousands of current piastres)
Source: Indochine Francaise (1930b, 15).

the most funds (on average 22 per cent of the total general budget during the period) followed by Cochinchina with an average of 19 per cent. Annam and Cambodia operated with smaller budgets, while the budget in Laos comprised a mere 3 per cent of the total.

The budgets of the local governments do not, however, show how much revenue was actually collected in each part of the federation. Tonkin had the largest budget for most of the years from 1914 to 1930, but it was not the largest revenue collector. Its budgets were balanced via transfers from the general budget. Bernard (1937, 52) estimated that Cochinchina provided 40 per cent of revenues of the central budget. These revenues, in turn, went to the weakest local budgets; in 1930, for instance, the subsidies to the local budget of Laos amounted to 59 per cent of the total revenues. In Annam, the subsidies were 33 per cent of the total; 23 per cent in Tonkin, 11 per cent in Cochinchina and only 7 per cent in Cambodia (Indochine Francaise 1930b). The evolution of the transfers from the federal budget to the local is summarized in Figure 4.3. The increases in the amounts accruing to Tonkin and Cambodia coincide with greater investments in infrastructure.

The 1920s were, in fact, one of the best decades for Indochinese economic and commercial interests as prices of commodities stabilized, rubber cultivation and export dramatically expanded partly as a result of the Stevenson plan (Robequain 1944, 201), and improvements in the government's institutional capacity were prioritized. The first population 'census' was carried out in 1921, although as Banens (2000) has argued, the figures were almost certainly understated. After Yves Henry was appointed as Director of Agriculture, attention was given to collecting agricultural statistics and implementing land surveys. But the inflexibility of the fiscal system still made it impossible to run local budgets without transfers from the federal budget, as shown in Figure 4.4, which constructs local budgets with direct taxes as their only source of revenue. This constraint, in turn, put significant pressure on local officials to increase their main sources of revenue, including all sources of direct taxation.

It is clear from Figure 4.4 that the annual growth rate of expenditure was greater than the annual growth of revenue from direct taxes in both Cochinchina and Laos during the 1920s. This meant that other sources of revenue, mainly transfers, had to increase in order to balance the budget. Touzet (1935, 156) presented a breakdown of local budget expenditures for 1914 and 1934, as shown in Table 4.1. The local governments were responsible for key welfare expenditures such as health and education, agrarian and commercial services and public works, which the French administration grouped as 'social and economic services' (Table 4.2). Even though these welfare expenditures increased modestly during the 1920s, they never gained real priority.

Why were local revenues so constrained? The main revenues were derived from head taxes, taxes on foreigners (mainly Chinese) and transfers from the federal budget. The introduction of a tax assessed on income was not attempted until 1938 (Robequain 1944, 149–56). But personal and land taxes for the majority population were collected by the village authorities in Vietnam and the canton (*khum*) in Cambodia. As there were no accurate population estimates, the French were unable to assess the full potential revenue from direct taxes at the village level. As in the case of indirect taxes, the geographical differences in collection were striking. In Laos, data provided by Guermeur (1909/1999) show that the total collection of direct taxes in 1900 was 25,000 piastres in land taxes (or 0.3 per cent of the total for all Indochina) and 258,000 piastres in head tax (or 6 per cent of the Indochina total). By 1910, direct taxation contributed just over one-third to a total budget of 900,000 piastres. Indirect taxes contributed a further 160,000 piastres, and the balance was transferred from the Indochinese central budget. The total budget had only grown by 12.5 per cent from 1896 to 1911 (Stuart-Fox 1997,

Table 4.1 *Local budgets for Indochina: decomposition of expenditures by type (%)*

	1914	1934
Debt	0.01	0.8
Subsidies to secondary budgets	0.29	0.7
Personnel	59.5	64.2
Materials, equipment	35.3	31.5
Public works	4.9	2.8

Source: Touzet (1935, 156)

Table 4.2 *Allocation of expenditures in 1930 for French Indochina (%) – local budgets*

	Annam	Cambodia	Cochinchina	Laos	Tonkin
Debt	0.45	0.46	0.64	0.32	0.86
Administration	38.84	33.98	25.77	40.20	36.72
Financial Services	2.56	5.67	6.38	2.44	3.43
Industrial Exploitations	16.10	31.79	23.98	21.61	19.99
Social & Economic Services	34.20	19.09	27.67	23.57	27.10
Undisclosed funds	0.14	0.13	0.10	0.14	0.24
Diverse	7.71	8.89	15.45	11.71	11.66
Total ('000 piastres)	11,043	13,386	19,762	4,189	20,328
Total per capita	**2.2**	**4.2**	**4.5**	**4.8**	**2.7**

Source: Indochine Francaise (1930b, 21–2).
Note: When small discrepancies arise in the source document, figures have been adjusted. Touzet (1935, 157) reports a similar table, based on the same source, and the greatest difference is that he includes the undisclosed fonds (*Fonds Secrets* in the original). There were small differences in the percentages for Cochinchinese administration. In the original, Government and Administration General are separated but following Touzet, we have grouped them. Population data: Ng (1974). Data for Cambodia are taken from Slocomb (2010, 46). In 1930, the piastre was set at 1:10 French francs.

32). Laos, as one of the poorest regions, was a net recipient of transfers during the whole period, but in limited amounts. Consequently, Laos did not play much of a role in increasing the fiscal capacity of the French colonial state in Indochina.

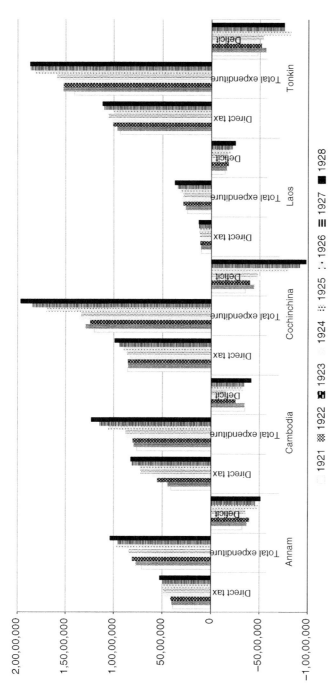

Figure 4.4 Constructed local budgets (direct taxes – total expenditures), 1921–8 (in piastres)

Source: Author's estimates based on Indochine Francaise (1930a, 87).

Legend: □ 1921 ▨ 1922 ▧ 1923 ▨ 1924 ▦ 1925 ⁞⁞ 1926 ≡ 1927 ■ 1928

The rates for direct taxation varied significantly. According to a report written for the Colonial Expo in 1930 (Indochine Francaise 1930c, 7), Cambodia charged 3.10 piastres per inhabitant, Tonkin charged 2.50 piastres for the registered and 0.30 for the non-registered population, and in Cochinchina the rate was 1 piastre. The differences were even larger for the foreign Asian population: 15 piastres in Cochinchina, 8 in Laos, 10 in Cambodia, between 3.5 and 10 in Tonkin and between 8 and 15 in Annam (Indochine Francaise 1930c, 10). As in the pre-colonial period, exemptions were given to the members of the royal families in different parts of the federation and to those holding honorific titles.

Another form of personal direct taxation was corvée labour, which predated colonial budgets and was normally employed for irrigation and other communal work. In Cochinchina, already from 1882, two-thirds of the corvée, fixed at thirty days per year per registered person, could be redeemed at the rate of 0.10 piastres per day and merged with the personal tax. These changes were made in 1918 for Annam and in 1920 for Tonkin (Brocheux & Hémery 2009, 91), but the number of days and the rates of redemption varied within and between the regions depending on ethnicity (Indochine Francaise 1930c, 9). The rates went from 0.06 to 0.30 piastres per day and the corvée days varied from five days (in Annam) to twenty days (in Laos). This variation in corveé days per eligible worker is similar to French West Africa (van Waijenburg 2018, 54). In Cochinchina, the revenues from direct taxes increased from 4.1 to 9.4 million piastres between 1904 and 1927. But, as a proportion of the total budget, direct tax revenues fell from 75.6 to 50.3 per cent (Fall 1985:179). Here, foreign Asians paid more than the Vietnamese or the Europeans. Cochinchina's per capita tax payments were higher than in Tonkin, even though the Tonkin tax rates (land and head tax) were higher. There, total revenues from direct taxes increased from 4.6 to 11.1 million piastres between 1904 to 1927, but as a percentage of the total budget, they fell from 70 to 59 per cent (Fall 1985, 178). Foreign Asians were unevenly distributed, even prior to colonization, as they were involved in the rice trade and thus concentrated in Cochinchina and Cambodia (Khanh 1993, 16). Robequain (1944, 149–56) refers to the inelasticity of the Indochinese tax system; in addition, taxes were unevenly distributed and broadly regressive. The other major source of revenue were land taxes, and these were assessed using a complex classification system. Rice fields were classified according to land productivity and use, and different rates were applied to indigenous and foreign populations. Normally, a higher rate was applied to the native population, which added to the regressivity of the tax system.

Summing up, each local colonial budget became dependent on different sources of revenue during the 1920s (Indochine Francaise 1930c, 21–5). In Annam, land taxes and indigenous direct taxes together amounted to four million piastres on average, almost the whole revenue collected. Tonkin depended on the same sources of revenue but the amounts were almost twice those in Annam. In Cambodia, the sources of revenue were more diversified, especially after 1922, when land taxes increased from less than 400,000 to 1.3 million piastres, and became the main revenue source (due to the rubber expansion). Most of the fiscal burden fell on the local indigenous population, followed by the Foreign Asian population. Cochinchina, by the 1920s, had the most diversified budget. As in Cambodia, revenues from land were the main contributor, reaching a maximum of 4.2 million piastres in 1930. Levies on foreign Asians, patents, and other imposts on the indigenous population amounted to under one million piastre per year, on average.

The real burden of direct taxes on population hence varied and the French adapted their policies to the economic differences in the different parts of the federal system. Due to the complexity of the system and inefficiency in tax collection, we can only give a rough estimate of the burden. If we take the total revenue from direct taxes in 1930 (Indochine Francaise 1930c, 19) and divide by the available population data, Cambodia had the highest tax collection at 2.6 piastres per inhabitant, followed closely by Cochinchina with 2.4 piastres. In contrast, in the most populated parts of the federation, the colonial government in Annam collected only 1.1 piastres per inhabitant, and in Tonkin 1.5 piastres.

What does this tell us about the impact of the French colonial state on the population? It is clear that French administrators lacked the capacity to collect land and income taxes, but the local populations were still subject to a range of imposts that did not enter the official statistics. The indigenous administrations were run on those taxes. The French did directly collect some land tax, especially in the concessions. But the colonial land registration system was not well developed. Popkin (1979, 170–2) has argued that in most parts of Indochina, French resources were limited and the French administrators were unable to gain control of political processes within the villages, which prevented effective registration. He also pointed out that in Cochinchina, when the French introduced new land registration procedures, they were poorly publicized and difficult to use. To understand the dual fiscal state in Indochina, I now consider the indigenous fiscal systems operated by local village elites.

The Peasantry and the Local Village Elites: Resistance and Change

The crux of the indigenous tax system was control over land. Khoi (1981, 128) has shown that there were three types of land in pre-colonial Vietnam: communal, private and granted (land given to mandarins, and soldiers as part of their salaries). Traditionally, all land belonged to the Emperor, but farmers, by cultivating the land and paying taxes, were granted access to the village or to communal land (in Vietnamese, *xa)*. The villages kept their autonomy through these communal lands, which were mainly rice fields exploited for the provision of public goods. Tax collection was a village, not an individual, responsibility.[3] There were other lands, within the communal area, such as temple land and land used for rituals (Ory, 1894). The distribution of land among these three types was anything but constant and a continuous source of conflict through Vietnamese history (Lan 1980, Khoi 1981, 306–7). The image of a peaceful and harmonious traditional village before the arrival of the French, as suggested by some authors (i.e. Wiegersma 1988), does not fit easily with these distributional conflicts.

A major area of disagreement about the effects of colonialism concerns the role of the communal lands. In a broad sense, communal lands refer to various types of land devoted to different purposes. But they should be distinguished from what is called *ruông công diên*, communal rice fields. These were rice lands, which were divided among taxpayers on an 'equal' basis within the class structure, as it existed at the village. They were the *commons* and inalienable. It might be expected that when new economic opportunities were opened up by French colonialism, processes of privatization would have occurred. Increase in rice prices and global demand for rice would have led to more intensive cultivation and the privatization of marginal land as McCloskey (1972) argued was the case in Europe.

But that was not the case in Vietnam, since the tendency to privatize these lands was evident even prior to the French presence (Chi 1980, Long 1991). As part of the contract between the Emperor and the farmer, dating back many centuries, those that paid their tribute had the right to access those lands, and every three years they were redistributed amongst the inhabitants of the village (Chinh & Giap 1974). Communal lands remained in Tonkin during colonial times and they were positively

---

[3] As taxation remained a village responsibility, understanding these units has been the focus of many studies. Those have shown that village institutions differed markedly across Indochina, and indeed across other parts of Southeast Asia. Murray (1980), Rambo (1973) and Hickey (1967) compared different parts of Vietnam, drawing on the work of French scholars including Henry (1932) and Gourou (1945). Hoadley and Gunnarsson (1996) examine the concept of the village across Southeast Asia.

correlated to the number of cultivators. That is, the larger the number of cultivators, the larger the number of communal lands (Gourou 1945). As long as farmers (males from approximately 18 to 60) paid their taxes, their households had the right to cultivate this land. But if farmers stopped paying taxes for three consecutive years, the land could be reclaimed and distributed amongst of the members of the village, including the non-registered ones such as widows and orphans. The distribution of communal lands was a village affair, and higher officials were not involved unless conflicts arose (Khoi 1981, 128). In the Red River Delta and parts of Annam, the cultivation of rice was among the most labour intensive in the world and hence the farming population could only be seasonally released.

In the village, we can identify three actors. The first was the village chief, who was one of the landed elite, and village administrators (normally three posts). The second were the tax payers who were registered villagers (cultivators who, by paying the head and land tax, had the right to cultivate the imperial land and communal lands). The third were the non-registered villagers. In order to become a resident in a traditional village, a person must have come from a family that had settled in the village for three generations and that person had to own land (Chi 1980, 69). This is indicative of the closed nature of the village structures. It is estimated from 1903 data, that only one-third of all eligible males had their names on the registers in Tonkin (Fall 1985, 165, Long 1991, 63). The better-off families in the village were part of the Council of Notables (Nghinh 1980, 177–9). They were in charge of the administration of the village and the link to the mandarins, who represented the Imperial state.

The village chief was not a single ruler, but part of the landed elite of the village. There were sometimes different family lineages (Papin 2002) and conflicts might have occurred. One might expect that when the time came for the village chief to decide on the distribution of communal lands, there was agreement within the elite to preserve the status quo, and maintain rents. This could be interpreted to mean that property rights were secure for the elite as argued by North, Wallis and Weingast (2009). For instance, Chinh and Giap (1974, 79) reported that, before the auction of the communal lands, the village chief had pre-arranged a grant of the fallow lands to an influential family in the village for 110 piastres. This family sublet the land to the village inhabitants making a substantial profit. Such abuses of power were repeatedly reported and were a source of conflict (Lan 1980, Long 1991). According to Popkin (1979, 155), 60 per cent of the families were either landless or cultivated less than 0.36 ha by 1930; in Tonkin, he argued that 20 per cent of families were completely landless. For a large part of the population, the existence of communal lands became the main source for survival or an important extra income. Those that had some rights to cultivation in their own name might consider the communal land as a bonus, but the landless (or non-registered) relied on these fields for their subsistence and became completely subordinated to the village elite.

Why would the landed elite have wanted to keep communal land? Moral economists such as Scott (1976) would argue that it was part of the reciprocity of the village society. In part, that could be understood as a self-reinforcing mechanism; the greater the population pressure, the more vulnerable the cultivator becomes, and the greater the need to keep communal lands. The existence of communal lands helped support population growth, and consequently provided a large supply of cheap labour for the landed elite. Since land distribution was more unequal in areas that were more densely populated, the power of the landed elite was positively correlated with the existence of communal lands. In Cochinchina, communal lands were less important; the area was small (60,000 ha compared to 235,000 ha in Tonkin and 195,000 ha in Annam) and a much smaller proportion of total land according to Henry (1932, 213). While this has been interpreted as a negative effect of colonialism, it might not always have been so. Farmers, whether tenants or owners, had access to larger landholdings than their northern counterparts and hence might not need communal lands for subsistence. In Cambodia, Henry (1932, 213) claimed that it was impossible to determine the amount of communal lands.

The communal lands certainly had a welfare function. But they also prevented mobility. If a village resident or non-resident stopped paying tax for three consecutive years, he lost his right to communal lands. This threatened his and his family's survival, and a break with his ancestors' land. The result was that the landed elite could keep a source of cheap and dependent labour, while simultaneously spreading the fiscal burden of the village, for which they were responsible, among a larger number of people. Indeed, the new market opportunities encouraged greater control over communal lands, but not their privatization. The fact that communal lands were proportionally lower in Cochinchina did not make the average farmer more vulnerable, especially if the land frontier was still open. In other parts of Vietnam, communal lands were a substantial barrier to modernizing the fiscal state, as one of the main assets of the economy, agricultural land, remained under village control and prevented the imposition of individual land taxes.

This meant that within the village, the payment of the land tax was a village responsibility. Popkin (1979, 147) argued that the village officials who assessed the tax had ample opportunity to avoid taxing themselves, and often imposed heavier taxes on poorer people. In effect, the smaller the holding, the larger the tax paid per hectare. This was also reported for Cambodia (Yuon 1982, 51). In Laos, Stuart-Fox (1997, 33) claims that the rather egalitarian access to available new land made the transformation from a barter to a monetized economy less disruptive than in other, more densely populated, parts of the federation, as people could sell opium, forest produce or extra rice to meet the fiscal demands. But corvée was burdensome in a labour-scarce economy. In Cochinchina, on the other hand, one of the effects of land expansion and increased commercialization of the economy was a more diverse socioeconomic structure, both in the villages and outside, though polarization occurred during the 1930s (Lopez Jerez 2014, 138–43). There seems to have been a greater division between the political and the economic elites in the village, and a tendency among richer rural families to delegate their administrative responsibilities and focus on their business activities (Brocheux & Hemery 2009, 101).

Seen from an inter-elite competition perspective, the political competition between the French and the village local elites was much reduced in Cochinchina as both parties gained with the commercialization and institutional transformation of the economy, while the traditional village elites in the more closed village economies in the north tended to resist French reform measures and collection efforts. A 1921 village reform in Tonkin attempted to reduce the power of the village notables and the landed elite, and favour more democratic elections by electing Clan representatives (and not Notables). But this was met with such resistance that it was reversed by 1928 (Chi 1980, 42).

Conclusion

This chapter has argued that indigenous institutions that were in place before the arrival of the French affected colonial fiscal development in Indochina. The colonial federal state was based on a complex, bureaucratic, and centralized administration, which allowed local colonial budgets to run without deficits, thanks to transfers from centrally levied custom duties and state monopoly earnings. In this system, the economic surpluses of Cochinchina subsidized the rest of the federation. The revenues of the central government were linked to levies on consumer goods and the expanding export economy that benefited from the remarkable investments in public works (which are visible even today). The outcome was a regressive colonial fiscal system, superimposed on the traditional domain estates that remained.

In the Tonkinese, Cambodian and Lao villages, the closed structures and the stability of social norms tended to prevent any change by the colonial powers, including changes in the tax regime, that could undermine traditional authority. It is probable that the northern parts of Vietnam suffered more from institutional persistence, and the existing landed elites benefited most from whatever new opportunities colonialism offered. In Cochinchina, the picture is more nuanced. The farmers there had access to land, but tenure conditions did affect incentives to invest in land improvements.

The conditions for fiscal modernization were better in Cochinchina, given the greater degree of commercialization after 1900. But the substantial transfers of funds from Cochinchina to other parts of the federation meant that the local government in Cochinchina was deprived of funds that could have *potentially* been used for productive investments, while at the same time the other parts of Indochina were supported by budgetary transfers, which prevented changes in local taxation. This, in turn, reduced the opportunity for socioeconomic investments, which potentially could have benefited a larger part of the predominantly rural population.

It could be argued that in the 1930s, as colonial officials struggled to cope with the aftermath of the Great Depression and the growing military threat from Japan, the conditions were present for change in Indochina's fiscal arrangements. However, the French administration tended to support the vested political and economic interests in the colony, mainly located in Saigon, and linked to the rubber plantations, big exporting houses and large landowners. Elsewhere, the French were unwilling to interfere in village government structures, although it was clear to at least some officials that these were holding back the economic modernization of the entire colony. This was a missed opportunity, not just for the socioeconomic development of Cochinchina, the economic engine of Indochina, but for other parts of the federation as well. The political division of the Union after the Geneva Accords in 1954, with Laos and Cambodia becoming separate states, and the division of Vietnam in two, indicated that the French had failed to create more than a fiscal federal state.

Bibliography

Acemoglu, D., Johnson, S., & Robinson, J. A. (2002). Reversal of Fortune: Geography and Institutions in the Making of the Modern World Income Distribution. *Quarterly Journal of Economics*, 117(4), 1231–94.

Anh, N. T. (1985). The Vietnamese Monarchy under French Colonial Rule 1884–1945. *Modern Asian Studies*, 19(1), 147–62.

Banens, M. (2000). Vietnam: A Reconstitution of Its 20th Century Population History. In J. P. Bassino, J. D. Giacometti & K. Odaka (Eds.), *Quantitative Economic History of Vietnam 1900–1990*. Tokyo: Hitotsubashi University, 1–42.

Bassino, J. P. (2000a). Public Finance in Vietnam under French Rule, 1895–1954. In J. P. Bassino, J. D. Giacometti & K. Odaka (Eds.), *Quantitative Economic History of Vietnam 1900–1990*. Tokyo: Hitotsubashi University, 283–304.

Bassino, J. P. (2000b). Estimates of Indochina's and Vietnam's Balance of Payments, 1890–1945: Investigating the Extent of the French Drain in Vietnam. In J. P. Bassino, J. D. Giacometti & K. Odaka (Eds.), *Quantitative Economic History of Vietnam 1900–1990*. Tokyo: Hitotsubashi University, 339–58.

Bassino, J. P., & Bui Thi Lan Huong (2000). Estimates of Indochina's and Vietnam's International Trade (1890–1946). In J. P. Bassino, J. D. Giacometti & K. Odaka (Eds.), *Quantitative Economic History of Vietnam 1900–1990*. Tokyo: Hitotsubashi University, 305–338.

Bernard, P. (1937). *Nouveaux aspects du problème économique indochinois*. Paris: Fernard Sorlot.

Brocheux, P. (1995). *The Mekong Delta: Ecology, Economy, and Revolution, 1860–1960*. Madison: Center for Southeast Asian Studies, University of Wisconsin-Madison.

Brocheux, P., & Hémery, D. (2009). *Indochina: An Ambiguous Colonization*. Berkeley: University of California Press.

Chi, N. T (1980). The Traditional Viet Village in Bac Bo: Its Organizational Structure and Problems. *Vietnamese Studies*, 61(1), 7–119.

Chinh, T., & Giap, V. N. (1974). *The Peasant Question (1937–1938)*. (Translated from the Vietnamese and introduced by C. Pelzer White). Ithaca: Department of Southeast Asian Studies, Cornell University.

Dommen, A. J (2001). *The Indochinese Experience of the French and the Americans*. Bloomington: Indiana University Press.

Doumer, M. P. (1902). *Situation de l'Indo-Chine (1897-1901)*. Hanoi: F. H. Schneider, Imprimeur-Éditeur.

Ennis, T. E. (1936). *French Policy and Developments in Indochina*. Chicago: The University of Chicago Press.

Fall, M. (1985). *Investissements publics et politique économique en Indochine, 1898–1930: (la commune vietnamienne dans la mise en valeur de l'Indochine)*. 2 vol. Paris, Thèse IIIe Cycle, Universite Paris VII.

Frankema, E., & van Waijenburg M. (2014). Metropolitan Blueprints of Colonial Taxation? Lessons from Fiscal Capacity Building in British and French Africa, c. 1880–1940. *The Journal of African History*, 55(3), 371–400.

Guermeur, H (1909/1999). *Le Régime Fiscal De L'Indochine*. Paris: L'Harmattan

Gourou, P. (1945). *Land Utilization in French Indochina*. New York: Institute of Pacific Relations.

Goudal, J. (1938). *Labour Conditions in Indo-China*. Geneva: International Labour Office.

He, W. (2013). *Paths toward the Modern Fiscal State: England, Japan, and China*. Cambridge, MA: Harvard University Press.

Henry, Y. (1932). *Économie agricole de l'Indochine*. Hanoi: Imprimerie d'Extrème-Orient.

Hickey, G. C. (1967). *Village in Vietnam*. New Haven and London: Yale University Press.

Hoadley, M., & Gunnarsson, C. (1996). *The Village Concept in the Transformation of Rural Southeast Asia*. London: Curzon Press.

Huillery, E. (2014). The Black Man's Burden: The Cost of Colonization of French West Africa. *The Journal of Economic History*, 74(1), 1–38.

Indochine Francaise. (1930a). *Histoire Budgétaire de L'Indochina* Hanoi: Imprimerie D'Extreme-Orient.

Indochine Francaise. (1930b). *Les Budgets Locaux en Indochine et Leurs Caisses De Réserve*. Hanoi: Imprimerie D'Extreme-Orient.

Indochine Francaise. (1930c). *Les Impots Directs en Indochine*. Hanoi: Imprimerie D'Extreme-Orient.

Isoart, P. (1961). *Le Phenomene National Vietnamien: De L'Independance Unitaire a L'Independance Fractionee*. Paris: Librairie générale de droit et de jurisprudence.

Khanh, T. (1993). *The Ethnic Chinese and Economic Development in Vietnam*. Singapore: Institute of Southeast Asian Studies.

Khoi, L.T (1981). *Histoire du Viet-Nam: Des origines à nos 1858*. Paris: Sudestasie.

Lan, T (1980). On Communal Land in the Traditional Viet Village. *Vietnamese Studies*, 61(1), 120–63.

Long, N. V (1991). *Before the Revolution: The Vietnamese Peasants under the French*. New York: Columbia University Press.

Lopez Jerez, M (2014). *Deltas Apart. Factor Endowments, Colonial Extraction and Pathways of Agricultural Development in Vietnam*. Lund Studies in Economic History 69. PhD Thesis, Lund University, Lund.

Luro, E. (1897). *Les pays d'Annam: étude sur l'organisation politique et sociale des Annamites* Paris: Ernest Leroux

McCloskey, D. N. (1972). The Enclosure of Open Fields: Preface to a Study of Its Impact on the Efficiency of English Agriculture in the Eighteenth Century. *The Journal of Economic History*, 32(1), 15–35.

Murray, M. J. (1980). *The Development of Capitalism in Colonial Indochina (1870–1940)*. Berkeley: University of California Press.

Ng, S. M. (1974). *The Population of Indochina: Some Preliminary Observations*. Field Report Series 7. Singapore: Institute of Southeast Asian Studies.

Nghinh, N. D (1980). Land Distribution in Tu Liem District According to Land Registers. *Vietnamese Studies*, 61(1), 164–87.

Nørlund, I. (1986). Social and Economic Studies on Vietnam: An Overview. In I. Nørlund, S. Cederroth & I. Gerdin (Eds.), *Rice Societies: Asian Problems and Prospects*. Riverdale: Curzon Press.

Nørlund, I. (1991). The French Empire, the Colonial State in Vietnam and the Economic Policy, 1885–1940. *Australian Economic History Review*, 31(1), 72–89.

North, D., Wallis, J., & Weingast, B. (2009). *Violence and Social Orders. A Conceptual Framework for Interpreting Recorded Human History*. New York: Cambridge University Press.

Ory, P. (1894). *La Commune Annamite au Tonkin*. Paris: Gallica.

Owen, N. G et al. (2005). *The Emergence of Modern Southeast Asia*. Honolulu: University of Hawai'i Press.

Papin, P. (2002). Who Has Power in the Village? Political Process and Social Reality in Vietnam. In G. Bousquet & P. Brocheux (Eds.), *Viêt Nam Exposé: French Scholarship on Twentieth-century Vietnamese Society*. Ann Arbor: University of Michigan, 21–60.

Popkin, S. L. (1979). *The Rational Peasant: The Political Economy of Rural Society in Vietnam*. Berkeley: University of California Press.

Rambo, A. T. (1973). *A Comparison of Peasant Social Systems of Northern and Southern Viet-Nam: A Study of Ecological Adaptation, Social Succession, and Cultural Evolution*. Carbondale: Center for Vietnamese Studies, Southern Illinois University.

Robequain, C. (1944). *The Economic Development of French Indo-China*. New York: Oxford University Press and The Institute of Pacific Relations.

Scott, J. C. (1976). *The Moral Economy of the Peasant: Rebellion and Subsistence in Southeast Asia*. New Haven: Yale University Press.

Slocomb, M (2010). *An Economic History of Cambodia in the Twentieth Century*. Singapore: NUS Press.

Stuart-Fox, M. (1997). *A History of Laos*. Cambridge: Cambridge University Press.

Thompson, V. (1968*). French Indo-China*. New York: Octagon Books Inc. (Reprint).

Touzet, A. (1935). *Fédéralisme Financier et Finances Indochinoises*. Paris: Librairie du Recueil Sirey.

Van Waijenburg, M. (2018). Financing the African Colonial State: The Revenue Imperative and Forced Labour. *The Journal of Economic History*, 18(1), 40–80.

Wiegersma, N. (1988). *Vietnam: Peasant Land, Peasant Revolution: Patriarchy and Collectivity in the Rural Economy*. Basingstoke: Macmillan Press

White, C. P. (1981). *Agrarian Reform and National Liberation in the Vietnamese Revolution, 1920–1957*. PhD Thesis, Cornell University, Ithica, NY.

Yuon, H. (1982). The Peasantry of Kampuchea: Colonialism and Modernization. In B. Kiernan & C. Boua (Eds.), *Peasants and Politics in Kampuchea 1942–1981*. London: Zed Press, 34–68.

5   Fiscal Development in Taiwan, Korea and Manchuria: Was Japanese Colonialism Different?

Anne Booth and Kent Deng

Historiography of Japanese Colonial Policies

This chapter examines government policies in the three principal Japanese colonies in the five decades up to 1945.[1] We examine the extent to which the Japanese colonial governments in Taiwan, Korea and Manchuria succeeded in centralizing tax and other revenues, in leveraging these revenues in order to borrow, in establishing accountable government fiscal systems and in using revenues from taxes, non-tax sources and from loans to fund not just administration and policing but also expenditures on capital works. In examining the development of fiscal capacity in the Japanese colonies, we have to bear in mind the important body of literature which has developed over the past five decades, and which argues that Japanese colonial policies were very different from those of the European powers, or the USA. Especially influential have been the writings of a group of American scholars, some based at Stanford University, who contributed to several edited volumes and also authored a number of journal articles examining the economic consequences of Japanese colonialism in Taiwan, Korea and Manchuria, as well as examining Japan's informal empire in Asia. These writers were not, for the most part, Japanese, although the majority had a deep knowledge of Japanese language as well as Western sources. They stressed the more positive aspects of the Japanese legacy, including the agricultural transformation, and especially the successful transfer of higher-yielding rice varieties, as well as the development of irrigation, industry and transport infrastructure. They also discussed the Japanese emphasis on expanding access to education.

In making these arguments about the developmental nature of Japanese colonialism, Peattie (1984, 23) emphasized the importance of the Meiji

---

[1] The chapter draws on Booth and Deng (2017).

137

experience in domestic reform in shaping Japan's subsequent colonial policies. Japan's per capita GDP was still quite low in the late 1890s, when it established control over the island of Taiwan, and in the early twentieth century, the economic gap between Japan and its colonies was narrower than that between the European powers and their Asian colonies, or between the USA and the Philippines. This had both positive and negative consequences for the Japanese colonies. On the one hand, several administrators who had been involved in formulating and implementing policy reforms in Meiji Japan were also crucial in shaping Japanese policy in both Taiwan and Korea after they became part of the Japanese empire. These men could draw on Japan's recent experience of economic modernization. But on the other hand, the Japanese also tended to view their newly acquired colonies as assets to be exploited in their race to catch up with the top industrial nations.

Those writers who stress Japanese exceptionalism claim that the Japanese colonial legacy was more positive, progressive and beneficial than that of the European powers, and indeed was an important reason for the stellar economic performance of both Taiwan and the Republic of Korea after 1945. A common assumption seems to be that British, Dutch, French and American colonial regimes in Asia were fiscally weak, did not promote economic growth and structural diversification, left behind institutions which were extractive rather than inclusive and did very little to improve living standards of the populations in their colonies. This chapter challenges these views by examining the evidence on the achievements of Japanese colonial policies in a comparative perspective, with particular emphasis on fiscal policies. But before examining government policies in detail, it is important to look at the evidence on growth and economic diversification in various Asian colonies in the decades from 1900 to 1940.

Growth and Structural Change in Asia: 1900–40

In 1913, the estimates given by the Maddison Project show that per capita GDP in colonial Asia (in 1990 international dollars) varied from $673 in India to $988 in the Philippines, and $1,367 in Singapore.[2] There was considerable variation in growth rates between 1913 and 1941. In per capita terms, growth was positive between 1913 and 1929 in most parts of colonial Asia, with Taiwan having the fastest growth and India the slowest. Korean growth until 1929 was no faster than in the Philippines, and

---

[2] These figures are taken from the revised figures given in the Maddison Project website; see www.ggdc.net/maddison/maddison-project/home.htm, 2013 version. Singapore did not exist as a separate entity before 1942; it was part of the larger territory known as the Straits Settlements, which, in turn, was one component in British Malaya.

Table 5.1 *Growth in per capita GDP in selected Asian colonies, 1902–40 (1929 = 100)*

Country	1902	1913	1929	1934	1940*	1940**
Korea	n.a.	77	100	112	145	893
Taiwan	54	65	100	101	100	1,250
Manchuria	n.a.	90***	100	81	121	n.a.
Philippines	47	74	100	95	106	1,507
Indonesia	64	80	100	86	104	1,127
India	90	92	100	96	94	686
Burma ****	77	68	100	93	82	740
Thailand	93	106	100	n.a.	104	826
Singapore	58	59	100	81	102	2,379

Sources: Korea: Kim et al (2008, 406–11); Taiwan: Sato et al (2008, 231–3); Manchuria: Chao (1983, table A-3); Philippines : Hooley (2005, table A.1); Indonesia: van der Eng (2013); India: Sivasubramonian (2002, 136); Burma: Aye Hlaing (1965, 289); Thailand: Sompop (1989, 251); Singapore: Sugimoto (2011, 49, 185); population data for the Philippines from Bureau of Census and Statistics (1941, 13).

Notes: * 1939 for Singapore; ** Per capita GDP figures in 1990 international dollars; 1938 for Thailand, 1939 for Singapore. Korea refers to South Korea only; *** 1924; **** Figures refer to 1901–2, 1911–12, 1931–32, 1936–7 and 1938–9.

not much different from Burma or Indonesia (Table 5.1). After 1929, there was a more obvious divergence between Korea and Manchuria compared with other parts of colonial Asia. All the European colonies in Asia, and in the Philippines, experienced a fall in per capita GDP between 1929 and 1934, although there was some recovery in Indonesia and the Philippines after 1934. Taiwan experienced little growth in per capita terms over the 1930s.

Manchuria, which had become the state of Manchukuo in 1932, under strict Japanese control, suffered a severe economic downturn in 1934. This was in part the result of the change of regime, although Chao (1979, 257) argued that the main reason for the poor performance was that Manchuria had fallen into a staple trap when the world market for its main export crop, soybeans, collapsed after 1930.[3] Both production and exports fell sharply.[4] The Japanese response was to implement a policy of economic diversification into mining and industry. This was also their strategy in both Korea

[3] Bix (1971, 178) argued that the reliance on one staple crop was an important reason for the widespread poverty in Manchuria even before prices fell in the 1930s.

[4] An analysis of the impact of the creation of Manchukuo on agricultural output is given by Sun (1969, 57ff). He argues that, after adjustments to the official data, the production of the main agricultural crops never regained the level of the late 1920s.

and Taiwan. The result was accelerated economic growth after 1934, especially in Korea, but also in Manchuria. In Taiwan, per capita GDP reached a peak in 1938. But after that there was a decline, and by 1940, per capita GDP was about the same as the 1929 estimate. In British India, per capita GDP in 1940 was still below the 1929 level, although in both Indonesia and the Philippines the estimates for 1940 were above those for 1929. Perhaps the most surprising result of all was from independent Thailand, where there was virtually no growth in per capita terms between 1913 and 1938.[5]

What explains the better growth performance in the Japanese colonies, especially in Korea and Manchuria, over the 1930s? The main reason was that their trade and investment flows were tightly linked to the Japanese economy which experienced faster growth over the 1930s, compared with the major economies in West Europe and America. Even before its formal annexation as a colony, Korea was conducting a very high percentage of its trade with Japan; by the late 1930s, both Korea and Taiwan were sourcing almost 90 per cent of their imports from Japan. The two colonies traded more intensively with the metropolitan power than any colony in Southeast Asia (Booth 2007, 91). Over the 1930s, the Japanese colonies, including Manchuria, continued to invest in both infrastructure (especially transport) and in directly productive activities, including agriculture, mining and manufacturing. By 1938, gross domestic capital formation in Manchuria was 23.5 per cent of GDP, although the proportion was lower in Taiwan and Korea.[6] In all parts of the Japanese empire, government played a key role in promoting investment in both infrastructure and in productive activities, offering considerable subsidies to the private sector. Comparative data show that length of road and railways in relation to area were higher in Taiwan and Korea than in any of the Southeast Asian colonies except Java (Booth 2007, 80).

While Dutch, French, British and American colonial administrations were all aware of the importance of investment in infrastructure, government investment was constrained by conservative fiscal policies, especially after 1930. Over the 1930s, the world slump had an adverse impact on export revenues, which, in turn, affected government revenues. In Indonesia, government spending on public works, including irrigation, harbour works, transport and railways, reached a peak in real terms in 1921, and fell thereafter. In the 1930s, spending on new projects was negligible (de Jong and Ravesteijn 2008, 66). But in spite of these cutbacks, in 1938, road and rail

---

[5] For a detailed discussion of growth in Thailand from 1870 to 1950, see Sompop (1989), and Booth (2016).

[6] The Manchurian figure is taken from Chao (1979, 258–61). Those from Taiwan and Korea are taken from Mizoguchi and Umemura (1988, 226–38).

Table 5.2 *Proportion of GDP from agriculture in selected colonies,*
1913–41

Country	1913	1924	1929	1934	1938–41*
Korea	66.9	56.9	52.3	49.7	36
Taiwan	45.2	47.2	42.2	45.6	39.1
Manchuria**	n.a.	49.7	50.7	36.2 (52.7)	33.9 (31.3)
Philippines	38.5	37.8	39.1	40.8	37.3
Indonesia	38.3	36.6	32.5	34.3	32.4
India	60	59.9	56.1	54.7	50.3
Burma***	68.6	55.6	55.6	59.9	54.3
Thailand	44.6	n.a.	43.8	n.a.	44.3

Sources: Korea: Kim et al (2008, 406–9); Taiwan: Sato et al (2008, 233 & 326);
Manchuria: Chao (1983, 16); Philippines: Hooley (2005, table A.1); population
data from Bureau of Census and Statistics (1941, 13). Indonesia: van der Eng
(2013); India: Sivasubramonian (2002, 136); Burma: Saito and Lee (1999, 7,
214); Thailand: Sompop (1989, 251).
Notes: * 1938 data for Thailand; 1940 data for Korea and the Philippines; 1941 for all
others except Burma; ** Figures in brackets are estimated from Yamanata et al
(2008); *** Burma percentages refer to 1911–12, 1921–2, 1926–7, 1931–2, 1938–9.

endowments in Java compared favourably with those in Taiwan and Korea,
although outside Java there was much less development. In Manchuria,
a rail system had been developed by the Russians, and was taken over by
the Japanese early in the twentieth century after the 1904–5 Russo–Japanese
War. The Japanese also developed the road system, although by the late
1930s the road density (36 kilometres per thousand square kilometres) was
about the same as in Indochina, and less than in Burma or the Philippines.
Investment in electricity generation in Southeast Asia was left to the private
sector, and, with the exception of British Malaya, installed capacity was
much lower in the Southeast Asian colonies than in Taiwan and Korea
(Booth 2007, 80). In the Japanese colonies, links between the government
and private investors were much tighter, to the extent that it was often
difficult to disentangle public and private initiatives.

As would be expected, the economic growth which occurred across
most of colonial Asia after 1900 led to some structural change in the
composition of both output and employment. The share of agriculture
fell as a percentage of total output, and that of industry (mining, manufacturing, construction and utilities) increased. The sharpest fall in the
share of agriculture occurred in Korea and Manchuria, while in the
Philippines and Thailand there was little change (Table 5.2). The decline

Table 5.3 *Proportion of GDP from industry* in selected colonies, 1913–41*

Country	1913	1924	1929	1934	1938–41**
Korea	6.4	10.4	12.3	15.6	27.9
Taiwan	12.1	15.7	21.3	20.6	23.7
Manchuria***	n.a.	14.7	12.9	19.8 (9.5)	20.3 (19.5)
Philippines	16.1	18.8	18.5	23.8	19.6
Indonesia	16.1	14.3	15.6	13.1	17.6
India	12.3	11.5	13.5	14.6	13.7
Thailand	17.1	n.a.	17.1	n.a.	17.3

Sources: Korea: Kim et al. (2008. 406–9); Taiwan: Sato et al. (2008, 233, 326); Manchuria: Chao (1983, 16); Philippines : Hooley (2005, table A.1); Indonesia: van der Eng (2013); India: Sivasubramonian (2002, 136); Thailand: Sompop (1989, 251).
Notes: * Mining, manufacturing, construction and utilities; ** 1938 data for Thailand; 1940 data for Korea and the Philippines; 1941 for all other countries; *** Figures in brackets from Yamanata et al (2008).

in the share of agriculture in the Japanese colonies was accompanied by an increase in the share of the industrial sector; by 1938, industry accounted for around 28 per cent of total GDP in Korea, 24 per cent in Taiwan and 20 per cent in Manchuria (Table 5.3). Industry accounted for around 20 per cent of total GDP in the Philippines, but a lower proportion in Indonesia, India and Thailand. The implications of these outcomes for revenue and expenditure policies will now be examined.

Government Revenue Policies in the Japanese Colonies

By the first decade of the twentieth century, all the colonial powers in East and South East Asia, were trying to establish effective administrative structures which prioritized the centralization and reform of fiscal systems. But there were considerable differences in outcomes of revenue policies in different parts of colonial Asia. In 1910, government revenues per capita varied between around one dollar per capita in Vietnam to 15 dollars in the Federated Malay States (FMS) (Table 5.4).[7] Although several of the colonies with low revenues per capita in 1910 improved their revenue performance over the next two decades, none caught up

[7] The very low figure for Vietnam could be partly the result of the exclusion of village-level imposts. See Chapter 4 for an examination of this point.

Table 5.4 *Government revenues per capita in South East Asia, Taiwan and Korea, 1910–38 (US$)*

Country	1910	1920	1929	1934	1938
Vietnam[a]	1	3	3	3	2
Netherlands Indies	2	5	5	4	4
Philippines	3	6	6	4	5
Thailand	3	3	4	3	4
Burma	3	5	6	6	4
UMS[b]	4	6	11	10	10
Straits Settlements	8	21	29	17	16
FMS	15	24	28	19	18
Taiwan	8	16	15	8	12
Korea	1	4	6	4	7

Sources: Vietnam: Bassino (2000): Netherlands Indies: Creutzberg (1976, table 4), population from van der Eng (2013); Philippines: Bureau of Census and Statistics (1941) and Birnberg and Resnick (1975, table A.38); Thailand: Ingram (1971 appendices B and C); Burma: Shein, Thant and Sein (1969, appendix II); Office of the Prime Minister (1958); Andrus (1948, tables 37 and 38); British Malaya (FMS, UMS and Straits Settlements): Emerson (1937, chapters 4, 5 and 6), with additional data from Lim (1967, appendix 9.2); Fraser (1939, appendix A) for the Federated Malay States; German (1936); Taiwan and Korea: Mizoguchi and Umemura (1988, 256, 288–93). Exchange rates: van Laanen (1980, table 8); Direction des Services Economiques (1947, 288); Ingram (1971); Emerson (1937, 522).

Notes: UMS refers to Unfederated Malay States, FMS to Federated Malay States (including Selangor, Perak, Negeri Sembilan and Pahang); a. Data refer to 1913, not 1910. Local and (after 1931) provincial revenues and expenditures are included; b. Data for the UMS refer to 1911 and 1921, not 1910 and 1920.

with either the FMS or the Straits Settlements. By 1929, government revenues in Taiwan were lower than in the FMS and the Straits Settlements, but higher than elsewhere (Table 5.4). Government revenues in Korea, along with Indonesia, the Philippines and Burma, were around five to six dollars per capita, more than in Thailand and Vietnam but still well below Taiwan, the Federated Malay States and the Straits Settlements. With the onset of the world depression, revenues fell in terms of dollars per capita in most colonies, and had not recovered to 1929 levels by 1938. Taiwan had higher government revenues per capita than both Korea and Manchuria through the 1930s; in 1932 government revenues per capita in Manchuria were very low, although they increased rapidly, and were almost as high as in Korea by 1938 (Table 5.5).

Table 5.5 *Revenues per capita in Japanese colonies,*
1925–38 (Yen)

Year	Taiwan	Korea	Kwantung*	SMR zone	Manchuria
1925	29	10	12	14	
1929	34	12	11	14	
1932	25	11			4
1934	28	14			9
1936	33	17			9
1938	42	25			21

Sources: Mizoguchi and Umemura (1988, 256, 291–3). Population figures
from Mizoguchi and Umemura (1988, 313–14).
Note: * Kwantung leased territory; SMR zone refers to land along the
South Manchurian Railway.

These differences in revenue performance can be explained partly by
differences in taxable capacity, as proxied by per capita GDP. The Straits
Settlements and the FMS had the highest per capita GDP in Southeast
Asia, and per capita GDP in Taiwan was higher than in Korea. But the
tax/GDE ratio (GDE = gross domestic expenditures) was higher in
Taiwan than Korea in the decades from 1911 to 1938, which suggests
that the Japanese government in Taiwan was better able to assess and
collect revenues. By the 1930s, the tax/GDE ratio in Taiwan was almost
the same as in Japan (Kimura 1989, table 4). In addition, there was
a reluctance on the part of several colonial regimes in Asia, including
the Japanese, to increase taxes on the indigenous populations too rapidly
for fear of provoking unrest. In both Taiwan and Korea, land taxes
accounted for a high share of total government revenues in the early
twentieth century, but fell in relative importance as the tax systems
became more diversified. Import duties also fell in both colonies, as
trade barriers were eliminated between Japan and her colonial possessions (Grajdanzev 1942, 134, Kimura 1989, 298). By 1940, income and
profits taxes accounted for 22 per cent of total tax revenues in Korea, and
a similar proportion in Taiwan (Grajdanzev 1942, 134, Grajdanzev
1944, 214).

But in spite of these changes, several analysts have argued that the
revenue regimes in both Taiwan and Korea were regressive, with a high
burden falling on the indigenous populations. Grajdanzev (1942, 134–5)
argued that 80 to 90 per cent of all taxes in Taiwan fell on the mass of the
population and only 10–20 per cent on the relatively wealthy, many of
whom were Japanese. He claimed that between 1935 and 1939, the

proportion of government revenues contributed by the well-to-do did rise, but was still only 22 per cent by 1939. He included among taxes on the well-to-do income and mining taxes and special profit and inheritance taxes; most of these were only introduced in the 1930s. Among those taxes which fell on the rest of the population he included land taxes, excises on sugar and alcohol and revenues from government monopolies. He also pointed out that the burden on the masses would be greater if provincial and local taxes were included.

In Korea, there is also a consensus that revenue policy was regressive. Kimura (1989, 301–4) argued that by the 1930s, wealthier people, whether Japanese or Korean, escaped quite lightly. In spite of the fact that land taxes fell as a proportion of total revenues after 1911, and a more progressive income tax was introduced in the 1930s, he found that only in 1938 did the average rate of tax on earnings in the non-agricultural sector catch up with that in the agricultural sector. Grajdanzev (1944, 215) also found that 'those who drew large incomes were treated with greater consideration than the poorer sections of the population'. Chung (2006, 158–9) argued that the burden of taxation rested more heavily on the Korean masses, many of whom were in agriculture, than on the indigenous middle and upper classes and on the Japanese. He argued that although land taxes fell as a proportion of total government revenues after 1920, more of the incidence fell on tenants rather than landlords. Korean consumers were also hit with new consumption taxes after 1920, including excises on liquor, sugar, soy products and textiles. In addition, the monopolies on tobacco, salt and ginseng accounted for a growing share of government revenues; by 1940, net revenues from monopolies were about the same as revenues from taxes on income and profits. A high proportion of these products were consumed by the poor, so the monopolies would have been regressive in their impact.

Government revenue policy in Manchuria after 1932 was initially concerned with unifying all tax collection organs under the control of the central government, and removing inequities between regions (Kanai 1936, 26, Myers 1982, 227–8). After 1932, revenues grew rapidly both in per capita terms and relative to GDP. Official policy was, in its initial phase, not to introduce any new taxes, and to avoid deficits which would necessitate government borrowing. Only after 1937 were state bonds introduced as a means of finance. Budget revenues and expenditures were divided into a general account and a special account; the latter grew in importance after 1937. General account revenues were dominated by revenues from taxation, of which import and export duties and tobacco and alcohol excises were the most important, together with revenues from monopoly profits. Land taxes were assessed but were a small share of total tax revenues; an income tax was introduced in 1938, but revenues were miniscule. The most important monopolies were those on salt, opium and oil. Overall, the tax system was probably regressive in its incidence. Special account revenues included loans and further incomes from government monopolies and investments (Manchoukuo Year Book 1941, 201–5).

Government Expenditure Policies in the Japanese Colonies

On the expenditure side, the Japanese colonial governments in both Taiwan and Korea assumed responsibility for a much broader range of activities than simply the maintenance of law and order and the collection of revenues. Kohli (2004, 40) describes the colonial state in Korea as a 'busy state' which became increasingly involved in many developmental activities, although expenditures per capita in Korea were not very different from those in most colonies in Southeast Asia (Table 5.6). In Taiwan, expenditures per capita were higher than in Korea, although not higher than in the Straits Settlements or the Federated Malay States. Kimura's estimates show that government expenditures were a higher proportion of GDE in Taiwan than in Korea until the end of the 1920s, but fell behind Korea in the 1930s (Kimura 1989, table 3). After 1930, Korean expenditures on economic services (mainly transport infrastructure, irrigation and agricultural research), as a proportion of GDE, were slightly higher than in Taiwan. Expenditures per capita in Manchuria increased after 1932 and by 1938 were almost as high as in Korea (Table 5.7).

A theme in much of the literature on Japanese colonialism is that budgetary expenditures were devoted to capital works, and to encouraging local industry, often through direct subsidies. In fact, the evidence is mixed. The functional distribution of government expenditures in Taiwan prepared by Ho (1978, 34) shows that fixed capital formation accounted for over half of total government expenditures in 1900, but fell rapidly after that. In 1930, around 27 per cent of government expenditure went on capital works, and a further 6 per cent on transfers to 'domestic sectors' (presumably subsidies to private enterprise). Both these percentages dropped after 1930.[8] By the mid 1930s, the share of budgetary expenditures going to public works and agricultural development was 28 per cent in Taiwan and 31 per cent in

---

[8] The series on the composition of government consumption expenditures (GCE) given in Sato et al. (2008, 340–1) shows that industrial subsidies peaked at 41 per cent of GCE in 1911, but had fallen to under 10 per cent in the 1920s. They rose again in the latter part of the 1930s.

Table 5.6 *Government expenditures per capita in South East Asia, Taiwan and Korea, 1910–38 (US$)*

Country	1910	1920	1929	1934	1938
Vietnam[a]	1	3	3	3	2
Netherlands Indies	2	7	5	5	4
Philippines	3	6	5	4	6
Thailand	3	6	5	4	6
Burma	2	4	4	3	3
UMS[b]	n.a.	8	11	7	10
Straits Settlements	6	20	19	15	18
FMS	13	33	29	15	28
Taiwan	6	13	12	6	9
Korea	1	4	6	4	7

Sources: As for Table 5.4.
Notes: a. Data refer to 1913, not 1910. Local and (after 1931) provincial revenues and expenditures are included; b. Data refer to 1911 and 1921, not 1910 and 1920.

Table 5.7 *Expenditures per capita in Japanese colonies, 1925–38 (Yen)*

Year	Taiwan	Korea	Kwantung[*]	SMR[*]	Manchuria
1925	22	9	7	14	
1929	27	11	7	14	
1932	20	10			4
1934	22	12			9
1936	25	15			9
1938	33	22			21

Sources: Mizoguchi and Umemura (1988, 256, 291–3). Expenditure figures from Kwantung and the SMR Zone from MYB (1933, 96–8). Population figures for Kwantung and the SMR Zone from Mizoguchi and Umemura (1988, 313–14).
Note: * Kwantung leased territory; SMR zone refers to land along the South Manchurian Railway.

Korea (Table 5.8). These were higher shares than in most Southeast Asian colonies except French Indochina and the Federated Malay States. The proportion going on public works in Manchuria was much lower, and the proportion on policing and defence much higher, although about the same

Table 5.8 *Percentage of budgetary outlays on law/police/defence, public works/ agriculture and education/health, 1930s*

Country (Year)	Law/Police/Defence	Public Works/ Agriculture	Education/Health
Japanese Colonies			
Manchuria (1934)	32	5*	3**
Korea (1936)	11	31	7
Taiwan (1935)	7	28	8
Southeast Asia			
Indonesia (1931)	32	7	12
Thailand (1931)	31	15	8
French Indochina (1931)	14	36	4
FMS (1931)	8	28	20
Philippines (1931)	8	18	36

Sources: Korea: Grajdanzev (1942, 218); Taiwan: Grajdanzev (1944, 137); Manchuria (MYB 1941, 203–4); Others: Schwulst (1931, 57).
Notes: * Expenditures on industry and communications; ** Expenditures on education only.

as in Indonesia and Thailand. Most of the rest of the general account budget in Manchuria was devoted to administrative expenditures; expenditures on infrastructure were taken from the special account and from other sources. Myers (1982, 240) argued that dependence on the special account to finance development expenditures continued throughout the period of Japanese control of Manchuria, but, after 1938, reliance on debt to fund special account expenditures grew.

Perhaps surprisingly, given the frequent claim that educational development was given high priority in the Japanese colonies, the proportion of budgetary expenditures devoted to health and education was considerably lower in all three Japanese colonies than in the Philippines, Indonesia or the Federated Malay States, although higher than in French Indochina (Table 5.8).[9] To some extent, these figures are misleading in that they do not take into account expenditures by local governments on health and education in Taiwan and Korea, or in some of the Southeast Asian colonies. Grajdanzev (1942, 140) argued that expenditures on health and education were modest in Taiwan, and fell as a percentage of the

---

[9] See Kobayashi (1996, 325) and Cumings (1999, 89). In Manchuria, Kanai (1936, 66) reported that by 1935 there were 770,000 children enrolled in primary schools, which was no doubt an increase over the pre-1930 figure but still low, relative to total population, compared with most other Asian colonies, although numbers did increase after 1935. Very few children were enrolled in middle schools, or in vocational schools.

total after 1935.[10] But he did point out that in 1939, local government spending on health and education was higher than that by the central government. The Japanese were quite successful in increasing school attendance in Taiwan at the primary level; by 1940, close to 60 per cent of school-age children attended primary school. But for the great majority of children in Taiwan, their education ceased after the primary cycle. Ten middle schools were located in the main towns; they were open to most Japanese but only carefully selected Taiwanese could attend (Kerr 1942, 53, Barclay 1954, 68). At the tertiary level, there were very few opportunities in Taiwan, although a small number went to mainland Japan. This contrasts with the situation in the Philippines where quite large numbers of young people were progressing through the school system and into tertiary education by the 1930s (Booth 2012a).

Budget Surpluses and Colonial Drains in Japanese Colonies

It has frequently been argued by critics of European colonialism, in both Asia and Africa, that policies were extractive, in the sense that more resources were taken out of colonial economies than were put in. Such critics have often based their arguments on balance of payments data.[11] If current accounts were in surplus, and the surplus was used to finance outward flows of capital on either government or private account, this was often interpreted as evidence of colonial exploitation. To what extent was there evidence of net outward flows of capital in the Japanese colonies? And to the extent that such outward flows did exist, were they the result of fiscal surpluses, or private sector outflows? In the early years of the Japanese occupation of Taiwan, the balance of payments was in deficit, which was funded by Japanese government transfers to the new colony (Grajdanzev 1942, 156–7, Mizoguchi & Yamamoto 1984, 407–11). But after 1909, the Taiwanese balance of payments became positive, and remained so for most years until the end of the 1930s. The surpluses were used to finance remittances on both government and private account to Japan. As Grajdanzev (1942, 158–9) has argued, these remittances represented interest and profits on the capital invested by the

---

[10] The series published in Sato et al. (2008, 340) shows that in most years from 1901 to 1938, the percentage of GCE devoted to education and public welfare was higher than that spent on law enforcement and public welfare, with the exception of 1910–14 and 1937–8.

[11] A review of the literature on, and statistical evidence for, both budget and balance of payments surpluses in Asia is given in Booth (2007, 85–87, 105–11). The key conclusion is that the evidence was very mixed, both across colonies, and over time within colonies.

Japanese in Taiwan. He claimed that by the 1930s, outward profits amounted to more than 100 million yen per year.

Did this represent a fair return on capital invested? Grajdanzev argued that the amounts remitted to Japan were rather more than a legitimate return on Japanese managerial and entrepreneurial ability, and reflected the protection from both local and foreign competition which was granted to Japanese companies in the colony. He concluded that the Taiwanese economy supported almost 300,000 Japanese at a much higher standard of living than they would have achieved at home. By 1935, Japanese comprised 5.7 per cent of the population in Taiwan, which was a much higher percentage than in any other Asian colony (Booth 2007, table 2.2).[12] Indigenous workers comprised around half of all workers in government and the professions in Taiwan, which was a much lower percentage than in most colonies in Southeast Asia, with the exception of British Malaya (Booth 2007, table 6.4). In many cases, locals could probably have done the jobs taken by Japanese, at lower remuneration.

In sharp contrast to Taiwan, the balance of payments in Korea was persistently in deficit for much of the period from 1910 onwards (Mizoguchi & Yamamoto 1984, 411). This was the result of the long-term government subsidy and private capital flows from Japan; Mizoguchi and Yamamoto estimate that these flows were large enough to cover government spending on capital formation for most years until 1935. They argued that these flows reflected the inability of the colonial government to mobilize funds from within the colony, rather than a lack of profits on the part of private investors. Kimura (1989, 305) while agreeing that there was a net inflow of funds into Korea from Japan, argued that the 'balance sheet was very different from industry to industry'. He stressed that the Japanese residents in Korea, who comprised almost three per cent of the population in 1939, secured considerable economic advantages, as did those Koreans who co-operated with them.

In Manchuria, as in Korea, imports exceeded exports over the 1930s, a tendency which was expected to persist for many years to come (MYB 1941, 311). Increasingly, imports of machinery and implements became more important than consumption goods such as cotton piece goods. Exports were mainly agricultural commodities, especially soybean, together with iron ore, sulphate of ammonia and hides. Critics have claimed that the terms of trade favoured Japanese enterprises. The price level of exports from Japan to Manchuria increased by up to 30 per cent

---

[12] Japanese comprised 3.8 per cent of the population in Korea and 1.6 per cent in Manchuria. In Java, Europeans accounted for 0.5 per cent of the population in 1930; in other colonies in Asia it was lower.

while the prices of exports to Japan declined (Xie 2007, 548). In the process, Japanese firms often earned high profits, especially in the mining sector (Li et al. 2009, 359). Wu (1955, 93) argued that large sums, worth over a third of Japan's total investment in Manchuria, were remitted back to Japan from 1932 to 1944.

In spite of the evidence that some Japanese investments in their colonies were very profitable, by the 1930s, both foreign scholars and Japanese business groups were voicing doubts about the net benefits of the colonies to the Japanese economy. An American study of the Japanese economy claimed that, at the end of the 1920s, from a fiscal point of view, 'the colonies as a whole have thus far clearly been a liability rather than an asset' (Moulton 1931, 180). In the early part of the 1930s, the private sector in Japan looked to the colonies, especially Manchuria, as providing relief from slowing growth at home (Young 1998, 201). In addition, the need for new markets for consumer goods exports became more pressing as access to markets in South and Southeast Asia and Africa was curtailed by the protectionist policies of Britain, France, the Netherlands and the USA. But demand in Korea and Manchuria was for producer goods; local populations were too poor to provide a large market for consumer products. Even the growing demand for capital goods was not viewed as an unmitigated blessing to Japan. Young (1998, 234) quoted a speech by the president of Mitsubishi Heavy Industries in 1940, pointing out that the diversion of plant and equipment to Manchuria was causing shortages at home. Bankers also complained at what were seen as excessive demands for loans in Manchuria which was causing problems in the Japanese financial market.

The Development of the Financial Sector in the Japanese Colonies

The development of a modern banking system and financial markets proceeded rather differently across the Japanese empire, reflecting the differences in flows of investment funds. Mizoguchi and Yamamoto (1984, 408–11) pointed out that the Bank of Taiwan, which had some of the functions of a central bank, loaned surplus funds back to Japanese firms, while at the same time the government held all its reserve funds in Japan. These flows must have retarded the development of the banking and financial sectors in Taiwan. Grajdanzev (1942, 128–30) argued that there was a rapid growth in deposits in local financial institutions from 1926 through to 1939, and the share taken by the post office and credit co-operatives grew relative to banks. As banks were mainly used by Japanese, while Taiwanese used credit co-operatives, this might suggest a growing propensity to save among the latter, although Grajdanzev did not think that this necessarily reflected growing prosperity among the Taiwanese, but rather a change in savings habits. He also argued that Taiwanese farmers and businesses were unable to access bank loans, and had to rely on other institutions which charged much higher interest rates.

In Korea, it appears that the establishment of Japanese rule led to a rapid expansion of bank credit after 1910, mainly through banks and credit co-operatives (Kimura 1986, 804–6). The Bank of Chosen was a private bank which performed the functions of a central bank while also lending to private firms. This bank and most of the other banks were in Japanese hands and mainly lent to Japanese companies. Kimura (1986, table 3) showed that the bank deposits and bank credit to Koreans did rise after 1915, but were smaller in absolute terms than the deposits made by, and credit granted to, Japanese in spite of the huge imbalance in numbers. Over the 1930s, loans made by credit co-operatives doubled and most of these were to indigenous Koreans, mainly in agriculture. But Grajdanzev (1944, 209) argued that much of the credit was used to finance consumption needs; only 23 per cent were for productive purposes. In Manchuria, Myers (1982, 250) argued that the Japanese faced considerable problems in establishing long-term capital markets, given the lack of a domestic entrepreneurial class, the dispersed indigenous population and their relative poverty. A central bank was established after 1932, together with an industrial bank. They dealt mainly with Japanese clients, and, after 1937, purchased a growing share of government debt.

In Korea, some studies pointed to the growing imbalance between government revenues and expenditures, especially after 1920. Between 1920 and 1939, revenues increased almost six-fold while expenditures increased more than seven-fold. It was argued that the growth in expenditures was mainly due to increases in the military budget together with grants from the Japanese to the Korean government which were used to fund subsidies to Japanese companies (Grajdanzev 1944, 210–11). The deficits were funded by borrowings, and debt service charges accounted for almost 20 per cent of total government expenditures in 1936, although the percentage fell thereafter. It seems that the loans were raised in Japan, although the Japanese-owned financial institutions in Korea may also have held government bonds.

In Manchuria, budgets were always in balance, in the sense that revenues from all sources equalled or exceeded expenditures. But as expenditures grew after 1937, debt issue grew; in the years from 1938 to 1940 debt issue covered 30 to 40 per cent of total government expenditures, although the proportion dropped in 1941 (Myers 1982, 247–8). By 1941, the cumulative total of debt issued since 1932 stood at slightly more than two billion yuan, or around 500 million dollars at the prevailing exchange rate (Myers 1982, 249). This growth in debt alarmed some Japanese bankers, who thought that the borrowings in Manchuria were causing problems in Japanese markets. In fact, after 1936, more than half the debt was held in Manchuria, mainly by the Central Bank and the Industrial Bank for Development. The indigenous commercial classes were too small to absorb much of the debt. In dollar terms, the total debt stock amounted to under 12 dollars per capita at the end of 1941, which was not a large amount by Asian standards. According to Myers, debt issue, together with surpluses generated by state enterprises, continued to fund much of the special budget to 1945.

Developments after 1945

In August 1945, Japanese colonial control of Taiwan, Korea and Manchuria came to an abrupt end with Japan's defeat. But the departure of the colonial power ushered in a period of instability in all three territories. A decision to divide the Korean peninsula was taken at the Yalta Conference of 1945; the south was occupied by American troops and the north by those of Soviet Russia. The termination of Japanese rule 'created extreme disorganization in every aspect of Korean society' (Kim & Roemer 1979, 25). The departure of most Japanese managers and technicians led to a fall in manufacturing output; many plants had to suspend production completely. The outbreak of open war between the north and the south led to the fall of Seoul and the arrival of United Nations troops, mainly from the USA. By the time a truce was signed in July 1953, it was estimated that between three and four million Koreans had perished, and there was substantial destruction of infrastructure and productive capacity. The two countries which emerged after the truce were both dependent on aid for reconstruction and development; in the south from the USA and in the north from the Soviet Union. It is probable that output from the two parts of the divided peninsula remained below 1940 levels until well into the 1950s.

Manchuria also faced massive problems in 1945. The Japanese government had ambitious plans for the further development of Manchuria's industrial capacity after 1942, when the second five-year plan was initiated.[13] Output of steel, pig iron and iron ore was to be nearly doubled by 1946. Further development of hydro electricity, coal and shale oil was also planned. Had these targets been achieved, Manchuria would have had a more developed industrial sector than any other part of Asia, with the

---

[13] On Japanese plans for the further growth of the modern factory sector, see Myers (1982, 142), Chao (1983, 32) and Sun (1969, 79–80).

exception of Japan itself. But the Soviet Army's invasion of Manchuria in 1945 led to considerable looting of both crops and industrial equipment, and massive falls in industrial output, from which the economy was slow to recover. Sun (1969, 88) quotes an American estimate which valued the loss of industrial assets at almost a billion dollars. This was confirmed by other estimates, by both Chinese and Western economists. The further development of Manchuria's fuel and mineral resources by the government in Beijing only began again in the latter part of the 1950s.

In Taiwan, the decision to hand the island back to the control of the mainland government was taken by the allied leaders during the war. There was no consultation with the population of Taiwan. After the Japanese surrender, the KMT government on the mainland installed General Chen Yi as High Commissioner. The result was three years of administrative misrule which severely hindered economic recovery (Kerr 1966, 97–142, Lin 1973, 27–33). There was substantial looting of Japanese assets by business people from the mainland. In addition, the arrival of thousands of poorly paid Chinese soldiers led to looting of property from indigenous Taiwanese. Food stockpiled by the Japanese was confiscated, and many Taiwanese farmers had to give rice and other produce to the government, leading to food shortages in what had been a food surplus island. Inflation accelerated and anger among many Taiwanese over conditions on the island led to an armed revolt in 1947, which was harshly suppressed.

The arrival of the KMT government in 1949 after its final defeat on the mainland finally led to economic recovery. Many skilled professionals, managers and technical workers came with the remnants of the KMT regime, and their expertise and capital began to revive manufacturing industry, utilities and parts of the service sector. In 1951, per capita GDE was only around 75 per cent of that in 1935, but the recovery after that was rapid and by 1960 output had surged past the peak level achieved in the Japanese period (Table 5.9). Substantial foreign aid, mainly from the USA, was used to repair infrastructure and boost productive capacity. Current government receipts as a proportion of gross domestic expenditures (GDE) exceeded the 1940 level in 1951, and grew further over the 1950s. While aid played an important role in increasing government receipts, tax revenues and revenues from state enterprises also increased. Gross domestic capital formation (GDCF) more than trebled in real terms between 1951 and 1960. By 1955, 46 per cent of GDCF came from government sources, although this percentage dropped in the latter part of the decade (Table 5.9). By 1960, the government had re-established fiscal and monetary control and Taiwan was ready to embark on a remarkable period of economic growth.

Table 5.9 *Government current revenues, government consumption expenditures and government gross domestic capital formation as a percentage of gross domestic expenditure (GDE), Taiwan, 1930–60*

Year	As percentage of Gross Domestic Expenditures			GDE per capita (1930 = 100)
	Current Revenues	Government Consumption	Government GDCF*	
1930	13.1	7.8	3.5 (31.2)	100
1935	14.9	6.4	3.1 (22.3)	110
1940	18.1	7.1	n.a	97
1951	21.1	17.6	4.8 (33.7)	82
1955	23.9	18.6	6.0 (45.9)	103
1960	23.1	19	7.8 (38.9)	119

Source: Sato et al. (2008), tables 2.1, 7.4, 7.6, 8.1, 8.2, 8.5.
Note: GDCF = Gross Domestic Capital Formation. Figures in brackets give the government share of total GDCF.

Conclusions

We return now to the question raised at the beginning of this chapter. To what extent did the Japanese manage to establish a modern fiscal state in their three colonies, replicating the achievements of the decades after the Meiji restoration? There can be no doubt that, in all three colonies, the Japanese managed to diversify government revenues by introducing new taxes and lucrative government monopolies and, especially in Korea and Manchuria, by increasing government borrowing. Several studies have argued that the tax systems were regressive, as they relied on consumption taxes which fell mainly on the lower income groups. But increased revenues did allow increased expenditures on the development of infrastructure and on social services, including health and education. By the late 1930s, Taiwan probably had one of the highest living standards in colonial Asia, only equalled by the Philippines and British Malaya (Booth 2012a). Although Korea was poorer, there was modest progress in at least some development indicators.

Over the 1930s, the development plans of the colonial governments in Taiwan, Korea and Manchuria were increasingly subordinated to the goals of the Japanese government which aimed to establish a powerful military-industrial complex across Northeast Asia, while turning Taiwan into a forward base for penetration into Southeast Asia. These policies produced the paradoxical result that while Taiwan resembled a 'typical'

colony in making substantial remittances to both the government and
private enterprises in the mother country, both Korea and Manchuria
experienced net inward flows of capital from Japan. It was true that
a considerable part of these flows were used to finance a large military
and police budget, and government subsidies to industrial ventures which
would probably not have been profitable without them. These policies led
to considerable criticism within Japan, but, by the late 1930s, the military
had the upper hand in the home government. The result was rapid
industrialization in both Korea and Manchuria, which continued until
the end of the Pacific War. In the longer run, many of the investments
made by Japanese companies in these colonies might have been profitable, had Japan not been defeated and deprived of its empire in 1945.

A complete assessment of the costs and benefits of the empire to Japan
has yet to be carried out. It is possible that such an assessment would
reach the same conclusion as that of Davis and Huttenback (1986) for the
British Empire. These authors concluded that the British economy as
a whole did not benefit from the empire, even if individual companies
did.[14] Those scholars who claim that Japanese colonial policies were more
developmental than those of the western powers in Asia argue that the
native populations in the Japanese empire benefited from improved infrastructure, accelerated agricultural development and increased provision
of credit, education and healthcare. Those who are sceptical about claims
of Japanese exceptionalism point out that these improvements also
occurred, to a greater or lesser extent, in other colonial empires. The
Japanese, like other colonial powers, actually did very little to encourage
indigenous Taiwanese, Koreans and Manchurians to participate in modern industry and commerce, either as entrepreneurs or employees.[15]

The conclusion must be that rapid economic modernization only
occurred after both western and Japanese colonialism was terminated in
Asia, from 1946 onwards. But because of the abrupt nature of the end of
Japanese colonial control, and the rivalries which emerged among the
various powers after 1945, all three colonies entered a period of political
instability and economic decline. Economic recovery was probably most
rapid in Taiwan. Certainly the island benefited from the influx of skilled
workers from the mainland after 1949, and from American assistance.
Government revenues and expenditures in real terms were above

[14] Kimura (1995) tried to establish who benefited from Japanese control of Korea in the
years from 1910 to 1939. He concludes that Japanese farmers were penalized by imports
of cheap rice, while Japanese workers benefited, but the total economic impact on the
Japanese economy was small. Non-economic motives dominated economic ones.
[15] Booth (2012b) and Booth and Deng (2017, 80–4) discuss the emergence of indigenous
entrepreneurs in the Japanese colonies, and in Southeast Asia.

pre-1940 levels by the mid-1950s. In Korea, recovery in both parts of the country was helped by aid from the USA and the Soviet Union. Manchuria's economy was badly damaged during the Soviet occupation, and by the civil war in China. After 1949, recovery appears to have been slow; it was only in the latter part of the 1950s that the Chinese government tried to build on the Japanese legacy and transform Manchuria into an economic powerhouse.

Bibliography

Andrus, J. R. (1948). *Burmese Economic Life*. Stanford: Stanford University Press.

Aye, Hlaing. (1965). *An Economic and Statistical Analysis of Economic Development of Burma under British Rule*. PhD Dissertation, University of London.

Barclay, G. (1954). *Colonial Development and Population in Taiwan*. Princeton: Princeton University Press.

Bassino, J-P. (2000). Public Finance in Vietnam under French Rule 1895–1954. In J-P. Bassino, J-D. Giacometti & K. Odaka (Eds.), *Quantitative Economic History of Vietnam 1900–1990*. Tokyo: Hitotsubashi University, 269–292.

Birnberg, T. B., & Resnick, S. A. (1975). *Colonial Development: An Econometric Study*. New Haven: Yale University Press.

Bix, H. P. (1971). *Japanese Imperialism and Manchuria 1890–1931*. PhD Dissertation, Harvard University.

Booth, A. (2007). *Colonial Legacies: Economic and Social Development in East and Southeast Asia*. Honolulu: University of Hawai'i Press.

Booth, A. (2012a). Measuring Living Standards in Different Colonial Systems: some Evidence from South East Asia, 1900–1942. *Modern Asian Studies*, 46(5), 1145–81.

Booth, A. (2012b). The Plural Economy and its Legacy in Asia. In E. Bogaerts & R. Raben (Eds.), *Beyond Empire and Nation. Decolonizing Societies in Africa and Asia, 1930s to 1970s*. Leiden: KITLV Press, 69–108.

Booth, A. (2016). Falling Behind, Forging Ahead and Falling Behind Again: Thailand from 1870 to 2014. *Economies*, 4(1), 2–17.

Booth, A., & Deng, K. (2017). Japanese Colonialism in Comparative Perspective. *Journal of World History*, 28(1), 61–98.

Bureau of Census and Statistics. (1941). *Yearbook of Philippine Statistics 1940*. Manila: Commonwealth of the Philippines, Bureau of Census and Statistics.

Chao, K. (1979). The Sources of Economic Growth in Manchuria, 1920–1941. In Chi-Ming Hou & Tzong-Shian Yu (Eds.), *Modern*

Chinese Economic History, Taipei: Institute of Economics, Academica Sinica, 255–63.

Chao, K. (1983). *The Economic Development of Manchuria: The Rise of a Frontier Economy*. Ann Arbor: Center for Chinese Studies, The University of Michigan.

Chung, Y-I. (2006). *Korea under Seige, 1876–1945: Capital Formation and Economic Transformation*. New York: Oxford University Press.

Creutzberg, P. (Ed.). (1976). *Changing Economy in Indonesia: vol. 2, Public Finance 1816–1939*. The Hague: Martinus Nijhoff.

Cumings, B. (1999*). Parallax Visions: Making Sense of American-East Asian Relations at the End of the Century*. Durham: Duke University Press.

Davis, L. E., & Huttenback, R. A. (1986). *Mammon and the Pursuit of Empire: The Political Economy of British Imperialism 1860–1912*. Cambridge: Cambridge University Press.

Direction des Services Economiques. (1947). *Annuaire Statistique de l'Indochine, 1943–46*. Hanoi: Government Printer.

Emerson, R. (1937). *Malaysia: A Study in Direct and Indirect Rule*. New York: Macmillan.

Eng, P. van der (2013). Historical National Accounts Data for Indonesia, 1880–2012. Mimeo, Australian National University.

Fraser, H. (1939). *Annual Report on the Social and Economic Progress of the People of the Federated Malay States for 1938*. Kuala Lumpur: FMS Government Press.

German, R. L. (1936). *Handbook to British Malaya, 1935*. London: Malayan Information Agency.

Grajdanzev, A. J. (1942). *Formosa Today: An Analysis of the Economic Development and Strategic Importance of Japan's Tropical Colony*. New York: Institute of Pacific Relations.

Grajdanzev, A. J. (1944). *Modern Korea*. New York: Institute of Pacific Relations.

Ho, S. P. (1978). The Development Policy of the Japanese Colonial Government in Taiwan, 1895–1945. In G. Ranis (Ed.), *Government and Economic Development*. New Haven: Yale University Press, 347–98.

Hooley, R. (2005). American Economic Policy in the Philippines, 1902–1940: Exploring a Dark Age in Colonial Statistics. *Journal of Asian Economics*, 16, 464–88.

Ingram, J. (1971). *Economic Change in Thailand, 1850–1970*. Kuala Lumpur: Oxford University Press.

Jong, F. de, & Ravesteijn, W. (2008). Technology and Administration: The Rise and Development of Public Works in the East Indies. In W. Ravesteijn & J. Kop (Eds.), *For Profit and Prosperity: The Contribution*

Made by Dutch Engineers to Public Works in Indonesia. Leiden: KITLV Press, 46–67.

Kanai, K. (1936). *Economic Development in Manchoukuo*. Tokyo: Japanese Council, Institute of Pacific Relations.

Kerr, G. H. (1942). Formosa: Colonial Laboratory. *Far Eastern Survey*, February 23, 50–5.

Kerr, G. H. (1966). *Formosa Betrayed*. London: Eyre and Spottiswoode.

Kim, K. S., & Roemer, M. (1979). *Growth and Structural Transformation; Studies in the Modernization of the Republic of Korea 1945–75*. Cambridge: Council on East Asian Studies, Harvard University.

Kim, N. N. et al. (2008). *Economic Growth in Korea 1910–1945* (Japanese translation). Tokyo: University of Tokyo Press.

Kimura, M. (1986). Financial Aspects of Korea's Economic Growth under Japanese Rule. *Modern Asian Studies*, 20(4), 793–820.

Kimura, M. (1989). Public Finance in Korea under Japanese Rule: Deficit in the Colonial Account and Colonial Taxation. *Explorations in Economic History*, 26(3), 285–310.

Kimura, M. (1995). The Economics of Japanese Imperialism in Korea, 1910–1939. *Economic History Review*, 48(3), 555–74.

Kobayashi, H. (1996). The Postwar Economic Legacy of Japan's Wartime Empire. In P. Duus, R. H. Myers & M. R. Peattie (Eds.), *The Japanese Wartime Empire, 1931–1945*. Princeton: Princeton University Press, 324–34.

Kohli, A. (2004). *State-Directed Development: Political Power and Industrialization in the Global Periphery*. Cambridge: Cambridge University Press.

Laanen, J. T. M. van. (1980). *Changing Economy in Indonesia: vol. 6, Money and Banking 1816–1940*. The Hague: Martinus Nijhoff.

Li, B., Gao, S., & Quan, F. (2009). *Riben Zai Dongbei Ruyi Laogong Diaocha Yanjiu* (*Investigation in Japanese Use of Slave-labourers in Manchuria*). Beijing: Social Science Academic Press.

Lim, C-Y. (1967). *Economic Development of Modern Malaya*. Kuala Lumpur: Oxford University Press.

Lin, C-Y. (1973). *Industrialization in Taiwan, 1946–72: Trade and Import-Substitution Policies for Developing Countries*. New York: Praeger Publishers.

Mizoguchi, T., & Umemura M. (Eds.). (1988). *Basic Economic Statistics of Former Japanese Colonies, 1895–1938: Estimates and Findings*. Tokyo: Toyo Keizai Shinposhain.

Mizoguchi, T., & Y. Yamomoto. (1984). Capital Formation in Taiwan and Korea. In R. H. Myers & M. R. Peattie (Eds.), *The Japanese Colonial Empire, 1895–1945*. Princeton: Princeton University Press, 399–419.

Moulton, H. G. (1931). *Japan: An Economic and Financial Appraisal*. Washington, DC: Brookings Institution.

MYB. (1933 and 1941). *The Manchoukuo Year Book 1941*. Hsinking: The Manchoukuo Year Book.

Myers, R. H. (1982). *The Japanese Economic Development of Manchuria, 1932 to 1945*. New York: Garland Publishing.

Office of the Prime Minister. (1958). *A Study of the Social and Economic History of Burma (British Burma), Part 6A 1897–1913*. Rangoon: Office of the Prime Minister.

Peattie, M. R. (1984). Introduction. In R. H. Myers & M. R. Peattie (Eds.), *The Japanese Colonial Empire, 1895–1945*. Princeton: Princeton University Press, 3–52.

Saito, T., & Lee, K. K. (1999). *Statistics on the Burmese Economy: The 19th and 20th Centuries*. Singapore: Institute of Southeast Asian Studies.

Sato, M. et al. (2008). *Asian Historical Statistics: Taiwan*. Tokyo: Toyo Keizai Inc.

Shein M., Thant, M. M., & Scin, T. T. (1969). 'Provincial Contract System' of British Indian Empire, in Relation to Burma: A Case of Fiscal Exploitation. *Journal of the Burma Research Society*, LIII, 1–27.

Sivasubramonian, S. (2002). Twentieth Century Economic Performance of India. In A. Maddison, D. S. Prasada Rao & W. F. Shepherd (Eds.), *The Asian Economies in the Twentieth Century*. Cheltenham: Edward Elgar, 102–42.

Sompop, M. (1989). *Economic Development of Thailand, 1850–1950*. PhD Thesis, University of Groningen, Groningen.

Sun, K. C. (1969). *The Economic Development of Manchuria in the First Half of the Twentieth Century*. Cambridge: East Asia Research Center, Harvard University.

Wu, C. (1955). *Diguozhuyi Zai Jiuzhongguode Touzi (Imperial Investments in pre-1949 China)*. Beijing: People's Press.

Xie, X. (2007). *Mantie Yu Huabei Jingji, 1935–1945 (South Manchuria Railway and the Economy of North China, 1935–1945)*. Beijing: Social Science Academic Press.

Yamanata, M., Makino, F., Quan, Z., & Guan Q. (2008). Economic Activities in Manchuria. In K. Odaka, O. Saito & K. Fukao (Eds.), *Asian Historical Statistics: China*. Tokyo: Keizi Inc, 478–513.

Young, L. (1998). *Japan's Total Empire: Manchuria and the Culture of Wartime Imperialism*. Berkeley: University of California Press.

6   From Coast to Hinterland: Fiscal Capacity Building in British and French West Africa, c. 1880–1960

Ewout Frankema and Marlous van Waijenburg

Introduction

With the exception of a string of coastal settlements, most of West Africa was incorporated into the expanding British and French African empires during the final two decades of the nineteenth century.[1] In West Africa, colonial conquest coincided with the expansion and development of embryonic fiscal systems that had financed the coastal settlements in earlier times. Since Britain and France were reluctant to channel large sums of domestic tax revenues into ever-growing empires, colonial governments were pressed to pay their own way as quickly as possible.[2] The lack of central funds to consolidate the newly acquired territories gave rise to what Crawford Young has called 'the revenue imperative' (1994, 38–9 and 124–33). Colonial state expansion depended crucially on the capacity to centralize revenue from *local* sources. This chapter compares the development of fiscal capacity in British and French West Africa from the 'scramble' to independence and discusses the opportunities and constraints that have shaped this process.

[1] We are grateful for the comments we received from Kleoniki Alexopoulou, Anne Booth, William Clarence-Smith, Kent Deng, Leigh Gardner, Abel Gwaindepi, Montserrat Lopez Jerez, Tirthankar Roy, Krige Siebrits and two anonymous referees on earlier versions of this chapter. We also acknowledge the generous financial support of the European Research Council under the European Community's Seventh Framework Programme (ERC Grant Agreement no. 313114), as part of the project 'Is Poverty Destiny? A New Empirical Foundation for Long-Term African Welfare Analysis'; the Netherlands Organisation for Scientific Research, as part of the project 'Is Poverty Destiny? Exploring Long Term Changes in African Living Standards in Global Perspective' (NWO VIDI Grant no. 016.124.307); the Economic History Association; and the Balzan Foundation/Center of Economic History at Northwestern University.
[2] The British converted part of the financial burden of military conquest into colonial government debt and thus passed part of the bill on to African taxpayers (Gardner 2017, 247). French military expenses were covered by the French treasury (Huillery 2014, 2).

Our narrative is structured around five interrelated arguments. First, the environmental conditions that had restricted pre-colonial state centralization also complicated colonial state-building efforts. However, the approach of colonial governments was somewhat different, as they had access to a combination of advanced transport and military technologies to enforce taxes and labour duties and to stimulate international trade, which had been unavailable to local African regimes.

Second, even though European pre-colonial trade relations with West Africa were more developed than in most other parts of Sub-Saharan Africa, the opportunities to use ocean-bound trade as a revenue basis for colonial state formation were very unevenly distributed. Within West Africa, the differences were most pronounced between parts of the coast and vast interior hinterlands. Whenever local conditions permitted, taxing trade became the default option (Frankema 2011, Frankema & van Waijenburg 2014). But in most places, colonial officials were mainly concerned with stimulating or 'enforcing' commercial production through labour taxes before they could start tapping revenues from custom duties (Frankema and van Waijenburg 2014, van Waijenburg 2017).

Third, British and French approaches to fiscal expansion in West Africa differed partly because opportunities to tax trade were lower in large parts of French West Africa, and partly because of different visions of imperial administration. Where the French pursued the idea of *assimilation* in their colonies through more direct forms of rule and a strong emphasis on 'emancipation' through (forced) 'civilization', British colonial governance was based on notions of 'indirect rule', which included a mission to civilize, but without visions of extending British 'citizenship' across the empire (Crowder 1968, 165–72, Conklin 1997). We will not dwell on the question whether this was a distinction in kind or rather one of degree, but we will discuss the implications for systems of revenue centralization.

Probably the most important difference in governance structure was the federal organization of French West Africa, which became operational in 1904. The introduction of a federal structure (*Afrique Occidentale Française*, or AOF) had implications for the allocation and flows of tax revenues that were levied on external revenues. Under the new system, individual colonies were asked to hand over all customs revenues to the federation, which then financed certain collective expenses (e.g. large public works) from these revenues. Additionally, albeit at a minor scale, the federation provided subsidies to fiscally struggling colonies.

This siphoning off of customs revenues to the federal level meant that direct taxes played a larger role in the individual colonies of the AOF, as they could no longer depend on customs revenues.[3] As an unintended result of a greater emphasis on direct taxes, the imposition of a federal system likely fostered the development of a more fine-grained fiscal administration in the French colonies. Additionally, the federal structure, which became the centre for colonial loan schemes, created tighter financial ties between the AOF and France than were seen in the British West African colonies, which in contrast, operated independent fiscal budgets. Cross-subsidies were largely restricted to investments in a joint colonial army (the West African Frontier Force [WAFF]).

Fourth, British administrations enjoyed scale advantages in revenue collection, because they ended up controlling four riverine areas that were relatively well integrated in the wider Atlantic economy, and at the same time included much larger populations than French West Africa. As Map 6.1 shows, the British territories were smaller, but in 1900, they contained roughly twice as many people (Frankema & Jerven 2014, online database). The physical distances that had to be bridged in French West Africa were much larger and the costs of fiscally integrating people in the distant hinterlands were higher. This variation in local conditions is important in explaining why the French opted for a federal system.

Fifth, it can be argued that in terms of revenue centralization, commercialization and monetization, the colonial state imposed a programme of fiscal 'modernization' onto a variety of West African societies. However, the central fiscal regimes remained too weak to function as a solid basis for sovereign debt creation after independence. In that sense, colonial rule bequeathed to African taxpayers a fiscal state that was limited in its reach. The difficulties in raising government loans were partly the result of central budgets remaining too small and too vulnerable to market shocks and political instability to serve as security. More important, however, was the fact that the prevailing system of colonial debt financing remained dependent on metropolitan capital markets (Coquery-Vidrovitch 1986, 381, Sunderland 2007). Unlike in British India (see Roy, Chapter 3, this volume), there was no tradition of 'national' African citizens investing in 'national' state bonds.[4] Despite tendencies to develop more

---

[3] These individual colonies, of course, did receive some revenues back through indirect means (e.g., investments that were made by the federation in public works), but lost autonomy over the allocation over these funds.

[4] That said, the introduction of a common colonial currency in the AOF, the Franc CFA, survived independence and gave former French African colonies a degree of monetary stability that was not witnessed in the former colonies of British West Africa. The *Franc des Colonies Françaises d'Afrique* (Franc-CFA) was introduced in 1945 with a value equal to 1.7 French Franc.

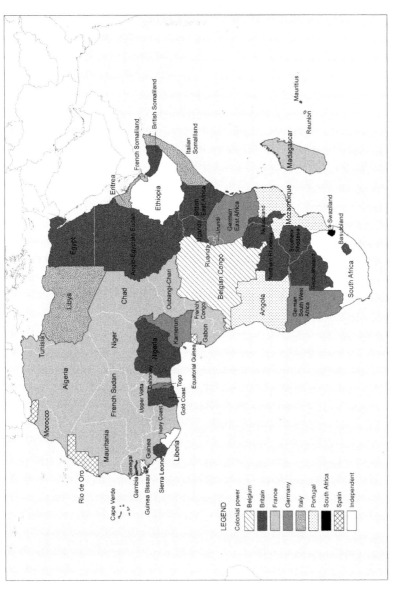

Map 6.1 Colonial borders in Africa in 1914

Source: Authors' own.

Notes: The status of Upper Volta changed several times during the colonial era, being subdivided between surrounding colonies at several moments.

accountable forms of colonial governance after the Second World War, the institutional foundations proved too weak to secure a stable post-colonial political environment.

The remainder of this chapter is organized as follows. We first discuss the fiscal challenges to pre-colonial and colonial state formation in (West) Africa in greater detail. Then we provide some descriptive statistics on colonial state revenue and highlight differences in the trends, the size and the sources of colonial state revenue. We proceed with a discussion of the role of forced labour services and then survey the main trends in expenditure patterns, focusing on trends in welfare spending (health and education). Finally, we analyse the structure of colonial government loans. In the concluding section we reflect on the legacies of colonial fiscal systems in West Africa, taking the broader comparative framework of this volume into account.

Environmental Constraints to Pre-colonial State Formation

Sub-Saharan Africa's low population density has often been regarded as a key constraint to state formation in the pre-colonial era. The basic idea, as put forward most powerfully by Herbst (2000), is that low densities complicate the broadcasting of state power from specific political cores into vast rural hinterlands. Building on the work of Tilly (1990), Herbst also points to the contrast between the territorial conception of the European nation state and the lack of well-defined territorial boundaries of African polities. African state borders were fluid and porous and most African polities were separated by vast open spaces inhabited by acephalous societies. Reasoning from a simple cost–benefit perspective, the control of territorial borders will be weaker where the expected marginal returns from additional tax revenues are outweighed by the expenses the state has to incur to defend its borders and secure the livelihoods of the inhabitants living in these more remote areas.

With the exception of a few areas of concentrated settlement in the Ethiopian highlands and parts of the Great Lakes region, the non-desert parts of pre-colonial West Africa were more densely populated than East, Central or Southern Africa. However, there is no denying that West Africa remained lightly populated compared to considerable parts of Europe and Asia. Comprising a land surface of a little over 5 million km^2, population guesstimates of 20 to 30 million people between the fifteenth to nineteenth centuries translate into an average of four to six people per square kilometre. To put this into perspective, around 1500, the average densities in Western Europe and China were about ten to fifteen people per square kilometre, while India could already have surpassed 30 per square kilometre (Frankema 2015).[5]

Yet, *average* densities may not be as important as some suggest, and fiscal capacity building in West Africa was certainly not constrained by an iron law of population scarcity. States are always characterized by uneven spatial distributions of population, and there are examples of extremely skewed spatial distributions in rural societies that have provided a basis for vigorous state building, especially if the costs of migration out of core regions are high. Carneiro (1970) formalized the idea of 'environmental circumscription' in a theory on the origins of the state. The clustering of population in ancient Egypt serves as a principle example: moving away from the densely settled Nile valley into the desert was extremely costly for farmers as it basically meant giving up their subsistence basis. This created favourable conditions for elites to extract surpluses and invest in the consolidation of state power. In other words, what matters is how human settlements are *distributed* across space and how centres of high population concentration (cities, or densely settled rural areas) were *connected* to one another.

Osafo-Kwaako and Robinson (2013) have shown that 'guesstimates' of historical population density and pre-colonial state centralization do not correlate well in Africa. To make this point more clearly, in nineteenth-century West Africa, the area that was to become British Nigeria may have contained about 15 to 20 million people (Frankema & Jerven 2014, 917–18); a level comparable to early-modern France (c. 1500–1800). With a possible density of sixteen to twenty people per square kilometre in Nigeria and twenty-three to thirty in France, it is not obvious why early-modern France would experience strong tendencies towards political unification and power centralization, while Nigeria would comprise of a combination of strong, but smaller states and large areas with acephalous societies. Moreover, Russia had far lower population densities, but this did not impose prohibitive barriers for the dissemination of state power via landed elites, as Domar (1970) noted in his famous study on slavery and serfdom.

---

[5] Population estimates for pre-colonial, colonial and post-colonial sub-Saharan Africa suffer from a high degree of uncertainty and are subject to ongoing debate, with different views on the comparative densities of West African populations over time and the possible effect of, amongst others, the Atlantic and trans-Saharan slave trades, the introduction of non-African diseases in the wake of intensifying contact with European traders, soldiers, missionaries and settlers.

What really mattered was the resilience of economic networks that could be used to impose taxes and centralize revenue flows. Hence, the largest and most powerful states emerged in the lightly populated West African savannah belt, where the commercial nodes of the trans-Saharan trade network were under control of horseback warriors who were effective in enforcing tribute from a range of vassal states. These states were tied together by Islamic law and associated identity politics (Lydon 2012). The general absence of feudal relations, and especially of inheritable land tenure, put these empires on a weaker footing in terms of elite control over resources than most Asian or European states (Goody 1971). Moreover, the smaller states that emerged in the tsetse infested forest zones were spatially more confined and their foot soldier armies had a much shorter reach (Reid 2012, 75–8). In the absence of horses and donkeys, military logistics depended on human porterage and opportunities for food storage to keep armies going. Warfare usually took the form of raiding and collecting booty, including human captives, rather than prolonged campaigns with the aim of establishing a permanent presence in alien territory. These raids had to be timed in the dry months and between agricultural peak seasons. Hence, environmental conditions, commercialization and the structure of social relations all shaped conditions for pre-colonial state formation, including their fiscal foundation.

Apart from major trade routes and local concentrations of specific mineral resources, such as salt and gold mines, pre-colonial states in West Africa tried to control human labour in the form of slaves, or alternative forms of bondage. The Sokoto Caliphate in Northern Nigeria promoted the construction of small fortified towns, known as *ribats*, to stabilize the frontier areas. These *ribats* provided a basic level of security to their inhabitants and served as local markets and centres of Islamic schooling. In order to extend the fiscal basis of the Caliphate, the state undertook deliberate attempts to settle the pastoral Fulani people and set up agricultural slave plantations (Lovejoy 2005, 179–80). These observations tie into a debate in the 1970s regarding the extent to which pre-colonial African states relied on direct taxation of farmer households, as opposed to taxing trade. Coquery-Vidrovitch (1969) and Hopkins (1973) have argued that there were few opportunities to extract feudal rents in West Africa, given extensive open land frontiers and the absence of land markets. Therefore, centralizing power depended on the presence of trade networks and the possibilities to monopolize the production of marketable handicraft, mineral resources or tropical cash crops such as palm oil and kola nuts. Ajayi, Ade and Smith (1971) have opposed this view, arguing that land and taxable peasants were much more important for the production of state revenue, and made their case in particular for Nigeria.

Law (1978) has added two arguments to this debate. First, he noted that West African leaders generally preferred to force people into slave-based food production in the vicinity of their courts, rather than collecting in-kind taxes from distant areas. Apparently, the perceived costs of raiding and maintaining considerable numbers of slaves were lower than the costs of transporting large quantities of food to the centre. Second, Law noted that the distinction between direct and indirect taxes was dubious anyway, since farm produce could be converted into money and tradable commodities (low weight, high value; i.e. cowry shells, copper rods, gold, salt, luxury textiles) in order to integrate decentralized collection systems into consolidated state funds.

The long-term growth in Atlantic trade in both slaves and commodities slowly widened the opportunities for this type of fiscal expansion. Slave raiding did not just undermine processes of state building as some have argued (Inikori 2003, Nunn & Wantchekon 2011, Obikili 2016), it also incentivized political leaders to pool resources and centralize revenue in order to invest in military power. Slave exports thus produced the rents needed to sustain the process of state building. Cases of societal disintegration, as among the Igbo in Eastern Nigeria, have to be set against cases of increasing state power, such as the militarized polities of Asante, Oyo and Dahomey (Manning 1982, Reid 2012, Dalrymple-Smith 2017). Moreover, the Atlantic slave trade also led to an expansion of the commodity trade in various regions (Dalrymple-Smith & Woltjer 2016). The expanding money supply, and the growing influx of gold, copper rods and cowry shells, facilitated the centralization of tax revenue in state centres.

The key point is that, contrary to British India, and parts of East and Southeast Asia, and to some extent Portuguese Africa as well (see discussion of the *prazo*-system in Mozambique by Alexopoulou, Chapter 8, this volume), sedentary food crop agriculture did not provide a tax base that colonial powers could exploit to finance the West African colonial state. The commercial transition, in which slave exports were gradually replaced by commodity exports, did create a modest foundation for early colonial states to generate trade revenues (Frankema & van Waijenburg 2014). As Figure 6.1 shows, commodity export growth accelerated after 'pacification', but it was preceded by an impressive terms of trade boom that started in the mid 1830s (Frankema et al. 2018). Indeed, without the deeper integration of West Africa into the Atlantic commodity trade, the economic rationale for colonization would have remained absent, and the possibilities to

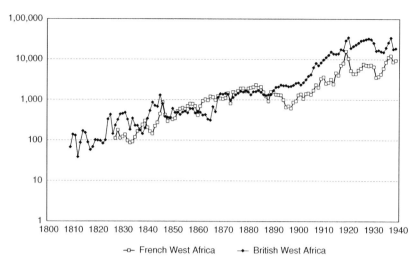

Figure 6.1 Total sea-bound exports from British and French West Africa, c. 1800–1940 (in British Pounds)
Source: Frankema et al. (2018, 243).

erect even the most rudimentary colonial state structures would have been too weak to shield metropolitan taxpayers against a real burden of empire.

Fiscal Challenges to Colonial State Formation in West Africa

The pre-colonial systems of revenue production were generally scattered and the chronically understaffed colonial governments found them difficult to integrate into centralized revenue systems. The challenge for the colonial state formation project in West Africa – and for many other parts of sub-Saharan Africa, as well as parts of Asia – was that substantial investments were needed to assess, monitor and collect taxes, while such investments, in turn, exceeded the available resources, both monetary and manpower.[6] Opportunities to bridge the resource gap between ex-ante investments and ex-post returns through debt creation via financial markets were low and dependent on metropolitan politics. Grants-in-aid helped to bridge this gap and helped to finance projects of 'utmost

---

[6] See for a similar argument, Gardner, Chapter 7 of this volume.

importance', but were quickly reduced as soon as local revenues started to rise (Frankema 2011, Gardner 2012).

Land taxes were absent in virtually all West African societies. Most of the land under cultivation was regulated by communal forms of land tenure, without centrally recorded registers of ownership. Practices of shifting cultivation and seasonal migration of pastoral communities also complicated the development of a formal system of land registration. Similar administrative constraints applied to the imposition of differentiated systems of income taxation. The prospects for levying indirect taxes were clearly better, although these should not be exaggerated. Trade taxes, and more specifically customs duties, had large cost advantages. Since exports and imports were passing through a limited number of port cities, the monitoring and collection of taxes was relatively easy to organize, although smuggling remained difficult to contain (Nugent 2002). Since the price effects of import tariffs were less obvious to consumers than the income effects of direct taxes to income earners, the risk of violent resistance and tax evasion was also lower. Moreover, given that imported goods mainly consisted of 'luxury' commodities such as textiles, alcohol, soap, tobacco and a range of other manufactured products, the duties were mainly borne by the wealthier strata of African consumers, as well as by small communities of European colonists.

A distinctive feature of colonial state formation in most parts of West Africa was the limited involvement of Europeans investors and entrepreneurs in African export production. Compared to the substantial numbers of European plantations set up in various parts of Central, East and Southern Africa, the production of exports crops, including plantation systems, was primarily undertaken by Africans (Tosh 1980). In some areas, such as the Gold Coast and Northern Nigeria, foreign land ownership was even formally prohibited. West Africa also lacked the big concentrated mining enclaves that attracted foreign investors in the Belgian Congo, Angola, the Rhodesias and South Africa. The French introduced schemes of forced cultivation of cotton and groundnuts in the savannah areas, and also experimented with European-owned cocoa plantations in the rainforests of Cote d'Ivoire, but the scale of European involvement remained low, and the economic viability of European investments in African cash-crop sectors was poor (Frankema et al. 2016, 256–60). Hence, African farmers, both smallholders and larger capitalist farmers, became the linchpin between the local economy and the colonial treasury.

Direct taxes usually took the form of a flat, albeit regionally differentiated, hut, head, or poll tax. Local chiefs were key in this process, as they had the political authority and inside information required to collect these direct 'native taxes'. The lack of legitimacy in the eyes of taxpayers could provoke serious resistance, and there are several examples of violent resistance against the imposition of direct taxes (Crowder 1968, 154–5, Martin 2006). In the context of such latent opposition, it was often difficult to adjust tax rates for inflation, so that real revenues could erode in periods of significant price hikes. And although reliance on indigenous rulers was generally an effective way to collect direct taxes, the information asymmetries between African chiefs and colonial officials also created new opportunities for corruption and tax evasion, or what Mamdani has called 'decentralized despotism' (1996, 37).

Prevailing levels of monetization complicated the centralization of taxes collected in distant provinces and districts. Especially in the early phases of colonial rule, tax obligations were often fulfilled in kind, which was inefficient given the leakages involved in converting agricultural commodities (including cattle) into the currencies needed to pay the wages, salaries and pensions of government staff. In landlocked colonies, where possibilities to raise custom duties were absent, forced labour and direct taxes were the only alternatives to meet the expenses of colonial state expansion. The uneven concentration of revenue collection thus raised issues of redistribution, which were particularly sensitive in the federation of French West Africa, where the coastal colonies, such as Dahomey, Côte d'Ivoire and Senegal in particular, contributed the lion's share of custom revenues (Frankema & van Waijenburg 2014, 384–6).

Even in coastal areas where international trade did offer a revenue basis, revenue possibilities remained limited, as colonial governments did not have the power to set tariffs. Tariffs were negotiated in the metropole, applied to imperial customs unions and sometimes even negotiated between metropoles to curb smuggling. Moreover, the negotiated *ad valorem* rates of 5 to 10 per cent were fairly low. Compared to import duties, export taxes were more contested as they often affected the profit margins of metropolitan enterprises, as well as indigenous African producers. Therefore, export taxes were less frequently imposed, and if they were, they tended to target a major commodity, rather than the full range of exports. The establishment of marketing boards since the 1930s, which set the purchase price of major export crops in order to dampen world market price volatility, proved another effective instrument to hive off large surpluses in times of rapid recovering markets, especially after the Second World War (Bauer 1956, Meredith 1986, Jones 1987, 378).

The main alternative to taxation and the creation of state mono-polies and monopsonies was the exploitation of human labour in order to produce rents for the state (Young 1994, van Waijenburg 2017). In pre-colonial Africa, political, spiritual and military leaders operating outside the 'productive economy' exploited labour in the form of slavery, debt bondage and human pawning, as well as through structural labour services, including military services. Colonial governments discarded the incorporation of African slaves into colonial systems of revenue production on moral grounds, but initiatives to abolish the use of slaves in African production systems were pursued with only modest pressure, in order not to damage the strategic relations with African political elites (Austin 2005). Moreover, colonial governments resorted to large-scale schemes of labour coercion, which were not always easy to distinguish from indigenous practices of slavery, as Klein (1998) has demonstrated for French West Africa.

Central Government Revenue: Levels, Trends and Sources

We now turn to a survey of the main trends of central government revenue (CGR). Since our focus is on *local* revenue-raising capacity, we exclude loans that governments raised on metropolitan financial markets, occasional grants-in-aid, reimbursements and withdrawals from the reserve funds from our series. Additionally, our CGR figures exclude railway receipts, which, although substantial in some colonies, were mostly balanced by equally large expenditures. Finally, the government revenues that were derived from state-enforced labour services neither appear in the fiscal records as part of the revenue account, nor as expenditure on public works. We will, however, dive deeper into this less visible component of taxation in the next section.

It should also be mentioned that central government accounts, of course, shed no light on decentralized taxes imposed by native administrations, chiefs or village heads. In British Africa, these consisted of two types. First, the state sanctioned and officially registered taxes, which were levied and kept by native administrations. The contribution of these revenues to the overall public budget were, in most places, relatively modest. Second, the additional local taxes and labour services that were imposed by chiefs and were not formally registered. The share of these contributions is impossible to estimate and will have varied from one community to another. Hence, the revenue series shown here give us an important part of the picture, but by no means a total overview of the 'public' revenues that were raised in West African colonial states.

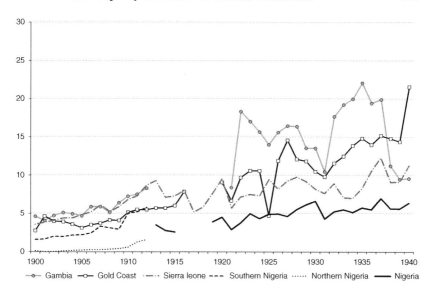

Figure 6.2a Central government revenue per capita/unskilled day wages, British West Africa, c. 1900–40.

Sources: Revenue data from Blue Books; wage data from Frankema and van Waijenburg (2012); population data from Frankema and Jerven (2014).

Notes: For our wage series we took the average of rural and urban unskilled wages. For Northern Nigeria, we only took the rural series, as separate wage observations for this area were not available. Based on other inland-coastal area series, wage differentials were observed for French West Africa, we thus assume that average wage rates were lower here. For years in which we were missing rural observations, we maintained the following principles: for a single missing year, we interpolated on the basis of the trend in surrounding years (both urban and rural). For more than one year, we interpolated rural wages on the basis of the trend in urban wages.

Figures 6.2a and 6.2b present the development of real per capita government revenues for the period 1880–1940 in British and French West Africa.[7] To deflate the nominal revenue series we have taken the day wage series for unskilled labour. Ideally, one would use a price index for government expenditures that takes both wages and unit prices of material expenses into account. However, while there is a rudimentary consumer price index based on a household subsistence basket, such indices do not capture commodities that governments are likely to consume in large quantities. Since colonial governments, like most other governments, spent most of their money on wages and salaries of government

[7] Our focus here is confined to the pre–World War II era, as the post-war period saw large amounts of development funds and loans come into the equation.

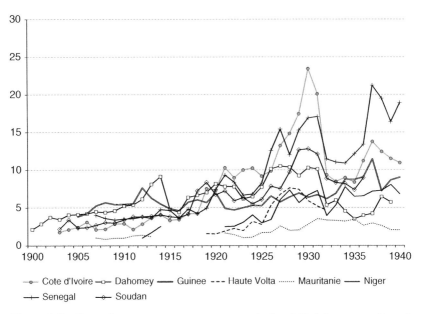

Figure 6.2b Central government revenue per capita/unskilled day wages, French West Africa, c. 1900–40.
Sources: Revenue data from van Waijenburg (2017); wage data from van Waijenburg (2018); population data from Frankema and Jerven (2014), with territorial adjustments for Upper Volta following van Waijenburg (2017).

employees, the wage series offer a better indication of the cost of government services. Hence, we may read Figures 6.2a and 6.2b as a reflection of the purchasing power of the colonial state, and, more precisely, its capacity to hire unskilled urban wage labour, controlled for the size of the theoretically taxable population.

Comparative Levels and Trends

Despite some significant volatility, especially around the era of the Great Depression, the series for both the British and French colonies show an upward trend, going from very small revenues early in the twentieth century to substantially higher revenues on the eve of the Second World War. The *variation* in growth rates of government revenue, however, was large, with colonies like the Gambia, the Gold Coast and Senegal reaching levels far higher than Nigeria, Mauritania and Soudan. What we cannot deduce from these graphs is whether *tax pressure* was also higher in colonies with greater fiscal capacity, as we do not know to what extent centralized revenues were complemented by revenues assessed at the local level. In the more autonomous region of Northern Nigeria, the British deliberately allowed indigenous leaders to levy and retain significant portions of direct taxes (Hailey 1939, 417–18). Reported difficulties in Sierra Leone of bringing local chiefs into the central system of revenue collection also suggest that the arm of the state was limited (Frankema 2010, 467–8).

In the AOF, the approach to revenue centralization was somewhat different. Customs duties of the individual colonies were levied at the federal level and subsequently allocated to the colonies and the federal administration in Senegal, while the remainder of tax and non-tax revenue stayed at the level of the individual colony. This structure gave the federal administration the opportunity to subsidize the fiscally less viable colonies and to finance commerce-boosting projects (e.g. railway construction) in specific parts of the federation. The extent to which the 'poorer' states benefitted from such transfers can be debated, especially because one of the richer colonies, Senegal, which hosted the federal government, attracted substantial amounts of additional revenue. But the public loans that were concluded through the federal structure would have been impossible to levy for places like Niger, Haute Volta, Mauritania or Soudan had they been independent fiscal entities.

In a wider comparative perspective, the real per capita revenue series suggests that the share of central public revenue in the total economy was not very large, especially before the Second World War. Assuming an average per capita income level equal to about 200 urban days of wage labour, total government revenues would, in most cases, have remained below 10 per cent of total national income. Of course, this is a rough calculation, but for the post-war era we can use GDP estimates to construct an alternative estimate of the relative weight of the public sector in the total economy. Figure 6.3 presents a bar graph of the share of CGR in total GDP. It shows that the state of Ghana, which was granted independence in 1957, had reached a revenue/GDP ratio of about 20 per cent around 1960. This was comparable to the highest levels that were reached by Britain in the late eighteenth century, and considerably higher than the share in Britain in 1850, as British government revenue collection in the nineteenth century did not keep pace with economic expansion. It was also higher than in mid-nineteenth-century France. However, in the other colonies, the development of fiscal capacity had progressed (much) more slowly, resulting in shares of 6 to 14 per cent of GDP, levels that were comparable to France and Britain around 1850.[8]

---

[8] The GDP data used to calculate these ratios are unlikely to be fully comparable, as margins of error will vary, so these figures should be taken as an indication of public sector size, rather than a precise estimate.

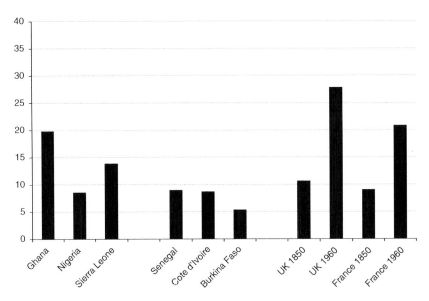

Figure 6.3 Central Government Revenue as percentage of total GDP, c. 1960
Sources: Central Government Revenue and GDP data from Mitchell (2007a and 2007b).
Note: Estimate for Ghana 1959, Nigeria 1959, Sierra Leone 1963, Senegal 1964, Cote d'Ivoire 1960, Burkina Faso 1962.

Revenue Sources

The most important distinction between British and French West Africa in the composition of government revenue was in the share of direct taxes, as Table 6.1 shows. These direct taxes mainly consisted of hut, head or poll taxes, including increasing buy-outs of labour services in the AOF. In British West Africa the share of direct taxes ranged from zero in the Gold Coast to 29 per cent in Sierra Leone in 1937.[9] In French West Africa the range was 12 per cent in Senegal in 1937 to 71 per cent in Mauritania in the same year. The regional averages show that there was a slightly declining trend in the AOF, from 51 per cent in 1911 to 46 per cent in 1937, but the AOF never reached the shares that were common in British West Africa. This is an important observation because it shows that British colonial governments in West Africa were relying to a greater extent on trade tax revenues. It would be wrong, however, to interpret this reliance on indirect taxes as a specifically 'British' type of colonial fiscal policy, for in British East Africa the share of

---

[9] The exception here is Northern Nigeria in 1911, where the share of direct taxes is much in line with Niger.

Table 6.1 *Share of direct native taxes in total government revenue, 1911–37*

French Africa	1911	1925	1937	British Africa	1911	1925	1937
Côte d'Ivoire	0.35	0.41	0.35	Gambia	0.05	0.04	0.04
Dahomey	0.20	0.20	0.27	Gold Coast	0.00	0.00	0.00
Guinée	0.57	0.61	0.51	Nigeria	0.19	0.15	0.14
Haute Volta		0.77		Sierra Leone	0.15	0.08	0.29
Mauritanie	0.66	0.64	0.71	**BWA average**	**0.10**	**0.07**	**0.12**
Niger	0.71	0.79	0.68				
Senegal	0.33	0.22	0.12	Bechuanaland	0.50	0.58	0.56
Soudan	0.72	0.54	0.58	Kenya	0.47	0.25	0.12
AOF average	**0.51**	**0.52**	**0.46**	Northern Rhodesia	0.69	0.30	0.12
				Nyasaland	0.52	0.35	0.24
				Tanganyika		0.36	0.30
				Uganda	0.61	0.29	0.35
				BEA average	**0.56**	**0.35**	**0.28**

Source: van Waijenburg (2017, appendix tables A5.1, A5.3, and A5.6).
Note: Regional averages are unweighted.

direct taxes exceeded that in French West Africa. As shown in the introduction to this volume, higher custom revenues strongly correlated with per capita values of international trade, and were thus mainly predicated on local economic conditions (Frankema and Booth, Chapter 1, this volume, Figure 1.1; see also Frankema 2011, Frankema & van Waijenburg 2014, van Waijenburg 2017).

There are three more observations to make on the revenue mix. First, states in the interior depended more on direct taxes than states at the coast, as a result of the latter's greater opportunities to rely on revenues from ocean-bound trade. This is not to say that there were no possibilities to tax trade in the West African interior – from the trans-Saharan trade network, for example – but the value of the trade was smaller and more difficult to tap into. Historians have long emphasized the pivotal role of direct taxes in achieving other colonial policy objectives, such as pushing Africans into the wage labour market, stimulating the monetization of the economy, and creating a 'governable subject' (Young 1994, Bush & Maltby 2004). But colonial governments did seem to reduce their relative reliance on such taxes as soon as more trade tax revenues became available (Frankema & van Waijenburg 2014).

Second, if the governments of Senegal and Côte d'Ivoire could have reserved the custom duties for their local budgets, their revenue mix would probably have had much more in common with the British West African colonies than with the remaining part of the AOF.[10] Third, in pastoral areas, where the mobility of people and taxable commodities added a further constraint to fiscal capacity building, the French tried to integrate existing taxes such as the *zekkat*, the traditional Muslim tax on wealth, including cattle, into the colonial tax system. It shows that colonial administrations were eager to adopt existing institutional arrangements, but on the whole the contribution of such taxes remained modest (Young 1994, 124–5). The exception is Mauritania, where the *zekkat* was the most important direct tax, and where alternative revenue sources were extremely limited.

Forced Labour

The financial records of the colonial state do not document a potentially large source of additional government revenues: that of forced labour

---

[10] The simple coast–interior distinction needs some further nuancing. What really mattered was the distance to existing infrastructural connections from the interior to the coast. That is to say, the costs of extracting revenues from farmers living in the remote forest areas in Guinea or pastoral groups living in the desert areas of Mauritania were prohibitive not because they were living so far from the coast, but rather because there was literally no way to reach out and integrate these people into a central fiscal system.

contributions (Fall 1993, van Waijenburg 2017, 2018). State-endorsed labour coercion schemes were implemented throughout all of colonial Africa, including British and French West Africa, and took on several forms. Of those generating direct government revenues, the two most important ones were corvée labour and conscript labour. Corvée labour, which had been practiced in many societies throughout history, obliged all adult males to work a fixed number of days per year on public works projects in the vicinity of their communities. In most places, this classic 'labour tax' concerned non-remunerated labour, although some payments were introduced in parts of British Africa by the 1930s.

Conscript labour, in contrast, was used to secure workers for longer periods of time and usually concerned work on larger projects located far away from home villages. These workers were compelled to sign long-term contracts, in which they agreed to carry out the requested labour for a fixed (and below market rate) wage, together with often-inadequate housing and rations. In some cases, such as the Congo-Ocean railway construction in French Equatorial Africa, the hazardous work sites and poor sanitary conditions resulted in excessive mortality rates (Sautter 1967). This system of conscript labour was also employed on a large scale by private companies. In the major mining areas for example, such as the Central African copperbelt, mining companies relied on the legal and military support of the state to garner recruits (Northrup 1988, Juif and Frankema 2018).

Despite the fact that all colonial powers relied on labour coercion, there were some differences in the way these systems were organized and administered. The French recorded the corvée component of their forced labour practice in a systematic way, documenting the number of days, as well as the money rates charged to those who wanted to pay off their labour duties, in the appended sections of their annual budgets. In British West Africa, in contrast, there was little formal registration of the incidence, type and spread of labour duties, although there is scattered evidence that it was practiced on a large scale (Akurang-Parry 2000). In both systems though, and much like regular tax collection, chiefs were made responsible for the implementation of labour taxes. As chiefs received compensation for their recruitment efforts, they maintained a major say in the communal distribution of the labour service tax.

The systematic recording by the French gives us the opportunity to get a better sense of the relative magnitude of these additional 'invisible' labour tax revenues. The most straightforward way of monetizing such revenues, is by asking how much the colonial state would have had to pay to hire the recruited amount of corvée labour for a cash wage (van Waijenburg 2018). Figure 6.4 shows the relative magnitude of corvée

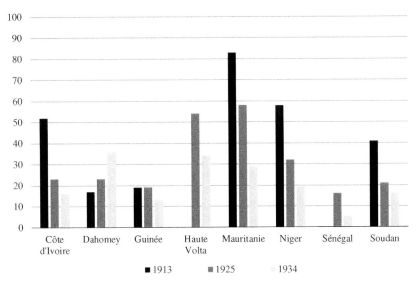

Figure 6.4 Additional per capita state revenue from corvée labour in French Africa, in 1913, 1925 and 1934 (in percentages)
Source: van Waijenburg (2018, 65).

revenues for three benchmark years: 1913, 1925 and 1934. The figure reveals that, in most colonies, these labour services contributed significant additional revenues to the cash component of the fiscal base, and that they were an especially vital source of fiscal capacity in the 'poorer' colonies, such Mauritania, Niger and Upper Volta. The declining trend over time, which is visible in most colonies, reflects the growing amount of cash taxes that were flowing in the treasury, most notably from trade revenues. It should be mentioned though, that this figure does not capture other revenues from forced labour schemes, such as conscript labour or abuse of the formal corvée rules. The figure should therefore be interpreted as a lower-bound estimate.

There are three major reasons why colonial states relied so heavily on forced labour in the early phase of colonial state formation. First, every bit of revenue that could be raised, whether monetary, in-kind, or 'in-service', aided the objective of fiscal self-reliance. Second, slavery and communal labour duties had been standard practice in large parts of the region. Even though one of the official 'justifications' for colonization was to outlaw slavery, the deeply rooted traditions of 'unfree' labour persisted as a foundation for the implementation, or integration, of labour taxes into the colonial fiscal regime. According to Klein (1998, 252–6), a substantial share of the population in Senegal, the French Soudan and Guinée remained enslaved until at least the 1920s, despite 'formal' emancipation policies. The strong grip indigenous authorities still had in such places on their enslaved populations likely facilitated the colonial state's efforts to coerce African labour through their cooperation. Finally, in order to enhance the commercialization of local economies, infrastructural investments (railways, roads, ports, telegraph lines) were key. For these construction works, large amounts of unskilled labour were required. But in the labour-scarce areas, labour was relatively expensive to hire at "market-clearing" rates (Frankema & van Waijenburg 2012). In other words, forced labour offered, in many respects, the key to relieving budget constraints in the short run and permanently solving the problem of revenue mobilization in the longer run (van Waijenburg 2017).

Expenditure Patterns

There were several trends in the way colonial governments in West Africa converted state revenues into expenditure budgets. These trends hold, to a greater or lesser extent, for most of the colonial empires in Africa and Asia. In the early phase of colonial state formation, most of the resources were allocated to securing law and order, to government administration, and to public works. Depending on the available funds, the shares allocated to social spending, in particular healthcare and education, increased gradually, but never gained priority. Moreover, at times of war, or during the severe depression of the early 1930s, these expenses were cut back. Colonial governments cut back on the financing of large railway construction projects, and for the most part did not engage in debt financing to give a major push to social provisions. Table 6.2 illustrates these patterns by showing the so-called resources-to-order ratio of government expenditure in British West Africa. This ratio divides the total amount spent on healthcare and education in the central government budget by the total amount spent on administration and security, including police and the army (for details on the construction of this ratio, see Frankema 2011).

Table 6.2 shows the growing share of welfare spending from 1910 to 1929.[11] It also shows that the Gold Coast government, which experienced the biggest rise in purchasing power during this period, spent a

---

[11] While fiscal literature often refers to education and health expenditure as "welfare spending", this may also be regarded as "investment in people", with the aim to increase the quality of labour. We thank Anne Booth for making this point.

Table 6.2 *Resources-to-order ratio in British West Africa, 1910–38*

	1910/13	1925	1929	1934	1938
Gambia	0.25	0.36	0.44	0.33	0.39
Sierra Leone	0.29	0.37	0.50	0.42	0.35
Gold Coast	0.29	0.48	0.59	0.50	0.52
Nigeria	0.21	0.23	0.37	0.35	0.39
Unweighted average	**0.26**	**0.36**	**0.47**	**0.40**	**0.41**

Source: Data from Frankema (2011, 144).

substantially higher share on health and education than the other three British West African colonies. In the early 1930s, when severe austerity measures were implemented, budget cuts on healthcare and education were larger than on other spending categories. In Sierra Leone, for instance, the budgets were reduced by 25 per cent between 1929 and 1934, and only after the Second World War did spending on health and education get back to pre-depression levels.

For French West Africa, the calculation of a resource-to-order ratio is complicated by the fact that the metropole incurred the costs of the military. Huillery has estimated that military expenditure accounted for about 80 per cent of the metropolitan contribution to the AOF (Huillery 2014, 5). Taking all financial flows into account, she found that the annual contribution of France to the AOF was about 0.29 per cent of the annual French budget. She argued that the costs of maintaining an exceptionally expensive government bureaucracy, in turn, placed a much heavier burden on African taxpayers (2014, 1). A similar argument applies to British Africa, where Frankema has shown that the expenses on the growing pension schemes of retired government officials took an increasing chunk out of local central budgets, which were financed from local revenues (Frankema 2011, 140).

Another way to compare trends in welfare spending in British and French West Africa is to calculate the per capita, or the per student, expenses on education. This approach reveals that spending levels in the 1920s and 1930s varied widely both between and within the colonial empires, but that they were nowhere impressive. The shares devoted to education ranged between 1 and 8 per cent of the annual budget. In the mid 1920s, the education budget of the Gold Coast was nearly as large as in Nigeria, while the Nigerian population was at least six times bigger. In absolute terms, the expenses in 1925 in the Gold Coast were about

£0.03 per capita, while the total budget in the AOF (including federal and local state expenses), was about £0.01 per capita.[12] This was considerably lower than in the Gold Coast, but twice as high as in Nigeria.

When we extend the comparison to the expenses *per student*, however, the AOF spent considerably more (Frankema 2012). Whereas public, state-funded education was an important tool for the French to train an African elite that could be employed in the bureaucracy, the British relied to a greater extent on private initiatives to extend primary education, most notable those of Christian missionaries. Before 1940, enrolment rates in the AOF were significantly lower, but they partially caught up to levels prevalent in British West Africa after the Second World War (Frankema 2012, supplementary table A2; see also attainment database of Barro and Lee, 2015).

The different approaches to missionary education were partly informed by the strong sentiment in French society that the state and the Church have a separate role, and that the provision of education was a state task (Cogneau & Moradi 2014). Decisions to allow missionary access should also be seen in relation to the influence of Islam and Islamic education. Muslims constituted a large proportion of the indigenous population in the AOF and the admission of Christian missions into Muslim territories provoked serious tensions. For similar reasons, the British prohibited activities of Christian missionaries in Northern Nigeria, and the Dutch colonial government remained reluctant to give Protestant or Catholic missions unlimited access to core Muslim areas in Indonesia. The provision of private missionary education, with or without government funding, also reflects a more persistent aspect of the African colonial and post-colonial state. NGOs still play a key role in the provision of health and education services, services which in the 'modernizing' fiscal states of the European metropoles from the late nineteenth century onwards were increasingly provided by government agencies.

Capital Investment and Public Debt

Perhaps the most convincing statistic underpinning our argument that the constraints to fiscal capacity building were higher in French than in British West Africa, was already provided by Frankel's classic study on *Capital Investment in Africa*, published in 1938. The data Frankel

---

[12] These estimates were obtained using official 1925 exchange rates: 1£ = 101 FFr. An alternative approach would be to use the PPP-based conversion rate from Frankema and van Waijenburg (2014, 395): 1£ = 49 FFr, which takes relative expenses on public sector salaries into account. In this case educational expenditures in FWA would compare more favourably to BWA, at around £0.02 per capita.

gathered reveal that almost four-fifth of total invested capital in Africa had gone into British controlled territories. More than 40 per cent of the 1.2 billion pounds he reports for 1935 went to South Africa alone. British West Africa had attracted 9.6 per cent (6.2 per cent for Nigeria, 2.9 per cent for the Gold Coast), while French West Africa only recorded 2.5 per cent, less than a quarter of the Belgian territories (11.7 per cent) and equal to Mozambique (2.8 per cent) and Angola (2.6 per cent). We cannot tell how large the margins of error in these estimates are, but given the fact that most of these investments were secured via recorded government loans, these figures probably have some factual foundation. Even if we take the differences in population size into account, the invested capital in British West Africa was twice the amount of the AOF (Frankel 1938, table 48, 202–3).

Comparing the histories of debt creation in British-ruled Sierra Leone and independent Liberia, Gardner (2017) has shown how colonial states benefitted from their connections to metropolitan capital markets. Whereas the Liberian regime faced great difficulties in attracting international loans, the government of Sierra Leone had access to cheap borrowing, since the backing provided by the British government removed most of the default risk.[13] This part of the so-called 'empire effect' should not be pushed too far, however, since imperial backing of loans also implied stronger metropolitan supervision. In the AOF, public loans could only be concluded by the federal government, and only through the governor-general, and not by the local colonial states (Crowder 1968, 179). Alexopoulou (Chapter 8, this volume) shows that the Salazar dictatorship in Portugal curtailed the possibilities of debt financing to tiny amounts.

Yet, compared to the small annual revenue base, the debt burden in West African colonies did take on significant proportions, also in comparison to other parts of British Africa (see Gardner, Chapter 7, this volume). Table 6.3 shows the accumulation of public debt in British and French West Africa as a ratio of total annual government revenue for a number of benchmark years between 1905 and 1935. The table shows that the debt burden increased in all colonies, and especially in the 1920s and 1930s. In French West Africa, public debt levels rose spectacularly because of the Great French Colonial Loan authorized in 1931, which injected 1.57 billion French Francs into the depressed economies of the federation (Frankel 1938, 342). The loan was substantial, but compared to current EU norms of state debt as a

---

[13] This argument has been made for the British Empire as a whole by, amongst others, Davis and Huttenback (1988) and Ferguson and Schularick (2006).

Table 6.3 *Ratio of accumulated public debt over total annual government revenue, 1905–35*

	1905	1913	1920	1929	1935
Sierra Leone	4.5	2.1	1.7	2.4	2.5
Gold Coast	3.9	1.9	2.0	3.5	3.6
Nigeria	1.9	2.5	1.5	3.9	4.7
French West Africa	2.3	3.1	1.9	1.8	6.2

Source: Frankel (1938, 316–47).

proportion of GDP (i.e. 60 per cent) the debt cannot be considered excessive. If government revenue did not exceed 10 per cent of GDP before the 1940s (see Figure 6.3), the share of government debt will have remained far below this bar.

With the exception of Nigeria, the share of debt servicing in the annual expenditure accounts also remained modest. This was partly due to favourable loan conditions – i.e. low interest rates. In the Gambia, Sierra Leone and the Gold Coast, debt servicing consumed less than 10 per cent of the budget in most years between 1900 and 1940, which was below the shares that were common in Britain during the interwar era (c. 20 to 30 per cent). Sierra Leone started out with a relatively high debt-to-revenue ratio in 1905 as a consequence of the Hut Tax War (1896–8), the costs of which were partly converted into colonial state debt. In French West Africa, debt payments were largely made from the federal budget. These payments rose from around 24 per cent of the federal budget in 1925 to about 40 per cent in 1936, but when we take the debt payments as a share of total consolidated revenue in the AOF (including the state budgets), the debt charges went up from about 8 per cent to 15 per cent. These shares remained well below Nigerian proportions. In Nigeria, the burden of debt payments increased from about 17 per cent in 1913 to 31 per cent in 1938. At this point the Nigerian ratio exceeded the share of debt servicing in the metropole.

Occasionally, grants-in-aid were provided by the metropole to fund infrastructural projects, but the amounts involved were, at least up to 1940, fairly small. In British West Africa, Nigeria again formed the exception. Between 1897 and 1919 it received c. £4.9 million in aid, in addition to £12.0 million of accumulated public debt (Frankel 1938, 317). Why Nigeria stands out is an interesting question and will require further in-depth research. One of the likely explanations, which would also make sense in view of the much higher levels of debt loaded onto the British Indian government (see Roy, Chapter 3, this volume) is that the economic potential of both societies, with vast populations, was assessed differently from those of the smaller states.

After the Second World War, grants-in-aid became more substantial and these transfers formed the basis for structural development aid in the post-independence era. It reflects changing visions on the main rationale of colonial rule. At the same time, rapidly growing funds were extracted via marketing boards controlling the export crop sectors (Meredith 1986, 77–8). Even though the intensification of financial transfers between the metropole and the West African colonies may not have delayed political independence, the financial dependence on the metropole and, later, on international institutions such as the IMF and World Bank, lasted much longer. At the eve of independence, the colonial office was forced to buy up large proportions of colonial state bonds in order to issue new colonial loans (Sunderland 2007). Increasing revenues from oil in the 1970s solved the credit constraint, at least in the short run, and enabled the Nigerian government to attract loans from Nigerian investors. At the same time, however, cheap credits sowed the seeds of a severe debt crises and a long period of retrogression, from which African economies have only recently recovered.

The question remains open to what extent the tendency to run budget deficits, especially in Ghana and Nigeria, in the years from 1900 to 1940, contributed to a 'fiscal management culture' that aggravated the post-independence debt crisis. The possibility to run deficits contrasted with the situation in Southeast Asia (Booth 2008, table 8) where, in several cases, revenues exceeded expenditures, even in the 1930s. These budget deficits were funded by government borrowing and the favourable terms in the London market may have contributed to this, even though fiscal affairs were closely supervised by the colonial office. It would be interesting to explore why budget surpluses and limited borrowing were the norm in some colonies (e.g. parts of British Malaya and Burma), and not in others (e.g. Nigeria).

Conclusions

Summing up, on the eve of independence, the centralization of state revenues had progressed substantially in both French and British colonies. Per capita revenues in 1960 were considerably larger in all colonies than in they had been in 1900, and most of the monetary revenues were collected into consolidated government budgets. The in-kind and in-service (i.e. labour duties) components of government revenue were largely phased out. Government borrowing had extended the fiscal leverage of the colonial state, and considerable infrastructural invest-ments had in many cases given a major impetus to commercial production.

Yet, state revenues were nowhere sufficient and stable enough to offer the degree of credibility required by global capital markets which would allow independent countries to continue to borrow at favourable inter-est rates. The disintegration of the imperial ties left the newly indepen-dent states in West Africa in a precarious situation. Their growing populations demanded more investment in infrastructure, education and health but resources were limited. Shifts to local investors and other foreign investors (the USSR and the Middle East) were made, but lack of experience in macro-economic management, corruption and a legacy of states that were not really nations put stable financial govern-ance on a very shaky footing. The inheritance of the CFA system in French West Africa (which was continued in most AOF colonies, except for Guinée) offered more stability, but also constrained possibilities to adjust exchange rates in line with swings in terms of trade and deterior-ating external trade balances.

The common currency adopted in French West Africa (*franc CFA*) was intended to offer an effective shield against the inflation monster that compromised state budgets and macro-economic stability in for-mer British West Africa which all adopted their own currencies at independence. But the CFA franc did not protect the former AOF colonies against the debt crisis of the 1980s, which was aggravated by collapsing world markets for primary commodities and the attractions of cheap credit in the wake of the oil crises of the 1970s. The collapse of West African state finances during the closing decades of the twentieth century was linked to the structural weaknesses inherent to the fiscal systems that were left behind after eight decades of European rule. There were no deeply rooted institutions to control state budgets, and insufficient mechanisms to prevent reckless debt accumulation. Nor was the legitimacy problem solved with the transfer of political autonomy.

On the expenditure side, there was a general trend in the decades from 1900 to 1960 towards increased spending on education and health, which was consistent with the growing commitment of metro-politan powers to their 'civilization' and 'development' missions. Yet, the white man's burden was never fully disconnected from the black man's burden. The growing revenue base was, in many cases, forged from the forced labour efforts of subjected African peoples, from forced cultivation programmes and from contested conceptions of the social contract held by African taxpayers, local tax collectors (chiefs) and state representatives, in which ethnic dividing lines, religious affiliations and class distinctions all played their part. Moreover, the extension of public services such as education and healthcare did not lead to an elaborate 'national' system of social security provisions. Many of the welfare services were supplied by private agents, principally European and African missionaries, who operated local schools and hospitals, rooted in local communities and finances. In this sense, state centralization only went half way. The independent states of West Africa are still wrestling with this legacy in the twenty-first century.

Bibliography

Ajayi, J., Ade, F., & Smith, R. (1971). *Yoruba Warfare in the Nineteenth Century.* 2nd ed. Cambridge: Cambridge University Press.

Akurang-Parry, K. O. (2000). Colonial Forced Labor Policies for Road-Building in Southern Ghana and International Anti-Forced Labor Pressures, 1900–1940. *African Economic History*, 28, 1–25.

Austin, G. (2005). *Labour, Land and Capital in Ghana: From Slavery to Free Labour in Asante, 1807–1956.* New York: University of Rochester Press.

Barro, R. J., & Lee, J-W. (2015). *Education Matters: Global Schooling Gains from the 19th to the 21st Century.* New York: Oxford University Press.

Bauer, P. T. (1956). Marketing Monopoly in British Africa. *Kyklos*, 9(2), 164–80.

Booth, A. (2008). West Africa in the Southeast Asian Mirror: The Historical Origins of the Post-1960 Divergence. *Itinerario* (European Journal of Overseas History), 32(3), 61–90.

Bush, B., & Maltby, J. (2004). Taxation in West Africa: Transforming the Colonial Subject into the 'Governable Person'. *Critical Perspectives on Accounting*, 15, 5–34.

Carneiro, R. L. (1970). A Theory of the Origin of the State. *Science*, 169 (3947), 733–38.

Cogneau, D., & Moradi, A. (2014). Borders That Divide: Education and Religion in Ghana and Togo since Colonial Times. *The Journal of Economic History* 74(3), 694–729.

Conklin, A. L. (1997). *A mission to civilize: the republican idea of empire in France and West Africa, 1895–1930.* Stanford, CA: Stanford University Press.

Coquery-Vidrovitch, C. (1969). Recherches sur un mode de production Africaine. *La Pensée*, 144, 61–78.

Coquery-Vidrovitch, C. (1986). French Black Africa. In A. Roberts (Ed.), *The Cambridge History of Africa, vol. 7: From 1905–1940.* Cambridge: Cambridge University Press, 347–49.

Crowder, M. (1968). *West Africa under Colonial Rule.* London: Hutchinson & Co.

Dalrymple-Smith, A. (2017). *A Comparative History of Commercial Transition in Three West African Slave Trading Economies, 1630 to 1860.* PhD Thesis, Wageningen University.

Dalrymple Smith, A., & Woltjer P. (2016). *Commodities, Prices and Risk the Changing Market for Non-slave Products in Pre-abolition in West Africa.* AEHN Working Paper No. 31/2016.

Davis, L. E., & Huttenback, R. A. (1988). *Mammon and the Pursuit of Empire: The Economics of British Imperialism.* Cambridge, MA: Cambridge University Press.

Domar, E. D. (1970). The Causes of Slavery or Serfdom: A Hypothesis. *The Journal of Economic History*, 30(1), 18–32.

Fall, B. (1993). *Le Travail Forcé En Afrique-Occidentale Française, 1900–1946.* Paris: Karthala.

Ferguson, N., & Schularick, M. (2006). The Empire Effect: The Determinants of Country Risk in the First Age of Globalization, 1880–1913. *The Journal of Economic History*, 66(2), 283–312.

Frankel, H. S. (1938). *Capital Investment in Africa: Its Course and Effect.* London: Oxford University Press.

Frankema, E. (2010). Raising Revenue in the British Empire, 1870–1940: How 'Extractive' Were Colonial Taxes? *Journal of Global History*, 5, 447–77.

Frankema, E. (2011). Colonial Taxation and Government Spending in British Africa, 1880–1940: Maximizing Revenue or Minimizing Effort? *Explorations in Economic History*, 48(1), 136–49.

Frankema, E. (2012). The Origins of Formal Education in Sub-Saharan Africa: Was British Rule More Benign? *European Review of Economic History*, 16(4), 335–55.

Frankema, E. (2015). The Biogeographic Roots of World Inequality. Animals, Disease, and Human Settlement Patterns in Africa and the Americas before 1492. *World Development*, 70, 274–85.

Frankema, E., Green, E., & Hillbom, E. (2016). Endogenous Processes of Colonial Settlement. The Success and Failure of European Settler Farming in Sub-Saharan Africa. *Revista de Historia Económica*, 34(2), 237–65.

Frankema, E., & Jerven, M. (2014). Writing History Backwards or Sideways: Towards a Consensus on African Population, 1850–2010.

The Economic History Review, 67(4), 907–31. Accessed www.aehnet work.org/data-research/.

Frankema, E., & van Waijenburg, M. (2012). Structural Impediments to African Growth? New Evidence from Real Wages in British Africa, 1880–1965. *The Journal of Economic History*, 72(4), 895–926.

Frankema, E., & van Waijenburg, M. (2014). Metropolitan Blueprints of Colonial Taxation? Lessons from Fiscal Capacity Building in British and French Africa, c. 1880–1940. *The Journal of African History*, 55(3), 371–400.

Frankema, E., Williamson, J. G., & Woltjer, P.J. (2018). An Economic Rationale for the West African Scramble? The Commercial Transition and the Commodity Price Boom of 1835–1885. *The Journal of Economic History*, 78(1), 231–67.

Gardner, L. A. (2012). *Taxing Colonial Africa: The Political Economy of British Imperialism*. Oxford: Oxford University Press.

Gardner, L. A. (2017). Colonialism or Supersanctions: Sovereignty and Debt in West Africa, 1871–1914. *European Review of Economic History*, 21 (2), 236–57.

Goody, J. (1971). *Technology, Tradition, and the State in Africa*. London: Oxford University Press.

Hailey, L. (1939). *An African Survey: A Study of Problems Arising in Africa South of the Sahara*. London: Oxford University Press.

Herbst, J. (2000). *States and Power in Africa: Comparative Lessons in Authority and Control*. Princeton, NJ: Princeton University Press.

Hopkins, A. G. (1973). *An Economic History of West Africa*. London: Longman.

Huillery, E. (2014). The Black Man's Burden: The Cost of Colonization of French West Africa. *The Journal of Economic History*, 74(1), 1–38.

Inikori, J. E. (2003). The Struggle against the Transatlantic Slave Trade: The Role of the State. In S. Diouf (Ed.), *Fighting the Slave Trade: West African Strategies*. Athens: Ohio University Press, 170–98.

Jones, W. O. (1987). Food-Crop Marketing Boards in Tropical Africa. *Journal of Modern African Studies*, 25(3), 375–402.

Juif, D., & Frankema, E. (2018). From Coercion to Compensation: Institutional Responses to Labour Scarcity in the Central African Copperbelt. *Journal of Institutional Economics*, 14(2), 313–43.

Klein, M. A. (1998). *Slavery and Colonial Rule in French West Africa*. Cambridge: Cambridge University Press.

Law, R. (1978). Slaves, Trade and Taxes: The Material Basis of Political Power in precolonial West Africa. *Research in Economic Anthropology*, 1, 37–52.

Lovejoy, P. E. (2005). *Slavery, Commerce and Production in the Sokoto Caliphate of West Africa*. Trenton, NJ: Africa World Press.

Lydon, G. (2012). *On Trans-Saharan Trails: Islamic law, Trade Networks, and Cross-Cultural Exchange in Nineteenth-century Western Africa*. Cambridge: Cambridge University Press.

Mamdani, M. (1996). *Citizen and Subject. Contemporary Africa and the Legacy of Late Colonialism*. Princeton: Princeton University Press.

Manning, P. (1982). *Slavery, Colonialism and Economic Growth in Dahomey, 1640–1960*. Cambridge: Cambridge University Press.

Martin, S. M. (2006). *Palm Oil and Protest: An Economic History of the Ngwa region, South-eastern Nigeria, 1800–1980*. Cambridge: Cambridge University Press.

Meredith, D. (1986). State Controlled Marketing and Economic Development: The Case of West African Produce during the Second World War. *The Economic History Review*, 39(1), 77–91.

Mitchell, B. R. (2007a). *International Historical Statistics: Africa, Asia & Oceania, 1750–2005*. 5th ed. Basingstoke: Palgrave Macmillan.

Mitchell, B. R. (2007b). *International Historical Statistics: Europe, 1750–2005*. 6th ed. Basingstoke: Palgrave Macmillan.

Northrup, D. A. (1988). *Beyond the Bend in the River: African Labor in Eastern Zaire, 1865–1940*. Athens: Ohio University Center for International Studies.

Nugent, P. (2002). *Smugglers Secessionists & Loyal Citizens on the Ghana-Togo Frontier*. Athens: Ohio University Press.

Nunn, N., & Wantchekon, L. (2011). The Slave Trade and the Origins of Mistrust in Africa. *American Economic Review*, 101(7), 3221–52.

Obikili, N. (2016). The Trans-Atlantic Slave Trade and Local Political Fragmentation in Africa. *The Economic History Review*, 69(4), 1157–77.

Osafo-Kwaako, P., & Robinson, J. A. (2013). Political centralization in pre-colonial Africa. *NBER Working Paper* No. 18770.

Reid, R. J. (2012). *Warfare in African History*. Cambridge, NY: Cambridge University Press.

Sautter, G. (1967). Notes sur la Construction du Chemin de Fer Congo-Océan (1921–1934). *Cahiers d'Études Africaines*, 7(26), 219–99.

Sunderland, D. (2007). *Managing British Colonial and Post-colonial Development: The Crown Agents, 1914–74*. Woodbridge, Suffolk: Boydell & Brewer.

Tilly, C. (1990). *Coercion, Capital, and European States, A.D. 990–1992*. Cambridge, MA: Blackwell.

Tosh, J. (1980). The Cash-Crop Revolution in Tropical Africa: An Agricultural Reappraisal. *African Affairs*, 79(314), 79–94.

Van Waijenburg, M. (2017). *Financing the African Colonial State: Fiscal Capacity and Forced Labor*. PhD Thesis, Northwestern University, Evanston.

Van Waijenburg, M. (2018). Financing the African Colonial State: The Revenue Imperative and Forced Labour. *Journal of Economic History*, 78(1), 40–80.

Young, C. (1994). *The African Colonial State in Comparative Perspective*. New Haven: Yale University Press.

7   New Colonies, Old Tools: Building Fiscal Systems in East and Central Africa

Leigh Gardner

Introduction

In East and Central Africa, colonial administrators faced a number of obstacles in building centralized fiscal systems and raising sufficient funds to support colonial rule. European trade with these regions was a small fraction of the more lucrative trades with West Africa or South Africa. Colonial expansion occurred relatively late, and wary metropolitan taxpayers were increasingly reluctant to devote public funds to the project. Further, new players like Belgium, Italy and Germany had less experience and sometimes fewer resources than older metropolitan states like Britain and France.

This combination of limited trade as well as a greater struggle for metropolitan resources had important implications for the public finances of colonial administrations. First, low levels of trade left new colonial governments without an easy source of revenue to support their expenditure. Colonies in this region remained dependent on metropolitan transfers of various kinds for a number of years after the beginning of colonial rule, which also delayed the process of financial development and meant that colonial borrowing took place in the less advantageous conditions of the interwar period.

Owing to this combination of circumstances, colonial fiscal systems in the region had three distinguishing features: (1) an early reliance on direct taxes driven primarily by low levels of trade in the early years of colonial rule; (2) the presence of expatriate settler communities, both European and Asian, which influenced local political debates and led to racial distinctions in the tax code; and (3) regional coordination in tax and trade policy, including federation. This chapter examines the emergence of these three features and presents fiscal data for seven colonial governments (Belgian Congo, Kenya, Nyasaland, Northern Rhodesia, Southern Rhodesia, Tanganyika and Uganda).[1]

The chapter proceeds as follows: the next section sketches out the economic conditions and fiscal institutions which existed in East and Central Africa prior to colonial rule, which shaped initial foundations of the colonial state. The following section focuses on the response of early colonial administrations to the challenges presented by these conditions, in particular the attempted revival of old techniques of European rule including settlement and the use of chartered companies. After that, the chapter addresses the process of revenue centralization in East and Central Africa, and highlights the comparative dominance of direct taxation in comparison to West Africa. Subsequent sections examine public spending and attempts to restructure the fiscal constitution prior to decolonization.

Pre-colonial Conditions

Recent research in African history has often emphasized the significance of colonial interventions, often at the expense of deeper histories of African societies and economies (Reid 2011, 135–6). In East and Central Africa, much like in other regions, the ultimate structure of colonial institutions reflected older patterns of governance, production and trade. This section reviews current knowledge of systems of public finance which existed in this region prior to European rule. This is a necessarily speculative exercise, as the types of administrative documentary sources used to understand fiscal systems in later periods are often lacking for Africa before the nineteenth century. However, studies of economic and political change in the region offer some clues.

The key sources of government revenue before European conquest were tribute and trade. The region includes both forest and savanna, a long coastline as well as numerous inland waterways, particularly in the interlacustrine areas of the East African Rift, which provided access to fish as well as canoe transport. Tsetse fly is endemic to much of the savanna, but some areas, particularly those at higher altitude, are suitable for keeping cattle. Such variety meant that even in areas of very low population density, such as in the forested areas of what is today the Democratic Republic of the Congo (DRC), there were at least sporadic exchanges between farmers, pastoralists, fishermen and hunters (Birmingham 1977, 254). Other essential resources, such as salt and iron, are also distributed

---

[1] Data are more sporadically available for the Belgian Congo and German Tanganyika, but they are included wherever possible.

unevenly through the region, which created centres of economic diversification and exchange. The salt mines of Katwe in Uganda formed the basis for what Stanley noted in 1889 was "a busy town of 2000 people supported by the winning and sale of salt, which they bartered for grain, millet, barkcloth, iron tools, weapons and foodstuffs" (Barrett-Gaines 2004, 20). Some centres also specialized in the production of manufactured goods, particularly textiles (Clarence-Smith 2014; Frederick 2017).

Such domestic economic diversification became one important source of revenue for African rulers in the form of tribute paid by subject chiefs who provided goods from their particular region. In 1847, the revenue of the Lunda empire, which at its peak stretched across the DRC, Northeast Angola and Northwest Zambia, came from thirty-six chiefs who contributed slaves, ivory, locally produced iron, copper, hoes, bows, spears, food, palm oil, skins, raffia, cloth and earthenware. The value of these goods was approximately £60,000, more than the colonial revenue of Portuguese Angola in the same year.[2] Similarly, the Lozi kingdom collected revenue from twenty-eight different "tribes", according to Silva Porto in 1853, which provided tribute in the form of specialized local produce (Birmingham 1977, 233–4).

Opportunities for international trade came mainly from the east. Monsoon trade winds connected the East African coast to Asia and the Middle East (Alpers 1975, 2, Austen 1987, 56, Coquery-Vidrovitch 2009, 85–6). From the medieval period, the east African coast was home to a number of urban trading centres with ties to both the mainland and to the wider Islamic world. One of the most important in the medieval period was Kilwa, which used its connections to the Zimbabwe gold trade to build a dynasty which remained powerful through the sixteenth century. Its commercial influence can partly be judged by the distribution of coins minted at Kilwa, which have been unearthed through archaeological research along the length of the East African coast (Wynne-Jones & Fleischer 2012, 23).

This international trade expanded in the nineteenth century with growing demand for slaves, ivory and spices. Caravans became larger and more financially sophisticated, drawing credit from Indian moneylenders in coastal centres. The search for elephants and slaves took caravans further into the interior, strengthening trade links between interior societies and coastal commerce promoting new patterns of commercialization in these regions. For example, the important settlement of Il Chamus on Lake

---

[2] Estimate by Rodrigues Graça, quoted in Birmingham (1977, 228). For further discussion of Portuguese Africa, see Alexopoulou, Chapter 8, this volume.

Baringo, along with surrounding villages, became an important supply centre for caravans travelling through the interlacustrine region from the East African coast from the middle of the nineteenth century (Anderson 2016, 51–2).[3] Demands from a growing population of African consumers influenced production patterns in Asia and the Americas (Prestholdt 2004, Pallaver 2016).

The expansion of trade networks in the interior, as well as growing trade with the coast, provided a foundation for the rise of increasingly bureaucratic regimes (Vail 1983, 202). In general, there was considerable variety in the structure of political institutions in the region. Brennan (2017) identifies what he calls three '"matrices of political power" in East Africa. First, there were those attached to *ntemi*, or rulers who had cleared particular areas first. Second were "stranger chiefs" who "stumbled upon already-settled but badly divided populations". Third, there were a number of societies organized by generational structures such as age-sets. Trade, both domestic and international, provided the material resources for some to centralize. For example, Buganda was comprised of clans under the rule of the kabaka, "head of the clan heads". The degree to which the king could exercise real authority over village chiefs or clan heads often varied, but the state became increasingly centralized as the kabaka gradually eroded the powers of the clan heads (Reid 2002, 3). For the Nyamwezi, ivory taxes were the most important revenue source and funded the territorial expansion of the kingdom from its base in western Tanzania, as well as a large military (Birmingham 1977, 245–7, Unomah & Webster 1977, 273).

This parallel rise of trade and state centralization proved difficult to sustain, and tension over resources combined with a series of ecological crises made the nineteenth century a turbulent period. As ivory became increasingly scarce, conflict over the remaining elephant herds increased. At the same time, the decline of the slave trade also stripped away an important source of revenue and imported goods. Compounding these problems further were a series of major droughts which helped reshape the political landscape across much of East Africa (Anderson 2016). Cultural influences from Islam and European missionaries also had a destabilizing effect (Reid 2002, 6–7). By the final decades of the nineteenth century, many of the centralized states which had emerged since 1750 had fragmented. This coincided with changes in the strategic interests of European powers in the nineteenth century.

---

[3] The extent to which caravan trades promoted changes in agricultural production and consumption remains the subject of debate. For a contrary argument, see Biginagwa (2012).

New Colonies, Old Tools

In contrast to West Africa, little of the nineteenth-century trade in East and Central Africa was in European hands. European colonial conquest in the region came only in the late nineteenth century, driven in large part by commercial competition amongst both existing and aspiring imperial powers. A newly united Germany attempted to safeguard external markets in the aftermath of the Depression of the 1870s in part by recognizing the dubious claims to territory by the eccentric explorer Carl Peters in what would become German Tanganyika (Koponen 1994, chapter 2, Iliffe 1979, chapter 4). In Belgium, another new European state, King Leopold faced similar imperatives, and explained his aggressive efforts to expand the boundaries of the Congo Free State in 1888–9 by predicting that "after next year there will be nothing more to acquire in Africa".[4] This section examines how this comparatively late beginning, along with the existing political and economic landscape in the region, shaped colonial rule in the region.

Figure 7.1 compares the countries featured here in terms of both exports and revenue per capita in c. 1900 with British territories in West Africa. Colonies in East and Central Africa were lower on both metrics. Initially, this meant that colonial governments had to be established without an easily accessible source of revenue to fund administrative and military costs. Deficits were large, particularly in the first years of colonial rule. In Northern Rhodesia, for example, local revenue in 1900 was only £1631, while expenditure totalled £31,226. Uganda was only slightly better off, with local revenue in 1901 of £73,998 and expenditure of £228,680. The Belgian Congo faced perhaps the steepest uphill climb, where revenue in 1886 was just 74,000 francs and expenditure 2,219,000 francs.

The difference had to be made up using external funds, which became increasingly difficult as the period progressed. In the Belgian Congo, King Leopold initially funded the deficits from his own personal resources, until these were insufficient and he had to turn first to a lottery loan and then to the Belgian government itself (Stengers & Vansina 1985, 318). In British colonies, grants-in-aid formed a substantial share of total revenue in the years before 1914. Kenya (then known as the East African Protectorate) received an average of just under £190,000 in Parliamentary grants compared with average local revenue of £320,000 across that period. Further support came from Treasury loans, which often carried at least some interest burden (unlike similar advances made

---

[4] Quoted in Stengers and Vansina (1985, 317).

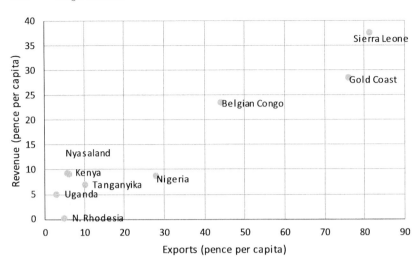

Figure 7.1 Exports and revenue pence per capita, c. 1900
In current British pence. For sources, see Appendix.

in earlier decades to West African colonies). Pressure to reduce these transfers placed strict limits on amounts and types of expenditure; in Nyasaland, for example, the colonial administration was denied permission to increase spending on agriculture and the railway until the grant-in-aid was eliminated (Gardner 2012, 26).

Another way to fund infrastructure and other development initiatives was through international financial markets. Colonies were, in general, able to borrow at lower cost than comparable independent countries. The reasons for this have been debated, but one explanation is that investors considered colonies to be subsidiary governments to metropolitan governments, and assessed the risk of default accordingly (Accominotti et al. 2011). However, colonies were not generally permitted to borrow until annual revenue was sufficient to pay interest and sinking fund contributions. Further, not all colonies were treated equally and active intervention was often required to generate demand for African bond issues (Gardner 2017). By the time colonial governments in this region were in a position to borrow, they had missed the crucial window offered by the era of 'financial globalization' up to 1914 (Flandreau & Zumer 2004). Instead, they borrowed mainly during the interwar contraction in capital flows.[5] This further dampened investor enthusiasm for debts of small,

---

[5] This region has been neglected in studies of colonial public debt.

poor countries. The underwriters of a Kenya loan wrote to the Crown Agents that "it should be remembered that the introduction of an entirely new stock such as Kenya does not appeal to underwriters in the same way that older issues and those in which there is already a large public interest do".[6] These same factors influenced the debt issues of other colonies in the region.

Lack of funds both internal and external meant that all three imperial governments in the region needed to reduce the costs of colonial rule. They revived several techniques of colonial conquest from the first period of imperial expansion, including using chartered companies and encouraging European settlement. Both had important implications for colonial fiscal systems in this region. Chartered company rule effectively delayed the process of revenue centralization as the proprietors attempted to reduce their administrative expenditure, rather than investing in a more comprehensive tax collection system. At the same time settler communities often represented powerful constituencies able to influence colonial policies in favour of their own interests.

Chartered companies had been a key means of colonial expansion in the first era of empire from the sixteenth century. In essence, metropolitan governments could outsource responsibilities for formal administration of colonies to private companies, which took on the burden in exchange for privileged rights over trade or particular resources. Once charters had been granted, metropolitan states could exert little control over their agents, and imperial history provides many examples of agents acting against the interests of the sovereign who had granted the charter, refusing to obey orders or recognize royal authorities (Burroughs 1999, 191, Benton 2010, 79). Unfortunately for most chartered companies, the costs of their administrative responsibilities exceeded their rather uncertain revenue sources, and their tenure did not last long. The Imperial British East Africa Company ceded control of the East African Protectorate (later Kenya) to the Foreign Office in 1895, just seven years after the charter was granted, citing bankruptcy as the cause (Mungeam 1966, 7–19). Bolstered by revenue from Cecil Rhodes' mining ventures, the British South Africa Company survived longer in its role, but eventually also handed over control of the Rhodesias to the British Government in 1924 (Gardner 2012, 23). Nor was this a particularly British problem. The chartered company charged with the early rule of Tanganyika, the DOAG, attempted to build a railway in 1891, but according to Iliffe (1979, 126), "they laid only forty kilometres of unsatisfactory track before its cost obliged them to abandon the project to the

[6] Scrimgeour to Crown Agents, 4 May 1921, in TNA CAOG 9/78.

government in 1899. By 1901 the DOAG had invested £169,000 in plantations and received only £13,650 in return."

Chartered company administration was more persistent, and often more infamous, in the Belgian Congo. Concessions were initially granted under the personal rule of the Congo Free State by Leopold II, who expanded his territorial claims beyond what his resources would allow him to administer himself. Instead, he offered concessions to Belgian companies in order to attract capital. The Comité Spécial du Katanga (CSK), for example, administered 45 million hectares in the Katanga region in exchange for rights over the produce of the region. Chartered companies also received guaranteed interest rates and other privileges. Unlike other colonies, however, chartered companies continued to play an important role in the Congo even after control shifted to the Belgian government in 1908, and through the rest of the colonial period (Peemans 1975, 178–9).

Having largely failed in their efforts to outsource the costs of colonial governance, imperial rulers next turned to strategies for developing the export industries that would finance their own administrations on the ground. This was easier in some places than in others. Some turned to settlers as a potential answer. Wrigley (1976, 213) notes that, owing to low population densities, it seemed natural to colonial administrators to "infer that there was ample room for immigrants and that without immigrants there could be little hope of a rapid growth of production and trade".

Economic historians have yet to form a consensus on the impact of settlers in Africa. In some cases, settlers imported beneficial new technologies and human capital which may have shaped patterns of local development (Acemoglu & Robinson 2012, chapter 9, Easterly & Levine 2016, Fourie & von Fintel 2014, Wood & Jordan 2000). However, settlers never amounted to a large share of the population. Table 7.1 gives percentages of the total population in 1960, dividing it into European, indigenous and other (primarily Asian). The country with the highest share of Europeans as a percentage of the population was Southern Rhodesia, and this was still less than 10 per cent. In others, the size of the European population was almost vanishingly small. Asian populations also varied, but were relatively substantial in Kenya, Uganda and Tanganyika. Expatriate groups therefore formed small, privileged oligarchies which used their influence with the colonial government to serve their own interest, often at the expense of the African majority. Supporting this view is evidence that, at least in British Africa, the indigenous population was worse off in terms of real wages and poverty rates than in colonies with no settler population (Bowden, Chiripanhura & Mosley 2008, Frankema & van Waijenburg 2012).

Table 7.1 *Shares of total population, c. 1960*

	European	Indigenous	Other
Kenya	1	95.6	3.3
Southern Rhodesia	7.1	92.2	0.5
Northern Rhodesia	3	96.7	0.4
Belgian Congo	0.8	99.2	
Nyasaland	0.3	99.3	0.4
Tanganyika	0.2	98.6	1.2
Uganda	0.1	98.8	1.1

Source: Mosley (1983, 7), Kettlewell (1965, 230–5); Uganda (1961); USDA (1965, 7).
Figures are approximate and may not total 100.

Settler communities differed substantially between colonies in terms of their occupations and level of economic and political influence. Decisions to encourage settlement were often controversial, with some officials afraid that settlers would need the colonial state to bail them out if their enterprises failed, which was not uncommon. Iliffe (1979, 128) writes that, "In 1903 Lushoto district office reported that not a single settler had yet made a profit", when the price of coffee, their main cash crop, declined. During downturns, settler enterprises, often heavily indebted, could be more vulnerable than African farms or commercial plantations (Gardner 2012, 71–2).

In an effort to insure against the possibility of needing to rescue settlers, some colonial administrations, like Kenya, imposed strict capital and income requirements for potential settlers. According to Kennedy (1987, 6), "a popular adage in British Africa held that Kenya was the officers' mess and Rhodesia the sergeants' mess among white settler colonies". Settlers in the 'officers' mess' wielded considerable political influence. The size and cohesiveness of settler communities influenced their ability to act collectively. Settlement was a dynamic process and the success of early groups of settlers shaped subsequent arrivals (Frankema, Green & Hillbom 2016). Distinctions between settler communities influenced the patterns of taxation and state budgets through the remainder of the colonial period.

The next section documents the growth and changing structure of public revenue in the Belgian Congo, Kenya, Nyasaland, Tanganyika, Uganda and the two Rhodesias. It shows that these colonies shared a reliance on direct taxation as opposed to trade taxes as the mainstay of the government budget. However, the structure and implementation of direct taxes varied between countries based on local resources and the politics of how to distribute the burden of funding the state.

Growth and Structure of Revenue

Despite local variations, the structure of taxation in all of these countries followed the same basic pattern over time (Hailey 1938, 676). In most colonies, metropolitan subsidies had been withdrawn before World War I as local revenue collections expanded. Direct taxation was introduced in the first few years of colonial administration, usually in the form of a hut tax followed by a poll tax, but collections were uneven, reflecting the sporadic extension of colonial administration. In this early period, collections from the non-African population were minimal, through taxes on imported goods or a separate system of poll taxes. The distribution of the tax burden increasingly became a source of political grievances.

Figure 7.2 shows revenue per capita during the colonial period, given in constant prices.[7] The figure shows a relatively gradual increase in revenues through the early colonial period and interwar period. Most colonies suffered a setback in revenue collections during World War I owing to

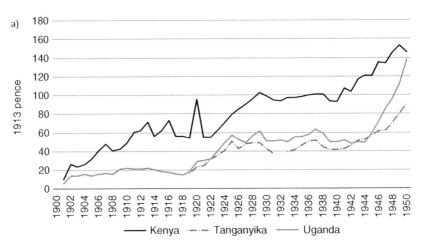

Figure 7.2a Per capita revenue, 1900–50: British East Africa (constant 1913 pence).
Source: See Appendix.

---

[7] Figures are deflated using metropolitan price series from Feinstein (1972) for Britain and Mitchell (1992) for Belgium. Use of alternative deflators does not alter the overall trend. Population statistics from Frankema and Jerven (2014).

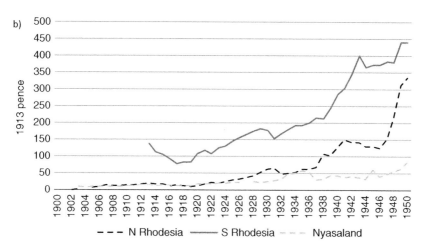

Figure 7.2b Per capita revenue, 1900–50: British Central Africa (constant 1913 pence)
Source: See Appendix.

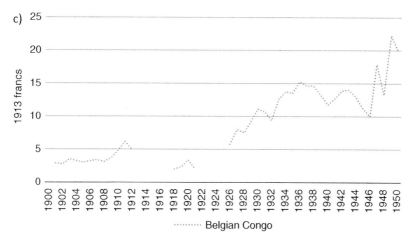

Figure 7.2c Per capita revenue, 1900–50: Belgian Congo (constant 1913 francs)
Source: See Appendix.

trade disruptions. More rapid increases occurred during and after World War II, when the war effort and post-war recovery led to rising prices for African commodities.

Figure 7.3 shows the share of trade taxes and direct taxes in total revenue over time. Compared to West Africa, where trade taxes were by

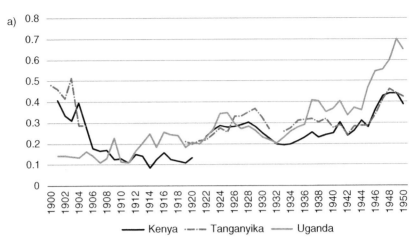

Figure 7.3a Indirect taxes as share of total – British East Africa
Source: See Appendix.

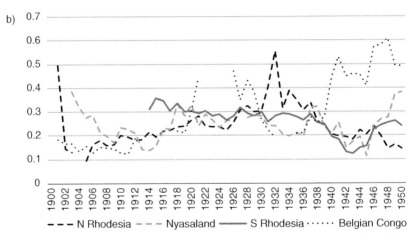

Figure 7.3b Indirect taxes as share of total – British Central Africa and Belgian Congo
Source: See Appendix.

far the largest source of revenue, they represented less than half of total revenue in East and Central Africa – sometimes substantially less. The only country which saw a majority of revenue from trade taxes was Uganda in the post-war period, after it had introduced lucrative export taxes on cotton and coffee. There is also a gap between the land-locked colonies and those on the coast (Tanganyika and Kenya), where trade

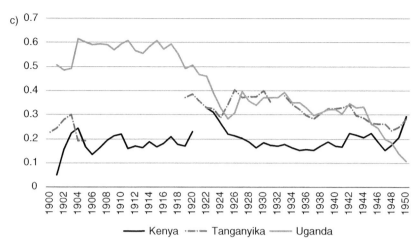

Figure 7.3c Direct taxes as share of total – British East Africa
Source: See Appendix.

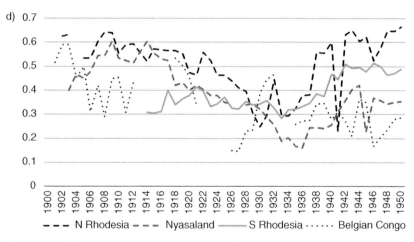

Figure 7.3d Direct taxes as share of total – British Central Africa and Belgian Congo
Source: See Appendix.

taxes were initially more important. In all cases, trade tax revenue increased faster than direct tax revenue in the interwar period as investments in infrastructure and export production began to bear fruit. During this period, the share of direct taxes decreased relative to indirect. However, this position was reversed again from the 1930s when revenues from income tax began to rise.

Table 7.2 *Hut and poll taxes*

Colony	Hut Tax		Poll Tax	
	Year Introduced	Initial Rate	Year Introduced	Initial Rate
Nyasaland	1891	6s		
Tanganyika	1897	3–12 rupees	1905	3 rupees
Southern Rhodesia			1904	£1
N-E Rhodesia	1900	3s	1914	10s
N-W Rhodesia	1904	£1		
Kenya	1901	2 rupees	1910	3 rupees
Uganda	1901	3 rupees	1910	10s
Belgian Congo			1910	Variable

Sources: Rates generally per adult male. See Gardner (2010b), Hailey (1938). In the period before World War I, the rupee/£ exchange rate was around 15 rupees per £.

Frankema and van Waijenburg (2014) show, for a wide sample of both French and British colonies, that the share of revenue from direct tax was closely related to the amount of revenue from trade taxes; where sufficient funds could be raised through indirect taxes, direct taxes were not imposed or at the very least were not very important as a source of revenue. Direct taxes across colonial Africa generally took the form of a flat-rate 'hut' tax on African dwellings, later replaced or supplemented by poll taxes on adult men. Whether in the form of hut or poll tax, the rates did not vary with income and the tax was inherently arbitrary and regressive (Fjeldstad & Therkildsen 2008, 116). Some colonial officials also argued that the imposition of such a tax would help compel Africans into the labour market, though levels of evasion were sufficiently high in most areas that it is questionable how effective this strategy was (Gardner 2012, 58–9).

By definition, the collection of direct tax required the extension of colonial governance into the interior and, in many cases, the end of the period of violent resistance. John Iliffe, writing about German Tanganyika, noted that "the imposition of tax in 1898 … initiated a transition to a second phase of administration" after the end of the conquest period (Iliffe 1979, 120). Tanganyika trailed Nyasaland, which had introduced a hut tax of six shillings per year in 1891. Uganda introduced a hut tax in 1900, followed by a poll tax five years later. Kenya's first hut tax of "not more than two rupees per annum" was imposed in 1901 (Fjeldstad & Thirkildsen 2008, 122, Gardner 2010b,

218, Gardner 2012, 47). Table 7.2 gives hut and poll taxes introduced in this region during the late nineteenth and early twentieth centuries.

However, the process was less even and more fitful than the legislative chronology suggests. Taxes were rarely imposed in full or across the whole country at the same time in the early years. In Northern Rhodesia, administrator Robert Coryndon proposed that district officers "while making it quite plainly understood that the rate of £1 per hut as laid down in Proclamation No. 18 of 1901 is the tax due and payable", should not "enforce a payment of say more than 5/- per hut for the first year, either 7/6 or 10/- for the second year, 16/- for the third and the full amount of 20/- per hut for the fourth and every subsequent year" (quoted in Gardner 2010b, 226). Similarly, in Kenya, the tax was imposed only in parts of Seyidie, Tanaland and Ukamba Provinces in 1901 (Gardner 2012, 55).

One former colonial official estimated that less than 5 per cent of the population paid direct tax in the first years (McGregor Ross 1927, 145). In 1891, the Foreign Office authorized the collection of direct taxes in Nyasaland "only on the clear understanding that it would be withdrawn if it gave rise to serious discontent".[8] German authorities in Tanganyika "were careful to levy tax only in the areas that were assumed to be safely under colonial control" (Koponen 1994, 216). Despite this gradual roll-out, tax revolts occurred in various parts of the region, including among the Kuba and other groups in the Belgian Congo, in the first years of the twentieth century (Stengers & Vansina 1985, 332–3).

Precisely who was taxed, and how, often reflected underlying resources in each colony. In the Congo Free State, under the so-called 'regime domaniale', also known as the 'red rubber' regime of the 1890s, taxes were collected not in cash but in rubber through often brutal coercion. Several factors coincided to bring about the red rubber regime, as later campaigners would label this period. One was the increasing financial desperation of King Leopold, who had been forced in 1890 to turn to the Belgian government for a series of loans to subsidize expenditure in the Congo Free State. As a result, he was under pressure to make the colonial government self-sufficient or lose control over its administration to the Belgian Parliament (Slade 1962, 175, Stengers & Vansina 1985, 318). The second factor was rising international demand for rubber linked to increasing industrial usage of rubber, the development of pneumatic bicycle tires and, finally, the automobile. This demand was filled largely by wild rubber before 1910, when plantation rubber came onto the market in larger quantities (Harms 1975, 74). During the 1890s, the Congo Free State

---

[8] Quoted in Gardner (2012, 55).

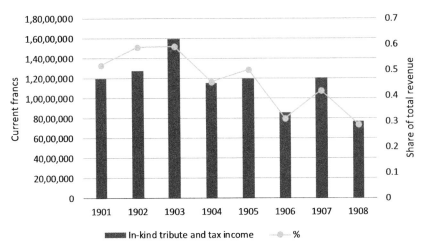

Figure 7.4 Value of in-kind revenue from rubber and ivory in the Belgian Congo
Source: De Roo (2017).

built on earlier policies which had claimed for the government all 'vacant lands', and forbade the sale of rubber and ivory to private traders (Slade 1962, 177). Figure 7.4 shows the contribution of such in-kind seizures to the budget of the Congo Free State.

While this system improved the financial position of the Congo Free State, it proved unsustainable owing to both falling rubber prices and an international outcry which ultimately ended Leopold's rule of the Congo and saw it transferred to the rule of the Belgian government.[9]

Resources also influenced the structure of taxation in the three colonies in this group with substantial mineral resources: Southern Rhodesia, Northern Rhodesia and the Belgian Congo. All three relied heavily on the mineral sector at various times in their history. The proceeds of gold mines gave Southern Rhodesia an early revenue advantage, shown in Figure 7.2.

In Northern Rhodesia and the Congo, a substantial share of revenue came, directly or indirectly, from the copper mines. In both, taxes on the profits of mining companies became an important source of revenue in the interwar period. In Northern Rhodesia, for example, copper mining companies paid 78 per cent of the total income tax revenue in 1936 (Pim

---

[9] This did not mean the end of colonial governments using forced labour, which remained an important method of resource mobilization through much of the colonial period, though one which is often hard to quantify. See, e.g., Okia (2017) on Uganda. For an attempt to calculate the value of forced labour to colonial governments in Francophone Africa, see van Waijenburg (2018).

Table 7.3 *Direct taxation per capita in 1934*

	Non-Africans	Africans	Ratio
S. Rhodesia	8.78	0.31	28.3
N. Rhodesia	7.6	0.08	95
Nyasaland	5.93	0.08	74.1
Tanganyika	2.38	0.12	19.8
Kenya	1.69	0.17	9.9
Uganda	1.56	0.15	10.4
Belgian Congo	1026 francs	8.6 francs	119.3

In pound sterling unless otherwise stated. *Source*: Hailey (1938, 547).

& Milligan 1938, 191). In the same year, the annual report on the finances of the Belgian Congo reported that income tax revenue had increased by 40 per cent from the year before. It noted that "the increase in value should be attributed mainly to the rise in commodity prices and to the development of the mining industry, which has led to an acceleration of recovery in all areas of the economic life of the colony".[10]

In addition to mining companies and mineworkers, expatriate communities formed another group which colonial states targeted, with mixed success. Table 7.3 gives approximate estimates of tax burdens for Africans and non-Africans in 1934. The ratio of non-African to African direct tax burdens varied considerably, with Kenya having the lowest non-African tax contribution. In part, this was due to Kenya's comparatively late introduction of income tax, which was fiercely resisted by the settler community. Settler representatives argued that settlers were already heavily taxed through customs tariffs, and that measurement of agricultural incomes was difficult. Further, they claimed that heavier taxation would inhibit future settlement. When the first income tax ordinance passed the Legislative Council in 1920, many of the settlers refused to pay, an act of collective disobedience so successful that out of an estimated £328,413, only £58,000 was paid, mostly by colonial officials (Hailey 1938, 550, Gardner 2012, 99). In response, the colonial government abandoned the income tax but increased tariffs on luxury imported goods such as perfume and wine which were consumed primarily by Europeans.

Racial distinctions in the tax system often had other perverse results. In 1936, the Isaq Somali community of Kenya, which had been classified as

---

[10] Chambre des Representants (1937, 55). Author's translation.

'other non-native' for the purposes of the non-native poll tax, began lobbying to pay the higher Asian rate in order to achieve Asian legal status in other areas such as labour law. Some groups of Abyssinians petitioned to pay the higher non-native tax, which the Crown Counsel argued would "not be a recognition of the right on the part of an Abyssinian to be treated as a non-native for the purposes of the Native Registration Ordinance, Native Arms Ordinance, etc. Probably this will be the next claim to be made" (Turton 1974, Gardner 2012, 108–9).

Historically, the imposition of direct taxes is often associated with a process of bargaining in which governments asking for revenue have to concede the provision of expanded services. In European history, at least, it is argued that "citizens were prepared to pay relatively high taxes in return for the public goods they desired, because they were more or less able to monitor the political process" (van Zanden & Prak 2006, 118). But how did this work under colonial rule? What sort of bargains were taxpayers able to strike, if any? And how did the racial hierarchies of political access and enfranchisement influence spending decisions? The next section examines the patterns of expenditure by colonial states and the ways in which they intersected with the taxation systems.

Dividing Assets in Divided Communities: Public Spending

This section examines the patterns of public spending in East and Central Africa. It shows that, in broad terms, these patterns were similar to those of the rest of Africa. However, there were two major exceptions: one is that the presence of settler communities prompted fierce debates about differences in service provision and the fair allocation of revenue, and the second is that federation introduced discussions about the division of resources between territories.

Public spending patterns in East and Central Africa, and in colonial Africa more generally, can be divided into three broad phases. The first, lasting approximately from the late nineteenth century until the outbreak of war in 1914, was a period of conquest and consolidation. Across much of that period, resistance to colonial rule continued, and colonial administrations pressed into new regions. As a result, the largest items in the colonial budgets were the costs of the administration and the military. The second phase, often referred to as the era of 'high colonialism' in the interwar period, saw spending on defence decrease as a share of total expenditure, replaced by investments in infrastructure, particularly railways, harbours and roads. These investments served several purposes. One was to increase exports and thus trade taxes. A second was to facilitate the expansion of

Table 7.4 *Expenditure allocations, 1900–10, 1925–9, 1945–9*

1900–1910	Admin	Defence	Education	Health	Infrastruct	Debt Svc
Belgian Congo[a]	12	46	2	2	8	0
Kenya	30	25	0	4	35	0
N Rhodesia	49	26	0	2	4	0
Nyasaland	37	30	0	6	13	0
Uganda	29	35	0	8	15	0
1925–29	Admin	Defence	Education	Health	Infrastruct	Debt Svc
Belgian Congo[b]	24		12		19	40
Kenya	16	11	5	8	12	11
N Rhodesia	39	16	4	9	19	0
Nyasaland	31	14	2	7	10	10
S Rhodesia	20	19	14	5	9	12
Tanganyika	24	14	3	10	25	2
Uganda	27	12	3	10	23	4
1945–49	Admin	Defence	Education	Health	Infrastruct	Debt Svc
Belgian Congo[c]	17	8	11	10	28	8
Kenya	13	13	7	6	12	6
N Rhodesia	39	6	7	7	15	4
Nyasaland	16	6	7	6	22	15
S Rhodesia	12	14	10	7	12	12
Tanganyika	22	8	5	8	9	3
Uganda	20	13	8	9	21	4

Notes: a. Data for 1891–7; b. for 1933–8; c. for 1955.

administration. Budgets also became more diverse in this period, particularly towards its end, as Africans suffering from the volatility of the global economy began to agitate for improved public services.

World War II marks the approximate beginning of the third phase. Wartime mobilization paved the way for a much more interventionist colonial state, and increasing African political activism convinced metropolitan states that maintaining stability in the empire required greater efforts to improve the development prospects of the colonies. Colonial resources were essential for European economies weakened by war, whether in themselves or as dollar-earners. In the British Empire, this

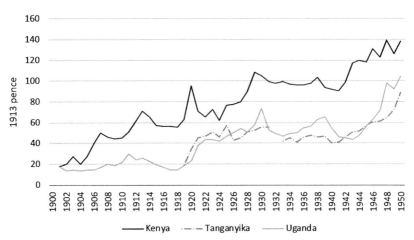

Figure 7.5a Total expenditure per capita: British East Africa (constant 1913 pence)
Source: See Appendix.

phase is often described as the 'second colonial invasion', for the expansion of the colonial civil establishment. Total expenditures went up, and the state took on a new range of development projects, including the wider provision of education and healthcare. Local governments also expanded their role. Figure 7.5 shows per capita expenditure over these three phases.

Table 7.4 shows how the allocation of these funds changed over the colonial period. It should be noted that the functional classification of colonial budgets is not an exact science. The presentation of expenditure data changes over time, and expenditures are often classified by department rather than by function, sometimes obscuring how much, for example, of the Education Department's expenditure is on the salaries of civil servants. More work is yet to be done with detailed records to calculate a true functional classification of spending. The figures below should therefore be taken as approximations only, and percentages may not total 100, particularly in later years when the range of government activity expanded. The principal omission is expenditure on agricultural services of various kinds.

Table 7.4 shows expenditure data for the first stage of colonial rule. Iliffe (1979, 119) argues for German Tanganyika that during this period the aims of colonial administration "were military security and political control". This is reflected in the expenditure statistics for all colonies, which show high shares in all cases devoted to the cost of administration and defence, which, in this case, includes both military and police expenditure. Other items of expenditure, particularly any kind of social provision, received few resources. Debt service was comparatively low or non-existent at this stage.

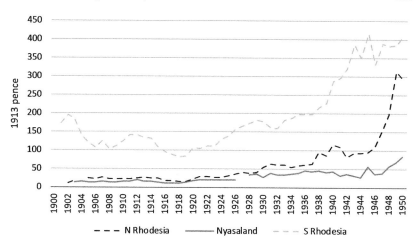

Figure 7.5b Total expenditure per capita: British Central Africa (constant 1913 pence)
Source: See Appendix.

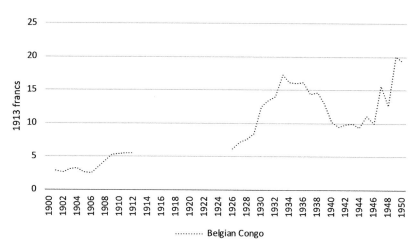

Figure 7.5c Total expenditure per capita: Belgian Congo (constant 1913 francs)
Source: See Appendix.

In the second period, infrastructure in particular increased as a share of the total budget. Infrastructure investments reduced transport costs for export goods, and new trade would increase revenue collections from both direct and indirect taxes. In addition, raw materials from the colonies could also contribute to metropolitan development (Constantine 1984, Havinden & Meredith 1993). In addition, infrastructure spending has the advantage of being relatively temporary in nature; the main expenditure is at the construction phase, with much less required for operation and maintenance. The same cannot be said of social services expenditures on education and healthcare, which require more permanent staffing with only distant potential returns to revenue.

The interwar period saw rising political activism across East and Central Africa, with African political groups lobbying for improved living standards. In response to these and other pressures, colonial governments committed to increasing spending on colonial development, particularly services to Africans. In 1940, the British government passed the Colonial Development and Welfare Act, which supplanted the 1929 Colonial Development Act. A new CDW Act was passed in 1945 with increased funding. These new priorities are reflected in public expenditures in the post-war period.

One way to characterize the changing patterns of public spending is to say that colonial governments aimed to maintain stability at the lowest possible cost, but that what was required to do this shifted over time with economic and political changes in the colonies. African taxpayers grew increasingly vocal about wanting to see some greater return for their taxes. For example, the Kavirondo Taxpayers Welfare Association of central Kenya wrote to the chair of a commission of inquiry in 1936 to say that: "About £250,000 is collected in this Province in the hut and poll tax ever year ... Every year this money goes out of the Reserve in taxes and every [sic] little comes back to Africans to be spent by Africans in the Reserves. This keeps us poor".[11] This early collective action by African taxpayers often provided the foundation for the emergence of larger political parties in the post-war period.

Controversies over the distribution of colonial budgets were often exacerbated by the presence of settlers. Bowden and Mosley (2012) disaggregate expenditures in settler and 'peasant' colonies, including Uganda and Ghana, to show that settler colonies spent less on the welfare of the African majority. They measure this in terms of what they call 'pro-poor' expenditure, or a combination of health, education and agriculture spending in African areas. Distributional debates were not restricted to racially defined communities. They could also be geographical. In Northern Rhodesia, the colonial government faced pressure for investing disproportionate amounts in the Copperbelt region, neglecting other parts of the country. In 1944, G. F. Clay, a Joint Development Adviser

---

[11] Quoted in Gardner (2012, 140–1).

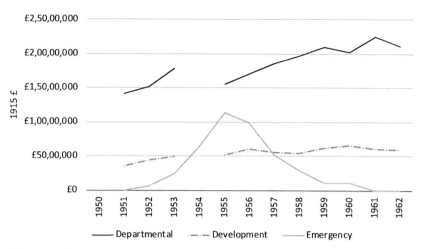

Figure 7.6 Emergency spending in Kenya
Source: Gardner (2010a, 70).

to Northern Rhodesia and Nyasaland argued that "it is only necessary to contrast the condition of the African labour on the Copperbelt and of the Askari on leave from the Forces, with that of the population remaining in rural areas to realise that one of the fundamental needs is for a large increase in the health services available in rural areas".[12]

These grievances fed the politically fraught atmosphere at the time. Unrest in various forms spread across most of Africa during the post-war period, and colonial officials drew an explicit link between political stability and development spending. At the same time, unrest itself could be costly. Perhaps the best example is Mau Mau in Kenya. Figure 7.6 shows Kenya's expenditure on the Emergency compared with ordinary and development expenditure across the 1950s. Revenue declined at the same time.

While the British government eventually stepped in to provide financial assistance, Kenya's development efforts were largely put on hold for the duration of the Emergency (Gardner 2012, 200–4). In asking for assistance from the British government, Kenyan officials repeatedly stressed the link between development projects and restoring peace. In a letter to the Secretary of State in 1953, Governor Evelyn Baring wrote, "I think most people would agree that the organization of successful peaceful development for Africans is part of the battle we are now fighting. If we can improve agriculture and education in Kikuyu areas then we are

[12] Clay (1945, 6). Quoted in Gardner (2012, 153).

fighting the revolutionary movement just as effectively as when we shoot up a gang". Another official described it as an "economic battle".[13]

In the end, the impact of this rhetorical shift in colonial policy on development outcomes was limited. Money was not always spent effectively, and there were some spectacular failures in which large sums were invested in projects which achieved little. This included the Tanganyika Groundnut Scheme (Hogendorn & Scott 1981) and the Vipya Development Scheme in Nyasaland (McCracken 2012, 244). Crises like the Mau Mau Emergency also diverted funds away from development and into defence. More broadly, however, the ambitions of colonial development planners frequently exceeded the resources at their disposal, and when there were questions about future revenues, projects with a more immediate revenue return were given priority. In a survey of the fiscal systems of the three East African territories, Wilfrid Woods noted with regard to education that all three governments had been "confronted with demands for schools which it would cost vast sums to satisfy", but that none could afford to accede to these demands "without drastic curtailment of what must, for the time being, be deemed to be the prior claims of economic development" (Woods 1946, 5–7).

In addition to limited, and sometimes unreliable, flows of revenue, colonial governments were also constrained by other factors, in particular a lack of financial development and autonomy. Monetary policy and borrowing were controlled by metropolitan governments, leaving colonial governments with little recourse in times of crisis except through the accumulation of reserves. In 1955, a Kenya Treasury official wrote that as a result of these constraints, "the role of the Finance Minister in a poor country cannot be that of a fairy godmother with a box full of Keynesian chocolates, but must rather be that of an unkind aunt who always – or almost always – says 'Jam tomorrow!'" (Butter 1955, 38). The next section examines the attempt to escape from this constraint by rethinking the structure of governments.

Regional Integration and Decentralization

The 'second colonial invasion' of the period after World War II placed considerable strain on the resources of both colonial and metropolitan governments. One strategy for coping with these problems involved rethinking the original boundaries established during the early colonial period, with an aim to create larger units more capable of sustaining development programmes. Lord Lugard (1922, 97–8) noted that "there are in British tropical

---

[13] Quoted in Gardner (2010a, 66).

Africa several blocks of territory under separate administrations which are contiguous to each other, and the question arises whether it would be more advantageous that they should be placed under a single directing authority, with a single fiscal system, a common railway policy, and identical laws".

There were various policies to encourage regional integration prior to World War II, including customs unions in both East and Southern Africa, but imperial authorities did not fully take his advice to heart until the last decades of the colonial period. At that point, they began more formal efforts to create larger territorial units. According to proponents, federation would allow wealthier territories to subsidize expenditure in poorer ones, diversify economic and fiscal foundations, and make government debt more attractive to investors (Gardner 2012, 207). This was controversial, and opponents argued that federated governments would merely serve the interests of settler communities in Kenya and the Rhodesias, and subject colonies like Uganda or Nyasaland to the discriminatory policies present in the settler colonies.

The outcomes of these efforts were disappointing for proponents. The Central African Federation, comprised of Nyasaland and the two Rhodesias, was established in 1953 but survived only a decade before splintering with the transfer of power a decade later. The level of political opposition to the Federation was summed up by a commission appointed to review its constitution in 1959: "the dislike of Federation among Africans in the two Northern Territories is widespread, sincere, and of long standing. It is almost pathological. It is associated almost everywhere with a picture of Southern Rhodesia as a white man's country."[14]

Proposals for East African federation failed, though common economic policies and services were strengthened through the creation of the East Africa High Commission in 1947. These were also controversial, as Kenya was seen to benefit disproportionately to Tanganyika and Uganda. Of the 21,000 jobs created by the common services provided by the EAHC, most went to people living in Kenya. At the same time, protective tariffs were thought to favour European producers in Kenya over the interests of African consumers in the other colonies. Given their short lives, it is unclear whether these new units achieved their aims. To take one example, namely the goal of lower borrowing costs, a 1954 World Bank memorandum on the Kariba Dam loan argued that "the creditworthiness of the Federation cannot be judged without further consideration: it is virtually a new country".[15]

---

[14] Quoted in Gardner (2012, 218).   [15] Quoted in Gardner (2012, 217).

Colonial Fiscal Systems and Colonial Legacies

The fiscal systems inherited by the former colonies when power was transferred to newly independent governments had been shaped by conditions of the pre-colonial and colonial periods. Colonial expansion in East and Central Africa came late, and faced particular challenges given limited overseas trade to serve as a revenue source. Some of the policies adopted by early colonial administrations, particularly the encouragement of settlement, had significant consequences for the politics of taxation and resource distribution in future years.

From the perspectives of government finance, these legacies were mixed. On the one hand, systems of direct taxation were much better developed by the 1960s, with income taxes and graduated personal taxes contributing substantial shares to revenue. Despite fears of tax revolts and the complications of a racially divided tax system, the early adoption of direct taxation may have served these colonies well through the economic turbulence of the decades after the outbreak of World War I. Trade taxes, though easier to collect, are more vulnerable to global price changes, especially the prices received for exports. Direct tax revenue was not immune to such trends – tax compliance often declined during downturns – but overall it offered a more stable revenue source over time.[16]

However, even direct tax revenue was subject to shocks, and the narrow economic base of some colonies in the region provided a weak foundation for fiscal growth in the post-independence period. This was most evident in Zambia and the DRC, which continued to rely heavily on the taxation of the mining industry after independence. In the case of Zambia, nationalization of the copper mines actually increased the state's dependence on mineral revenues just as the copper price declined during the 1970s.

Further, the neglect of investment in African living standards and education also left post-independence governments with major gaps to fill, and a key focus of post-independence regimes was expanding provision of education and other government services (Simson 2017). Regional policies also left their mark. The attempted secession of Katanga in the Congo also highlighted tensions over the redistribution of resources from wealthier mining areas to other parts of the country, as well as over continuing relationships with expatriate enterprise (Newbury 2012, 133). However, regional units proved difficult to dismantle, with shared infrastructure and administrative systems. When Zambia cut ties with Southern Rhodesia after the latter unilaterally declared independence in 1965, one of the biggest costs to the government was replacing

---

[16] Coefficients of variation are lower for direct tax revenue over time than for trade tax revenue. See also Mkandawire (2010).

the energy and transport infrastructure which it had previously accessed through its southern neighbour (Gardner 2012, 236–7).

Current research on colonial fiscal systems has not, in general, paid much attention to how these fiscal systems responded to the shock of decolonization, and the expansion of the franchise. However, the history of east and central Africa shows that the development of colonial fiscal systems must be understood both in light of the lasting impacts of early policies as well as in the reactions of colonial governments to 'winds of change' coming from both within and outside individual colonies. The severe constraints faced by colonial administrations which struggled to build centralized fiscal systems out of existing political and economic foundations led to both delayed financial development and the creation of a number of interest groups which shaped the tax system in unpredictable ways. These early decisions were difficult to reverse even as colonial governance entered a more interventionist phase in the decades before decolonization.

Bibliography

Accominnotti, O., Flandreau, M., & Rezzik, R. (2011). The Spread of Empire: Clio and the Measurement of Colonial Borrowing Costs. *Economic History Review*, 64(2), 385–407.

Acemoglu, D., & Robinson, J. A. (2012). *Why Nations Fail: The Origins of Power, Prosperity and Poverty*. London: Profile Books.

Alpers, E. (1975). *Ivory and Slaves: Changing Patterns of International Trade in East Central Africa to the Later Nineteenth Century*. Berkeley: University of California Press.

Anderson, D. (2016). The Beginning of Time? Evidence for Catastrophic Drought in Baringo in the Early Nineteenth Century. *Journal of Eastern African Studies*, 10(1), 45–66.

Austen, R. (1987). *African Economic History: Internal Development and External Dependency*. Oxford: James Currey.

Barrett-Gaines, K. (2004). The Katwe Salt Industry: A Niche in the Great Lakes Regional Economy. *African Economic History*, 32, 15–49.

Benton, L. (2010). *A Search for Sovereignty: Law and Geography in European Empires 1400–1900*. Cambridge: Cambridge University Press.

Biginagwa, T. J. (2012). *Historical archaeology of the nineteenth century caravan trade in North-Eastern Tanzania: a zooarchaeological perspective*. PhD Thesis, University of York.

Birmingham, D. (1977). The Forest and the Savannah of Central Africa. In J. E. Flint (Ed.), *The Cambridge History of Africa, vol. 5: from c. 1790 to c. 1870*. Cambridge: Cambridge University Press, 232–69.

Bowden, S., Chiripanhura, B., & Mosley, P. (2008). Measuring and Explaining Poverty in Six African Countries: A Long-Period Approach. *Journal of International Development*, 20(8), 1049–79.

Bowden, S., & Mosley P. (2012). *Politics, public expenditure and the evolution of poverty in Africa, 1920–2009*. Sheffield Economic Research Paper Series 2012003.

Brennan, J. (2017). Popular Politics in East Africa from Precolonial to Postcolonial Times. In T. Spear (Ed.), *Oxford Research Encyclopedia of African History*. Oxford: Oxford University Press, 1–28.

Burroughs, P. (1999). Imperial institutions and the government of empire. In A. Porter (Ed.), *Oxford History of the British Empire, vol. III: The Nineteenth Century*. Oxford: Oxford University Press, 170–97.

Butter, J. H. (1955). Problems of Colonial Financial Policy. *East African Economics Review*, 2, 24–38.

Chambre des Representants (1937). *Rapport annuel l'administration de La colonie Congo Belge*. Bruxelles: Les Anciennes Imprimeries van Gompel.

Clarence-Smith, W. G. (2014). The Textile Industry of Eastern Africa in the Longue Duree. In E. Akyampong et al. (Eds.), *Africa's Development in Historical Perspective*. Cambridge: Cambridge University Press, 264–94.

Clay, G. F. (1945). *Memorandum on Post War Development Planning in Northern Rhodesia*. Lusaka: Government Printer.

Constantine, S. (1984). *The Making of British Colonial Development Policy, 1914–1940*. London: Frank Cass.

Coquery-Vidrovitch, C. (2009). *Africa and the Africans in the Nineteenth Century: A Turbulent History*. London: M.E. Sharpe.

De Roo, B. (2016). *Colonial taxation in Africa: a fiscal history of the Congo through the lens of customs (1886–1914)*. PhD Thesis, University of Ghent.

De Roo, B. (2017). Taxation in the Congo Free State: An Exceptional Case? (1885–1908). *Economic History of Developing Regions*, 32(2), 97–126.

Easterly, W., & Levine, R. (2016). The European Origins of Economic Development. *Journal of Economic Growth*, 21(3), 225–257.

Feinstein, C. (1972). *National Income Expenditure and Output of the United Kingdom 1855–1965*, vol. 6. Cambridge: Cambridge University Press.

Fjeldstad, O-H., & Therkildsen, O. (2008). Mass taxation and state-society relations in East Africa. In D. Bräutigam, O-H. Fjeldstad & M. Moore (Eds.), *Taxation and State-Building in Developing Countries: Capacity and Consent*. Cambridge: Cambridge University Press, 114–34.

Flandreau, M., & Zumer, F. (2004). *The Making of Global Finance, 1880–1913*. Paris: OECD.

Fourie, J., & von Fintel, D. (2014). Settler Skills and Colonial Development: The Huguenot Wine-Makers in Eighteenth-Century Dutch South Africa. *Economic History Review*, 67(4), 932–63.

Frankema, E., Green, E., & Hillbom, E. (2016). Endogenous Processes of Colonial Settlement: The Success and Failure of European Settler Farming in Sub-Saharan Africa. *Revista de Historia Economica*, 34(2), 237–65.

Frankema, E., & Jerven, M. (2014). Writing History Backwards or Sideways: Towards a Consensus on African Population, 1850–2010. *Economic History Review*, 67(4), 907–31.

Frankema, E., & van Waijenburg, M. (2012). Structural Impediments to African Growth? New Evidence from Real Wages in British Africa, 1880–1965. *The Journal of Economic History*, 72(4), 895–926.

Frankema, E., & van Waijenburg, M. (2014). Metropolitan Blueprints of Colonial Taxation? Lessons from Fiscal Capacity Building in British and French Africa, c. 1880–1940. *Journal of African History*, 55(3), 371–400.

Frederick, K. (2017). Global and Local Forces in Deindustrialization: The Case of Cotton Cloth in East Africa's Lower Shire Valley. *Journal of Eastern African Studies*, 11(2), 266–89.

Gardner, L. (2010a). An Unstable Foundation: Taxation and Development in Kenya, 1945–63. In D. Branch, N. Cheeseman & L. Gardner (Eds.), *Our Turn to Eat: Politics in Kenya Since 1950*. Berlin: Lit Verlag, 52–75.

Gardner, L. (2010b). Decentralization and Corruption in Historical Perspective: Evidence from Tax Collection in British Colonial Africa. *Economic History of Developing Regions*, 25(2), 213–36.

Gardner, L. (2012). *Taxing Colonial Africa: The Political Economy of British Imperialism*. Oxford: Oxford University Press.

Gardner, L. (2017). Colonialism or Supersanctions: Sovereignty and Debt in West Africa, 1871–1914. *European Review of Economic History*, 21(2), 236–57.

Hailey, W. M. H., & Royal Institute of African Affairs (1938). *An African Survey: A Study of Problems Arising in Africa South of the Sahara*. London: Oxford University Press.

Havinden, M., & Meredith, D. (1993). *Colonialism and Development: Britain and Its Tropical Colonies*. London: Routledge.

Harms, R. (1975). The End of Red Rubber: A Reassessment. *Journal of African History*, 16(1), 73–88.

Hogendorn, J. S., & Scott, K. M. (1981). The East African Groundnut Scheme: Lessons of a Large-Scale Agricultural Failure. *African Economic History*, 10, 81–115.

Iliffe, J. (1979). *A Modern History of Tanganyika*. Cambridge: Cambridge University Press.

Kennedy, D. K. (1987). *Islands of White: Settler Society and Culture in Kenya and Southern Rhodesia, 1890–1939*. Durham: Duke University Press.

Kettlewell, R. J. (1965). Agricultural Change in Nyasaland: 1945–1960. *Food Research Institute Studies* 5.

Koponen, J (1994). *Development for Exploitation: German Colonial Policies in Mainland Tanzania, 1884–1914*. Helsinki: Raamuttutalo Pieksämäki.

Lugard, F. J. D. (1922). *The Dual Mandate in British Tropical Africa*. London: W. Blackwood and Sons.

McCracken, J. (2012). *A History of Malawi, 1859–1966*. Oxford: James Currey.

McGregor Ross, W. (1927). *Kenya from Within: A Short Political History*. London: Allen & Unwin.

Mitchell, B. R. (1992). *International Historical Statistics: Europe 1750–1988*. London: Palgrave Macmillan.

Mkandawire, T. (2010). On Tax Efforts and Colonial Heritage in Africa. *Journal of Development Studies*, 46, 1657–69.

Mosley, P. (1983). *The Settler Economies: Studies in the Economic History of Kenya and Southern Rhodesia, 1900–1963*. Cambridge: Cambridge University Press.

Mungeam, G. H. (1966). *British Rule in Kenya, 1895–1912: The Establishment of Administration in the East Africa Protectorate*. Oxford: Clarendon Press.

Newbury, D. (2012). The Continuing Process of Decolonization in the Congo: Fifty Years Later. *African Studies Review*, 55(1), 131–41.

Okia, O. (2017). Virtual Abolition: The Economic Lattice of Luwalo Forced Labor in the Uganda Protectorate. *African Economic History*, 45, 54–84.

Pallaver, K. (2016). From Venice to East Africa: History Uses and Meanings of Glass Beads. In K. Hofmeester & B. S. Grewe (Eds.), *Luxury in Global Perspective: Commodities and Practices, c. 1600–2000*. Cambridge: Cambridge University Press, 192–217.

Peemans, J.-P. (1975). Capital Accumulation in the Congo under Colonialism: The Role of the State. In P. Duignan & L. H. Gann (Eds.), *Colonialism in Africa, 1870–1960: The Economics of Colonialism*. Cambridge: Cambridge University Press, 165–212.

Pim, S. A., & Milligan, S. (1938). *Report of the Commission Appointed to Enquire into the Financial and Economic Position of Northern Rhodesia*. London: HMSO.

Prestholdt, J. (2004). On the Global Repercussions of East African Consumerism. *American Historical Review*, 109(3), 755–81.

Reid, R. (2002). *Political Power in Pre-Colonial Buganda*. Oxford: James Currey.

Reid, R. (2002). Past and Presentism: The 'Precolonial' and the Foreshortening of African History. *Journal of African History*, 52, 135–55.

Simson, R. (2017). *(Under)privileged Bureaucrats?: The Changing Fortunes of Public Servants in Kenya, Tanzania and Uganda, 1960–2010*. PhD Thesis, London, London School of Economics.

Slade, R. (1962). *King Leopold's Congo: Aspects of the Development of Race Relations in the Congo Independent State*. Oxford: Oxford University Press.

Stengers, J., & Vansina, J. (1985). King Leopold's Congo, 1886–1908. In J. D. Fage & R. Oliver (Eds.), *The Cambridge History of Africa: vol. 6 from 1870 to 1905*. Cambridge: Cambridge University Press, 315–58.

Turton, E. R. (1974). The Isaq Somali Diaspora and Poll-Tax Agitation in Kenya, 1936–41. *African Affairs*, 73(292), 325–81.

Uganda. (1961). *Uganda Census 1959*. Entebbe: Ministry of Economic Affairs.

USDA. (1965). *The Agricultural Economy of Tanganyika*. Washington, DC: USDA.

Unomah, A. C., & Webster, J. B. (1977). East Africa: The Expansion of Commerce. In J. E. Flint (Ed.), *The Cambridge History of Africa, vol. 5: from c. 1790 to c. 1870*. Cambridge: Cambridge University Press, 270–318.

Vail, L. (1983). The Political Economy of East-Central Africa. In D. Birmingham & P. Martin (Eds.), *History of Central Africa*, vol. 2. London: Longman, 200–50.

Van Waijenburg, M. (2018). Financing the African Colonial State: The Revenue Imperative and Forced Labor. *Journal of Economic History*, 117(469), 543–568.

Van Zanden, J. L., & Prak, M. (2006). Towards an Economic Interpretation of Citizenship: The Dutch Republic between Medieval Communities and Modern Nation-States. *European Review of Economic History*, 10(2), 111–45.

Wood, A., & Jordan, K. (2000). Why Does Zimbabwe Export Manufactures and Uganda Not? Econometrics Meets History. *Journal of Development Studies*, 37(2), 91–116.

Woods, W. (1946). *A Report on a Fiscal Survey of Kenya, Uganda and Tanganyika*. Nairobi: Government Printer.

Wrigley, C. C. (1976). Kenya: The Patterns of Economic Life 1902–1945. In V. Harlow & E. M. Chilver (Eds.), *History of East Africa*. Oxford: Oxford University Press, 209–64.

Wynne-Jones, S., & Fleisher, J. (2012). Coins in Context: Local Economy, Value and Practice on the Ast African Swahili Coast. *Cambridge Archaeological Journal*, 22(1), 19–36.

Data Appendix

Table A1 *Total revenue (current prices)*

	Belgian Congo	Kenya	N. Rhodesia	Nyasaland	S. Rhodesia	Tanganyika	Uganda
	BEF	£	£	£	£	DM/£	£
1900			1,631				
1901	23,108,000	68,453	2,992		439,412	2,917,000	73,998
1902	21,590,000	95,283	10,438		498,960	3,035,000	176,158
1903	26,972,000	108,856	19,007	65,895	437,175	3,218,000	181,473
1904	25,519,000	154,756		62,202	456386	3,267,000	199,557
1905	23,998,000	270,362	48,032	69,388	528547	6,029,000	179,755
1906	27,574,000	461,362	59,138	74,756	544937	6,680,000	203,818
1907	28,541,000	474,759	88,899	67,197	554029		189,326
1908	26,637,000	485,668	81,829	70,533	564399		197,202
1909	28,907,000	503,039	86,633	68,647	626172		268,259
1910	38,290,000	609,585	100,636	86,980	784909		287,094
1911	50,388,000	919,077	97,474	97,355	818355		267,657
1912	41,745,000	787,404	116,921	128,272	769978		282,787
1913		1,123,798	126,335	124,848	777008		289,844
1914		984,755	137,992	118,522	718126		292,138
1915		1,165,561	134,743	137,911	744629		285,411
1916		1,533,783	121,504	148,283	736127		314,064
1917		1,368,328	143,972	144,239	737442		326,366
1918	35,956,254	1,548,703	139,097	187,645	887800		351,834
1919	48,928,471	1,726,435	152,099	186,926	1053395		495,548
1920	76,954,135	2,978,785	169,715	267,969	1367827	669097	777,084
1921	50,556,839	1,722,239	235,403	259,116	1488606	946844	803,173
1922		1,649,032	279,104	247,347	1326469	978191	820,365
1923		1,839,447	258,008	281,044	1521881	1228586	999,750
1924		2,111,565	309,794	293,055	1599455	1315187	1,239,789
1925		2,430,509	371,046	322,160	1842283	1558981	1,479,284
1926	309,713,335	2,627,222	421,034	348,320	2009628	1975400	1,389,641
1927	504,034,161	2,846,110	474,683		2165208	1691451	1,292,306
1928	475,047,770	3,020,693	541,605	374,967	2333246	1904107	1,519,237
1929	593,107,071	3,333,742	672,288	372,507	2487185	1972858	1,682,918
1930	634,032,941	3,241,599	830,254	400,923	2449283	2002982	1,412,241
1931	525,164,463	3,066,929	856,376	443,535	2110280	1749478	1,399,912
1932	387,345,079	3,010,213	616,998	486,664	2268910	1522368	1,402,527
1933	507,779,031	3,121,496	646,283	598,777	2465380		1,350,069
1934	529,210,147	3,182,938	693,337	643,672	2722038	1564538	1,527,672
1935	593,769,301	3,304,026	833,484	777,785	2820526	1720285	1,566,688
1936	744,659,093	3,496,388	863,255	831,635	3059858	1973863	1,712,939
1937	835,891,551	3,667,393	981,894	542,035	3437266	2206417	1,959,533
1938	782,768,854	3,776,030	1,593,504	590,943	3514032	2345004	1,863,863
1939	735,067,845	3,811,773	1,674,369	817,485	4371551	2113294	1,717,926

Table A1 *(cont.)*

	Belgian Congo	Kenya	N. Rhodesia	Nyasaland	S. Rhodesia	Tanganyika	Uganda
	BEF	£	£	£	£	DM/£	£
1940	851,207,765	4,111,412	2,245,084	910,997	5619909	2133345	1,870,914
1941	1,172,758,552	5,348,888	2,979,613	902,984	6763810	2308108	2,178,283
1942	1,560,789,508	5,595,024	3,072,512	1,054,261	8350986	2674558	2,190,065
1943	1,883,650,577	6,801,859	3,274,178	1,025,421	10422944	3146939	2,428,658
1944	2,023,947,020	7,734,332	3,338,618	1,029,567	10521764	3729766	2,658,241
1945	1,999,566,278	8,034,196	3,433,507	1,894,089	11096123	4207397	3,366,424
1946	2,002,034,303	9,057,390	3,362,141	1,211,349	11214278	4768397	4,053,236
1947	3,926,683,662	9,876,888	4,439,730	1,566,250	12700414	5146761	5,331,221
1948	3,237,425,200	11,411,664	6,715,517	1,870,607	13530621	5776796	6,401,346
1949	5,223,085,784	13,030,650	10,583,863	2,378,201	16910773	6965058	8,094,383
1950	5,028,376,000	13,244,018	12,059,219	2,999,988	17999217	8585645	11,036,702

Table A2 *Expenditure*

	Belgian Congo	Kenya	N. Rhodesia	Nyasaland	S. Rhodesia	Tanganyika	Uganda
	BEF	£	£	£	£	DM/£	£
1900			31,226				
1901	23,463,000	278,151	60,688		736,859		228,680
1902	20,989,000	311,469	72,026		841,700		173,528
1903	24,519,000	418,877	111,778	102,525	812,396		186,800
1904	25,638,000	302,559		122,771	624,053		171,869
1905	20,814,000	418,839	150,176	108,682	549,057		185,919
1906	21,798,000	616,088	139,908	111,563	501,474		191,502
1907	28,526,000	691,676	150,182	105,586	543,597		195,077
1908	37,256,000	703,102	138,230	103,032	508,915		256,837
1909	41,035,000	669,404	135,839	108,728	553,041		240,240
1910	43,848,000	682,041	143,389	112,368	648,684		276,156
1911	45,908,000	772,353	149,084	118,069	737,949		382,175
1912	46,491,000	961,978	164,542	166,360	770,867		318,215
1913		1,115,898	178,043	133,105	763,916		342,874
1914		1,151,729	186,169	143,160	848,611		340,643
1915		1,072,916	192,769	125,665	768,953		304,332
1916		1,197,396	160,672	128,272	751,085		297,574
1917		1,368,329	184,131	143,676	838,597		292,913
1918	43,775,874	1,548,703	188,121	150,198	888,913		330,972
1919		2,024,081	199,170	217,659	1,082,371	790,025	497,594
1920		2,976,960	300,186	261,812	1,350,005	1,389,353	616,151

Table A2 *(cont.)*

	Belgian Congo	Kenya	N. Rhodesia	Nyasaland	S. Rhodesia	Tanganyika	Uganda
	BEF	£	£	£	£	DM/£	£
1921		2,222,380	363,518	305,494	1,335,040	1,807,889	1,014,271
1922		1,972,212	367,374	312,298	1,357,442	1,811,871	1,110,530
1923		2,137,633	338,983	282,800	1,355,928	1,901,157	1,079,050
1924		1,861,510	340,326	295,481	1,591,745	1,747,578	1,065,921
1925		2,339,995	394,145	301,933	1,752,254	2,233,626	1,203,457
1926	338,750,586	2,414,681	455,959	318,899	2,006,957	1,671,201	1,330,355
1927	451,210,213	2,515,101	518,806		2,168,954	1,782,076	1,430,976
1928	484,010,373	2,834,646	496,399	528,312	2,273,827	2,049,235	1,368,188
1929	547,559,734	3,505,050	532,367	557,247	2,470,518	2,147,624	1,607,174
1930	714,962,530	3,438,874	704,986	428,901	2,453,286	2,297,881	2,040,293
1931	656,612,306	3,216,096	820,056	578,994	2,228,822	2,257,403	1,451,562
1932	574,577,945	3,119,722	794,039	505,799	2,176,565		1,332,751
1933	694,352,582	3,168,034	778,878	528,361	2,500,246	1,694,828	1,275,593
1934	626,081,056	3,180,795	712,902	571,674	2,636,542	1,871,496	1,361,666
1935	706,628,075	3,252,783	806,429	622,874	2,888,424	1,750,068	1,440,094
1936	785,575,282	3,340,381	857,417	754,216	3,017,573	2,029,824	1,624,073
1937	826,521,099	3,565,976	909,252	745,543	3,173,221	2,173,922	1,740,888
1938	782,768,854	3,876,952	1,417,776	819,260	3,591,203	2,186,032	2,019,654
1939	725,928,340	3,808,079	1,382,363	806,806	4,083,210	2,388,821	2,259,576
1940	741,856,030	4,064,465	2,026,037	924,137	5,646,950	2,255,915	2,056,543
1941	873,710,001	4,511,274	2,161,365	740,565	6,607,061	2,550,190	1,937,925
1942	1,108,888,182	5,341,551	1,779,971	918,225	7,763,731	3,132,026	2,063,528
1943	1,329,495,874	6,782,466	2,157,033	875,614	10,020,070	3,725,042	2,136,553
1944	1,449,003,079	7,629,087	2,363,826	857,194	10,050,177	4,180,939	2,597,659
1945	1,981,076,004	7,815,928	2,543,370	1,771,453	12,392,815	4,756,258	3,199,421
1946	1,999,741,349	8,795,237	2,898,788	1,136,882	10,001,039	5,140,442	3,574,193
1947	3,426,551,000	9,023,624	4,534,132	1,375,645	12,899,754	5,664,952	4,473,773
1948	3,072,172,100	10,966,892	6,208,455	2,104,904	13,602,085	6,381,963	6,530,443
1949	4,698,593,879	10,761,675	10,600,457	2,745,295	14,828,537	7,772,440	6,686,865
1950	4,808,519,000	12,503,798	10,591,694	3,598,195	16,726,257	10,122,799	8,000,382

Table A3 *Indirect tax revenue*

	Belgian Congo	Kenya	N. Rhodesia	Nyasaland	S. Rhodesia	Tanganyika	Uganda
	BEF	£	£	£	£	DM/£	£
1900						1,403,000	
1901	4,208,000	27,892	1,486		121,323	1,396,000	10,473
1902	3,580,000	31,906	1,521		128,383	1,347,000	5,828
1903	4,505,000	34,124	2,483	25,377	126,573	1,681,000	6,996
1904	3,381,000	61,520		19,918	105,934	1,722,000	8,026
1905	3,743,000	75,800	4,508	19,131	129,456	1,913,000	12,553
1906	3,528,000	81,302	9,581	21,343	156,867		13,187
1907	4,306,000	78,717	15,853	14,515	162,456		11,355
1908	3,979,000	81,655	12,979	13,872	194,015		13,144
1909	4,161,000	63,593	14,017	11,503	208,412		37,573
1910	4,858,000	78,123	20,337	20,189	273,759		21,385
1911	6,129,000	101,088	18,861	22,035	297,904		21,851
1912	7,981,000	146,085	20,859	26,543	235,431		39,782
1913		158,637	23,143	17,492	254,204		51,995
1914		85,544	29,538	16,448	224,076		69,806
1915		145,397	26,087	21,570	265,816		52,329
1916		243,770	26,513	34,143	254,058		79,863
1917		170,509	31,903	32,617	224,174		79,063
1918	7,888,770	181,261	32,648	62,582	298,091		84,148
1919	10,353,512	186,218	36,420	52,509	315,765	140,708	90,849
1920	23,422,469	399,657	44,779	87,758	417,209	188,199	161,118
1921	22,610,533		66,891	62,563	437,289	209,866	157,980
1922		387,530	66,718	71,407	403,338	267,939	190,056
1923		492,128	60,652	74,848	431,738	325,676	272,000
1924		607,350	72,720	68,732	461,573	426,725	427,262
1925		679,726	83,056	84,269	486,809	501,065	513,619
1926	145,952,890	741,373	107,917	93,357	569,674	562,623	409,362
1927	176,983,779	830,550	146,500		686,194	631,708	348,082
1928	205,647,055	915,281	175,964	103,512	681,148	697,881	432,062
1929	228,565,959	949,725	202,000	106,073	704,693	739,670	439,375
1930	167,983,532	815,286	251,330	113,309	739,607	565,997	324,763
1931	115,809,280	698,583	344,314	106,545	543,160	411,354	304,127
1932	73,218,044	597,262	342,017	117,476	644,466		284,377
1933		600,416	204,018	122,863	720,478	404,730	308,968
1934		631,509	270,662	127,747	790,566	476,267	393,693
1935	123,759,724	715,211	291,956	165,502	791,725	612,563	436,539
1936	157,771,590	802,638	266,793	159,979	809,424	697,133	496,709
1937	234,516,517	932,853	331,982	172,701	998,870	751,288	800,267
1938	199,227,771	878,608	414,120	190,616	895,594	644,748	752,866
1939	205,446,994	918,258	403,995	189,933	1,072,961	684,200	604,289
1940	382,117,587	1,038,311	461,801	190,254	1,097,304	631,200	691,654
1941	623,722,124	1,614,465	587,218	230,384	1,244,550	783,430	878,965
1942	701,091,176	1,325,423	599,205	155,835	1,090,310	769,693	731,600
1943	863,158,431	1,780,359	604,154	178,723	1,294,741	1,049,267	901,367
1944	922,164,434	2,398,401	738,790	198,427	1,551,901	1,209,224	954,371
1945	822,278,071	2,256,139	696,831	212,352	1,706,300	1,372,988	1,585,443

Table A3 *(cont.)*

	Belgian Congo	Kenya	N. Rhodesia	Nyasaland	S. Rhodesia	Tanganyika	Uganda
	BEF	£	£	£	£	DM/£	£
1946	1,147,993,528	3,314,879	806,257	295,392	2,522,366	1,759,378	2,098,670
1947	2,287,428,642	4,254,210	863,377	418,059	3,074,414	2,373,477	2,838,178
1948	1,969,480,300	5,040,281	976,725	514,923	3,454,605	3,220,378	3,499,721
1949	2,583,407,000	5,733,012	1,697,913	893,573	4,406,010	3,800,311	5,391,288
1950	2,463,805,000	5,130,791	1,723,677	1,149,907	4,329,683	4,416,145	6,882,320

Table A4 *Direct tax revenue*

	Belgian Congo	Kenya	N. Rhodesia	Nyasaland	S. Rhodesia	Tanganyika	Uganda
	BEF	£	£	£	£	DM/£	£
1900						662,000	
1901	11,961,000	3,328				738,000	37,504
1902	12,741,000	14,698	6,532		104,150	902,000	19,936
1903	15,971,000	24,177	12,041	26,276		984,000	25,356
1904	11,577,000	37,655		29,023		1,145,000	36,700
1905	12,004,000	44,541	25,598	31,074	184,261	1,274,000	46,297
1906	8,625,000	61,333	31,499	35,619			54,399
1907	12,041,000	77,561	53,919	36,605			61,957
1908	7,721,000	94,752	52,553	38,388			60,371
1909	13,002,000	106,563	55,584	41,530			94,241
1910	17,284,000	134,446	55,876	46,533			113,440
1911	15,560,000	146,215	57,716	50,970			123,462
1912	18,064,000	167,541	69,543	65,684			134,709
1913		183,001	70,562	69,809	218,745		141,646
1914		185,978	71,759	71,754	221,539		165,144
1915		193,914	77,199	76,679	226,022		173,640
1916		275,603	69,156	78,478	228,090		180,189
1917		287,515	81,758	75,448	294,266		193,676
1918	19,212,559	272,935	78,895	79,303	301,191		195,704
1919	24,663,842	294,777	83,848	80,582	383,948	249,817	243,892
1920	35,181,078	683,956	80,732	107,194	519,335	366,535	392,633
1921	16,987,773		109,065	109,022	616,967	349,554	375,187
1922		541,805	155,706	99,611	524,516	406,549	376,187
1923		575,089	135,248	106,623	508,248	426,333	394,162
1924		561,629	143,076	110,948	550,991	446,900	406,324
1925		537,478	172,087	112,490	681,973	674,973	419,007
1926	45,987,099	558,044	184,777	119,934	652,764	682,106	427,333
1927	73,114,424	570,783	195,375		695,047	708,533	513,250
1928	109,267,179	564,405	214,091	127,026	826,926	736,970	545,500
1929	137,816,209	539,641	207,600	128,165	842,738	748,734	573,593
1930	247,157,735	591,424	207,142	129,087	839,058	700,852	522,971
1931	234,481,156	530,877	251,712	128,757	751,908	537,033	516,801
1932	181,199,025	515,277	274,830	123,857	740,959		519,354

Table A4 *(cont.)*

	Belgian Congo	Kenya	N. Rhodesia	Nyasaland	S. Rhodesia	Tanganyika	Uganda
	BEF	£	£	£	£	DM/£	£
1933		557,791	193,246	111,651	700,825	590,231	528,047
1934		514,480	202,670	129,562	865,688	592,119	535,698
1935	153,633,838	502,302	271,541	129,059	906,931	632,330	550,298
1936	204,096,705	544,897	327,881	131,608	1,022,475	657,305	560,660
1937	231,352,493	552,523	374,579	132,120	1,191,532	663,241	580,291
1938	267,474,765	636,798	890,825	145,027	1,359,795	643,369	571,395
1939	256,164,408	712,480	930,550	195,947	1,642,531	696,604	552,077
1940	236,759,437	702,194	1,352,658	233,748	2,631,765	754,000	601,259
1941	366,885,643	887,710	690,864	280,428	3,019,304	883,887	660,250
1942	423,244,171	1,244,193	1,951,280	375,585	4,256,492	1,069,739	758,043
1943	392,286,448	1,478,742	2,128,196	413,005	5,126,152	1,106,158	795,577
1944	737,809,858	1,578,775	2,018,477	435,059	5,230,116	1,206,598	884,623
1945	699,751,731	1,798,699	2,135,277	425,889	5,297,923	1,265,559	885,226
1946	330,959,931	1,715,697	1,755,687	447,581	5,750,216	1,350,108	934,128
1947	808,985,791	1,498,121	2,584,173	559,872	6,321,957	1,521,362	1,015,163
1948	757,212,000	1,979,133	4,347,014	641,328	6,256,872	1,636,607	1,068,989
1949	1,466,376,175	2,660,884	6,842,177	832,360	7,940,537	2,115,910	1,056,686
1950	1,443,694,000	3,911,890	8,015,654	1,066,434	8,769,384	2,936,123	1,115,300

Sources:
DRC:
De Roo, Bas. (2016), '*Colonial taxation in Africa: a fiscal history of the Congo through the lens of customs* (1886–1914)', PhD thesis, University of Ghent.
Chambre des Representants (various), *Rapport annuel l'administration de La colonie Congo Belge* (Bruxelles: Les Anciennes Imprimeries van Gompel).
Kenya:
Kenya Colony (various), *Financial Reports* (Nairobi: Government Printer).
Zambia:
British South Africa Company (various), *Directors' Report and Accounts* (London).
Northern Rhodesia (various), *Blue Books* (Lusaka: Government Printer).
Northern Rhodesia (various), *Financial Reports* (Lusaka: Government Printer).
Nyasaland:
Nyasaland (various), *Blue Books* (Zomba: Government Printer).
Nyasaland (various), *Financial Reports* (Zomba: Government Printer).
Zimbabwe:
Southern Rhodesia (various), *Report of the Auditor General* (Salisbury: Government Printer).
Tanzania:
Koponen, J. (1994), *Development for Exploitation: German Colonial Policies in Mainland Tanzania, 1884–1914* (Helsinki: Raamuttutalo Pieksamaki).
Tanganyika (various), *Blue Books* (Dar-es-Salaam: Government Printer).
Tanganyika (various), *Financial Statements by the Accountant-General and Report Thereon by the Direct of Audit* (Dar-es-Salaam: Government Printer).
Uganda:
Uganda (various), *Blue Books* (Entebbe: Government Printer).
Uganda (various), *Financial Reports* (Entebbe: Government Printer).

8   Local Conditions and Metropolitan Visions: Fiscal Policies and Practices in Portuguese Africa, c. 1850–1970

Kleoniki Alexopoulou

Introduction

Three major developments spurred Portuguese interests in Central Africa during the mid-nineteenth century.[1] First, Portugal was severely hurt by the independence of Brazil in 1822. For most of the eighteenth century, over 50 per cent of Portuguese state revenues had been derived from Brazil (Maxwell 2000, 1). It was hoped that an extension of the Portuguese strongholds in Central Africa could compensate for part of this loss. Second, the abolition of the slave trade in 1836 and the international ban on slavery in 1876 dealt another blow to the Portuguese economy. Portugal and Portuguese Brazil were the largest slave traders in the Atlantic world and the transfer of slaves from Angola to the mines and plantations of Brazil accounted for an overwhelming share of the colonial budgets (Capela 1979, 85–6, Lains 1998, 236). At the same time, Britain gained ground by the expansion of legitimate commerce, the shift to steam shipping and by increasing exports of industrial commodities and financial services during the nineteenth century. Expansion in Africa was part of a strategy to curb the growing British domination in the Southern hemisphere (Newitt 1995, 333). Third, there was an emerging

[1] I would like to thank Ewout Frankema, Elise van Nederveen Meerkerk, Maciel Morais Santos, Filipa Ribeiro da Silva, Barbara Direiro, Leigh Gardner, Philip Havik, Nuno Valério, Anthony Gerald Hopkins, William Clarence Smith, Corrado Tornimbeni, Anna Maria Gentili and Dácil Juif. I also owe deep gratitude to Diogo Paiva for his assistance in data collection; to the participants of the 9th New Frontiers in African Economic History Workshop at London School of Economics (October 2014); to the participants of the World Economic History Congress 'Diversity in Development' in Kyoto (August 2015); and to the participants of the workshop on Lusophone Africa in World Politics at Bologna University (May 2017) for their insightful comments. Last but not least, I am grateful for the financial support provided by the Netherlands Organization for Scientific Research (NWO) as part of the VIDI project 'Is Poverty Destiny? Exploring Long-Term Changes in African Living Standards in Global Perspective'. The usual disclaimer applies.

bourgeoisie in the urban centres of Portugal – Lisbon and Porto in particular – with roots in the banking and trade sectors. This group gained political influence and lobbied continuously for new industrial investments and the promotion of capitalist entrepreneurship (Clarence-Smith 1979, 167, 170). In their view, Africa offered opportunities for such capital investments if the Portuguese government would stimulate the exploration of Africa's interior resources and develop institutions to regulate wealth extraction (Newitt 1995, 334).

These three factors in combination with the increasing threats posed by King Leopold's explorations in the Congo and German incursions in the south of Angola during the 1880s, created a need to safeguard the informal Afro-Portuguese trade empire through a more direct form of control over African resources (Newitt 1995, 332). At the Berlin Conference (1884–5) the Portuguese stressed that their claims to Central African territory were based on prior discovery and a long-term presence in the region. Yet, the principle of "effective occupation" prescribed that territorial claims had to be backed up by treaties with local leaders, by planting flags and by the establishment of an administration and police force to keep order (Herbst 2000, 71–2). With the benefit of hindsight, these visions of a unified Central African territory under Portuguese rule, connecting the Atlantic with the Indian coasts, proved illusionary. The political negotiations with Britain about overlapping territorial claims were never an equal game. Britain ruled the waves, while Portugal had lost a great deal of its former imperial power and the costs of occupation pressed hard on its impoverished economy.

Indeed, Portuguese–African trade relations had deep roots in what later became Angola and Mozambique.[2] The Portuguese were the first to arrive in Central West Africa, and already in the sixteenth century the king of the Kongo kingdom converted to Christianity. The Portuguese dominated the slave trade south of the equator and drew parts of the Eastern coast of Central Africa into the trans-Atlantic slave trade during the second half of the seventeenth century (Klein 2010). Portuguese merchants settled at the coast, albeit in small numbers, and some also went further inland to establish plantations in the central zone of Mozambique under the so-called *prazo* system. Yet, Portugal was forced into a scramble for the vast hinterlands stretching beyond the coastlines where most of their trade had concentrated. The Portuguese government knew that if it waited to move, other European nations would stake out

---

[2] Throughout this chapter, I will refer to the territories of Angola and Mozambique using the names they obtained under colonial rule. I am aware of the anachronism. I will use more specific geographic indications when the context requires.

their claims. British fears of French and German incursions gave Portugal some room to manoeuvre, but the occupation involved significant warfare and went against considerable vested interests. This context of contested occupation shaped the evolution of a specific "Portuguese African" colonial fiscal system.

The military and economic competition extended far beyond the negotiation tables in Berlin. On the ground, private concession companies such as the *Companhia de Moçambique* and the *British South Africa Company* both aimed to get access to mineral deposits in the areas of Zambezia, Manica and Sofala. The efforts of the Company of Mozambique to reach an agreement with Rhodes' BSA Company pushed the Portuguese authorities to develop a vision of colonial administration which was closely aligned with the British 'model' of indirect rule through concession companies. It also spurred investments in military and administrative capacity and infrastructure to defend Portugal's territorial claims against the British (Costa 1902, 9).

There are four specific features of fiscal state formation in Portuguese Africa that I will highlight in the remainder of this chapter. First, a central colonial budget had existed from 1845 onwards for Angola and 1854 for Mozambique (*Governo Geral da Provincia de Moçambique*, various issues, 1850–1910), but the process of revenue centralization only gained steam in the early twentieth century.[3] Second, even though custom revenues, as in most other African colonies, were the single biggest item of state revenue, the revenue mix did contain some categories that were more common to Asian colonial fiscal systems than to colonial Africa. These included a corporate income tax, a range of sales taxes and excises and an urban property tax.[4] Third, both Portuguese African states were highly militarized. Even though the governments of Angola and Mozambique were certainly not among the poorest in colonial Africa in terms of comparative per capita revenues, the share of welfare spending (i.e., health and education) remained low and only expanded modestly during the First Portuguese Republic (1911–26) and after 1950. Security, infrastructure (also serving security objectives) and administration remained the key spending categories, and especially military spending remained high up to the 1930s (Alexopoulou & Frankema 2019). Fourth, even though many colonial economies included poorly integrated production

---

[3] In the metropole, centralization and regulation of government accounts was achieved by 1859 (Dincecco 2011, 22). However, budgets of Portugal were already published in Diario do Governo since early 1820s: https://dre.pt/web/guest/conheca-o-diario-da-republica.

[4] Attempts to introduce a land tax in 1868 failed in the metropole as well as the colonies (Cardoso & Lains 2010, 263).

and trade enclaves, fiscal unification in Portuguese Africa proved very complicated, and was actually never achieved in Mozambique. The civil wars that devastated both countries in the immediate post-colonial era reflected this lack of integration (Newitt & Tornimbeni 2008, Alexopoulou & Juif 2017).

This chapter investigates in a largely chronological order how colonial fiscal policies and practices evolved, and how these were shaped by local conditions as well as by regime changes in Portugal. I will present data from primary and secondary sources to reveal the main trends in taxation and expenditure and highlight the main differences between Angola and Mozambique. The period under examination spans from the later settlements of Portuguese merchants and land owners in the mid-nineteenth century under the *prazo* system (in central Mozambique), to the official incorporation of the two colonies into the Portuguese Empire in the 1890s, to the shifts of power in Portugal in the 1910s to 1930s, to the post-war era up to the independence wars of the 1960s and 1970s.

The Onset of Colonial Occupation, 1850s–1910s

The change from tribal rule to military occupation was violent, politically complicated and had remained far from completed at the start of the twentieth century. In Angola, changing coalitions of African kings and chiefs supported and resisted colonial occupation. Earlier military campaigns during the sixteenth to nineteenth centuries had never led to permanent occupation, but had influenced local expectations about Portuguese intentions. Especially the Kingdom of Kongo, which tried to benefit from 'peaceful' trade in ivory and slaves with the Portuguese, and absorbed forms of 'cultural colonization', experienced frequent military confrontations in case it failed to meet Portuguese demands. Wheeler (1972, 68) has even claimed that "the traditional form of African resistance against Portuguese rule in Angola, was armed violence repeated on countless occasions over a period of 300 years".

These confrontations enhanced a type of micro-nationalist identity in the Kongo long before the emergence of the Angolan state. Kings of the Kongo were writing protest letters against Portuguese slave traders in the early seventeenth century, in order to protect their communities. In the mid-nineteenth century, this micro-nationalism triggered resistance against newly imposed taxes by the Portuguese. In 1841 Prince Alexus, brother of King Henry II of Kongo, ordered a major chief not to pay a new Portuguese tax in Dembo territory (Wheeler 1972, 68). The Dembo lived northeast of Luanda and were part of the Mbundu peoples, who consisted of an assembly of Bantu-speaking tribes in north-western Angola that were part of a paramount chiefdom. The Dembo were the last of the Mbundu tribes to be defeated by the Portuguese in a war that officially lasted for three years (1907–10), but in reality continued up to 1917. The conflict demanded considerable numbers of lives on both sides. Such violent resistance urged the colonial government to channel substantial resources into military campaigns, placing a large burden on the central budget, as I will show later on. However, after 'pacification' was attained and local chiefs were willing or forced to cooperate with the colonial administration, the existence of a semi-centralized political structure facilitated colonial control.

The colonial administration adopted a system of indirect rule in which privileges were provided to native chiefs who were loyal to the colonial administration and cooperated in local tax collection. Up to 1925, the armed forces of Angola consisted of a first-line army staffed by European soldiers and a larger second-line force of African auxiliary forces named the *guerra preta* (Wheeler 1969, 426). This system was supported by loyal *sobas* (chiefs) and its principal strength was its capacity of rapid mobilization of African troops whenever a crisis broke out (Wheeler 1969, 427).

The colonies were primarily supposed to provide the metropole with raw materials and markets for Portuguese exports. In 1898, a report of the Ministry of Marine and Overseas Affairs stated that "in countries, such as the Portuguese colonies, where the agriculture and industrial sectors are least developed, commercial movement is the best indicator of their economic progress" (Dias Costa 1898a, 9). Infrastructural investments were key to encourage trade and local production (Dias Costa 1898a, 10). In reality, however, imperial trade consisted largely of re-exports of colonial produce to other European countries via Lisbon. This invited continuous manipulation of trade margins, especially after the end of the liberal era in Portuguese politics. From a metropolitan viewpoint, these trade policies were successful. For most of the colonial era the African colonies contributed positively to Portugal's balance of payments and formed an important source of foreign currency for the Portuguese economy (Lains 1998, 243).

Angola received the lion's share of private investments by agricultural, mineral and commercial corporations. It had been the main area for the trade in slaves, it held tracts of highly fertile soils and it had more developed markets for industrial goods from Portugal (Dias Costa 1898a, 56). Individual traders and white settlers (Portuguese, Greek, Lebanese) were also more active in Angola than in Mozambique. Yet, the colonial state in Mozambique benefitted from its proximity to the Rand mines in South Africa. This connection offered larger scope for a rapid expansion of public revenue through custom duties levied on cross-border trade, as well as direct taxes on circular migrant workers who went back and forth between Southern Mozambique and the Rand (Lains 1998, 254). Non-tax revenues from government-controlled railways and ports also formed an important source of revenue. Because of the 'Rand effect', wage labour in Mozambique was more expensive than in Angola, and this may also explain a preference of private investors for Angola, especially in the labour-intensive plantation sector.

Portuguese inroads in the lower Zambezi region in central Mozambique followed a more gradual pattern and resistance against conquest was broken earlier than in Angola. The defeat of the Gaza Kingdom in southern Mozambique in 1895 allowed the Portuguese to develop a fiscal administration, which was mainly run by concession companies. The use of private intermediaries had deep roots. From the sixteenth to the nineteenth century, large land tracts had been granted by the Portuguese Crown to Portuguese merchants under the so-called *prazo* system. The *prazeros* were regarded as delegates of the Portuguese Crown and were granted rights of feudal landlords as well as a major stake in local slave and ivory trades. The Zambezi chiefs (*mambos*) retained ownership over the lands cultivated by their peoples and preserved their judicial authority, a vivid example of legal pluralism. All the inhabitants within the chiefdom had to pay an annual tax in kind, called *mutsonko* (Isaacman 1972, 26) to their chief, who supervised the tax collection at harvest time. The content of this tax varied from one area to another. The collected taxes were transferred to the *prazero*, who redistributed a percentage to the chief and his subordinates (ibid., 29, 31). *Prazeros* disposed of slave armies governed by *achikunda*s, who policed indigenous farmers and controlled migration (ibid., 33–34). Few landlords could sustain their power without consent of indigenous leaders. *Prazeros* who bypassed a chief risked revolt (ibid., 28) and in cases of abusive treatment, African chiefs sent petitions to the Portuguese government to explain their refusal to pay taxes (ibid., 37, 39).[5]

In the mid-nineteenth century, the *prazo* system went into decline due to the Ngoni invasions, the curtailing of the slave trade and new legislations such as the 1832 decree which reformed the land tenure system and ended the use of Zambezi as a penal settlement (Newitt 1969, 79–80). From the 1840s, Portugal fought wars against the *prazo* families who tried to hold on to their 'traditional' privileges. The idea that *prazo* holders represented the interests of the Portuguese Crown had long evaporated.

---

[5] Armed runaway slaves posed another threat to the stability of the *prazos*. In 1762, for instance, the governor of Mozambique stated that many *prazeros* abandoned their estates due to peasant revolts.

Through accumulation of wealth and intermarriages, *prazo* families had obtained a large degree of autonomy and a mixed race identity. By the end of the century, in 1895, the Portuguese army attained control over the central zone of Mozambique, with the support of British imperial troops. However, the *prazos* survived as fiscal agents up to the early twentieth century (ibid., 85).

By the 1890s, the control of the *prazeros* over central Mozambique had given way to large private concession companies such as the *Companhia de Moçambique*. In the period 1891–1942, the Mozambique Company obtained a number of privileges, including the right to levy and collect taxes and manage the treasury of *Manica* and *Sofala* districts. Similarly, the Niassa Company ruled over the largest part of the northern zone of Mozambique from 1891 to 1929. During the 1930s and 1940s, these tasks passed on to colonial officials, who were appointed by the Portuguese government. As I will show below, these transfers of power had a notable effect on revenue and expenditure policies and practices. When the frontiers of the Portuguese African colonies were eventually demarcated, Lisbon shifted from a relatively free-trade policy towards a "new colonial system", which aimed at maximizing trade revenues through stricter regulation (Lains 1998, 238).

Colonial State Revenue: Sources and Trends

Clarence-Smith has argued that during the mid-nineteenth century, the Liberal party in Portugal regarded Angola as a potential source of public revenue to be invested in metropolitan infrastructure (1979, 167), in a similar way as the Dutch used surpluses from the East Indies to invest in canals, railways and to amortize part of their massive state debt (see Frankema & Booth, Chapter 1, this volume). However, in this period, colonial state revenues never grew to extractable proportions and occasional deficits had to be covered by Lisbon via loans or subsidies. Especially in the 1880s, when the military occupation started, transfers from Portugal to the colonies were substantial (Governo Geral da Provincia de Moçambique, 1889). Only from the 1910s onwards, the shares of Portugal's budget invested in the colonies declined, but were still ranging from 1 per cent to 14 per cent (the latter only in wartimes). In the 1960s, Portugal again allocated higher shares of its domestic government budget to the colonies (Ferreira & Pedra 1988).

Lains (1998, 241) has argued that, on the whole, Portugal did not have to spend excessive sums to retain its colonies, and that the trade benefits through price and exchange rate controls largely outweighed these investments. Based on data from Mata (1993) he concluded that metropolitan expenditures on the colonies remained below 5 per cent of annual total expenditures for most of the 120 years between the 1850s and 1970s. Metropolitan expenditures only spiked during the military campaigns of the 1890s, the First World War and the independence wars, and particularly in the case of Angola. Up to World War I, the share of colonial spending in the metropolitan budget reached about 12 per cent (Lains 1998, 249). That said, 5 per cent of annual expenditures is far more than the 0.29 per cent that Huillery (2014) has calculated for France pouring into French West Africa (see also Frankema & van Waijenburg, Chapter 6, this volume).

Throughout the nineteenth century, the single most important source of public revenue for Portugal, as well as the emerging colonial administrations in Africa, consisted of the *alfandegas*, the customs houses. Import and export taxes were imposed in 1838 (Repartição Superior de Fazenda 1908, 15) and accounted for roughly two-thirds of total revenue (Monteiro 1941, 46). In the recession years of the 1890s, preferential tariffs were promulgated, favouring the shipment of colonial commodities via Lisbon (Clarence-Smith 1985, 85–6). By the early twentieth century, the African colonies accounted for c. 15 per cent of total Portuguese exports (Lains 1998, 239). Yet, the predominance of custom duties in the revenue mix changed after the occupation of the interior regions in Mozambique, as Figure 8.1 demonstrates. Figure 8.2 shows that direct taxes also gained ground in Angola, especially after the First World War. The rise of non-tax revenues was mainly driven by railway revenues.

Throughout the colonial era, Angola's state budget relied more on trade taxes than on other forms of direct and indirect taxation. As Figures 8.3 and 8.4 show, in the 1930s to 1970s, the contribution of export taxes was almost equal to the contribution of import taxes in Angola, whereas in Mozambique export taxes remained quite small and the gap with import taxes kept growing, especially after 1945. Angola's export sector expanded impressively after 1945 and *ad valorem* taxes on principal export commodities such as coffee, sugar, cotton and sisal were a significant revenue source for the Angolan colonial government (see Appendix Figures A.8.1 and A.8.2). Moreover, whereas Mozambique was a net food importer, Angola was a net food exporter (Kyle 1999, 2). In Mozambique, the ports of Lourenço Marques and Beira functioned as transit ports for import goods destined for South Africa and Southern Rhodesia respectively, while domestic export revenues remained low (Frankel 1938, 368–69). In view of this transit function, imports were a more effective fiscal target.

However, one of Angola's most significant export products, diamonds, remained untaxed. The *Companhia de Diamantes de Angola* (Diamang)

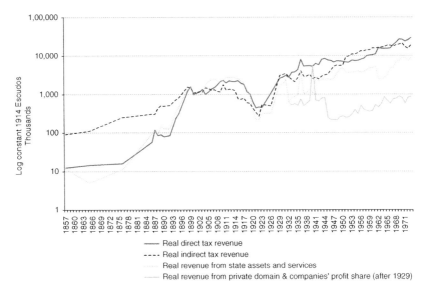

Figure 8.1 Real tax and non-tax revenue in Mozambique, 1850s–1970s
(constant 1953 escudos)

Sources: Boletim Official, Orçamentos Gerais (General Budgets) and Anuários
Estatísticos (Statistical Yearbooks) of Mozambique and Angola, various issues
between 1857 and 1973.

Notes: For the figures referring to the early colonial period or the whole colonial
era, I used the consumer price indexes (CPI) constructed by Valério and Tjipilica
(2008) especially for Mozambique and Angola, with 1939 and 1914 as base years
respectively and extrapolated them based on the CPI constructed by Valério
(2001) for Portugal. I deflated all past currencies used by the two colonies for
the respective periods: Real (1430–1911), Mozambican Escudo (1914–80),
Angolan Escudo (1914–28, 1958–77) and Angolar (1928–58). Both the
Mozambican and the Angolan Escudo were almost equivalent to Portuguese
Escudo (1911–99). In the case of Reis (1 Escudo=1,000 Reis) and Angolares
(1 Angolar=1,25 Escudos), I first converted them to Escudos before deflating
them. For the figures referring only to the late colonial period, I used the
extrapolated wholesale price index (WPI) based on data provided by Mitchell
(2008), with 1954 as base year.

engaged in mining activities in colonial Angola from 1917 until independence in 1975.[6] The 1921 agreement between the Portuguese state of
Angola and Diamang "called for the company to grant to the colony 40
per cent of its net profits, 100,000 shares of Diamang stock, and a series of

---

[6] After the independence, in 1977, Diamang was nationalized and, in 1988, it was officially
dissolved.

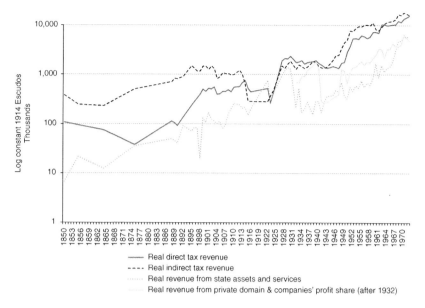

Figure 8.2 Real tax and non-tax revenue in Angola, 1850s–1970s (constant 1953 escudos)
Sources: Boletim Official, Orçamentos Gerais (General Budgets) and *Anuários Estatísticos* (Statistical Yearbooks) of Mozambique and Angola, various issues between 1850 and 1972; for the conversion of nominal into real revenues, see notes at Figure 8.1.

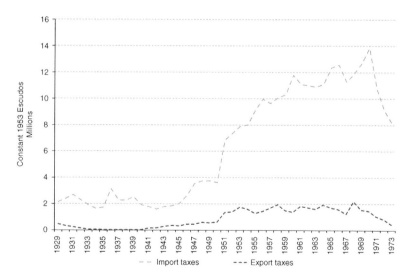

Figure 8.3 Import and export taxes in Mozambique, 1930s–70s (constant 1953 escudos)
Source: Anuários Estatísticos (Statistical yearbooks) and Contas de Gerência (Accounts) of Mozambique, various issues 1929–73; Price deflator: WPI from Mitchell (2008, table H1).

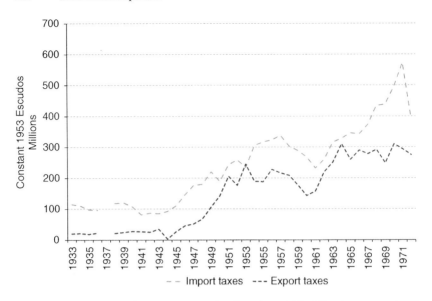

Figure 8.4 Import and export taxes in Angola, 1930s–70s (constant 1953 escudos)
Source: Anuários Estatísticos (Statistical yearbooks) and Contas de Gerência (Accounts) of Angola, various issues 1933–73; Price deflator: WPI from Mitchell (2008, table H1).

loans at very favourable repayment rates. Moreover, the pact formally exempted Diamang from all current and future tax obligations on profits, imports, and all of its diamond exports-an arrangement not even enjoyed by missionaries operating in the colony" (Varanda & Cleveland 2014, 93).

As Tables 8.1 and 8.2 show, the direct taxes that emerged with the expansion of the colonial state consisted of three main sources. First, the indigenous population paid a hut or head tax and labour migrants in Mozambique also paid a migration tax.[7] These direct taxes paid by 'indigenous' Africans formed the bulk of direct tax revenue. Second, enterprises and individual entrepreneurs (white settlers) operating in the colonies paid a corporate income tax, also named as 'industrial tax' (*contribuição industrial*). Third, there was a property tax (*contribuição predial*) levied on urban and rural real estate (especially buildings or land in urban zones), exempting state assets, church property and

---

[7] For reasons unclear to me, over the early colonial era these migration taxes were recorded in the broad category of *proprios nacionais* in the Portuguese records (Repartição Superior de Fazenda 1908, 21).

Table 8.1 *Direct tax revenue in Mozambique, 1920–60*

	1920		1930		1940		1950		1960	
	Escudos (×1,000)	%	Escudos (×1,000)	%	Escudos (×1,000)	%	Escudos (×1,000)	%	Escudos (×1,000)	%
Property tax	110	3	3,580	6	6,310	5	15,492	6	24,645	6
Indigenous tax	2,400	66	39,630	64	110,000	85	205,681	77	342,540	80
Corporate tax	194	5	8,681	14	12,988	10	30,186	11	48,864	11
Other direct taxes	911	25	9,923	16	..	..	14,540	5	10,883	3
Total direct taxes	3,615	100	61,814	100	129,298	100	265,899	100	426,932	100

Source: Anuários Estatísticos (Statistical Yearbooks) and Contas de Gerência (Accounts) of Mozambique, various issues, 1920–60.

Table 8.2 Direct tax revenue in Angola, 1920–60

	1920		1930		1940		1950		1960	
	Escudos (×1,000)	%	Angolares (×1,000)	%	Angolares (×1,000)	%	Angolares (×1,000)	%	Escudos (×1,000)	%
Property tax	550	8	1,740	3	3,074	5	4,439	2	20,581	5
Indigenous tax	6,000	86	51,000	89	45,169	71	88,744	46	120,733	32
Corporate tax	315	5	4,782	8	10,686	17	42,603	22	97,949	26
Other direct taxes	135	2	..	..	5,053	8	58,427	30	139,725	37
Total direct taxes	7,000	100	57,522	100	63,982	100	194,213	100	378,988	100

Source: Anuários Estatísticos (Statistical Yearbooks) and Contas de Gerência (Accounts) of Angola, various issues, 1920–60.

residences of indigenous people.[8] Especially in Angola, the capacity of the concession companies to collect these taxes and manage the *fazendas* (treasuries) was limited. Contrary to the chartered companies in Mozambique, the *Companhia de Mossamedes* operating in the southern part of Angola did not obtain the right to levy custom duties, nor to tax local Africans. Only in 1923, when the colonial state had secured control over this area, was their charter abolished (Clarence-Smith 1979, 173, 177). In 1928, both the metropolitan and the colonial governments introduced a progressive tax *(imposto de salvação pública)* on the income of civil servants (Havik 2013, 168). However, it remained of minor importance.

The *dizimos* – after 1883, the hut tax *(imposto de palhota)* – were annual taxes imposed on indigenous households at fixed rates (Repartição Superior de Fazenda 1908, 13). Colonial fiscal policies followed the trends in Portugal, where the government failed to foster a modern direct tax system and higher-income classes achieved exemption from income tax that was introduced in 1880 (Cardoso & Lains 2010, 263). In the 1910s to 1930s, the rate was set at 2.5 Escudos to be paid by Africans who "squatted" on settler farms. The "squatters" were forced to either pay the tax and become tenants, or to move into one of the native reserves, where the soils were poorer (Direito 2013a, 365). By 1918, the hut tax was renamed as "indigenous tax" *(imposto indigena)* and had to be paid by all African adult men. It became the most important revenue source for the colonial state of Mozambique.[9] According to the 1946 legislation on the indigenous tax, 30 per cent of the collected revenue had to be spent on indigenous affairs (sanitation and agriculture assistance) of which 20 per cent was managed by the municipalities *(Colónia de Moçambique* 1946). After the end of the *indigenato* system (the informal colour bar) in 1958, this tax was renamed as "personal tax" *(taxa pessoal).*[10]

[8] The same direct taxes were introduced in Portugal by early 1840s. *Décima* tax was replaced by three separate taxes on property, production and personal income (Cardoso & Lains 2010, 261).

[9] In the years 1901 to 1908, the total "peasant tax" *(imposto campones)* constituted only 13 per cent of the total revenue of the overseas provinces Mozambique, Angola and Guinea. The peasant tax results from the hut tax and the property tax, plus the license tax for the plantation of palm and cashew trees (Santos 2015, 52).

[10] From the 1920s to 1950s, Mozambique was characterized by a dual system of colonial governance. As Mamdani points out, the so-called *Indigenato* subordinated Mozambican subjects to tribal chiefs and Portuguese citizens to colonial administrators (O' Laughlin 2000, 16). The code of the Indigenato was formally adopted in 1928 and it concerned principally labour relations (O' Laughlin 2000, 12), but it was based on previous per-ennial arrangements of citizenship and governance. As in parts of British Africa, it aimed at legitimizing the new system of governance by drawing in existing political structures. *Regulos* and *cabos* were responsible for hut tax collection, land distribution and forced-labour recruitment and were paid by the colonial state through commissions (ibid., 17).

In Angola, the pressure to implement direct taxes was lower, and the constraints were higher given the lack of a pre-existing network of settlers or planters that could aid tax collection. The so-called *tributos* were collected by tribal chiefs, while the *dizimos* were collected by the colonial government. The latter was a fixed annual tax on each household and on each unit of cattle the household owned, plus a percentage of the value of its crop production and of its property income each year. There is evidence showing that in the late nineteenth century, poor indigenous families used to burn their houses and leave their villages in order to avoid paying the *dizimos* (*Governo Geral de Angola* 1920, 7). In 1888, this tax was replaced by the hut tax (*imposto sobre cubatas*), which was reformed in 1907 (Melo 1953, 72). The hut tax had to be paid by the headmen of all indigenous families (Legislação administrativa 1918, 27).

In 1919, the hut tax was renamed as a "head tax" (*imposto de capitação*) and, in 1920, as indigenous tax (*imposto indigena*) which, according to legislation of 1931, could only be paid in money and no longer in kind (Melo 1953, 72). In 1920, the individual tax in Angola was set at two Escudos and concerned the black and mixed race residents. As high as 70 per cent of the collected revenue had to be reserved at the national treasury, to be redistributed by the state, and only 10 per cent out of the remaining 30 per cent could be spent by the municipalities on public assistance (Governo Geral de Angola 1920, 14–15). In 1949, the indigenous tax was replaced by the personal annual tax (*taxa pessoal anual*) levied on all "black, non-civilized" adult males, who didn't contribute through other types of taxation (Melo 1953, 73). After 1950, the revenue derived from the corporate income tax caught up quickly with the indigenous tax revenue. The corporate tax was paid by individual entrepreneurs or businesses involved in trade, construction, food and arts. State companies, service companies and the naval industry were exempted (*Angola Repartição Técnica de Estatística Geral* 1954, 3).

From the evidence presented, I draw the conclusion that the management of tax revenue in Angola was more centralized than in Mozambique, where concession and private companies as well as municipalities played a more important role. The organization of direct taxes differed between Mozambique and Angola in another respect. Whereas in Angola the system was eventually enrolled on a 'national' level, in Mozambique the system never attained uniformity in geographic terms. Alexopoulou and Juif (2017) have shown that in Mozambique different systems operated in

Although there was some space for negotiations between local African leaders and colonial officials, in tax affairs the chiefs were mainly used as instruments by the colonial state.

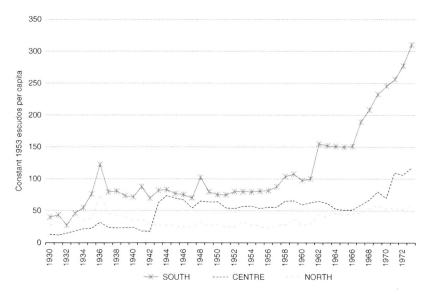

Figure 8.5 Real direct tax revenue per capita and per zone in Mozambique, 1930s–70s (constant 1953 escudos)
Sources: Contas de Gerência (Accounts of Mozambique); Population estimates from Frankema and Jerven (2014); price deflator: Valério (2001, table 8.1).

the north, the centre and the south of the country, which were closely related to different systems of agricultural production (Bowen 2000, 32) and labour recruitment. Figure 8.5 shows the contribution of the three zones to direct tax revenue in the 1930s to 1970s.

The north (Cabo Delgado, Niassa and Nampula provinces) consisted of a rather poor indigenous peasant economy which received a tiny share of public funds. In the years 1891–1929, the British-controlled Niassa Company was active in the region, but it was forced to give up its operations during the depression of the early 1930s. The central zone (Zambezia, Manica, Sofala and Tete provinces) had an expanding plantation economy, producing export crops such as sugar and sisal. These plantations were also largely run by the British-controlled *Companhia de Moçambique* and the British-owned *Companhia de Zambezia* (Paton 1994, 140). The Company of Mozambique had obtained the exclusive right to collect taxes, while the company itself enjoyed a twenty-five-year tax exemption (Isaacman & Isaacman 1983). The so-called *Guarda fiscal*, a branch of the public police/military force, was authorized to inspect the collection of custom duties in the territory of the Mozambique Company (Dias Costa 1898b).[11] A hut tax was also used to raise revenue, and to force indigenous labour to work on plantations or infrastructural projects.

The southern zone (Inhambane, Gaza and Maputo provinces) was dominated by private settler farms, rather than concession companies, and developed into the major sending area of migrant workers into the mines of South Africa. While the south had the fiscal features of a typical 'labour reserve economy' dominated by direct taxes, the centre relied much more on trade taxes, despite the gradual increase of indigenous tax revenue. Although the colonial state of Mozambique increased its military and administrative control across these three zones, the existing, differentiated patterns of taxation were largely kept intact (Alexopoulou & Juif 2017).

The persistence of this divergence was caused by two factors. First, the rise in wage labour migration from southern Mozambique to the South African mines enabled the state to levy higher direct taxes. Second, the increase of imperial subsidies to the Portuguese settlements from the 1930s (O' Laughlin 2000, 10) and the migration boom from Portugal in the 1940s (Castelo 2007) strengthened the settler farm economy in the southern zone. As a result, this zone became more competitive in terms of production and trade and thus generated more revenue from indirect taxes. In the other two zones, and particularly in the north, the concessions ended and forced cotton cultivation was introduced by the colonial state and smaller private companies. This shift in colonial policy intensified the dynamics that were already in place, instead of reversing them.

From the 1870s to the 1900s, the direct taxes levied on Africans in the 'pacified' parts of Angola could be paid either in kind or in money (Castro & de Morais 1948, 37–8). In the *Regulation on registration and collection of indigenous tax* these taxes were described as "a valuable element of politics for the affirmation of Portuguese sovereignty, and a practical means of collecting subsidies for the organisation of provincial censuses" (Governo Geral de Angola 1920, 5). It took a long time before this system was entirely monetized, but the arguments for direct taxation were similar to those used in other African colonies (see Bush & Maltby 2004, Gardner 2012).

In the 1890s, the regional commissioner of Mozambique, Antonio Enes, had linked the ideas of fiscal monetization to the enhancement of forced and voluntary wage labour schemes in order to stimulate agricultural development and expand "civilization" (Ferreirinha 1947, 5). In the early twentieth century, the governor of Lourenço Marques (Mozambique)

---

[11] There were no duties on overland domestic trade (also because of the lack of an adequate bureaucratic machine), so *Guarda fiscal* was principally concerned with the custom duties that were collected on the port of Beira in the account of the Company.

complained about the transportation and storage costs related to in-kind taxes as well as price fluctuations of crops and also argued that endemic labour scarcity could be lifted by monetary taxes, which would stimulate the growth of a wage labour market (Aguiar n.d., 75–6).

Regime Changes in Portugal and the Dogma of Fiscal Balance

So far, I have focused attention on how local conditions, and especially the contested process of colonial occupation, shaped the revenue side of the fiscal systems that emerged in Angola and Mozambique. In this section, I will highlight the impact of political changes in the metropole, especially with regard to some major reforms of imperial finances in the 1910s to 1930s.

In 1910, the republican revolution toppled the Portuguese monarchy. The republican era was characterized by a more liberal view on colonial rule, and included the adoption of the so-called decentralization policy, which was comparable to the idea of fiscal self-sufficiency that Britain promoted in colonial Africa (De Oliveira Marques 2001, 22). The African "provinces" – a term introduced under the monarchy – had to gain autonomy in administrative and financial terms and the *Leis Organicas* adopted in 1914 and the *Cartas Organicas* of 1917 arranged the legal dimension of this autonomy: the Portuguese colonies obtained their own police, military and marine forces as well as transportation services (Vasconselos 1920, 179). Moreover, the capacity of the colonies to borrow from metropolitan and international credit markets and serve their own public debt (*divida*) was one of the arguments for their autonomy (Costa 1903, 155–6, cited in: Santos 2015, 39). Law 278 of 1914 made *Caixa Geral de Depósitos* (Portugal's largest public sector banking corporation established in Lisbon in 1876) the preferential creditor of colonial governments.[12] The reasons for decentralization may have been ideological as well as pragmatic. Since colonial budget deficits had grown substantially during the occupation efforts up to 1910, greater autonomy also meant a stricter separation between Portuguese and African taxpayers.

The Republicans aimed to strike a balance between the British system of indirect rule and the French system of direct rule, by giving administrative and fiscal autonomy to the colonial state and African chiefs (who were involved in tax collection), while on the other hand pursuing an

---

[12] This is based on email correspondence with Professor Nuno Valério. I thank him for his insights into these issues.

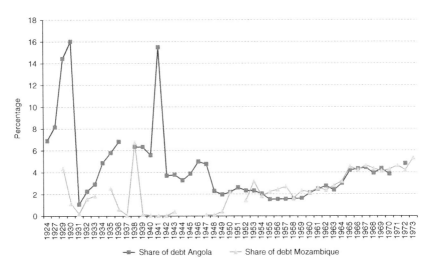

Figure 8.6 Shares of debt service in total expenditure of Angola and Mozambique, 1920s–70s
Source: Orçamentos gerais (Budgets) and Contas de Gerência (Accounts) of Angola and Mozambique; price deflator: Valério (2001, table 8.1).

assimilationist agenda promoting the 'civilization' of natives through civil law, and by constraining the influence of the clerical missions. In practice, the financial autonomy of the colonies from 1914 implied limited transfers from Lisbon, increasing direct taxation as well as contracting loans on the international market and accumulating debt (Havik 2013, 178–9). Decentralization did not help much to keep imperial finances under control. The military investments incurred during the First World War and the ensuing post-war hyper-inflation depleted colonial state budgets too. In the 1920s, the financial crisis in Angola led to the replacement of the *Banco Nacional Ultramarino* by the Bank of Angola as an issuing bank of the Angolan Escudo (the *Angular*) which was devalued against the Portuguese Escudo in 1928 (Valério 2002, 4).[13]

Figure 8.6 shows that the interest payments on Angolan government debt exploded after the appointment of Norton de Matos as High

---

[13] BNU was created in 1864 as a step towards the building of a coherent economic space, based on the French model of colonial banks. BNU enjoyed the monopoly of banknote issuing in the whole Empire and, until 1901, also enjoyed the monopoly over banking activities (Valério 2002, 4).

Commissioner of the Republic (1921–3).[14] However, from an international perspective, it was not uncommon to spend 15 per cent of the state budget on debt service (see Frankema & van Waijenburg, Chapter 6, this volume). Most of the loans were provided by Lisbon and were used to finance investments in infrastructure. In contrast to Angola, the government of Mozambique struggled to obtain international loans. According to Vail and White (1978), South Africa did much to block such loans in order to retain the migration flows of Mozambican workers to the South African gold mines. For example, in 1922, when it was rumoured that J. P. Hornung, the head of Sena Sugar Estates Ltd., was negotiating a loan of 5 million pounds for Mozambique, General Smuts, prime minister of the Union of South Africa, put pressure on 'American capital' in Whitehall and succeeded in having the loan blocked. After the overthrow of the Republicans in 1926 by a coup d'état, Portugal attempted to raise a loan of 12 million pounds from private banks and the League of Nations. The South African government argued that such a loan should be blocked "because it would fund development projects undertaken by forced labour" (Vail & White 1978, 242).

Decentralization policies were halted after the military coup of 1926 and the establishment of Salazar's *Estado Novo* in 1933 (De Oliveira Marques 2001, 23). In the midst of the great depression, Salazar strove to re-unify the empire and obtain stricter control over imperial finances, including the imposition of austerity measures and social repression (e.g. forced cultivation) in order to curb colonial deficits. The Portuguese Ministry of the Colonies had to approve the general budgets of all colonies every year. The main financial principle of the "New State" was the so-called *politica de equilibrio orçamental*, the policy of balanced budgets (Conceição 1967, 3). Monetary flows were strictly controlled (Lains 1998, 251). Colonial policies had to be in line with the national interests of Portugal and the Lisbon government was regarded as the principle authority. The 1930 Colonial Act created a juridical and political union that was supposed to harmonize the economic interests of the colonies and the metropole (Antologia Colonial Portuguesa 1946, 331–2). Ironically, Salazar himself extensively used the term "self-sufficiency" (*autosuficiencia*), but for him it referred to the sufficiency of the Portuguese Empire as a whole, as a united economic system.

From 1931 onwards, Salazar carried out a re-centralization programme in order to redress the putative administrative "chaos" and

---

[14] De Matos became high Commissioner after having served as General Governor of Angola (1912–15) and as Minister of War (1915–17). In the 1940s, he became a leading opposition figure against the Salazar regime.

financial deficits caused by the Republicans. In 1932, a new corporate income tax was levied on private and state-run companies. In Mozambique, the contribution remained negligible, but in Angola it gained some importance. In theory, the Salazar regime promoted a "minimalist" state, with low taxes and minimal expenses. Salazar denied any financial aid to Angola and propagated stability over growth in the overseas territories. Colonial officials in key positions were reshuffled (Smith 1974, 663). In practice, however, direct tax revenues increased right from the beginning of Salazar's governance, while public investments remained low until the 1940s. "No matter how pressing their needs, areas such as rural development, the health services and education would have to wait until the necessary surplus was in hand" (Smith 1974, 662).

With the exception of wartime expenditure in the early 1940s, the New State retained the debt position of both colonies at very low levels. The colonial records of both countries demonstrate an almost absolute equation of revenue and expenditure. It is difficult to assess whether these records fully represent fiscal reality, and to what extent these were artificial 'constructions' of colonial governments that needed to abide by metropolitan directives. What seems clear, however, is that the capacity of the colonial states of Angola and Mozambique to invest in welfare services was severely constrained. Exports and re-exports via the metropole were stimulated so that "the colonies were often well supplied with unnecessary commodities from Portugal, while starving for essentials which could only be obtained from elsewhere" (Smith 1974, 666).

In 1949, new tax reforms in Angola were adopted to further raise the contribution of direct taxes, especially income taxes. The reforms were propagated as a policy to enhance wealth and income redistribution (Conceição 1967, 10–11). However, the idea that direct taxation would contribute to social justice more than indirect taxation was inspired by the Western fiscal regimes, where income and property taxes were increasingly made progressive. In Portuguese Africa, the main form of direct taxation, the hut/poll tax, was uniformly applied to indigenous adult males at fixed rates, regardless of their income. Havik (2013, 185) stresses that the actual sum of taxes paid by heads of households was notably greater than the monetary value of the huts.

As Vail and White (1983) have shown, in Mozambique the indigenes expressed their resistance against the Portuguese rule and rising taxes also in indirect ways, for example via singing songs such as the Katini's ngodo of 1940: "It is time to pay taxes to the Portuguese/The Portuguese who eats eggs /And chicken/ Change that English pound!" (Tracey 1970). There is evidence showing that tax rates were regionally differentiated, especially in the case of Mozambique (Inspecção superior dos negocios indígenas 1951). For instance, in northern Mozambique the tax rates were lower. The colonial state attempted to broaden the tax base by obliging women to pay taxes, but revolts broke out (Inspecção superior dos negocios indígenas 1951, 186). Property taxes always formed a minor source, and included a fixed and progressive rate from 1940 onwards. Only in the 1960s was a new tax levied on white settlers *(imposto profissional)*.

To further centralize revenue collection and promote tight treasury management, Salazar removed the fiscal powers from the chartered companies. The concessions in the central zone of Mozambique were terminated in 1942. The private leasing companies, which operated plantations using forced labour, were no longer allowed to keep the money they collected from the hut tax "in exchange for an annual rental fee paid to the government" (Smith 1974, 664). The charter of Niassa Company in the north was already terminated in 1929 and the government obtained authority for the collection of taxes, while the Banco Nacional Ultramarino was converted into a partner of the state (Smith 1974, 665). Only the "Diamang Company" in Angola retained the concession for diamond mining from 1917 until independence. However, Diamang did not obtain any parastatal or political rights within its concession area, where the state always maintained the authority to collect taxes. In this sense, the Diamang monopoly over the mining of, and trade in, diamonds was consistent with Salazar's policy to end the concessions to private companies.[15] Smith is clear on the two main legacies of Salazar's colonial policy: a rationalization of exploitation for the benefit of the mother country and structural underdevelopment of the African colonies (Smith 1974, 667).

Expenditure Priorities and Redistributive Effects

The expenditure budgets of Mozambique and Angola consisted principally of expenses on military and marine forces, as well as on general administration *(administração geral)*. As elsewhere in colonial Africa, the military forces were used not only to combat external threats but also to secure domestic order (Alexopoulou & Frankema 2018). In the early

---

[15] In any case, the circulation of economic and political elites in Mozambique was such that even when the concessions ended, the same people who ruled the companies could later work for the state administration. For example, in the 1920s José Ferreira Bossa was director of the Negócios Indígenas of the Mozambique Company in Manica e Sofala, while in the 1930s he became briefly Minister of the Colonies and in the 1940s he was appointed Governor of Portuguese India (Direito 2013b, 72).

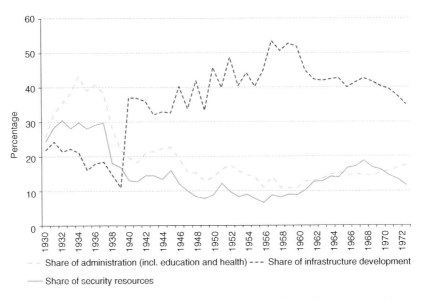

Figure 8.7 Shares of public ordinary expenditure in Mozambique, 1930s–70s
Sources: Anuários Estatísticos (Statistical Yearbooks) and Contas de Gerência (Accounts) of Mozambique, various issues, 1930–73.

colonial era (1850s–1920s), investments in education and health were not even a distinct expenditure category in the aggregated annual statistics of the Portuguese colonies presented at *Boletim Official*, as they were included in civil administration services. However, colonial accounts (*Contas da Gerencia*) of the following period (1930s–70s) offered a more detailed classification, including the distinction of social or welfare services.

In any case, the fact that social services were not distinguished from the general administration, while financial and justice services were, indicates the low priority of welfare spending in Portuguese Africa. In 1920, in Mozambique, education and health received only 10 per cent of the budget while by 1960 the share dropped to 5 per cent. During the same period (1920–60) in Angola, the share of expenditure on education and health ranged from 7 to 15 per cent. Until the 1920s, infrastructural investments were classified as extraordinary expenses, and mainly funded by loans and subsidies from Portugal as well as private capital. However, from the 1930s the colonial states took over the control of most public works (Alexopoulou 2018). In the post-war era, spending priorities

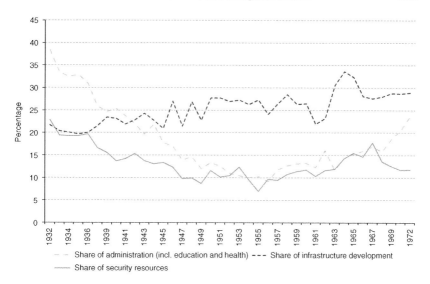

Figure 8.8 Shares of public ordinary expenditure in Angola, 1930s–70s
Sources: Anuários Estatísticos (Statistical Yearbooks) and Contas de Gerência
(Accounts) of Angola, various issues, 1932–73.

started to change, with infrastructure (roads, railways, ports, irrigation)
gaining priority. As Figures 8.7 and 8.8 show, infrastructural development services (*fomento*) acquired a growing share of the expenditure
budget, while the shares spent on security and administration (colonial
government, fiscal administration, justice services, military and marine
forces) and social services (education, health, pensions and indigenous
affairs) dropped and then remained relatively stable at similar levels in
both Angola and Mozambique.

Infrastructure development aimed principally at facilitating the commodity trade with the metropole, South Africa and the neighbouring
British colonies. Increasing investments in transportation and communication by the colonial states of Mozambique and Angola can be perceived as a concern for material development, but not necessarily for
welfare development. Investments in both infrastructure and social services targeted the urban areas and, most importantly, the capital cities
and the ports of the colonies (Luanda and Benguella in Angola, Lourenço
Marques and Beira in Mozambique). Besides serving the trade interests
of the metropole and the private capital, the development projects aimed

to increase the mobility of armed forces and improve the living standards of the settlers. In other words, they did not serve the needs of the vast majority of the indigenes, who lived mostly in the rural areas (Alexopoulou 2018).

The same applies to the six-year Development Plans that Portugal initiated in the late colonial era. The first (1953–8), invested about $55 million in Mozambique and $100 million in Angola, mainly in ports, roads, railways and telecommunications (Penvenne et al. 2005, 84). The second plan invested $125 million in Mozambique and targeted health, education and agriculture. However, both aimed at increasing white settler migration from Portugal and serving the interests of the existing settler communities in trade, agriculture and irrigation. The threat of African independence movements in the 1960s further motivated these infrastructural investments and settler schemes (Newitt 1995, 461–4).

Concerning welfare spending services, it should be noted that the Catholic Church played a major role in the provision of schooling and healthcare, sending off missionaries to run many of the schools and hospitals. Janeiro (2013) has shown that the religious missions were mainly funded by the colonial states, even though these subsidies remained below 5 per cent of expenditure budgets in both colonies between 1850 and 1920. From the First Portuguese Republic to Salazar's New State, colonial officials advocated education as a tool to transform the natives into 'civilized' and cooperative subjects (Cayolla 1912), but educational expenses never gained priority. According to one source, in Mozambique "only 33 people had graduated from college by the withdrawal of the Portuguese forces and the granting of independence in 1975" (Kyle 1999, 2).

The law of 1917 (Portaria Provincial No 317) stipulated that indigenous people had to fulfil a series of requirements in order to become Portuguese 'citizens', such as being fluent in Portuguese and completing basic education (Zamparoni 2000). Under the New State the requirements continued to be highly exclusionary. Moreover, the role of education in the colonies was not always to reduce the gap between the 'native' and the 'civilized'. In Mozambique, native children attended 'rudimentary' schools focusing on Portuguese culture and manual arts to prepare for manual jobs and were discouraged from attending secondary education (O' Laughlin 2000, 15).

Besides the arbitrary criteria set for citizenship and the questionable role of education, the Africans who attained the status of *assimilado*, had to pay more taxes and continued to be discriminated against in everyday life. In contrast with the French model of governance, which integrated the African elites, Salazar's regime did not encourage the participation of African elites (Keese 2007). The increasing number of settlers migrating from the metropole to the colonies in the period after World War II (Castelo 2007) added another impediment: the colonial states had to recruit the settlers rather than the assimilated elites for the administrational positions in the public sector (Keese 2012, 231). Assimilation partly remained a dead letter and this also lowered incentives to increase educational investments. Therefore, the objective of assimilation could not sufficiently motivate the colonial states to spend more on welfare services.

The increase of public spending on human resources in both Mozambique and Angola during the 1960s was driven by two forces. First, Portuguese colonial policies met with increasing international criticism. In the 1950s Portugal became a member of multilateral and international organizations such as the United Nations, which "subjected Portugal's colonial policies to international condemnation" (Pinto & Teixeira 2004, 113). Portugal was asked to reconsider its policies concerning forced and migration labour, heavy taxation and preferential trade (on the latter, see Lains 1998). Also, Portugal was criticized for its military operations against the guerrillas fighting for independence, who started to gain ground in the 1960s, especially in Angola. "What Portugal feared most was further isolation. Criticism from abroad had already begun to hurt" (Venter 2013, 223).

Second, Salazar's "New State" was aging, and his successor, Marcello Caetano, started to liberalize some of Salazar's imperial policies from 1968 onwards. In view of the increasing support of the indigenes for the independence movements of UNITA, MPLA and FNLA in Angola, as well as FRELIMO in Mozambique, Caetano foresaw the nearing end of the Portuguese Empire. Liberalization policies and investments in public goods could place the metropole in a better position to negotiate its future relations with the colonies. Ironically, the independence wars in both colonies forced Portugal to raise its military and security expenditures to about 45 per cent of its annual budget (Pinto & Teixeira 2004, 117).

Conclusion

This chapter has discussed the decisive role of the metropole in determining the colonial fiscal policies, as well as the importance of local conditions and disparities between and within the two colonies. To what extent did these influence the development of a modern fiscal state?

On the first condition of fiscal modernization, the capacity of the state to centralize revenue collection, the conclusion is that it took a long time before the colonial state broke through the stakes of private concession companies and local African leaders, who employed diverse strategies from resistance to cooperation in order to keep the state at arm's length. In the 1890s, certain areas of central Mozambique passed from the authority of *prazeros* to the control of large concession companies which mainly invested in plantation agriculture. As a result, certain zones were administered by private actors and remained out of the supervision of the colonial state apparatus. This led to less centralization in decision-making and tax management. The consolidation of the fiscal state was eventually enforced by the Salazar regime.

The Portuguese based their colonial rule on military superiority. Spending on military forces dominated the early colonial budgets, especially in Angola. The Portuguese used both direct violence and a system of indirect rule, delegating tax collection to native chiefs and rewarding them for their services. The ethnic diversity and the existence of multiple centres of power, especially in nineteenth-century Mozambique, played a dual role: on the one hand, they hindered administrative unification; on the other hand, they may have belated the eventual overthrow of the colonial power. Nevertheless, the revenue mix became more diversified than in many other African colonies. Indirect taxes played a major role, especially in Angola, but the development of property taxes, corporate income taxes and sales taxes did induce a more fine-grained system of income and asset assessment over time.

On the second condition of fiscal modernization, the creation of long-term debt and the ability of the state to fund larger development projects, it can be concluded that fiscal modernization was curbed by the straitjacket of Portugal's imperial dictatorship. Debt elimination and the dogma of budget balance were core principles of Salazar's authoritarian regime. Most of the loans were offered by the metropole and the degree of monetization and financial development in both Mozambique and Angola were low. Throughout the colonial era, the Portuguese metropole swung between administrational autonomy, following the British approach to empire, and power centralization, adopted by the French Empire. Administrative and financial autonomy was given to the colonies during the Republicans' governance in Portugal, while during Salazar's governance fiscal controls by the metropole were intensified, including restrictions on colonial government borrowing.

The same applies to the third modernization condition: public investments in welfare services remained very low. Only in the late colonial years, under the pressure of international organizations and independence movements, did the colonial governments initiate development projects aimed at improving African living standards. Public revenues that were not allocated to military and administrative capacity building, went mainly into infrastructural projects that facilitated imperial trade. Catholic missionaries filled part of the gap, but the subsidies they received for their mission schools and hospitals remained tiny.

Finally, the fourth condition of fiscal modernization – the existence of a representative government, with a system of checks and balances, to ensure legitimacy and tax compliance – was a requirement that colonial rule by definition could not meet. However, this condition was also not met in the metropole. In the framework of "compulsory globalisation" (Hopkins 2002), Portuguese Africa passed from peasant or feudalist societies to capitalist production, but this transformation was not accompanied by the emergence of modern political and fiscal institutions.

Bibliography

Aguiar, Francisco Roque de. (n.d.). *Imposto de palhota*. Distrito de Lourenço Marques.

Alexopoulou, K., & Juif, D. (2017). Colonial State Formation Without Integration: Tax Capacity and Labour Regimes in Portuguese Mozambique (1890s–1970s). *International Review of Social History*, 62(2), 215–252.

Alexopoulou, K. (2018). *An Anatomy of Colonial States and Fiscal Regimes in Portuguese Africa: Long-Term Transformations in Angola and Mozambique, 1850s–1970s*. PhD Thesis. Wageningen University.

Alexopoulou, K., & Frankema E. (2019). Imperialism of Jackals and Lions? The Militarization of Portuguese Africa in the British African mirror, 1850–1940.

Angola – Repartição Técnica de Estatística Geral (1954). *Estatística das Contribuições e Impostos*. Luanda: Imprensa Nacional.

Bowen, M. L. (2000). *The State against the Peasantry: Rural Struggles in Colonial and Postcolonial Mozambique*. Charlottesville: University of Virginia Press.

Bush, B., & Maltby, J. (2004). Taxation in West Africa: Transforming the Colonial Subject into the 'Governable Person'. *Critical Perspectives on Accounting*, 15(1), 5–34.

Capela, J. (1979). *As burguesias portuguesas e a abolição do trafico de escravos, 1810–1842.* Porto: Afrontamento.

Cardoso, J. L., & Lains, P. (2010). Public Finance in Portugal, 1796–1910. In J. L. Cardoso & P. Lains (Eds.), *Paying for the Liberal State: The Rise of Public Finance in Nineteenth-Century Europe.* Cambridge: Cambridge University Press, 251–78.

Castelo, C. (2007). *Passagens para África: o povoamento de Angola e Moçambique con naturais da metrópole (1920–1974).* Porto: Afrontamento.

Castro, A. A. G., & de Morais, E. (1948). *Economia, Finanças e Geografia Económica. Ligeiro esboco histórico do sistema de pagamento de imposto na colonia de Angola.* Mensário administrativo: publicação de assuntos de interesse ultramarino / direcção dos Serviços de Administração, 14, 37–40.

Cayolla, L. (1912). *Sciencia de colonisação* (vol. 1). Lisboa: Typographia da Cooperativa Militar.

Clarence-Smith, W. G. (1979). The Myth of Uneconomic Imperialism: The Portuguese in Angola, 1836–1926. *Journal of Southern African Studies,* 5(2), 165–80.

Clarence-Smith, W. G. (1985). *The Third Portuguese Empire, 1825–1975: A Study in Economic Imperialism.* Manchester: Manchester University Press.

Colonia de Angola. (1921–1941). *Orçamento Geral.* Luanda: Imprensa Nacional.

Colonia de Angola, Repartição Central de Estatística Geral. (1933–1973). *Anuário Estatistico.* Luanda: Imprensa Nacional.

Colonia de Moçambique. (1946). *Legislação sobre Imposto Indígena.* Lourenço Marques: Imprensa Nacional de Moçambique.

Colonia de Moçambique. (1912–1941). *Orçamento Geral.* Lourenço Marques: Imprensa Nacional.

Colonia de Moçambique, Repartição Central de Estatística Geral. (1926–1973). *Anuário Estatístico.* Lourenço Marques: Imprensa Nacional.

Conceição, Lourenço Mendes da. (1967). Trinta e Quatro Anos de Administração Financeira a proposito do Orçamento Geral de Angola para 1965. *Separata da Revista "Angola".* 174 (Janeiro/Junho).

Costa, E. (1902). *O Território de Manica e Sofala e a Administração da Companhia de Moçambique, 1892–1900.* Lisboa: Typ. da Companhia Nacional Editora.

Costa, E., & Congresso Colonial Nacional. (1903). *Estudo sobre a administração civil das nossas possessões africanas: Memoria.* Lisboa: Imprensa Nacional.

De Oliveira Marques, A. H. R. (2001). *O império africano, 1890–1930* (vol. 3). Lisboa: Editorial Estampa.

Dias Costa, F. F. (1898a). *Relatório do Ministro e Secretario d'Estado dos Negócios da Marinha e Ultramar apresentado a Camara dos Senhores Deputados na Sessão Legislativa de 1898.* Lisboa: Imprensa Nacional.

Dias Costa, F. F. (1898b). *Regulamento Orgânico da Guarda Fiscal nos Territórios da Companhia de Moçambique approvado por Decreto de 12 de Maio de 1898,* Lisboa: Imprensa Nacional.

Dincecco, M. (2011). *Political Transformations and Public Finances: Europe, 1650–1913.* Cambridge: Cambridge University Press.

Direito, B. (2013a). Land and Colonialism in Mozambique–Policies and Practice in Inhambane, c. 1900–c. 1940. *Journal of Southern African Studies,* 39(2), 353–69.

Direito, B. (2013b). *Políticas coloniais de terras em Moçambique: o caso de Manica e Sofala sob a Companhia de Moçambique, 1892–1942.* PhD Thesis. Lisbon: Lisbon University.

Ferreira, L., & Pedra, C. (1988). Despesas coloniais do Estado Português, 1913–1980. *Revista de História Económica e Social,* 24, 89–103.

Ferreirinha, F. (1947). Antonio Enes e o seu pensamento colonial. In Sociedade de Estudos da Colonia de Mocambique. *Teses Apresentadas ao 1o Congresso realizado de 8 a 13 de Septembro de 1947* (vol. 1). Lourenço Marques: Tip. Minerva Central.

Frankel, H. S. (1938). *Capital Investment in Africa: Its Course and Effect.* London: Oxford University Press.

Frankema, E., & Jerven, M. (2014). Writing History Backwards or Sideways: Towards a Consensus on African Population, 1850–present. *Economic History Review,* 67(4), 907–31.

Gardner, L. A. (2012). *Taxing Colonial Africa: The Political Economy of British Imperialism.* Oxford: Oxford University Press.

Governo Geral da Provincia de Moçambique. (Various issues between 1850 and 1910). *Boletim Official.* Lourenço Marques: Imprensa Nacional de Moçambique.

Governo Geral de Angola – Secretaria Geral. (1920). *Regulamento do recenseamento e cobrança do imposto indígena.* Loanda: Imprensa Nacional.

Havik, P. J. (2013). Colonial Administration, Public Accounts and Fiscal Extraction: Policies and Revenues in Portuguese Africa (1900–1960). *African Economic History,* 41(1), 159–221.

Herbst, J. (2000). *States and Power in Africa: Comparative Lessons in Authority and Control.* Princeton, NJ: Princeton University Press.

Hopkins, A. G. (2002). The History of Globalization – and the Globalization of History. In A.G. Hopkins (Ed.), *Globalization in World History*. New York: Norton, 11–46.

Huillery, E. (2014). The Black Man's Burden: The Cost of Colonization of French West Africa. *The Journal of Economic History*, 74(1), 1–38.

Inspecção superior dos negocios indígenas. (1951). *Lourenço Marques*. In Arquivo Histórico de Moçambique (AHM).

Isaacman, A. F. (1972). *Mozambique: The Africanization of a European Institution: The Zambesi Prazos, 1750–1902*. Madison: University of Wisconsin Press Madison.

Isaacman, A. F., & Isaacman, B. (1983). *Mozambique: From Colonialism to Revolution, 1900–1982* (vol. 3). Boulder, CO: Westview Press.

Janeiro, H. P. (2013). The First Portuguese Republic and the Catholic and Lay Missions in Angola: Finance and Power. *Historia y Politica*, 29, 161–91.

Keese, A. (2012). The Constraints of Late Colonial Reform Policy: Forced Labour Scandals in the Portuguese Congo (Angola) and the Limits of Reform under Authoritarian Colonial Rule, 1955–61. *Portuguese Studies*, 28(2), 186–200.

Keese, A. (2007). *Living with Ambiguity: Integrating an African Elite in French and Portuguese Africa, 1930–61*. Stuttgart: Steiner.

Klein, H. S. (2010). *The Atlantic Slave Trade*. Cambridge: Cambridge University Press.

Kyle, S. (1999). Economic development in Angola and Mozambique. *The Africa Notes*.

Lains, P. (1998). An Account of the Portuguese African Empire, 1885–1975. *Revista de Historia Económica / Journal of Iberian and Latin American Economic History*, 16(01), 235–63.

Mata, M. E. (1993). *As finanças públicas portuguesas da Regeneração à primeira Guerra Mundial*. Lisbon: Banco de Portugal

Maxwell, K. (2000). *Why Was Brazil Different? The Contexts of Independence*. Cambridge, MA: David Rockefeller Center for Latin American Studies, Harvard University.

Melo, A. A. G. (1953). *Economia e Finanças. Noticia dos impostos lançados sobre os indígenas angolenses desde os tempos da conquista ate hoje*.

Mitchell, B. R. (2007). *International Historical Statistics: Africa, Asia & Oceania, 1750–2005*. New York: Palgrave Macmillan.

Mitchell, B. R. (2008). *International Historical Statistics: Europe 1750–2005*. 6th ed. New York: Palgrave Macmillan.

Monteiro, Manuel, (1941, de Junho). A Evolução do Mecanismo Pautal Ultramarino durante um Seculo. *Boletim Geral das Colonias*, 192, 43–86.

Newitt, M. D. (1969). The Portuguese on the Zambezi: An Historical Interpretation of the Prazo System. *Journal of African History*, 10(1), 67–85.

Newitt, M. D. (1995). *A History of Mozambique*. Bloomington: Indiana University Press.

Newitt, M., & Tornimbeni, C. (2008). Transnational Networks and Internal Divisions in Central Mozambique. *Cahiers d'études africaines* 4, 707–40.

O' Laughlin, B. (2000). Class and the Customary: The Ambiguous Legacy of the Indigenato in Mozambique. *African Affairs*, 99(394), 5–42.

Paton, B. (1994). *Labour Export Policy in the Development of Southern Africa*. London: Palgrave Macmillan.

Penvenne, J. M., Elkins, C., & Pedersen, S. (2005). Settling against the Tide: The Layered Contradictions of Twentieth Century Portuguese Settlement in Mozambique. In C. Elkins & S. Pedersen (Eds.), *Settler Colonialism in the Twentieth Century*. New York: Routledge, 79–94.

Pinto, A. C., & Teixeira, N. S. (January 1, 2004). From Atlantic Past to European Destiny: Portugal. In *European Union Enlargement: a Comparative History*. London: Routledge, 112–130.

Província de Angola (1918). *Legislação administrativa*. Loanda: Imprensa Nacional. Província de Angola, Direcção dos Serviços de Fazenda e Contabilidade. (1931–1972). *Contas da Gerência*. Luanda: Imprensa Nacional.

Província de Moçambique, Direcção dos Serviços de Fazenda e Contabilidade. (1934–1973). *Contas da Gerência*. Luanda: Imprensa Nacional.

Provincia de Moçambique, Repartição Superior de Fazenda (1908). *Estatística dos Rendimentos da Provincia. Annos de 1897–1898 a 1906–1907*. Lourenço Marques: Imprensa Nacional.

Santos, M. (2015). Peasant Taxation and the Funding of the Colonial State in the Portuguese Colonies (1900–1939). In P. J. Havik, A. Keese & M. Santos (Eds.), *Administration and Taxation in Former Portuguese Africa: 1900–1945*. Newcastle upon Tyne, UK: Cambridge Scholars Publishing, 28–81.

Smith, A. K. (1974). António Salazar and the Reversal of Portuguese Colonial Policy. *Journal of African History*, 15(4), 653–67.

Tracey, H. (1970). *Chopi Musicians: Their Music, Poetry, and Instruments*. London: Oxford University Press.

Vail, L., & White, L. (1978).'Tawani, Machambero!': Forced Cotton and Rice Growing on the Zambezi. *Journal of African History*, 19(02), 239–63.

Vail, L., & White, L. (1983). *Forms of Resistance: Songs and Perceptions of Power in Colonial Mozambique*. Grahamstown: Rhodes University, Institute of Social and Economic Research.

Valério N. (2001). *Estatísticas históricas portuguesas: Portuguese Historical Statistics*. Lisboa: Instituto Nacional de Estatística.

Valério, N. (2002). *The Escudo Zone: A Failed Attempt at Colonial Monetary Union (1962–71)*. In session thirty-nine of the 13th International Economic History Congress. Buenos Aires.

Valério, N., & Tjipilica, P. (2008). Economic Activity in the Portuguese Colonial Empire: A Factor Analysis Approach. *Economies et sociétés*, 42(9), 1765–1807.

Varanda, J., & Cleveland, T. (2014). (Un) healthy Relationships: African Labourers, Profits and Health Services in Angola's Colonial-Era Diamond Mines, 1917–75. *Medical History*, 58(01), 87–105.

Vasconselos, E. de. Sociedade de Geografia de Lisboa (1920). *Questões Coloniais e Económicas: Conclusões e Pareceres 1913–1919*. Lisboa: Topografia da Cooperativa Militar.

Venter, A. (2013). *Portugal's Guerrilla Wars in Africa: Lisbon's Three Wars in Angola, Mozambique and Portuguese Guinea 1961–74*. Solihull: Helion.

Wheeler, D. L. (1969). The Portuguese Army in Angola. *The Journal of Modern African Studies*, 7(03), 425–39.

Wheeler, D. L. (1972). Origins of African Nationalism in Angola: *Assimilado* Protest Writings, 1859–1929. In R. H. Chilcote (Ed.), *Protest and Resistance in Angola and Brazil: Comparative Studies*. Berkeley and Los Angeles: University of California Press.

Zamparoni, V. D. (2000). *Frugalidade, moralidade e respeito: A política do assimilacionismo em Moçambique, c. 1890–1930*. In X Congresso Internacional da Associação Latino-Americana de Estudos Afro-asiáticos.

Appendix

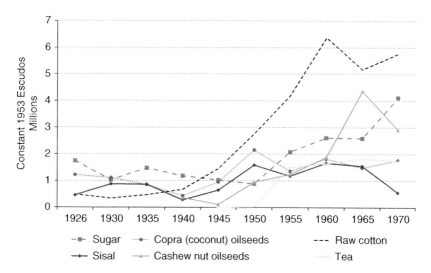

Figure A.8.1 Revenues from main export commodities, Mozambique, 1926–70
Source: Statistical Yearbooks of Mozambique, Price deflator: Mitchell (2007, table H2).

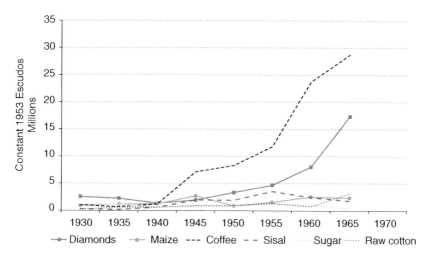

Figure A.8.2 Revenues from main export commodities, Angola, 1930–70
Source: Statistical Yearbooks of Angola, Price deflator: Mitchell (2007, table H2).

9 How Mineral Discoveries Shaped the Fiscal System of South Africa

Abel Gwaindepi and Krige Siebrits

Introduction

Between 1850 and 1961, South Africa evolved from a politically fragmented and economically backward territory into a unified country with a diversified economy and a modern fiscal state. Economic historians (e.g. De Kiewiet 1957, Feinstein, 2005) have long emphasized the pivotal role of the discovery of rich diamond and gold deposits in the second half of nineteenth century in the subsequent political and economic development of South Africa. This chapter focuses on a particular aspect of this role, namely the influence of the burgeoning mining sector on the modernization of the country's fiscal system. It follows the introduction to this volume in using four criteria to assess progress towards fiscal modernization. These criteria are the capacity to centralize revenue collection, the ability to establish and maintain a floating debt position, the channelling of a large portion of government revenue into public spending programmes that promote general well-being and the development of accountable government.

Economic theory and empirical evidence both suggest that the modernization of a country's fiscal system might be boosted or retarded when it hits the jackpot in what Blattman, Hwang and Williamson (2007) labelled the "commodity lottery". Natural resources broaden the tax base and the scope for government borrowing and welfare-enhancing government spending programmes. Primary commodity exports can spur economic diversification via various channels (Auty 2008, 391). These include fiscal linkage effects: taxes levied on commodity-extracting sectors can finance public provision of physical infrastructure and social services directly, and, by improving governments' access to borrowed funds, indirectly as well.[1] However, a large body of research has highlighted that natural

---

[1] Sunderland (2004, 149) stated that limited access to capital markets condemned colonies without sufficient tax revenues to a catch-22 situation as far as the financing of physical

resources may undermine economic development. Early writings on the resource curse emphasized macroeconomic mechanisms: the export demand and foreign capital inflows associated with a booming commodity sector might cause exchange rate appreciation that stymies the competitiveness of other tradeable sectors (Auty 2008, 390–91). The resource curse might also manifest in kleptocracy (Wenar 2008) or recurrent violent conflict over resource rents (Ross 2004).

Another body of research suggests that institutions determine the economic effects of natural resources and, hence, implications for the fiscal modernization process. Mehlum, Moehne and Torvik (2006) distinguish between "production-friendly institutions" that reward growth-boosting activities and "grabber-friendly institutions" that hinder growth by creating incentives for unproductive rent-seeking. "Grabber-friendly institutions" can include elements of fiscal systems. According to Robinson, Torvik and Verdier (2006), politicians may abuse resource rents for growth-inhibiting forms of redistribution to groups of supporters unless institutional constraints ensure accountability and competence in government. Sokoloff and Zolt (2007) provide an historical example of the distorting effects of inappropriate institutions on fiscal systems. They claim that the political institutions in resource-rich Latin American colonies cemented the power of elites and that skewed distributions of political power are reflected in extreme income inequality levels and low levels of tax mobilization and social spending. The possibility that mineral and other natural resources have benign or malign effects on fiscal modernization processes underscores the importance of case studies that delve into key mechanisms and establish the relevance of theoretical arguments. This chapter on the experience of South Africa from 1850 to 1961 provides such a case study.

Political and Economic Context

This section contextualizes the subsequent discussion of the fiscal modernization process by providing a synopsis of the wide-ranging political and economic effects of the mining boom. Figure 9.1 depicts Fourie and Van Zanden's (2013, 489–90) estimates of the real gross domestic product (GDP) per capita for the Cape Colony (1701–1909) and South Africa (1910–1994).[2]

---

infrastructure was concerned: "Funds were required to build infrastructure, but the very lack of transportation networks and economic activity reduced the likelihood that they would be forthcoming at a price the colonies could afford."

[2] Magee, Greyling and Verhoef (2016) recently published estimates of GDP per capita at 1861 prices in the Cape Colony and Natal Colony from 1861 to 1909. At the time of this

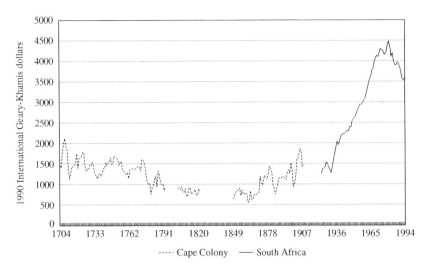

Figure 9.1 Estimates of the real GDP per capita of the Cape Colony (1701–1909) and South Africa (1910–2001)
Source: Fourie and Van Zanden (2013, 489–90).

By the middle of the nineteenth century the European settler population controlled the bulk of modern-day South Africa. The territory was politically fragmented, however, and this had not changed by the time of the mineral discoveries (cf. Map 9.1). The settler-controlled areas consisted of two coastal British colonies – the Cape Colony and Natal – and several inland Boer republics. The Cape Colony, which had been under British rule since 1806, elected its first parliament in 1854. Natal was settled in the 1830s by the Voortrekkers – settlers of Dutch descent who had moved out of the Cape Colony – but was annexed by Britain in 1843. It lacked a legislative council until 1856. The Voortrekkers also established several Boer republics which crystallized into two fledgling states. The Orange Free State had been under Voortrekker control from the second half of the 1830s onwards. It was annexed by Britain in 1848, but obtained independence in 1854. The second major Boer republic, the South African Republic (or Transvaal), came into existence after the British annexation of the Orange Free State induced some Boers to move beyond the Vaal River. Britain recognized its independence in 1852. The South African Republic later absorbed some smaller Boer

writing, similar estimates for other parts of present-day South Africa are not available for years before 1910.

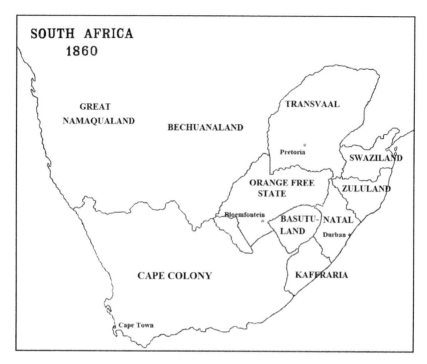

Map 9.1 South Africa, c. 1860
Source: Authors' own.

territories between the Vaal and Limpopo Rivers. Only a few independent African territories had remained at that stage, including Basutoland (between the Orange Free State and Natal), Kaffraria (between the Cape Colony and Natal), Zululand (to the north of Natal) and Swaziland (to the east of the South African Republic). In addition, the mixed-race Griquas controlled Griqualand West – a sparsely settled area to the north of the Cape Colony and the west of the Orange Free State.

The economies of these territories were poorly developed at the onset of the mineral discoveries. As Feinstein (2005, 2–3) put it: "Prior to the discovery of this mineral wealth, South Africa was a relatively backward economy, almost entirely dependent on agriculture . . . . Markets were small, conditions difficult, and progress slow." This was true even of the Cape Colony – the oldest and economically most advanced area under settler control. To be sure, recent research suggests that the GDP per capita of the Dutch Cape Colony reached levels comparable to those of England and Holland in the early eighteenth century (Fourie & Van Zanden, 2013, 477–80). According to Fourie and Van Zanden (2013, 484), this reflected a "strong demand for Cape products by the passing European ships in Table Bay, and a large slave society that increased productivity and caused a low dependency burden". Nonetheless, Figure 9.1 shows that the average income of the settlers decreased, on balance, from the early years of the eighteenth century until the mid–nineteenth century. This trend probably reflected longer-term effects of the Cape Colony's reliance on slave labour, such as high levels of inequality and weak incentives for technological innovation and accumulation of capital goods (Fourie 2013, 446). In the first half of the nineteenth century, economic progress was also hindered by the undiversified nature of economy activity; the lack of infrastructure, capital and skilled labour; and the high prevalence of subsistence farming and barter trade (Schumann, 1938, 31, Hobart-Houghton 1971, 1–4).

Feinstein's (2005, 3) claim that "[t]he situation was then totally transformed by the discovery of diamonds and gold in the late nineteenth century" was devoid of hyperbole. For one, the mineral discoveries played a major role in the political unification of South Africa. Prior to the 1870s, the frequency and cost of conflict between settlers and indigenous African peoples was the sole reason why some in the Imperial Government favoured expansion of the area under British control.[3] Their intention was to establish a self-governing federation responsible for its own defence (Davenport & Saunders 2000, 203). In the late 1860s, for example, the motivation of members of the government of William Gladstone to advocate responsible government for the Cape Colony was to begin the process of creating a South African confederation consisting of the Cape Colony, the Natal Colony, Griqualand West, Basutoland, the South African Republic and the Republic of the Orange Free State (Davenport and Saunders 2000, 105). Others, however, feared the fiscal burden of such a step.

The balance of views on this issue changed completely after the mineral discoveries.[4] Despite opposition from the Cape Government, the British High Commissioner, Sir Henry Barkly, annexed the diamond mining area around Kimberley as the Crown Colony of Griqualand West in 1871. In 1874, the British Colonial Secretary, Lord Carnarvon, launched a plan to realize the envisaged confederation. This led to a series of so-called

---

[3] According to Welsh (2000, 229), the Cape Colony absorbed more than a quarter of all British colonial military spending in the 1860s despite holding only 4 per cent of the British colonial population. The so-called Frontier Wars against the amaXhosa in Kaffraria accounted for a large portion of these outlays.

[4] The first diamond was found at Hopetown in 1866, while the large deposits around modern-day Kimberley were discovered in 1870. Gold was discovered in the Witwatersrand area around modern-day Johannesburg in 1886.

Confederation Wars in various parts of Southern Africa, including Basutoland, Kaffraria, Matabeleland and Zululand. The discovery of gold in the South African Republic further raised the stakes. British control over the whole of present-day South Africa was finally established when the Boer Republics were defeated in the South African War, which was fought from 1899 to 1902.

Britain initially governed South Africa as four separate colonies (the Cape, Natal, the Orange River Colony and the Transvaal) and maintained Basutoland, Bechuanaland and Swaziland as separate protectorates. Various considerations, including administrative costs and economic interdependence, led to the unification of the four colonies in 1910 (cf. Davenport and Saunders 2000, 255–62). The four areas became provinces of the Union of South Africa – a self-governing dominion of the British Empire. Although the Union was a unitary state, the provinces retained significant revenue powers and expenditure responsibilities (we will return to this issue). The Union came to an end in 1961 when South Africa became a republic and left the Commonwealth.

On the economic front, the mineral discoveries boosted international trade and government revenue, which enabled higher levels of public spending on infrastructure. In addition, the mining sector's demand for goods and services stimulated manufacturing, as well as commercial, financial and transport services (Gilbert 1933, Schumann 1938, 37–58, Hobart-Houghton 1971, 12–14). Figure 9.1 confirms that these effects ended the long spell of economic retrogression and initiated an extended period of rapid, albeit at times volatile, growth in per capita incomes that continued until the early 1970s. The mining sector generated 27.1 per cent of the gross national income of the Union in 1912, and its contribution exceeded 15 per cent in every year until 1944. Furthermore, employment in the mining sector increased from 325 thousand workers in 1912 to 548 thousand in 1957 (Bureau of Census and Statistics 1960, S-3). More generally, the mineral discoveries initiated several structural changes in the South Africa economy that Chenery (1979) and others later identified as elements of modern economic growth. These included urbanization, the shift from agricultural to industrial production, and the accumulation of physical capital.

The seemingly impressive growth in per capita income until the early 1970s masked two undesirable outcomes. The first was the extreme skewedness in the distributions of income and wealth that remain prominent features of modern-day South Africa (cf. Nattrass & Seekings 2011, 518–19). The second was South Africa's failure to capitalize fully on the opportunities presented by the so-called golden age after the Second World War: Table 9.1 reveals that the South African economy performed

Table 9.1 *Growth rates of GDP per capita in 1990 international dollars in South Africa and selected countries and groups of countries, 1913–94*[1]

	Average annual percentage changes		
	1913–50	1950–73	1973–94
South Africa	1.3	2.2	−0.6
Latin America	1.2	2.7	1.1
UK Dominions	1.1	2.5	1.5
Japan	0.9	8	2.6
Europe	0.6	5.2	2
Other African[2]	0.6	2	0.8
Other Asian[3]	0	3.5	4.3
Total sample	0.5	4	2

Source: Feinstein (2005, 7), based on Maddison (2001, 185, 195, 215, 224, 276–9, 288–9, 304–5 and 322–6).
Notes: 1. Sample countries: Latin America – Argentina, Brazil, Chile, Colombia, Mexico, Peru; UK Dominions – Australia, Canada, New Zealand; Europe – Austria, Finland, Greece, Ireland, Italy, Portugal, Spain; Other African – Algeria, Egypt, Ghana, Morocco, Nigeria; Other Asian – Indonesia, Malaysia, Pakistan, Philippines, South Korea, Taiwan, Thailand; 2. 1913–1950: Egypt, Ghana and Morocco; 3. For South Korea, 1913–40 population and GDP are assumed to have grown at same rate as for Korea as a whole; for Pakistan, 1913 population is based on census data for corresponding areas of India, and per capita GDP is assumed to have grown at same rate for 1913–50 as in total pre-partition India.

markedly less well than those of many other countries from 1950 to 1973 (cf. also Moll 1991, Feinstein 2005, 7–9). The sustained decrease in per capita income from 1975 until 1994 depicted in Figure 9.1 shows a further economic deterioration.[5] Other sections of this chapter link these undesirable outcomes to the economic and political ramifications of the apartheid system.

Progress towards Fiscal Modernization

Reference was made earlier to the four criteria for assessing progress towards fiscal modernization outlined in the introduction to this volume.

---

[5] The boom conditions associated with the sharp increase in the gold price in 1980 briefly interrupted this trend.

These criteria provide the contours of a narrative that suggests that South Africa made remarkable progress as far as the creation of a modern fiscal state was concerned, albeit in the context of non-inclusive political and economic institutions.

Accountable Government

Although the emergence of accountable government is often considered as a later development in the process of fiscal modernization, its roots in South Africa were comparatively early, especially when compared to the rest of colonial Africa. The four parts of the Union of South Africa exhibited elements of accountable government in varying degrees before 1910. The Cape Colony, which was the oldest of the four territories, obtained representative government in 1854 and responsible government in 1872. These developments were accompanied by the modernization of financial management and other governance institutions (cf. McCracken 1967). Institutional development also occurred in Natal after it obtained representative government in 1856 and responsible government in 1893. The Orange Free State and the South African Republic had democratic constitutions (Thompson, 2000, 101–2), but Hobart-Houghton (1971, 8) pointed out that "the difficulties of creating a modern administrative machine without trained staff or adequate finance proved almost insuperable in both". More progress occurred in the Orange Free State than in the South African Republic (Du Plessis & Du Plessis, 2017). The British Government extended responsible government to the Transvaal Colony and the Orange River Colony in 1907.

A thirty-member National Convention drafted the South Africa Bill, which the British Parliament adopted in 1909 to establish the Union of South Africa (Davenport & Saunders 2000, 255–62). The next two decades were marked by what Nattrass and Seekings (2011, 525) described as "a remarkable process of state-building" in which the basic institutions of a modern fiscal state were established. Nattrass and Seekings (2011, 525) emphasized the Union government's capacity to manage the economy:

In its fiscal capability, its capacity to collect and to use statistics, its strategic interventions in industrial development and social welfare and perhaps, above all, in its interventions in wage determination and the regulation of employment, the South African state adopted the form of the modern economic state, empowering it in its dealings with the powerful capitalist elites in gold mining and other sectors.

The fiscal institutions of the Union mattered greatly for the revenue-, public debt- and spending-related dimensions of fiscal modernization.

The Constitution of the Union of South Africa mandated the creation of well-structured budgeting and financial management processes in which critical roles were played by Parliament, the Minister of Finance, the Department of Finance (including two branches responsible for revenue collection, namely the Department of Inland Revenue and the Department of Customs and Excise), the Public Debt Commissioners and the Controller and Auditor-General.[6] Capable ministers and secretaries developed the Department of Finance into a small but effective organization with a durable tradition of "enlightened conservatism" (cf. Browne 1983) that enabled South Africa to avoid fiscal crises during the period under review. Moll (1993, 255) also acknowledged the effectiveness of fiscal policymaking and macroeconomic policymaking more generally:

Apartheid South Africa was blessed with competent economic policymakers and policy implementers. Political leaders were consistently committed to macroeconomic prudence and low inflation, the government enjoyed the degree of unity, continuity and bureaucratic competence necessary to implement most of its macroeconomic policies.[7]

The Union of South Africa closely resembled an independent country (Freund 2011, 211). The combination of a high degree of autonomy and solid democratic institutions ensured that its governments were accountable to voters. The vast majority of voters, however, were members of the white minority. Whites already had a near monopoly on political power when the Union came into being: blacks had neither citizenship nor voting rights in the Boer Republics and much attenuated rights in the Cape Colony and Natal (Thompson 2000, 150). Moreover, the drafters of the South Africa Bill – the document that determined the nature of the political institutions of the Union – did not include any blacks. The result was that all decisions regarding the establishment of the Union and its political institutions were taken by the representatives of some 20 per cent of the South African population. The National Convention agreed after much debate to allow the Cape and Natal to retain limited voting rights for blacks, but rejected proposals to extend these rights to the other two

---

[6] De Kock (1927, 332–57) and Van Waasdijk (1964, 83–9, 289–99) provided useful overviews of the fiscal management of the Union of South Africa.

[7] The effectiveness of other parts of the Union's civil service varied. According to Posel (1999), "Afrikanerization" (attempts to replace liberal civil servants with loyal Afrikaner nationalists) and expansion to staff the increasingly unwieldy apartheid structures reduced the efficacy of the bureaucracy over time. Hyslop (2005, 780–2) argued that little overt corruption occurred in the higher echelons of the Union bureaucracy, but added that junior officials often exploited the elaborate restrictions on the movements of blacks to extract bribes.

provinces or to allow the election of blacks to Parliament (Davenport & Saunders 2000, 260).[8] Discontent among the majority led to the formation of the South African Native National Congress – which later became the African National Congress – but this had no immediate effect on the exclusionary nature of the institutions. Hence, the accountability structures in the Union resulted in a trajectory of institutional development and economic policies that focused overwhelmingly on the interests of white voters.

One outcome of this focus was the further disenfranchisement of South African blacks. In 1936 and 1951, respectively, Africans and Coloureds were placed on separate voters' rolls and restricted to choosing a few white representatives to the House of Assembly (Davenport & Saunders 2000, 308, 395-6). The seats reserved for representatives of African voters were abolished in 1960, when the focus of the Union government had shifted to the establishment of ethnically based "homelands" for Africans. The Union period also brought the adoption of a series of other laws underpinning the apartheid system; these ranged from restrictions on the movement of blacks in so-called "white areas" to severe discrimination in the allocation of public expenditures and measures to prevent social interaction between whites and blacks.

The economic policies of successive Union governments reflected a similar focus on the interests of whites. One of the major policy priorities was to ensure the availability of labour with required skills at desired wage levels to various sectors of the economy whilst protecting white labourers from competition by black workers. Feinstein (2005, 47-89) outlined how Union governments pursued these aims by combining coercive measures to ensure cheap black labour, ranging from taxes to dispossession of land and restrictions on movement and industrial organization, with the imposition of an elaborate colour bar to protect so-called "civilized labour". The effects of these policies on the performance of the South African economy was the subject of a protracted debate (cf. Nattrass 1991). Liberals (e.g. Horwitz, 1967, Hobart Houghton 1971) acknowledged that apartheid policies at times benefitted some capitalists – for example, by depressing the cost of black labour. More generally, however, they argued that apartheid undermined capitalism because it implied various government interventions that distorted the allocation of labour and other productive resources (Nattrass 1991, 657-61). Radicals

---

[8] In 1909, the composition of the registered voters in the Cape Colony was as follows: Africans – 5 per cent, Coloureds – 10 per cent, and Whites – 85 per cent (Thompson 2000, 150). Yet at the time of the 1911 census (the first after the establishment of the Union), 59 per cent of the population of the Cape Province were Africans, 18 per cent Coloureds and 23 per cent Whites (Bureau of Census and Statistics, 1960, A3-A5).

(e.g. Johnstone 1976) initially claimed that apartheid served the interests of capitalists, capitalism and whites by underpinning an exploitative yet highly profitable form of capitalism based on cheap black labour (Nattrass 1991, 664–7).[9] The deteriorating performance of the South African economy from the 1970s onwards necessitated a reconsideration of this position. Later contributions to this debate by radical economists, for example that by Saul and Gelb (1986), pointed out that the effects of apartheid policies changed over time: the measures adopted from the late 1940s onwards initially benefitted capitalists by boosting profitability, but in the longer run gave rise to secular increases in the capital intensity of the economy and a constrained domestic market.

Hence, there is now agreement across the ideological spectrum that apartheid policies were inimical to long-run economic development in South Africa. Lipton (1986) showed that the economic policymaking aspects of apartheid revolved around the evolving and, at times, conflicting needs of agricultural capital, mining capital, manufacturing capital and white workers. At first, the availability of cheap unskilled black labour benefitted agriculture and mining; in fact, these sectors actively used their political influence to lobby for the adoption of key apartheid measures. Yet both sectors eventually were hampered by a side-effect of the colour bar, namely intensifying skills shortages that arose because blacks were prevented from accessing more skilled jobs (Lipton 1986, 94, 116–17).[10] This affected mining first, but later became a constraint in agriculture as well, especially when mechanization and increasing farm sizes brought a growing demand for younger, more educated workers from the late 1950s onwards. An additional problem for the mining sector was that the colour bar exerted upward pressure on the cost of employing semi-skilled and skilled white labour (Lipton 1986, 110).

The manufacturing sector was more skill-intensive than mining and agriculture and required large and diverse domestic markets (Lipton 1986, 139). Hence, ramifications of apartheid policies such as the high cost of skilled labour, the high prevalence of poverty and the extremely skewed distribution of income had particularly pernicious effects on the development of manufacturing in South Africa. To be sure, manufacturing activity expanded rapidly in the period under review; its share of the national income

---

[9] The profitability of the gold-mining industry, which could not influence the price of its output, depended heavily on cost containment (while South Africa's gold deposits are extensive, extraction generally require deep-level mining and the application of expensive physical and chemical processes) (Feinstein, 2005: 104). Hence, the cost of unskilled labour assumed great significance.

[10] Skills shortages would have constrained these and other sectors of the economy of the Union even in the absence of the colour bar because of the devastating effects of inferior "Bantu education" on the schooling of blacks – an issue to which this chapter will return.

increased from 6.7 per cent in 1912 to 25.4 per cent in 1925 and 24.6 per cent in 1959 (Bureau of Census and Statistics 1960, S-3). The election victory of the Pact Government (a coalition of the National Party and the Labour Party) in 1924 gave considerable impetus to the growth of the manufacturing sector. This government launched a wide-ranging import substitution programme based on customs tariffs to create new jobs for core supporter groups (poor, urbanizing whites and other Afrikaners), promote economic self-sufficiency and diversify economic activity away from the extraction of exhaustible minerals (Feinstein 2005, 117–18). It also used large parastatals – including South African Railways and Harbours, the Electricity Supply Commission (established in 1923) and the Iron and Steel Industrial Corporation (established in 1929) – to provide inputs and infrastructure to private industries (Nattrass & Seekings 2011, 547). The effects of inefficiency (a function of high levels of protection and skills shortages) and the small domestic market became increasingly clear over time: profit rates in manufacturing and South Africa's share of world man-ufactured exports fell from the 1960s onwards, and the sector's share of GDP dropped precipitously after 1990 (Nattrass & Seekings 2011, 543–4).

The economic development literature emphasizes the importance of industrialization to avoid excessive dependence on depletable natural resources (cf. Szirmai 2012, 409–10). While the development of various service sectors partly compensated for the decline of the primary sectors, the limited achievement of manufacturing development was one of the major reasons why the South African economy ran out of steam from the mid-1970s onwards (for detailed expositions of this argument, see Fedderke 2014, Feinstein 2005, 200–23). In addition, protests against the apartheid system intensified from the early 1960s onwards, and increasingly stifled confidence and investment. The combination of the direct effects of apartheid policies and the indirect effects of resistance to the political system thus undermined sustained economic growth in South Africa after 1960.

Centralized Government Revenue Collection

Prior to the mineral discoveries, the two British colonies and the two Boer republics relied on various forms of tax and non-tax revenue to finance public spending. These included customs duties, stamp duties, transfer duties, hut taxes and land rents (De Kock 1924, 386–9, 394–401). With the exception of hut taxes, the tax systems of these territories were similar to those of England in the mid-nineteenth century (cf. Tames 2005, 124). Government revenues generally sufficed in the Cape Colony and the Colony of Natal, in part because the Imperial Government defrayed the

Table 9.2 *Government revenue and expenditure in British colonies and Boer republics in South Africa, selected years 1870–1910*

Total (Thousands of pounds)		1870	1882/3	1890/1	1898/9	1909/10
Cape Colony	Revenue	668	2,408	2,398	3,416	4,828
	Expenditure	642	2,832	3,106	4,830	5,646
Natal Colony	Revenue	127	483	764	1,100	1,661
	Expenditure	118	472	994	2,458	2,483
Transvaal	Revenue	32	83	1,216	4,184	6,004
	Expenditure	31	91	1,486	4, 424	5,080
Orange Free State	Revenue	64	212	378	393	991
	Expenditure	53	200	313	441	975
"South Africa"	Revenue	891	3,186	4,756	9,093	13,484
	Expenditure	844	3,595	5,899	12,153	14,184
Per capita (pounds)		1870	1882/3	1890/1	1898/9	1909/10
Cape Colony	Revenue	0.96	2.06	1.61	1.81	1.96
	Expenditure	0.92	2.42	2.09	2.56	2.29
Natal Colony	Revenue	0.41	1.09	1.43	1.43	1.47
	Expenditure	0.38	1.06	1.87	3.19	2.2
Transvaal	Revenue	1.1	0.16	1.67	4.06	3.83
	Expenditure	0.09	0.17	2.05	4.29	3.24
Orange Free State	Revenue	0.73	1.37	1.58	1.21	2.06
	Expenditure	0.61	1.3	1.31	1.36	2.13
"South Africa"	Revenue	0.63	1.38	1.59	2.26	2.4
	Expenditure	0.59	1.56	1.97	3.03	2.53

Sources: Revenue and expenditure data from De Kock (1924, 388, 392, 395, 398, 401); Union of South Africa (1921, 816); population data: own estimates based on De Kock (1924, 136, 139, 141–2).

bulk of these territories' military expenditures. In the Transvaal and the Orange Free State, by contrast, public finances tended to be in perilous states because of low levels of economic activity, weak tax administration, low levels of tax compliance and the costs of frequent wars with surrounding African groups (De Kock 1924, 396–401).

Table 9.2 reveals that the emergence and growth of mining from the 1870s onwards brought marked increases in the non-railway government revenues of all four territories (cf. Schumann, 1938, 49–53).[11] The per

---

[11] All amounts in this chapter are in pounds sterling. The currency of the Cape Colony was linked to that of Britain in 1825, when British silver and copper coins were introduced and the paper Rixdollar was made convertible (De Kock 1924, 91). The Union of South Africa adopted the South Africa pound in 1910. Apart from the period September 1931 to December 1932, when the Union remained on the gold standard after Britain had

capita figures in the bottom panel of the table show these increases less clearly than the totals in the top panel. This reflects large population changes caused by war-related displacement and territorial expansion. Moreover, the population estimates are subject to large margins of error. Be that as it may, the growth in government revenue was accompanied by similar increases in public spending (see also next section). The direct contributions of mining activities to government revenues varied. In the Transvaal, the lack of other revenue sources and the disenfranchized status of the "Uitlander" (literally "foreigner") mine-owners made heavy reliance on prospecting and diggers' licences necessary and feasible. The Transvaal Colony also introduced a tax on the net profits of goldmines in 1902 (De Kock 1924, 424).

A more developed economy and the vital role of its ports and railways in trade throughout South Africa endowed the Cape Colony with a wider government revenue base than that of the Transvaal. Furthermore, a number of men with interests in diamond mining became influential politicians in the Cape Colony, and succeeded in limiting the tax burden on the industry.[12] All four territories, however, benefitted from the general increases in economic activity and trade associated with the mineral discoveries. Customs revenues increased everywhere, but special benefits accrued to the two coastal colonies from increased traffic through their ports.[13] Such traffic also elevated railway receipts to vital sources of public revenue in the Cape Colony and Natal (De Kock 1924, 391–5).

The productivity of customs and railway revenues and strong opposition to direct taxation of income worked against further diversification of the tax base in pre-1910 South Africa. In the Cape Colony, for example, tax revenue grew little in per capita terms after 1875, whereas gross non-tax revenues soared (cf. Table 9.3). In 1904, the Cape Colony became the first territory in South Africa to introduce an income tax (De Kock 1924, 423), but its share of total government revenue until 1909 ranged between 4 and 6 per cent. Natal followed suit in 1908.

All four territories imposed taxes on Africans: The Cape Colony and Natal opted for hut taxes, while the Orange Free State and Transvaal used poll taxes (De Kock 1924, 430–1). These taxes never became such important sources of revenue as they did in Kenya and Northern

abandoned it, the South African pound was approximately at par with the pound sterling until it was replaced by the Rand in 1961 (Hobart-Houghton 1964, 196).

[12] These politicians included Joseph Robinson (Member of Parliament from 1881 to 1885) and Cecil John Rhodes (Member of Parliament from 1880 to 1896, including two terms as Prime Minister from 1890 to 1896).

[13] The customs agreement concluded between the Orange Free State and the Cape Colony in 1889 provided for the remittance of 75 per cent of the revenues collected on transient trade (Plant 1936, 785).

Table 9.3 *Government tax revenue and non-tax revenue in the Cape Colony in pounds per capita at current prices, selected years 1853–1904*

Per capita revenues	1853	1865	1875	1891	1904
Tax revenue	1.14	0.81	1.49	1.34	1.6
Non-tax revenue	0.22	0.2	0.38	1.54	1.85
Total revenue	1.36	1.01	1.87	2.88	3.45

Source: Own calculations based on revenue and population information in *Blue Books* for the Colony of the Cape of Good Hope, various years.

Rhodesia (Gardner 2012, 48–9). In the Cape Colony, for example, the hut tax peaked at 1.5 per cent of total government revenue in 1908. However, as was the case elsewhere, the hut tax became an important instrument in attempts to solve labour supply problems in the mining and other sectors by coercing Africans into wage labour. In the Cape Colony, the hut tax was complemented from 1894 onwards by the Glen Grey Act – a piece of legislation conceived and enthusiastically promoted by Rhodes (cf. Rotberg 1988, 467–72). This Act introduced a system of individual land tenure in areas with large concentrations of amaXhosa, but it limited the size of individual holdings to an uneconomical four acres and imposed a labour tax on non-titleholders (Davenport & Saunders 2000, 190).

The rapid growth in government expenditure in the first two decades after the establishment of the Union of South Africa necessitated important tax reforms that set the contours of a modern tax system.[14] These included the expansion of the excise tax system from 1911 onwards and the introduction of a fully fledged income tax system in 1914. The income tax, which was levied on individuals and companies, included a dividend tax and a supertax on incomes in excess of £2,500 (De Kock 1924: 404). Various mining tax laws were consolidated in 1910, and in 1917 a consolidated income tax was adopted that subjected the mining profits to income tax. Henceforth, the mining sector made a markedly larger direct contribution to the coffers of the Union government. Meanwhile, the levying of hut and poll taxes was

---

[14] Elsewhere in this chapter we show that various factors contributed to this trend, including the creation of new administrative structures, South Africa's involvement in the First World War and the expansion of economic infrastructure and the education and health-care systems.

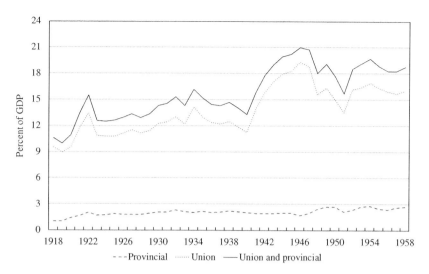

Figure 9.2 Union and provincial government revenue as percentages of GDP, 1918–58
Source: Own calculations based on information in Bureau of Census and Statistics (1960, H-23, Q-2, Q-9; S-3).

continued. The four provinces had differentiated systems until 1925, when a uniform poll tax was introduced. This tax remained in place until well after 1961, and eventually complemented the pass laws as an element of a wide-ranging system of controls on the movement of Africans in urban areas of South Africa (Savage 1986).

These and other changes, including the introduction of a diamond export levy in 1916 and a temporary excess profit tax in 1917, significantly boosted government revenue. The total revenue of the Union and provincial governments increased from 10.6 per cent of Gross National Income in 1918 to 18.7 per cent in 1958 (cf. Figure 9.2). Revenue collection was relatively centralized: provincial revenues only occasionally exceeded 15 per cent and from time to time fell below 10 per cent of the total. The South Africa Act assigned some large expenditure responsibilities to the provinces, most notably education, healthcare and the construction of roads and bridges. The revenue sources assigned to these entities in the early decades of the Union – which included direct taxes for provincial purposes; property taxes; motor vehicle, dog and other licences; betting and other entertainment taxes; and transfer duties – proved inadequate and left them dependent for roughly one-half of their total revenues on transfers from the Union government. Although subsequent legislative changes expanded the provinces' own revenue sources

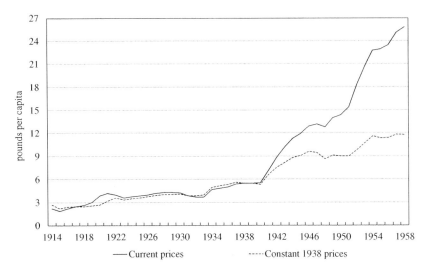

Figure 9.3 Union and provincial government revenue in pounds per capita, 1914–58
Source: Own calculations based on Bureau of Census and Statistics (1960, A-8, H-23, Q-2, Q-9).
Note: Constant-price figures were calculated by deflating the total revenues with the all-items retail price index.

to include surcharges on personal income tax collections by the Union government, auction sales taxes and user charges for the provision of education and healthcare services, this high level of dependence on transfers continued to pose risks for the maintenance of fiscal discipline at the provincial level (Browne 1973, 9–11).

Figure 9.3 shows trends in Union and provincial government revenue per capita from 1914 to 1958. In nominal terms, revenue grew from £2 per person in 1914 to £5½ per person in 1940. The growth in revenue per capita accelerated thereafter, and receipts reached £25¾ per person in 1958. While it is clear from Figure 9.2 that prices also increased significantly in this period, the constant-price estimates suggest that real revenue per capita more than doubled. On balance, these trends are indicative of an impressive revenue-collection effort in a territory in which widespread poverty among the majority African population and a large "poor white" community markedly curtailed the income and consumption tax bases.[15]

---

[15] It should be noted that the revenue figures presented in this section exclude the incomes of local authorities. The data published by the Bureau of Census and Statistics (1960, Q19) do not make it possible to distinguish between the own revenues of local authorities

The growth depicted in Figures 9.2 and 9.3 was accompanied by important changes in the composition of Union government revenue (cf. Table 9.4). Reflecting growth in personal incomes and business activity, the revenue share of income taxes grew steadily – in the 1950s, such taxes represented almost one-half of all Union government revenues. According to the Bureau of Census and Statistics (1960, Q-3), the number of tax assessments issued to individuals increased from 58 thousand in 1917 to 658 thousand in 1957; the corresponding increase for companies was from 2 thousand to 21 thousand. For similar reasons, revenues from excise taxes also grew in relative terms, especially in the 1940s and 1950s. Compensatory decreases were recorded in the shares of the formerly main source of revenue, namely customs duties, and, to a lesser extent, receipts from the provision of postal, telegraphic and telephone services. Tax and other revenues from mining increased rapidly until the 1930s, but declined thereafter as gold mining became less profitable. Although revenue from the mining sector undoubtedly was important in the Union of South Africa, the government never became as dependent on resource revenues as those of modern-day economies such as Angola, the Republic of the Congo, Iraq, Kuwait, Libya, Saudi Arabia and the United Arab Emirates.[16]

An international comparison for 1959 (Tun Wai 1962, 431, 434) confirms the unusual salience of direct taxes in the tax structure of the Union of South Africa. In that year, direct tax revenue amounted to 50 per cent of total central government revenue in South Africa – a ratio that exceeded the medians for seventeen high income countries with per capita incomes above $500 per annum (43 per cent), fifteen other medium-income countries with per capita incomes between $200 and R500 per annum (28 per cent) and nineteen low-income countries with per capita incomes below $200 per capita (20 per cent).[17] Furthermore,

---

and transfers from other levels of government. Nonetheless, it is clear that local authorities mobilized large amounts of revenue. The total revenues of local authorities (inclusive of transfers received) increased from £6.5 million in 1919 to £101.7 million in 1957. These figures represented 35.8 per cent and 33.3 per cent of the revenues of the Union government, respectively. Collections from one of the key revenue sources, property taxes, increased from £4.9 million in 1938 (the first year for which data are available) to £21.7 million in 1957. In the latter year, the revenues from the trading departments of local authorities yielded a further £51.5 million. This amount included revenue from public transport and abattoir services, as well as the provision of power and water. See also Van Waasdijk (1964, 114–17).

[16] A database published by the International Centre for Tax and Development (2017) contains statistics on the composition of government revenue in most countries.

[17] The medium- and low-income comparator countries included the following (direct tax shares are provided in brackets): Malaya (15 per cent), Burma (25 per cent), Thailand (21 per cent), Indonesia (18 per cent), India (17 per cent) and Ghana (10 per cent).

Table 9.4 *Contribution of selected revenue sources to Union government revenue, average decadal percentage shares 1910–59*

	1913–19	1920–9	1930–9	1940–9	1950–9
Income tax	9.9	22.9	28	33.1	48
Mining tax	10.6	10.2	18.5	20.2	10.3
Other mining revenue	5.9	8.2	10.5	4.6	2
Net customs revenue	33.8	28.6	25.7	13.6	10.4
Net excise revenue	5.7	6.9	6.2	10.9	12.9
Posts, telegraphs and telephones	12.7	12.3	13	8.9	9.4

Source: Own calculations based on Bureau of Census and Statistics (1960, Q-2, Q-4, Q-5, Q-6).

the total revenue share of taxes on foreign trade in the Union (15 per cent) lagged those for fourteen other medium-income countries (26 per cent) and twenty low-income countries (30 per cent).

Frankema and Booth (Chapter 1, this volume) refer to two factors that rendered most colonies heavily reliant on indirect taxes, namely widespread poverty and the legitimacy problem of colonial governments. Compared to most other colonies, these constraints on the raising of direct tax revenue were less acute in South Africa after 1910. The growth in incomes and wealth initiated by the mineral discoveries made it possible to introduce income taxes that soon yielded large portions of the government's revenues. Moreover, the high level of autonomy and perceived effectiveness of the Union government endowed it with considerable legitimacy in the eyes of whites, who constituted the bulk of the voters and direct taxpayers.

Government Borrowing

The mineral discoveries also had major implications for the ability of the South African state to establish long-term floating debt positions. Before the discoveries, authorities borrowed to finance exceptional outlays and endeavoured to redeem debt when tax revenues sufficed. Thus the government of the Cape Colony incurred various forms of debt in the first half of the nineteenth century, including inconvertible paper money and occasional borrowing from the Imperial government, the East India Company and various local boards (De Kock 1924, 393). It used the proceeds to establish the Lombard Bank and to construct buildings and public works. By 1835, the outstanding debt of the Cape government amounted to £265 thousand. John Montagu succeeded in redeeming virtually the entire amount during his term as Colonial Secretary (1843–52), but the Cape government resorted to borrowing again from 1859 onwards.

The positive effects of the mineral discoveries on tax revenues improved the ability of the two British colonies and the Boer republics to obtain loans on reasonable terms. In the Cape Colony, for example, the public debt increased rapidly from £2,8 million in 1875 to £23,7 million in 1890 and £52,6 million in 1910 (De Kock 1924, 394). This increase reflected the influence of the mineral discoveries on the colony's credit-worthiness as well the "empire effect" discussed by Accominotti et al. (2010): the public debts of the Cape and other self-governing colonies were guaranteed, in de facto terms, by the Imperial government, which improved these territories' borrowing terms and access to the capital market in London.[18] This provided financing for the construction of railway lines between the mining areas around Kimberley and Johannesburg and three ports in the Cape Colony (Cape Town, Port Elizabeth and East London). These transport links greatly increased the beneficial economic effects of the mineral discoveries for the Cape Colony. The Natal Colony also ensured a share of the benefits of the mining booms by mobilizing foreign capital to improve Durban harbour and to construct rail links. Hence, its public debt mushroomed from £263 thousand in 1872 to £22,7 million in 1910 (De Kock 1924, 396).

The situation was different in the Boer republics, which had to do without the "empire effect" and had to carry the full burden of the Confederation Wars and other conflicts with indigenous peoples. Before the mineral discoveries, puny tax revenues forced both republics to issue paper money to defray government expenses (cf. De Kock 1924, 396–7, 400–1). Apart from the major increases in taxes and other govern-ment revenues referred to earlier, the benefits of these discoveries included improved access to loans. Thus the Transvaal secured funding from Dutch and German investors for the construction of a railway from the goldfields to Delagoa Bay (Van Helten 1978, 369–73), while bor-rowed funds enabled the Orange Free State to purchase railways in the Republic that were built earlier by the Cape Government (De Kock 1924, 402). Both territories required funding for reconstruction and develop-ment after the South African War. An amount of £35 million was raised for this purpose in London in 1903; reflecting the new status of the two

[18] While the entry of the so-called Imperial banks (Standard Bank, the Oriental Banking Corporation and the African Banking Corporation) from 1861 onwards was a major boost to banking in South Africa, the financing of large infrastructure projects remained beyond the capacity of the domestic financial sector.

territories as British colonies, the loan had favourable terms and was guaranteed by the Imperial Government (De Kock 1924, 400).

Mainly because of the construction of railways and reconstruction programmes after the South African War, the Union came into being with a sizeable public debt of £116 million (De Kock 1924, 404). In 1912, the public debt amounted to £19.25 per capita (some 7.5 times the revenue per capita of the Union government) or 88.3 per cent of the national income (Bureau of Census and Statistics 1960, A-8, Q-8, S-3). It transpires from Figure 9.4 that the nominal debt stock grew modestly in per capita terms until 1940, when it reached £28. The Second World War caused a steep upward trend that continued in the late 1940s and 1950s. By 1958, public debt per capita amounted to £78.33 The fiscal authorities did not accumulate debt in an unsustainable manner, though. In fact, a markedly different trend emerges when the size of the economy is used to gauge the extent and growth of the public debt. Figure 9.4 shows that the debt burden increased from 95.5 per cent of the national income in 1918 to a peak of 121.6 per cent in 1932. It then entered a secular decline (briefly interrupted during the Second World War) and stood at a moderate 54.3 per cent in 1958. According to Browne and Jones (1961, 181), loans incurred from 1910 to 1961 mainly financed spending on railways and harbours (33 per cent of all borrowed funds), war and defence (17 per cent), infrastructure programmes by provincial authorities and land purchases by the South African Natives Trust (11 per cent), housing (7 per cent) and telegraphs and telephone systems (7 per cent).

A strong commitment to fiscal prudence and effective institutions contributed to the authorities' success at limiting the growth of public debt below the growth of South Africa's national income. One of the manifestations of this "enlightened conservatism" in the Department of Finance was an acute awareness of the dangers of excessive borrowing. The following statement by the Secretary of the Treasury who held the office from 1937 to 1950, was a clear example of the prudent approach of fiscal policymakers in the period under review: "Annual budgeting . . . involves certain corollaries if it is to be a successful instrument in sound finance. One of these is that if a deficit emerges, steps must immediately be taken to extinguish it. Another is that if a surplus emerges it must not be an incentive to increased expenditure" (Holloway 1954, 107). This conservatism enabled the Treasury to negotiate the challenges posed by the Great Depression and two world wars. It also precluded systematic recourse to anti-cyclical Keynesian fiscal policy until the 1950s (Calitz, Du Plessis & Siebrits 2009, 16). Hence, the Union of South Africa largely eschewed the policy approach blamed by some economists (e.g. Buchanan & Wagner 1977) for

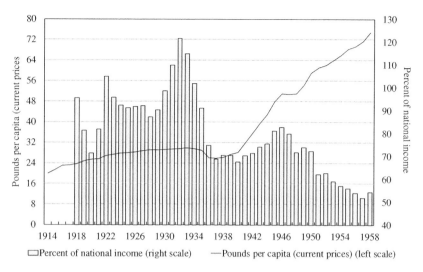

Figure 9.4 Public debt of the Union government in pounds per capita at current prices, 1914–58 and as a percentage of gross national income, 1918–58
Source: Own calculations based on Bureau of Census and Statistics (1960, A-8, Q-8. S-3).

the public debt burdens of high-income countries in the 1960s and the 1970s.

Two aspects of the fiscal policymaking framework complemented the resolve of the authorities. A dual-budget system required the government to finance all current spending from tax and other current revenues via the Revenue Account, while capital expenditure had to be financed by borrowing via the Loan Account. This system was in force in South Africa throughout the period from 1910 to 1961.[19] It was designed to balance current government expenditure with current government revenue. The distinction between the two accounts became blurred from the early 1950s onwards (Calitz, et al. 2009, 18). Nonetheless, the dual-budget system was an effective barrier to excessive debt accumulation: it forced the fiscal authorities to adhere to the 'golden rule of fiscal policy' by preventing borrowing to finance current outlays.

---

[19] Several countries (including Canada, Ecuador, India, Sweden and the United Kingdom) used similar systems in the first half of the twentieth century. In addition, many African countries also adopted dual-budget systems after obtaining independence (Lienert 2003, 38–9).

Table 9.5 *Public debt in a sample of countries in pounds per capita at current prices, selected years 1930–60*

Per capita public debt	1930	1939	1950	1955	1960
Canada	50	68	403	399	412
New Zealand	173	147	337	337	352
Australia	165	150	285	324	317
Union of South Africa	28	27	37	34	–
Malaya	–	–	6	12	25
Ceylon	–	2	6	9	17
Turkey	–	6	17	22	16
Philippines	–	–	7	9	11
India	3	3	5	6	10
Egypt	7	6	8	10	–
Ghana	–	–	–	4	8
Thailand	1	1	2	4	4
Burma	–	–	4	2	–
Kenya	–	–	–	–	1

Sources: Own calculations based on the following: for South Africa, Bureau of Census and Statistics (1960, A-8, Q-8. S-3); other countries, Maddison (2003, 82–3), Mitchell (1998, 48–66), United Nations (1948), United Nations (various issues).

Note: All the United Nations publications from which the public debt data were sourced point out that the figures are not necessarily fully comparable (e.g. some are for gross and others for net debt stocks). Such differences, however, are unlikely to affect the inferences in the text.

The General Sinking Fund, which was established by the Public Debt Commissioners (Amendment) Act of 1926, also constrained the accumulation of public debt. The Act stipulated that the Fund was to receive £1.3 million from general revenue per annum for forty fiscal years starting in 1926/7; in addition, it was to be allowed to earn interest at 4.5 per cent per annum on moneys used to repay government debt. While the effect of the Sinking Fund on the public debt burden was not as large as was foreseen when it was established (Van Waasdijk 1964, 74), it definitely contributed to the sustained decrease in the debt-to-GDP ratio from the early 1930s onwards.

Table 9.5 shows per capita debt figures in pounds sterling for the Union of South Africa and other territories in selected years from 1930 to 1960. The public debt burden of the Union was higher in per capita terms than those of colonies and other developing territories in Africa and Asia, yet markedly lower than those of Australia, Canada and New Zealand. As was pointed out by Frankema and Booth (Chapter 1, this volume), South Africa and India were exceptional among colonies with regard to the extent to which debt was used to finance government expenditure programmes.

The growing reliance on domestic borrowing from 1910 onwards was vital for a sustainable management of South Africa's public finances. In 1914, domestic debt constituted only 11.5 per cent of the outstanding debt of the Union government (Bureau of Census and Statistics 1960, Q-8). The domestic component of the public debt stock exceeded the foreign component for the first time in 1936, however, and reached 91.7 per cent in 1958 (Bureau of Census and Statistics 1960, Q-8). External events (such as pressure on the British capital market during the two world wars) played a part in eroding the Union government's reliance on foreign borrowing. Browne and Jones (1961, 197–9) emphasized two additional factors behind this trend: the domestic capital market expanded steadily as the economy of the Union grew, and the Government substituted domestic for foreign debt when large volumes of investment capital accumulated during periods of extraordinary prosperity.[20] These boom periods were largely driven by the mining industry, most notably the boom after the Union left the gold standard in 1932.

Welfare-Enhancing Government Expenditure

The literature on colonial fiscal development (e.g. Booth 2007, Frankema 2011) has shown great variation between states that mobilized little revenue and provided few services apart from protection against external and domestic threats (i.e. night watchman states) and those that imposed high tax burdens but invested large portions of the proceeds in growth-promoting infrastructure and social services. A superficial interpretation of statistics from the years 1850 to 1861 would suggest that South Africa increasingly resembled the so-called developmental colonial state: an earlier part of this section pointed out that the overall tax burden increased markedly over the period as a whole, and it will be shown that growing portions of government revenue were invested in infrastructure and social spending. However, this subsection will also highlight the extreme skewedness in the racial distribution of social expenditure. Such discrimination in the allocation of public resources served to

---

[20] An important reason for substituting domestic for foreign debt was the danger that surpluses of investable funds could have fuelled inflation (Browne and Jones, 1961: 198).

Table 9.6 *Functional classification of central government spending in the Cape Colony in pounds per capita at current prices, selected years 1856–1904*

Per capita expenditures	1853	1865	1875	1891	1904
Administration	0.16	0.09	0.11	0.11	0.19
Debt service	0.11	0.56	0.33	0.83	0.69
Health, education and welfare	0.16	0.13	0.14	0.21	0.34
Law, order and defence	0.42	0.35	0.29	0.48	1.13
Public works	1.3	1.57	1.44	2.87	4.46
Total	2.15	2.7	2.31	4.5	6.81

Source: Own calculations based on expenditure and population information in *Blue Books* for the Colony of the Cape of Good Hope (various years).

legitimize the state in the eyes of taxpaying white voters. At the same time, it constituted one of the cornerstones of the apartheid system which, as argued earlier, proved incompatible with sustained economic development in the longer run.

Table 9.2 has shown that the growth in government revenues caused by the mineral discoveries led to marked increases in the public expenditures of the two British colonies and the two Boer republics. The availability of additional revenue gave rise to rapid growth in infrastructure spending (especially the construction of railways) and initial steps towards general provision of education and healthcare. Data for the Cape Colony illustrate these trends. Table 9.6 shows the composition of government expenditure in the Cape Colony in selected years from 1853 to 1904. The major expenditure categories before the mineral discoveries were public works (mainly infrastructure items such as roads, bridges and dams); law, order and defence; and, periodically, debt-service costs. Outlays on administration and health, education and welfare were significantly smaller. The 1891 and 1904 figures for public works reflected the effects of railway construction – the Cape government obtained legislative authority to undertake large-scale expansion of the railway network in 1874 – but outlays on roads, bridges and harbour facilities and the telegraph and postal systems also absorbed considerable resources. Spending on healthcare, education and welfare were also significantly higher in per capita terms in these years, albeit starting from a low base.

As was the case in other colonies and, indeed, the metropole itself, public provision of social services remained poorly developed throughout the years leading up the establishment of the Union of South Africa.[21] Education was a case in point. Compulsory education for white children aged seven to fourteen was introduced in the Cape Colony in 1905, and the Natal Colony, Free State Colony and Transvaal Colony followed soon. Yet school enrolment of white South African children barely exceeded 50 per cent by 1910 (Duff 2012, 275). Enrolment rates were much lower among African and Coloured children, for whom education was not compulsory.[22] Racial disparities in the allocation of government resources were evident throughout this period. In 1895, for example, 57 per cent of the children enrolled in schools in the Cape Colony were black (Malherbe 1925, 174). Yet the budget for that year provided slightly less than £19 thousand for the education of African children, compared to almost £175 thousand for that of others. Such disparities reflected the particular purposes of the education of indigenous peoples, namely exposure to the values of the settlers, undermining of the authority of their traditional leaders and acceleration of their integration into the settler economy as manual labourers. As Molteno (1984, 53) put it: "Schooling in the 19th century helped to undermine the unconquered, while incorporating the already conquered into the structure of settler society".

Reflecting the fiscal authorities' prudent approach, the consolidated expenditures of the Union government and the four provinces closely mirrored the revenues depicted in Figures 9.2 and 9.3. Factors such as the consolidation of the institutions of the four former colonies, the development of new national policies, the First World War and the economic turbulence of the 1920s led to considerable instability in the composition of government spending. Nonetheless, capital spending by the Union government increased from an average of £3.3 million per annum from 1910 to 1914 to £13.2 million in 1937/8 (Van Waasdijk 1964, 161). Further expansion of the railway network accounted for a large portion of the increase in capital spending, while water infrastructure and capitalization of the Land Bank (an agency established to support farmers) and government enterprises and corporations also absorbed significant fractions. In addition, Union and provincial expenditure on education and on health and social security each tripled in per capita terms between 1911/12 and

---

[21] According to Tanzi and Schuknecht (2000, 34, 38), government spending on education and health in Britain amounted to 1.1 per cent of GDP in 1910 and 0.3 per cent of GDP in 1913, respectively.

[22] The situation was different in some areas as far as school enrolment numbers were concerned. Black children outnumbered white children in schools in the Cape Colony in 1865 and in the Natal Colony in 1885 – the first years for which Malherbe (1925, 174, 218) provided disaggregated data. The vast majority of black children were in mission schools, many of which received government grants (Hunt-Davis 1984, 130–1).

Table 9.7 *Composition of Union and provincial government spending in per capita terms in pounds, selected years 1927/28–1959/60*[1]

Expenditure category:	1927/8	1937/8	1950/1	1959/60
Administrative services	0.37	0.5	1.14	2.18
Defence, justice and police	0.65	0.68	1.76	3.05
Education, arts and science	0.99	0.93	2.71	4.82
Health, housing and social security[2]	0.64	1.07	4.2	6.95
Economic services[3]	1.73	2.99	6.01	10.55
Interest on public debt	1.22	1.1	1.86	3.47
Miscellaneous expenditure	0.18	0.33	0.78	1.92
Total	5.78	7.6	18.46	32.94
Of which:				
Current expenditure	4.13	4.68	13.43	23.36
Capital expenditure	1.65	2.92	5.03	9.58
Total	**5.78**	**7.6**	**18.46**	**32.94**

Sources: Own calculations based on information in Van Waasdijk (1964,155, 161, 224) and Bureau of Census and Statistics (1960, A-8).
Notes: 1. The expenditure figures provided in this table were calculated as the sum of current expenditure by the central government less subsidies to provinces, capital expenditure by the central government less loans to provinces, and total expenditure of the provinces; 2. Social security expenditure were calculated as the sum of the following items: Labour, social welfare, social insurance payments, and pensions and relief; 3. Expenditure on economic services were calculated as the sum of the following items: agriculture and land; mining, commerce and industry; and food, agricultural and transport subsidies.

1925/6.[23] School enrolment rates increased sharply among all population groups in the first two decades after 1910. This development was accompanied by strong growth in the number of teachers and their average salaries, the construction of many schools and school hostels, and the expansion of teacher training facilities (cf. De Kock, 1927, 59–60). The growth in social security expenditure from 1910 to 1930 largely reflected the establishment and expansion of a consolidated pension fund for civil servants and the introduction of military pensions from 1916 onwards. The effects of the devastating influenza epidemic in 1918 included the marked expansion of public health programmes and outlays (cf. De Kock 1927, 74–9, 88–9).

Table 9.7 demonstrates that expenditure on infrastructure and social services continued to grow from 1927/8 to 1959/60. To be sure, the

[23] These per capita figures were calculated using the aggregate social spending statistics in De Kock (1927, 29) and the mid-year population estimates in Bureau of Census and Statistics (1960, A-8).

growing complexity of the South African economy and the duplication of governance functions inherent in the apartheid system raised administrative expenditures as well. Furthermore, the growth in public spending on defence, justice and police after the Second World War testified to the growing tensions caused by this system. Yet, public spending on education, arts and science increased in per capita terms from slightly less than £1 in 1927/8 to nearly £5 in 1959/60. Per capita outlays on health, housing and social security increased from £0.6 to almost £7. The introduction of means-tested social pensions in 1928 marked the genesis of what became an unusually large social assistance system for a developing country. It was expanded to provide grants for the blind in 1936 and the disabled in 1937 and allowances for large low-income families in 1947 (cf. Van der Berg 1997, 484–8). The increase in capital expenditure per capita from £1.7 in 1927/8 to more than £9.5 in 1959/60 was indicative of large-scale infrastructural investment. However, it is an incomplete measure of such investment: while reflecting capital spending on transport and water infrastructure, inter alia, it excludes spending in other areas such as electricity provision.

Per capita social spending figures for this period masked large racial disparities that resulted from differential funding of strictly separated systems and facilities. The growth in interracial social spending gaps from 1910 onwards was interrupted from 1939 until 1948, when the policies of the Union Party government led by Jan Smuts brought "limited progress towards incorporation and equality" (Bromberger 1982, 172). Such policies included the extension of social pensions to Africans and Indians, the introduction of school-feeding programmes for children of all races, and abolition of the practice of coupling the level of education spending on Africans to that group's direct tax payments (Bromberger 1982, 172–4). Yet, the election victory of the National Party in 1948 led to a swift reversal of these gains. The National Party government proceeded to cement existing discriminatory measures and adopt the remaining elements of the mature apartheid system.

The degree of racial discrimination in the allocation of public education spending is shown in Figure 9.5, which gives government expenditure on primary, secondary and tertiary education per head of the total population for each population group between 1910 and 1960. In 1910, spending per capita on Africans amounted to a mere 0.3 per cent of spending per capita on whites. The corresponding figures for coloureds and Indians were 1.1 per cent and 3.9 per cent, respectively. By 1960, spending per coloured person had increased to 24.0 per cent of spending per white person, while that on each Indian had reached 24.9 per cent. The corresponding figure for Africans was still only 3.5 per cent. These

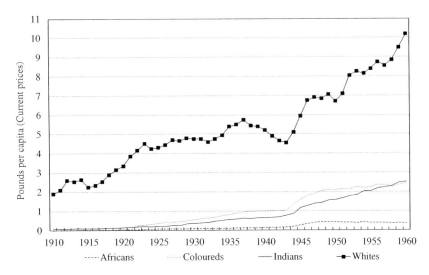

Figure 9.5: Government spending on education in per capita terms in pounds, 1910–60
Source: Own calculations based on information in Malherbe (1977, 735–42).
Notes: Expenditures are expressed per head of the population (not per learner).

discrepancies were mirrored in the facilities and opportunities available to children of the four groups, education outcomes and various quality indicators. To name but one example: 10,665 learners passed the matriculation examination (the final school-leaving assessment that determines eligibility for university) in South Africa in 1960. Fully 94 per cent of them were whites (Malherbe 1977, 724–6). In the same year, whites constituted only 21 per cent of the South African population (Bureau of Census and Statistics 1960, A-8).[24]

Similar racial discrimination characterized all social expenditure programmes. For example, only whites and coloureds initially qualified for social pensions. When the extension of such pensions to Africans occurred sixteen years later, the value of the grant was less than one tenth of that given to whites and the eligibility test was markedly more

---

[24] Similar racial disparities existed in other British colonies. Frankema (2012, 344) presented data on disparities in spending per student and students per teacher in Kenya, Northern Rhodesia, Southern Rhodesia, Tanzania, Nyasaland and Bechuanaland in 1938.

stringent (Van der Berg 1997, 487). Healthcare, housing and other social assistance programmes also exhibited massive racial spending gaps. Apart from devastating social effects, these social spending disparities contributed greatly to wholly inadequate human capital development in the South African economy.

Conclusion

South Africa made remarkable progress from 1850 to 1961 with the establishment of a 'modern' fiscal state. By the end of this period, the South African state exploited a diversified revenue base and a well-developed floating debt position to finance infrastructure provision as well as essential social and other public services. Lucrative mineral discoveries in the second half of the nineteenth century provided the impetus for territorial consolidation and modern economic growth in South Africa. For much of this period, the mining sector was the backbone of the South African economy, having a strong influence on the economic policy agenda.

That said, the white minority used its political and economic power to infuse the organization and activities of the South African state with the ideology of racial segregation. Besides its many achievements, the state also created and maintained the apartheid system. This system negated vital potential benefits of the fiscal modernization process. The inhumane and repressive character of apartheid meant that the South African state could not achieve the legitimacy needed for political stability and long-term economic development. Furthermore, timely diversification is essential for sustained progress in economies built on the extraction of exhaustible resources. The extent of diversification achieved in South Africa was inadequate despite intensive state-led efforts to foster manufacturing activity. Implementation errors contributed to this failure, but the hampering effects of apartheid measures on policy priorities and the inadequate use of social spending programmes to build the country's human capital base were pivotal. It is ironic that the needs of the mining sector in the early years of the Union period motivated the adoption of some of these measures.

By and large, the South African experience confirmed the version of the "resource curse" argument that emphasizes links between institutions and the economic and other effects of natural resources. The mineral discoveries generated vast resources that reshaped the political and economic development of South Africa. The details of these effects clearly reflected the influence of institutions, however: whites' political power gave them a high degree of control over the development of the fiscal system as well as the evolution of political institutions, economic institutions and economic outcomes. Sadly, the ideology of apartheid distorted these processes and institutions to such an extent that South Africa failed to capitalize on the opportunities afforded by its mineral wealth and otherwise solid governance foundations.

Bibliography

Accominotti, O., Flandreau, M., Rezzik, R., & Zumer, F. (2010). Black Man's Burden, White Man's Welfare: Control, Devolution and Development in the British Empire, 1880–1914. *European Review of Economic History*, 14(1), 47–70.

Auty, R. (2008). Natural Resources and Development. In A. K. Dutt & J. Ros (Eds.), *International Handbook of Development Economics*. Cheltenham: Edward Elgar, 288–403.

Blattman, C., Hwang J., & Williamson, J. G. (2007). Winners and Losers in the Commodity Lottery: the Impact of Terms of Trade Growth and Volatility in the Periphery 1870–1939. *Journal of Development Economics*, 82(1), 156–79.

Booth, A. (2007). Night Watchmen, Extractive, or Developmental States? Some Evidence from Late Colonial South-East Asia. *Economic History Review*, 60(2), 241–66.

Bromberger, N. (1982). Government Policies Affecting the Distribution of Income, 1940–1980. In R. Schrire (Ed.), *South Africa: Public Policy Perspectives*. Cape Town: Juta, 165–203.

Browne, G. W. G. (1973). Fiscal Policy in South Africa. In J. A. Lombard (Ed.), *Economic Policy in South Africa: Selected Essays*. Cape Town: HAUM Publishers, 1–25.

Browne, G. W. G. (1983). Fifty Years of Public Finance. *South African Journal of Economics*, 51(1), 134–73.

Browne, G. W. G., & Jones, J. (1961). Die staat se leningsuitgawes and hul finansiering. In D. H. Steyn (Ed.), *Inleiding tot die Suid-Afrikaanse Staatsfinansies*. Pretoria: J.L. van Schaik, 173–214.

Buchanan, J. M., & Wagner, R. (1977). *Democracy in Deficit: the Political Legacy of Lord Keynes*. Indianapolis: The Liberty Fund.

Bureau of Census and Statistics. (1960). *Union Statistics for Fifty Years*. Pretoria: Bureau of Census and Statistics.

Calitz, E., du Plessis S. A., & Siebrits F. K. (2009). *Institutions and the Sustainability of Fiscal Policy in South Africa, 1960–2008*. Unpublished paper delivered at the 15th World Economic History Congress in Utrecht (The Netherlands). 3–7 August 2009.

Chenery, H. B. (1979). *Structural Change and Development Policy.* Washington, DC: The World Bank.

Davenport, T. R. H., & Sanders, C. (2000). *South Africa: a Modern History.* 5th ed. Basingstoke: Macmillan Press.

De Kock, M. H. (1924). *Selected Subjects in the Economic History of South Africa.* Cape Town: Juta.

De Kock, M. H. (1927). *An Analysis of the Finances of the Union of South Africa.* 2nd ed. Cape Town: Juta.

De Kiewiet, C. W. (1957). *A History of South Africa: Social and Economic.* Cape Town: Oxford University Press.

Duff, S. E. (2012). 'Education for Every Son and Daughter of South Africa': Race, Class, and the Compulsory Education Debate in the Cape Colony. In L. Brockliss & N. Sheldon (Eds.), *Mass Education and the Limits of State Building, c.1870–1930.* Basingstoke: Palgrave Macmillan, 261–82.

Du Plessis, S. A., & du Plessis S. W. F. (2017). *Which Comes First: Good Governance or Prosperity? A Historical Experiment from the South African Republic and the Orange Free State.* ERSA Working Paper No. 691. Cape Town: Economic Research Southern Africa.

Fedderke, J. W. (2014). *Exploring Unbalanced Growth in South Africa: Understanding the Sectoral Structure of the South African Economy.* ERSA Working Paper No. 468. Cape Town: Economic Research Southern Africa.

Feinstein, C.H. (2005). *An Economic History of South Africa: Conquest, Discrimination and Development.* Cambridge: Cambridge University Press.

Fourie, J. (2013). The Remarkable Wealth of the Dutch Cape Colony: Measurements from Eighteenth-Century Probate Inventories. *Economic History Review,* 66(2), 419–48.

Fourie, J., & van Zanden, J. L. (2013). GDP in the Dutch Cape Colony: the National Accounts of a Slave-Based Society. *South African Journal of Economics,* 81(4), 467–90.

Frankema, E. (2011). Colonial Taxation and Government Spending in British Africa, 1880–1940: Maximising Revenue or Minimising Effort? *Explorations in Economic History* 48(1), 136–49.

Frankema, E. (2012). The Origins of Formal Education in Sub-Saharan Africa: Was British Rule More Benign? *European Review of Economic History,* 16(4), 335–55.

Freund, W. M. (2011). South Africa: the Union years, 1910–1948: Political and Economic Foundations. In R. Ross, A. K. Mager & B. Nasson (Eds.), *The Cambridge History of South Africa, vol. 2: 1885–1994.* Cambridge: Cambridge University Press, 211–53.

Gardner, L. (2012). *Taxing Colonial Africa: the Political Economy of British Imperialism*. Oxford: Oxford University Press.

Gilbert, D. W. (1933). The Economic Effects of the Gold Discoveries upon South Africa: 1886–1910. *Quarterly Journal of Economics*, 47(4), 553–97.

Government of the Cape Colony. (Various years). *Blue Books*. Cape Town: Government Printer.

Hobart-Houghton, D. (1964). *The South African Economy*. Oxford: Oxford University Press.

Hobart-Houghton, D. (1971). Economic Development, 1865–1965. In M. Wilson & L. Thompson (Eds.), *The Oxford History of South Africa, vol. 2: South Africa, 1870–1966*. Oxford: Oxford University Press, 1–48.

Holloway, J. E. (1954). South African Public Finance and Taxation, 1933–1953. *South African Journal of Economics*, 22(1), 107–14.

Horwitz, R. (1967). *The Political Economy of South Africa*. London: Weidenfeld and Nicolson.

Hunt-Davis, R. (1984). The Administration and Financing of African Education in South Africa, 1910–1953. In P. Kallaway (Ed.), *Apartheid and Education: The Education of Black South Africans*. Johannesburg: Ravan Press, 127–38.

Hyslop, J. (2005). Political Corruption: Before and after Apartheid. *Journal of Southern African Studies*, 31(4), 773–89.

International Centre for Tax and Development. (2017). *Government Revenue Dataset* (July 2017 version). Brighton: Sussex University, Institute of Development Studies. www.ictd.ac/datasets/the-ictd-gov ernment-revenue-dataset (accessed 25 January 2018).

Johnstone, F. A. (1976). *Race, Class and Gold*. London: Kegan Paul.

Lienert, I. (2003). A Comparison between Two Public Expenditure Management Systems in Africa. *OECD Journal on Budgeting*, 3(3), 35–66.

Lipton, M. (1986). *Capitalism and Apartheid: South Africa, 1910–1986*. Cape Town: David Philip.

Maddison, A. (2001). *The World Economy: A Millennial Perspective*. Paris: Organisation for Economic Co-Operation and Development.

Maddison, A. (2003). *The World Economy: Historical Statistics*. Paris: Organisation for Economic Co-Operation and Development.

Magee, G.B., L. Greyling & G. Verhoef. (2016). South Africa in the Australian Mirror: Per Capita Real GDP in the Cape Colony, Natal, Victoria, and New South Wales, 1861–1909. *Economic History Review*, 69(3), 893–914. Online data appendix: http://onlinelibrary.wiley.com/doi/10.1111/ehr.12125/suppinfo.

Malherbe, E.G. (1925). *Education in South Africa (1652–1922)*. Cape Town and Johannesburg: Juta and Company.

Malherbe, E. G. (1977). *Education in South Africa (1923–1975)*. Cape Town and Johannesburg: Juta and Company.

McCracken, J. L. (1967). *The Cape Parliament, 1854–1910*. Oxford: Clarendon Press.

Mehlum, H., Moehne, K., & Torvik, R. (2006). Institutions and the Resource Curse. *Economic Journal*, 116(508), 1–20.

Mitchell, B. R. (1998). *International Historical Statistics: Africa, Asia and Oceania*. 3rd ed. London: Macmillan.

Moll, T. (1991). Did the Apartheid Economy 'Fail'? *Journal of Southern African Studies*, 17(2), 271–91.

Moll, T. (1993). Macroeconomic Policy in Turbulent Times. In M. Lipton & C. E. W. Simkins (Eds.), *State and Market in Post-Apartheid South Africa*. Johannesburg: Witwatersrand University Press, 235–69.

Molteno, F. (1984). The Historical Foundations of the Schooling of Black South Africans. In P. Kallaway (Ed.), *Apartheid and Education: The Education of Black South Africans*. Johannesburg: Ravan Press, 45–107.

Nattrass, N. (1991). Controversies about Capitalism and Apartheid in South Africa: An Economic Perspective. *Journal of Southern African Studies*, 17(4), 654–77.

Nattrass, N., & Seekings, J. (2011). The Economy and Poverty in the Twentieth Century. In R. Ross, A. K. Mager & B. Nasson (Eds.), *The Cambridge History of South Africa, vol. 2: 1885–1994*. Cambridge: Cambridge University Press, 518–72.

Plant, A. (1936).Economic Development, 1795–1921. In A. P. Newton, E. A. Benians & E. A. Walker (Eds.), *The Cambridge History of the British Empire, vol. 8: South Africa, Rhodesia and the Protectorates*. Cambridge: Cambridge University Press, 759–807.

Posel, D. (1999). Whiteness and Power in the South African Civil Service: Paradoxes of the Apartheid State. *Journal of Southern African Studies*, 25(1), 99–119.

Robinson, J. A., Torvik R., & Verdier, T. (2006). Political Foundations of the Resource Curse. *Journal of Development Economics*, 79(2), 447–68.

Ross, M. L. (2004). What Do We Know about Natural Resources and Civil War? *Journal of Peace Research*, 41(3), 337–56.

Rotberg, R. I. (1988). *The Founder: Cecil Rhodes and the Pursuit of Power*. Oxford: Oxford University Press.

Saul, J., & Gelb, S. (1986). *The Crisis in South Africa*. London: Zed Books.

Savage, M. (1986). The Imposition of Pass Laws on the African Population in South Africa 1916–1984. *African Affairs*, 85(339), 181–205.

Schumann, C. G. W. (1938). *Structural Change and Business Cycles in South Africa, 1806–1936*. London: P.S. King and Son.

Sokoloff, K. L., & Zolt, E. M. (2007). Inequality and the Evolution of Institutions of Taxation: Evidence from the Economic History of the Americas. In S. Edwards, G. Esquivel & G. Márquez (Eds.), *The Decline of Latin American Economies: Growth, Institutions, and Crises.* Chicago: University of Chicago Press and National Bureau of Economic Research, 83–136.

Sunderland, D. (2004). *Managing British Colonial and Post-Colonial Development: The Crown Agents, 1914–1974.* Woodbridge: Boydell and Brewer.

Szirmai, A. (2012). Industrialisation as an Engine of Growth in Developing Countries, 1950–2005. *Structural Change and Economic Dynamics*, 23(4), 406–20.

Tames, R. (2005). *Economy and Society in 19th Century Britain.* London: Routledge.

Tanzi, V., & Schuknecht, L. (2000). *Public Spending in the 20th Century.* Cambridge: Cambridge University Press.

Thompson, L. (2000). *A History of South Africa.* 3rd ed. New Haven: Yale University Press.

Tun Wai, U. (1962). Taxation Problems and Policies of Underdeveloped VCountries. *IMF Staff Papers*, 9(3), 428–48.

United Nations. (1948). *Public Debt, 1914–1946.* New York: United Nations, Fiscal Division of the Department of Economic Affairs.

United Nations. (Various years). *Statistical Yearbook.* New York: United Nations, Statistics Division of the Department of Economic and Social Affairs.

Van der Berg, S. (1997). South African Social Security under Apartheid and Beyond. *Development Southern Africa*, 14(4), 481–503.

Van Helten, J. J. (1978). German Capital, the Netherlands Railway Company and the Political Economy of the Transvaal 1886–1900. *Journal of African History*, 19(3), 369–90.

Van Waasdijk, T. (1964). *Public Expenditure in South Africa: A Study of the Growth, Co-Ordination and Control of Budgets.* Johannesburg: Witwatersrand University Press.

Welsh, F. (2000). *A History of South Africa.* London: Harper Collins Publishers.

Wenar, L. (2008). Property Rights and the Resource Curse. *Philosophy and Public Affairs*, 36(1), 2–32.

Index